Richard III and the Battle of Bosworth

Mike Ingram

Helion & Company

The Series Editor would like to express his thanks to the talented artist Gambargain, for her illustration of the armour of Sir Thomas Martyn.

Helion & Company Limited
Unit 8 Amherst Business Centre
Budbrooke Road
Warwick
CV34 5WE
England
Tel. 01926 499 619
Email: info@helion.co.uk
Website: www.helion.co.uk
Twitter: @helionbooks
Visit our blog at http://blog.helion.co.uk/

Published by Helion & Company 2019
Designed and typeset by Mach 3 Solutions Ltd (www.mach3solutions.co.uk)
Cover designed by Paul Hewitt, Battlefield Design (www.battlefield-design.co.uk)
Printed by Henry Ling Limited, Dorchester

Text © Mike Ingram 2019
Illustrations © as individually credited, otherwise Open Source
Maps drawn by Dr Lesley Prince © Helion & Company 2019
The cover illustration is entitled "As His Own Champion", depicting King Richard III in his cavalry charge at the Battle of Bosworth, by historical illustrator Matthew Ryan. Image © Matthew Ryan. Signed prints of this and more are available direct from the artist's website www.matthewryanhistoricalillustrator.com

Every reasonable effort has been made to trace copyright holders and to obtain their permission for the use of copyright material. The author and publisher apologise for any errors or omissions in this work, and would be grateful if notified of any corrections that should be incorporated in future reprints or editions of this book.

ISBN 978-1-912866-50-2

British Library Cataloguing-in-Publication Data.
A catalogue record for this book is available from the British Library.

All rights reserved. No part of this publication may be reproduced, stored in a retrieval system, or transmitted, in any form, or by any means, electronic, mechanical, photocopying, recording or otherwise, without the express written consent of Helion & Company Limited.

For details of other military history titles published by Helion & Company Limited, contact the above address, or visit our website: http://www.helion.co.uk

We always welcome receiving book proposals from prospective authors.

For my Grandparents
Long gone but never forgotten

Herein may be seen noble chyvalrye, curtoseye, humanitye, friendlynesse, hardynesse, love, frendship, cowardyse, murdre, hate, virtue, and synne.
William Caxton's preface to
Sir Thomas Malory's 'Morte d'Arthur, 1485

Contents

Acknowledgements		vi
Foreword		vii
Introduction		viii
Timeline		xviii
1	The Wars of the Roses	27
2	Weapons and Warfare in the Reign of Richard III	46
3	Richard: Duke of Gloucester	84
4	Henry Tudor	105
5	France, Brittany and Henry Tudor	116
6	Richard: The King	127
7	Rebellions	148
8	Preparations	173
9	Invasion	200
10	The Battle of Bosworth Field 22 August 1485	216
11	King Henry VII	252
Epilogue		262
Appendices		
I	Finding the Battlefield	263
II	Finding Richard	267
III	Order of Battle	272
Colour Plate Commentaries		278
Bibliography		281
Index		285

Acknowledgements

Firstly, I would like to thank my family for their support and patience whilst writing the book, and Dr. Phil Stone, Chairman of Richard III Society, for his foreword and comments. Also thanks to Matthew Ryan for allowing me to use his brilliant Bosworth illustration on the cover and Graham Evans for his comments. I would like to thank all those who were involved in finding both the actual battlefield and Richard III himself, without their amazing painstaking work this book would not have been possible.

I would also like to thank all those who have visited the battlefield with me. It was all your questions that helped me hone the book before you. The only way to truly understand a battle is to walk in the footsteps of those who were there, so please keep visiting the site. I would also like to express my thanks to all those people who protested against the development of part of the battlefield in 2018. Our battlefield heritage is important, we must not let it be chipped away and destroyed.

Finally, I would like to thank Charles Singleton and all the team at Helion for making the book happen.

Foreword

Yet another book on Richard III and the Battle of Bosworth? Yes, but one that gives a different and interesting perspective on the combatants and the battle that saw a change of regime and the death of the last of the Plantagenet kings.

In this work of considerable scholarship, Mike Ingram avoids telling us what the principal characters thought, since we cannot possibly know what was in anyone's mind five hundred or more years ago. We get the facts as can be found in contemporary chronicles and archaeological findings.

There is a useful account of how a medieval army was made up, how it was armed and how it worked. The overview of warfare as fought in England compared with France and Flanders is a bonus.

For many years, the account of the Battle we know as Bosworth has been based on accounts by historians rather than contemporary or near contemporary sources, with authors trying to make their theories fit the then known topography. Thanks to the work of Glenn Foard et al. in 2010, we have a clearer idea of where the battle of Bosworth was actually fought and can see how some of these earlier accounts can no longer be made to work. The author enables us to see a way that the battle may have been fought that fits with what we now know to be the true battlefield site.

It is good to find another debunking of the hunchback myth using the findings from the discovery and analysis of Richard III's remains.

This is a fascinating book giving another perspective on one of the most important battles ever fought on English soil. It tells of how it came about as the allegiance of fifteenth century magnates flowed from one side to another, enabling the reader to understand so much more as to why King Richard came to his untimely end. It is an interesting read and the author is to be thanked for this.

Dr Phil Stone
Chairman, Richard III Society

Introduction

With his death at the Battle of Bosworth on 22 August 1485, Richard III entered the realm of legend. Moore's, John Rous's and Shakespeare's, image of the last Plantagenet king of England as a misshapen monster and their versions of events have always clouded opinion of Richard III's life and death. Since then there have been many tomes written by both the supporters and detractors of Richard III; of the mysterious death of the Princes in the Tower, (if they did indeed die) and the usurpation of the throne itself. And scholars and historians will no doubt continue to debate Richard's character and life for many years to come.

However, first, the discovery of the true site of the battle and then the spectacular and unlikely discovery of Richard's remains in 2012, which have proved beyond doubt that at least Tudor descriptions of his physical appearance have been wrong, have meant that the history books will now have to be rewritten.

This book is therefore primarily concerned with Richard the soldier and military leader and his death at Bosworth in 1485 in light of this new evidence. It will be seen that Henry Tudor's invasion was not just a battle for the throne of England, but part of a wider war between England, Burgundy, Brittany and the French that began in the reign of Edward IV. It was also about French politics. After the death of King Louis XI there was minor on the throne. Anne of Beaujeu, the new king's sister, also known as Madame la Grande, took control of the King and the government. Anne was opposed by Louis d'Orléans, the first Prince of the Blood, who claimed the regency himself. Anne refused to give her position up leading to what is now known as the Mad War. The book also looks at Richard's relationship with the Stanley brothers, Thomas and William, and how it would ultimately lead to his downfall. From the seventeenth century to today, largely due to Hutton's book on the battle, the Stanleys have been portrayed as the ultimate fence-sitters. However, nothing could be farther from the truth. As this book will show they were intimately involved in the plots against Richard from the very beginning.

The Battle of Bosworth (or Redemoor) was fought on 22 August 1485 and was the penultimate battle of the Wars of the Roses. It was one of, if not the, most important battle in English history after the Battle of Hastings in 1066. It is often regarded as the end of the middle ages, and the beginning of the English Renaissance although in reality the change was much more gradual. But it does

INTRODUCTION

mark the beginning of the reign of the Tudors. By the end of the day, Henry VII would be on the throne, and his son Henry VIII and his granddaughter Elizabeth I, would go on to lead the country to previously unknown greatness.

Considering its importance, very little was written about the battle either at the time or during Henry's reign. In addition, most surviving accounts were written by people with either little or no concern for military tactics, making any reconstruction of the battle difficult. Added to that, Tudor writers were determined to disguise, or write out entirely, the importance of the French to the campaign and battle, so their involvement has to be unpicked from Continental sources. It is also an old adage that history is written by the victor, but in the medieval period, it usually was, and as such was heavily biased. Only by studying the landscape, the contemporary accounts and the archaeology can the battle be reconstructed.

Sources

Of all the accounts, *The Croyland Chronicle* is probably the most contemporary. It was commissioned by the Benedictine Abbey of Croyland (or Crowland) in Lincolnshire and was written in two parts known as the *First* and *Second Continuations*. *The Second Continuation*, which details the battle and the events leading up to it, was probably written the year after. Its author was most likely John Russell, Bishop of Lincoln, who was the keeper of the privy seal for Edward IV and chancellor under Richard III. He probably accompanied Richard III on the campaign and as such was well-informed. However, he was not an eyewitness to the battle and does little to disguise his dislike of Richard's rule.

Dominic Mancini was an Italian scholar who visited England in 1483. His account of the dramatic events in England from the death of Edward IV to the coronation of Richard III was originally called *De Occupatione Regni Anglie per Riccardum Tercium* ('The Occupation of the Throne of England by Richard III') and was written for Angelo Cato, Archbishop of Vienne. Cato was one of King Louis XI of France's counsellors and therefore Mancini was quite possibly a French spy. Although generally regarded as one of the primary sources for events leading to Richard's coronation, it is not clear how much English Mancini understood. It is unlikely he met many officials or key players and his account seems to have relied heavily on gossip, rumours and unsubstantiated reports, some of which probably came from Italian merchants in London. His report must therefore be treated with extreme caution. Mancini returned to France soon after Richard III's coronation on 6 July 1483 and he delivered his report in December the same year. Based on his report, Guillaume de Rochefort, Lord Chancellor of France, repeated the rumour of the Princes' death in the Estates General in Tours in January 1484.

Polydore Vergil was an Italian who came to England in 1502 as a deputy to the collector of papal taxes, Cardinal Adriano Castelli. He wrote his description of the battle in his *Historiae Anglicae* between 1503 and 1513, probably at the request of Henry VII. Unusually for the time, he gives a detailed description of events during the battle.

Vergil drew on an impressively wide range of sources for his work, including published books and oral testimony. He claimed to have been diligent in collecting materials and to have drawn on the work of foreign as well as English historians. Vergil himself says that his account is truthful, although may have had some direction as the French involvement in events are played down or not included. There are, however, four distinct versions of his text with small but significant differences. The manuscript in two volumes was written in 1512–13, covering events up to 1513 and is now held in the Vatican Library. It was presented to the ducal library at Urbino in 1613 by Vergil's grand-nephew: the first edition was completed in 1512–13, but not published until 1534, and covered events up to 1509: the second edition, Basel, 1546, folio, covered events up to 1509 and the third edition, Basel, 1555, folio, covered events up to 1537.

Both the Tudor chroniclers Hall and Holinshed made use of it, in turn, Shakespeare would use these two texts to write his history of Richard III. Another source for the battle is Jean Molinet's *Chroniques*. Molinet was the historian to the Burgundian court and sympathetic to the Yorkist cause. His account of Bosworth was written around 1504, probably based on stories told by French troops and tales recounted at the court.

The Burgundian nobleman Philippe de Commines (or Commynes), wrote his eight-volume *Memoirs* during the 1490s. He was one of Louis XI of France's most trusted advisors, so unsurprisingly his account of the battle and the events leading up to it are biased towards Louis, Henry Tudor and his supporters. Although well written, his account has to be treated with caution because his information would have been based on rumour and second- or third-hand accounts. It also appears that in parts he was guilty of altering events to suit his own ends. A further foreign account was written for the Spanish king and queen, Ferdinand and Isabella, in March 1486, by Diego de Valera, a Castilian courtier. Much of his information appears to come from Spanish merchants returning from England and is in places, confused.

Completed around 1504 and first published in 1516 by Richard Pynson without attribution as *The New Chronicles of England and France*, the work now commonly known as *Fabyan's Chronicle*, presents 'parallel histories of England and France', and covers the period from the arrival of the legendary Brutus of Troy in England to the death of Henry VII. Fabyan, a London cloth merchant and city alderman, was the first of the London chroniclers to cite his sources, which included The Brut, Bede, William of Malmesbury, Ranulf Higden, Henry of Huntingdon and numerous others, as well as records of the City of London. John Bale claimed that the 1516 edition was burned by Cardinal Wolsey. A second edition printed after Wolsey's death in 1533 by William Rastell has Fabyan's name on the title page. Two further editions were printed in 1542 and 1559 by John Kyngston. The 1559 edition was revised and extended for the years 1542–1559. Kyngston acknowledged the assistance of Robert Recorde, the Tudor mathematician and sage, whose work he had previously printed and the German scholar, Johann Funck. It is probable that Kyngston's narrative also drew on the work of another contemporary printer and chronicler, John Mychell of Canterbury. Today Kyngston's work is the most widely cited sixteenth century edition of *Fabyan's Chronicle*. Two manuscripts are extant

(Holkham Hall, MS 671, and BL, Cotton MS Nero C.xi). The anonymous *Great Chronicle of London* has also been tentatively ascribed to Fabyan. Like many of the chronicles of the day, it is strewn with errors, particularly in the chronology of events and contradictions in facts. Both accounts focus on London and the author does seem to have been an eyewitness to some of the events there, however he only mentions Bosworth in passing.

John Rous was a chantry priest of Guy's Cliffe in Warwickshire and a supporter of the Neville family. In 1483 he was commissioned, possibly by Anne Neville wife of Richard III, to create what is now known as *The Rous Roll*, an illustrated armorial roll-chronicle for the Beauchamp family commemorating the deeds of the Earls of Warwick, as well as Edward IV and Richard III. The roll, Add MS 48976, held at the British Library, is 335 mm wide × 7 metres long on eight membranes and contains 65 brief biographies in at least three different hands, each with unframed pen drawings and the coats of arms of the individuals. There are also several genealogical charts in a different hand to the text. Richard is included twice, first on membrane two, in which he is wearing armour whilst holding a sword in his right hand and Warwick Castle in his left hand, with a charter looped over his wrist and a boar at his feet. In the second, on membrane eight, Richard is again wearing armour, holding a sword in his right hand and an orb in his left hand, a boar at his feet, and six helms and crests alongside his wife Anne and son Edward also wearing armour and a boar at his feet. As Edward is described as 'Prince of Wales', this dates the roll to no earlier than April 1483. In it, Richard is described as a 'mighty prince', an upholder of the law and beloved of his subjects. A second Latin version has been held at the College of Arms since 1786. However, Richard was not included on the roll, other than as the husband of Anne. It has been speculated that it was made or changed by Rous after Richard was deposed in 1485. There are a number of early copies in existence such as the Lansdowne MS 882, ff. 6r-23b, 67r-v, 83r-v, an anonymous early sixteenth century copy giving the text and painted coats of arms (all in shields) and MS Ashmole 839, ff. 8r-31r. held by the Bodleian Library, Oxford.

Rous began work on his *Historia regum Angliae* (History of the Kings of England), around 1480. He seems to have initially intended to be a general history of England and to give Edward IV information about kings and high-ranking clergy who might be commemorated with statues in St. George's Chapel, Windsor. However, Rous didn't finish the work until 1486 and turned it into anti-Ricardian propaganda in an attempt to win favour with the new king. It was Rous who invented the legend of Richard's unnatural and monstrous birth. He also compares Richard to the Antichrist and accuses him of a list of injustices and murders, although he praises Richard's bravery at Bosworth, his building works, founding of chantries and financial generosity with his people.

Edward Hall, a London lawyer, wrote *The Union of the Two Noble Families of Lancaster and York* in around 1550. The majority of his text follows Vergil, with other parts from Commines, Fabyan and other now unknown sources. Throughout his work Hall includes lengthy speeches, no doubt dramatic invention. Shakespeare derived some of his history from here.

Bernard André, also known as Andreas, was a French Augustinian friar and poet. He is repeatedly called 'the blind poet' in the accounts of Henry VII's payments. He was probably introduced to Henry VII by Richard Fox, later Bishop of Winchester, whom he calls his Mæcenas and received his appointment as poet laureate and a pension from the crown soon after Henry came to the throne. André began to write a life of Henry VII around 1500 but of Bosworth he only says 'Rather than affirm anything rashly, therefore, I pass over the date, place and order of battle, for as I have said I lack the illumination of eye-witnesses. Until I am more fully instructed, for this field of battle, I shall leave blank a space…' He does however, give useful detail of Henry's early reign, particularly the Cornish rebellion of 1495.

Thomas More's unfinished work, *The History of Richard III*, was found after his death and was subsequently published by his son-in-law in 1557. More was only a child of seven at the time of the Battle of Bosworth, so he must have obtained his information from elsewhere. He had spent a considerable amount of his youth in the home of John Morton, Bishop of Ely and after the battle Archbishop of Canterbury. Morton was a fanatical Lancastrian and both Margaret Beaufort's and her son's main confidant and supporter. It has been suggested that the book was not written by More but Morton, and More only copied it. There is a high level of detail that could have only come from an eyewitness such as Morton. George Buck, writing in the seventeenth century, also states that 'Doctor Morton made the book and Master More … set it forth, amplifying it and glossing it.' Whilst it lacks historical accuracy it is, however, noted for its literary skill and adherence to classical principles. It would blacken Richard's character completely. Since then there have been many books written about Richard and the fate of the Princes in the Tower, some generally agreeing with More, others saying Richard was a good king, and a victim of Tudor propaganda.

Holinshed's Chronicles was first published in 1577 and it soon became a standard history of England. It appears that Holinshed gathered his material from Thomas More, Polydore Vergil and Hardyng. Shakespeare made extensive use of Holinshed as source material for his plays.

We cannot complete a survey of the sources without mentioning the Elizabethan plays. Although they are just that – plays – they have heavily influenced public perceptions ever since they were first performed. The first was *The True Tragedy of Richard III*, an anonymous play first performed in 1594, another was *Richardus Tertius*, a drama written in Latin by Dr Thomas Legge, and performed in 1597. The most famous, however, is Shakespeare's *Richard III*, written in the 1590s. Despite the mounting evidence to the contrary, many of the public's perceptions of Richard III and Bosworth still seem to come from the play and films and TV based on it. For its sources, Shakespeare seems to have drawn his inspiration from Holinshed and Hall. However, Margaret Hotine, in her 1991 article in *Notes and Queries*: 'Richard III and Macbeth: Studies in Tudor Tyranny?' suggests that the play was actually written about the Elizabethan courtier Robert Cecil, Earl of Salisbury. Elizabeth I was ageing and had no heir. She was also refusing to name her successor. The Queen's long-serving advisor Sir William Cecil was also ageing. His son, Robert Cecil, was being groomed to take his father's place. Motley's *History of the Netherlands*, printed in 1588, describes Cecil as 'A slight, crooked, hump-backed young gentleman, dwarfish in stature, but with a face not irregular in feature, and thoughtful and subtle in expression without doubt, a hunchback.' Hotine points out that 'Salisbury … was far too powerful to be criticised openly while he was alive, but as soon as he was dead the libels and damning squibs began pouring forth.' Quoting Hotine, M.G. Aune, in his 2006 article in the *Shakespeare Bulletin*, 'The Uses of Richard III', also points out that 'Cecil's ambitions and his regular promotions as connected to, if not a cause of, the printings of the first five of the eight Richard III quartos.'

Was Shakespeare, then, less concerned with telling the history Richard III and instead providing a morality tale for the Queen and country about the perils of relying on a scheming, unpopular hunchback and of failing to secure the succession?

Written in the early sixteenth century, *The Ballad of Bosworth Fielde* gave a poetic account of the battle in over 600 lines. It was commissioned by a member of the Stanley family, with Lord Thomas and Sir William Stanley playing a central role. Its accuracy has long been debated, although it does contain information collaborated by other sources as well as detail not found anywhere else. Its author remains unknown but because it gives a detailed list of nobles and gentry fighting on Richard's side, it is likely that it was written by a herald, possibly Thomas Stanley's own. Today, the ballad only exists as a single later manuscript, the last line of which is to King James. However, it has all the indications of having been composed very soon after the battle by one who knew at first hand many of the details about which he was writing. The opening lines welcome the new King and it continues by first calling Richard and then Henry '*our Kinge*' in turn, suggesting the author lived in Richard's time. Events also appear to be narrated from an eyewitness point of view and he uses the words 'we' and 'see' several times.

The Song of Ladye Bessiye includes an account of the battle with a strong Stanley bias, but like the Ballad has been considered suspect by some historians. However, examining both these sources in the light of the discovery of the true location of the Battle of Bosworth has made them both of prime importance as parts which were once considered incorrect (particularly those relating to the landscape) can be seen to be far more relevant. *Ladye Bessiye* has no statement of authorship, but it is thought that the most likely author was Humphrey Brereton. According to *Ladye Bessiye*, Brereton, who probably came from Malpas in Cheshire, was an 'esquire' in service with Lord Stanley. He takes a central role in the poem, so he appears to have been involved in its writing at the very least. In addition, its author also lapses into the first-person narrative while describing the actions of Brereton. The earliest of the surviving manuscripts of *Ladye Bessiye* is from around 1600, however it is probable that it was written much earlier. The poem mentions the death of Sir William Stanley, but not Thomas Stanley, so this seems to suggest that it was written between February 1495 and July 1504. Three different versions exist: *Bishop Percy's Folio Manuscript* (P) called '*Ladye Bessiye*': Harley 367 (B) titled *The Most Pleasant Song of Ladye Bessy, the eldest daughter of King Edward the Fourth; and how she married King*

Henry the Seventh of the House of Lancaster, and the Bateman MS (H), now lost, but entitled *Ladye Bessie, or the Princesse Elizabeth, after wife of King Henry VII*. Halliwell recognised that the versions in MSS B and H were so different as almost to be two separate poems, so he printed both in the 1847 edition of his book for the Percy Society.

About 1562, a metrical chronicle charting the history of the house of Stanley was written by Thomas Stanley, Bishop of Sodor and Man, who was an illegitimate son of Edward Stanley, Lord Mounteagle, or possibly a minstrel named Richard Sheale. It is called the *Stanley Poem* and part of it tells the story of the Thomas Stanley. There are five manuscripts which contain versions of this poem, including B.L. Harley 541, fols. 183a–206b and B.L. Add. 5830, fols, 105a–121a. The only printed copy of this poem is in J.O. Halliwell-Phillip's *Palatine Anthology* (London, 1850). Much of it denigrates Richard in the same ways as other Tudor writers and firmly blames him for the death of the Princes. However, it does give a good insight into Richard's deteriorating relationship with Stanley and contains detail not found elsewhere.

Another poetic account of the battle was written by Baronet Sir John Beaumont around 1600 and called *Bosworth Field*. Beaumont studied at Broadgates Hall (now Pembroke College) Oxford and lived at Thringstone, not far from the battlefield. He was a descendant of both William Hastings, who was executed by Richard III, and the Earls of Oxford, whilst his father was a Justice of the Common Pleas. It was written in the style of the heroic poems of old and much of what he wrote is found in other sources such as Hall. However, there are a few interesting sections that are not recorded anywhere else. Maybe these parts come from another source, now lost, as it goes into extraordinary detail.

It was William Hutton who wrote the first detailed study of the battle, *The Battle of Bosworth-Field* in 1788. Often using local hearsay as sources, he placed the location of the battle as Ambion Hill, largely based on a comment by *Holinshed's Chronicles* written in 1577 that: 'King Richard pitched his field on a hill called Anne Beame, refreshed his souldiers and took his rest'. For many years to come, this would be the accepted site. Hutton's ideas were developed and continued in John Nichols' *The history and antiquities of the county of Leicester*, Vol. 4, published in 1811. According to Nichols, during the demolition of an old wainscot in Sutton there was discovered a large number of old writings which were found to contain an account of the Battle of Bosworth Field. However, little notice was taken of the manuscript and it was actually destroyed by the cook. Nichols also reproduced a letter that stated:

> Mrs. Jane Dixie has many times stated that she could remember reading in the papers alluded to; and that she recollected something about the king stopping at the Well; and about his natural son being placed on such a hill, and of the king being set fast in a bog; how another man gave him his horse, and the king mounted a second time; likewise the king cleaving sir William Brandon the earl's standard bearer down the head at one blow. She mentioned, that she read of Henry being quite in the rear (who seemed a coward to the king); and that the king, being on the hill with his son, declared he was betrayed, but that he would a die a hero, or wash his hands in Henry's blood.

INTRODUCTION

To the literary sources, we can now add the archaeology, as the actual site of the battle was identified in 2010 (see Appendix I). A considerable amount of debris from the battle, ranging from cannonballs to a broken sword chape, plus that all-important boar badge, have been discovered, allowing a more detailed analysis of how events unfolded. However, battles are notoriously difficult to interpret, and we still do not know exactly what happened during many of the battles of the First World War, even with the huge amounts of documentation and plentiful eyewitness testimony available. So for the medieval period it is almost impossible to say what happened with any degree of certainty. Bosworth is a prime example and, until very recently, events have all been based on Ambion Hill being the site of the battle. Until the discovery of the actual battlefield, the majority of historians made the events fit the site. Even now, the dispositions of the three armies; their locations before and during the battle; the location of the artillery; and how events unfolded that day are all open to a number of differing interpretations due to the scarcity and ambiguities of the sources. Added to this was the discovery of Richard's remains announced in 2012. His remains were subjected to an unprecedented scientific investigation allowing us to study the life and death of the last Plantagenet king of England.

A Note on Currency

The currency of medieval England was divided into pounds (l), shillings (s) and pence (d), with 20 shillings to the pound and 12 pence in a shilling. However, there was no pound coin or note, and the first shilling coin was not minted until the reign of Henry VII (called a testoon). The noble, introduced by King Edward III, was the first English gold coin to be produced in quantity. The angel was introduced in 1464 and was worth six shillings and eight pence. Another unit of currency was the mark, and although there was no coin of this value, it was a common amount used for accounting purposes. It is almost impossible to compare prices at the time of Bosworth with today due to legislation, perceived values and scarcity of supply. This is exacerbated by the effects of Great Slump which lasted from 1440 to approximately 1480 and the Wars of the Roses. However, to give some measure of comparison, in 1480 one pound could purchase two cows, two bushels of wheat, and two yards of best woollen cloth, whilst a skilled craftsman earned 6d per day and a labourer approximately 3d per day. The National Archives Currency Converter as a general guide, suggests that one pound in 1480 was the equivalent of £691.29 and £10,000 almost £7 million in 2017.

The currency of France was the livres tournois. Like English coinage, there were 20 sol to the livre and 12 dernier to the sol. Between 1360 and 1641, coins worth 1 livre tournois were known as francs. The French equivalent of the Angel was the Écu, first minted in 1266 during the reign of Louis IX of France. Although the value fluctuated over time, it was generally the equivalent of six livres tournois.

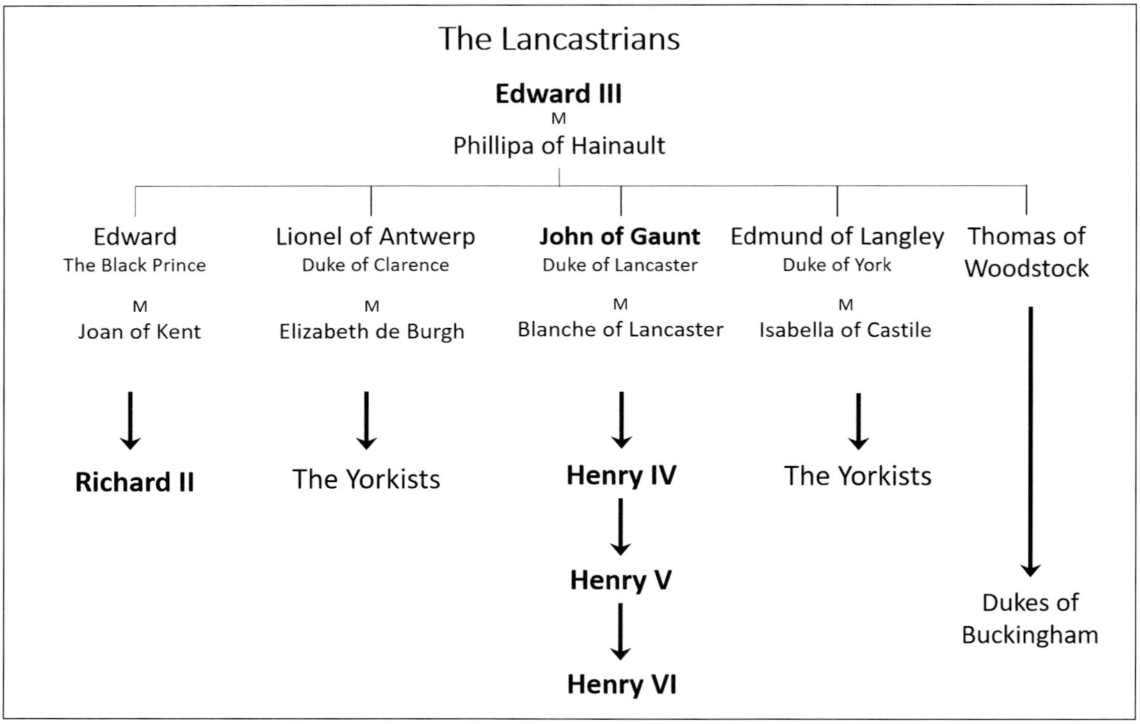

RICHARD III AND THE BATTLE OF BOSWORTH

The Lancastrians

Edward III
M
Phillipa of Hainault

- Edward, The Black Prince — M Joan of Kent → **Richard II**
- Lionel of Antwerp, Duke of Clarence — M Elizabeth de Burgh → The Yorkists
- **John of Gaunt**, Duke of Lancaster — M Blanche of Lancaster → **Henry IV** → **Henry V** → **Henry VI**
- Edmund of Langley, Duke of York — M Isabella of Castile → The Yorkists
- Thomas of Woodstock → Dukes of Buckingham

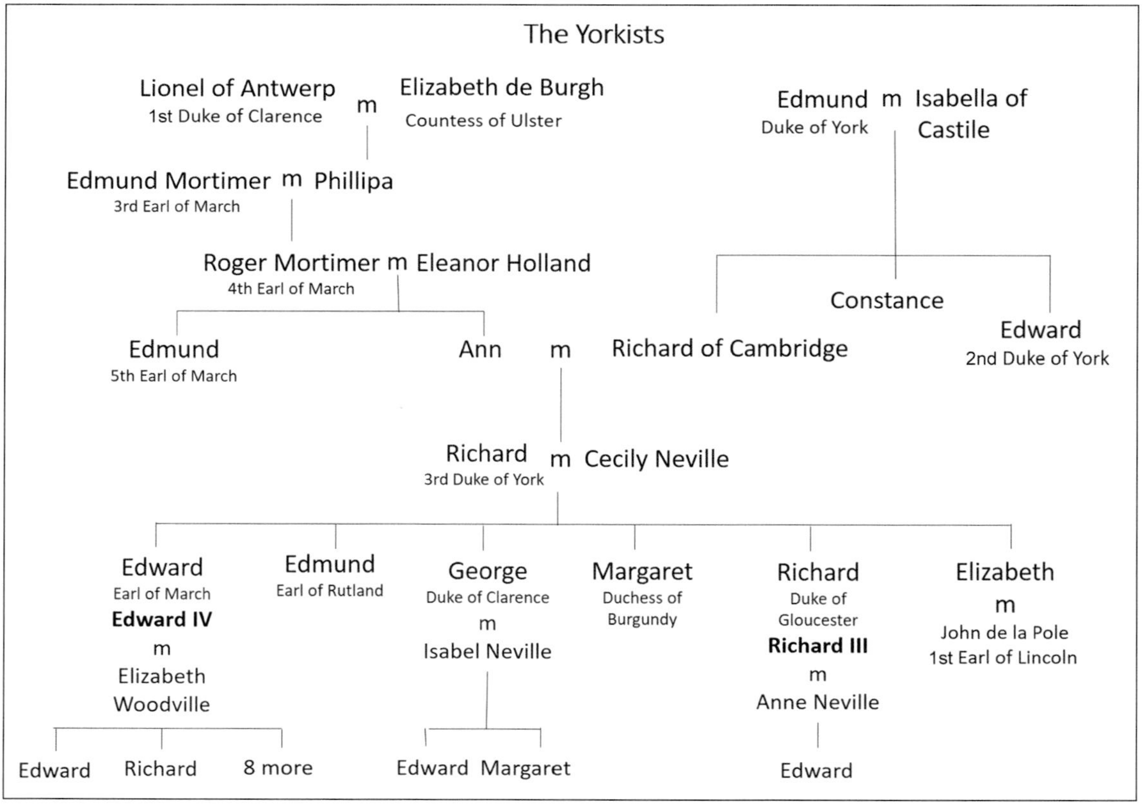

The Yorkists

Lionel of Antwerp, 1st Duke of Clarence m Elizabeth de Burgh, Countess of Ulster

Edmund Mortimer, 3rd Earl of March m Phillipa

Roger Mortimer, 4th Earl of March m Eleanor Holland

Edmund, 5th Earl of March

Ann m Richard of Cambridge

Edmund, Duke of York m Isabella of Castile
- Constance
- Edward, 2nd Duke of York

Richard, 3rd Duke of York m Cecily Neville

- Edward, Earl of March — **Edward IV** m Elizabeth Woodville
  - Edward
  - Richard
  - 8 more
- Edmund, Earl of Rutland
- George, Duke of Clarence m Isabel Neville
  - Edward
  - Margaret
- Margaret, Duchess of Burgundy
- Richard, Duke of Gloucester — **Richard III** m Anne Neville
  - Edward
- Elizabeth m John de la Pole, 1st Earl of Lincoln

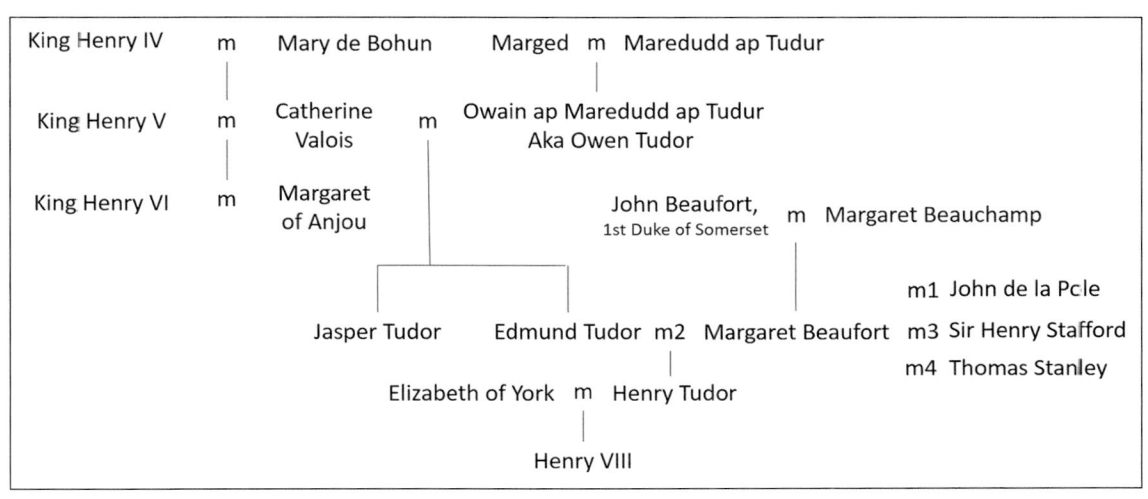

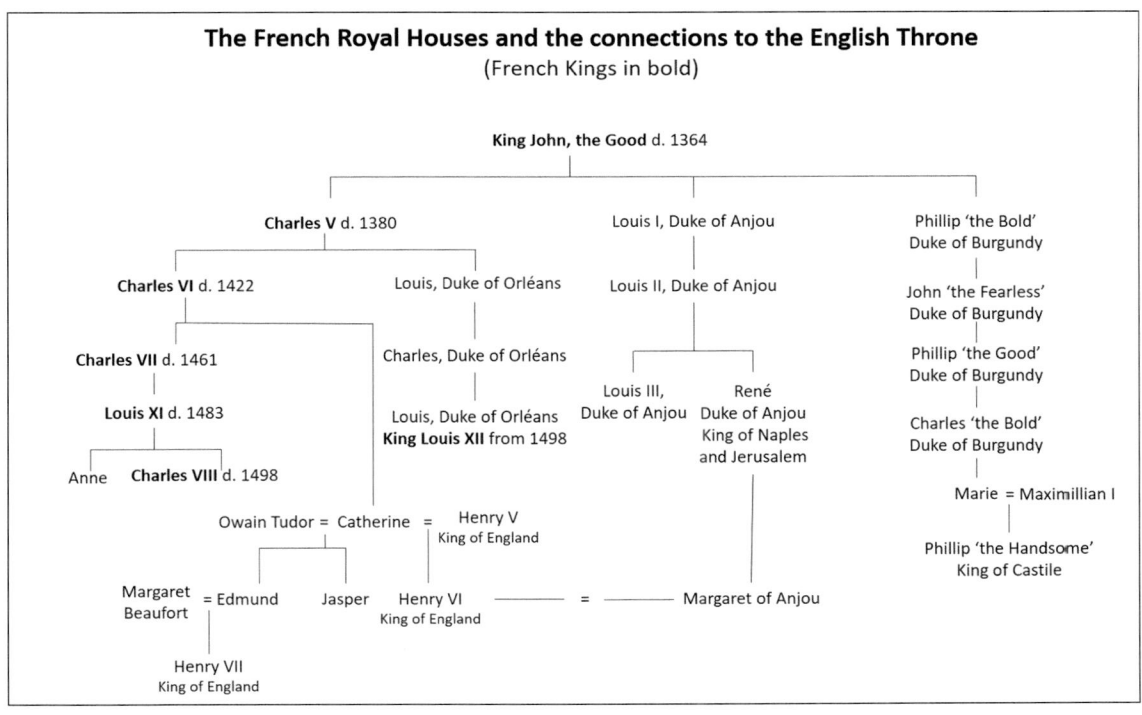

Timeline

1399	29 September. Deposition of Richard II; Henry of Bolingbroke as Henry IV, first king of the House of Lancaster.
1411	22 September. Birth of Richard Plantagenet, future Duke of York.
1420	22 May. Treaty of Troyes recognises Henry V as heir to Charles VI of France, disinherits the Dauphin Charles, future Charles VII.
	2 June. Henry V marries Catherine of Valois, daughter of Charles VI of France.
1421	6 December. Prince Henry, son of Henry V and future Henry VI, is born at Windsor.
1422	31 August. Death of Henry V; uncontested accession of nine-month-old Henry VI, third king of the House of Lancaster.
	21 October. Death of Charles VI of France; Charles VII accepted as king in areas of France outside Anglo-Burgundian control.
1426	May. The 'Parliament of Bats' held in Leicester.
	19 May. The Duke of Bedford knights the four-year-old Henry VI, who in turn knighted 36 others, including the 14-year-old Richard, third duke of York.
1428	28 November. Birth of Richard Neville, future Earl of Warwick.
1429	17 July. Charles VII is crowned King of France at Rheims.
	6 November. Henry VI is crowned King of England at Westminster. Richard Duke of York marries Cecily Neville
1435	20/21 September. The second Treaty of Arras is signed ending the longstanding feud between King Charles VII of France and Duke Philip III of Burgundy (Philip the Good). The treaty breaks the alliance between Burgundy and England, and Charles VII consolidates his position as King of France against the rival claim by Henry VI of England.
1436	York is appointed commander of the English forces in France. He arrives in Normandy on 7 June.
1437	Henry VI aged 16, is declared of age to rule.
1442	28 April. Birth of Edward, future Earl of March and King Edward IV, eldest son of Richard Duke of York at Rouen, Normandy.
1443	17 May. Birth of Edmund, future Earl of Rutland, second son of Richard Duke of York at Rouen, Normandy.

TIMELINE

1445 23 April. Henry VI marries Margaret of Anjou.

1447 9 December. York appointed lord lieutenant of Ireland.

1449 21 October. Birth of George, son of Duke of York; future Duke of Clarence.

29 October. The Duke of Somerset surrenders Rouen, the capital of Normandy, to the French

1450 June–July. Jack Cade's rebellion.

12 August. French capture Cherbourg and end English rule in Normandy.

1452 Feb–March. York's uprising.

2 October. Birth of Richard, future Duke of Gloucester and King Richard III, youngest son of Richard Duke of York.

November. Henry VI ennobles his uterine half-brothers, Edmund and Jasper Tudor, as Earls of Richmond and Pembroke, respectively.

1453 17 July. French victory at Castillon ends English rule in Gascony; Calais is the only remaining English possession in France.

*c.*1 August. Onset of Henry VI's first bout of mental illness.

24 August. Percy and Neville families clash at Heworth Moor in Yorkshire.

13 October. Birth of Edward of Lancaster, son of Henry VI and Margaret of Anjou.

1454 27 March. York is named Lord Protector during the King's illness.

*c.*31 October. Percy and Neville families clash at Stamford Bridge near York.

*c.*25 December. Henry VI recovers.

1455 January. York surrenders the office of Protector.

22 May. First Battle of St. Albans – a Yorkist victory. York and his allies, the Neville Earls of Salisbury and Warwick, win control of the King and kill their chief enemies: Somerset, Northumberland, and Clifford.

19 November. York is appointed Lord Protector for the second time.

1456 25 February. York resigns as Lord Protector.

August. Court travels to Coventry and the Midlands.

1457 28 January. Birth of Henry Tudor, Earl of Richmond, the future Henry VII.

1458 25 March. Loveday

1459 23 September. Battle of Blore Heath – a Yorkist victory. Army under Richard Neville, Earl of Salisbury, defeats a Lancastrian army that tries to block its move to Ludlow.

12–13 October. Heavily outnumbered, the Yorkist lords flee from the royal army at Ludford Bridge outside Ludlow; York goes to Ireland, and Warwick, Salisbury, and March go to Calais.

20 November. Lancastrian-controlled Parliament opens at Coventry. The Yorkists are attainted.

1460 26 June. Yorkist Earls of Warwick, Salisbury, and March land in England from Calais.

	10 July. Battle of Northampton – a Yorkist victory. Warwick captures Henry VI and control of the government.
	3 August. James II of Scotland killed by a cannon fired to celebrate the arrival of his wife, Mary of Guelders, at the siege of Roxburgh; accession of eight-year-old James III.
	30 December. Battle of Wakefield – a Lancastrian victory. Deaths of York, Salisbury, and York's second son, Edmund Plantagenet, Earl of Rutland.
1461	2 February. Battle of Mortimer's Cross – a Yorkist victory.
	17 February. Second Battle of St. Albans – a Lancastrian victory. Margaret of Anjou and her son are reunited with Henry VI.
	4 March. Edward, Earl of March, York's eldest son, takes coronation oath and is proclaimed king as Edward IV at Westminster.
	27–28 March. Battle of Ferrybridge – a Yorkist victory. Lancastrian attempts to prevent a Yorkist crossing of the River Aire.
	29 March. Battle of Towton – a Yorkist victory. Edward IV wins throne and Henry VI and his family flee into Scotland.
	28 June. Official coronation of Edward IV.
	22 July. Charles VII of Frances dies; accession of Louis XI.
1464	25 April. Battle of Hedgeley Moor – a Yorkist victory in the north.
	1 May. Edward IV secretly marries Elizabeth Woodville at Grafton Regis, Northants.
	15 May. Battle of Hexham – a Yorkist victory leads to the execution of Henry Beaufort, the Lancastrian Duke of Somerset.
	25 December. Elizabeth Woodville is publicly introduced to the court as Queen.
1465	13 July. Henry VI is captured in Lancashire and imprisoned in the Tower of London.
1467	15 June. Death of Philip the Good, Duke of Burgundy; accession of Charles the Bold.
1468	3 July. Margaret of York, sister of Edward IV and Richard, marries Charles the Bold, Duke of Burgundy.
	3 August. Edward IV concludes an alliance with Burgundy, agreeing to send English troops to support the Duke against France.
1469	20 March. Battle of Nibley Green. Thomas Talbot, 2nd Viscount Lisle and William Berkeley, 2nd Baron Berkeley fight over land. Lisle is killed, ending in a victory for Berkeley. Last private battle in England.
	April–July. Robin of Redesdale's Rebellion is fomented by Warwick.
	11 July. Clarence marries Warwick's daughter, Isabel Neville, at Calais.
	24 July. Battle of Edgcote Moor – William Herbert, Earl of Pembroke, and other Yorkist lords are defeated by rebel forces under the direction of Warwick. A young Henry Tudor escapes the battlefield.
	27 July. William Herbert, Earl of Pembroke, and his brother Richard are executed by Warwick and Clarence at Queen Eleanor's Cross, Northampton.

TIMELINE

	29 July. Edward IV is taken into custody by Warwick's brother, George Neville, Archbishop of York, who places the king under the earl's 'protection'. Warwick now has control of two kings, earning him the title 'The Kingmaker'.
	c.10 September. Warwick is forced to release Edward IV from custody.
1470	12 March. Battle of Losecote Field – Edward IV defeats rebels led by Sir Robert Welles, operating under the direction of Warwick and Clarence.
	early April. Warwick and Clarence flee England.
	22 July. Warwick and Margaret of Anjou meet in Angers to conclude a formal accord known as the Angers Agreement.
	25 July. Prince Edward of Lancaster is formally betrothed to Warwick's daughter, Anne Neville.
	c.15 September. Warwick and Clarence land in West Country and declare for Henry VI.
	1 October. Elizabeth Woodville, wife of Edward IV, flees into sanctuary with her children at Westminster.
	2 October. Isolated in the north, Edward IV and a small party of supporters flee England for Burgundy.
	6 October. Warwick enters London in triumph.
	2 November. Birth in sanctuary of Prince Edward, eldest son of Edward IV; future Edward V.
	26 November. Readeption Parliament meets at Westminster
	c.13 December. Prince Edward of Lancaster marries Anne Neville.
1471	14 March. Edward IV and his supporters land in England at Ravenspur.
	3 April. Clarence abandons Warwick and is reconciled with his brothers, Edward IV and Richard.
	14 April. Battle of Barnet – Yorkist victory. Warwick is killed; Margaret of Anjou and Prince Edward of Lancaster land in England at Weymouth.
	4 May. Battle of Tewkesbury – a Yorkist victory. Prince Edward of Lancaster is killed on the field.
	7 May. Margaret of Anjou is captured and taken to the Tower of London.
	21 May. Edward IV enters London in triumph; Henry VI dies in the Tower of London.
	2 June. Jasper Tudor, Earl of Pembroke and Henry Tudor, Earl of Richmond escape from England. They head for France but possibly due to storms land in Brittany.
1472	Richard, Duke of Gloucester, marries Anne Neville, daughter of Warwick.
	Margaret Beaufort marries Thomas Stanley.
	11 September. Anglo-Breton Treaty of Châteaugiron agreed but not ratified by Edward until 24 October.

1473		c.17 August. Birth of Richard, second son of Edward IV and future Duke of York.
		30 September. John de Vere, the Lancastrian Earl of Oxford, seizes St. Michael's Mount, Cornwall.
1474		25 July. Treaty of London concludes a formal alliance between England and Burgundy against France.
1475		4 July. Edward IV crosses to Calais to begin invasion of France.
		29 August. Edward IV concludes Treaty of Picquigny with Louis XI, ending the English invasion of France.
1476		21 December. Death of Isabel, Duchess of Clarence.
1477		5 January. Death at the battle of Nancy of Charles the Bold, Duke of Burgundy, ally and brother-in-law of Edward IV.
		16 August. Charles the Bold's daughter and heiress marries Maximillian Habsburg, son of Frederick III, the future Holy Roman Emperor.
1478		18 February. George, Duke of Clarence, is executed for treason in the Tower of London
1480		August. Edward sends 1,500 archers and 30 men-at-arms under Sir John Milton, Sir Thomas Everingham and Sir John Dichefeld to Burgundy in support of Maximillian.
1481		June. Louis forces Edward IV to terms. They are ratified in secret by Edward in November 1481.
1482		27 March. Death of Mary, Duchess of Burgundy, begins ultimate division of Burgundy between France and Maximilian Habsburg of Austria – Mary's husband and eventual ruler of the Netherlands.
		11 June. Treaty of Fotheringhay is concluded between Edward IV and the Duke of Albany, brother of James III of Scotland.
		July. English army led by Richard, Duke of Gloucester invades Scotland.
		4 August. Peace Treaty with Scotland signed. Berwick falls 22 August.
		29 August. Death of Margaret of Anjou, widow of Henry VI, in France.
		23 December. Maximillian is forced to sign the Treaty of Arras with the French.
1483		9 April. Death of Edward IV; accession of Edward V.
		30 April. Richard, Duke of Gloucester, takes charge of his nephew, Edward V, at Stony Stratford on the road to London. They spend three days at Northampton before returning to London.
		13 June. Summary execution of William Hastings, Lord Hastings.
		17 June. Richard, Duke of York, leaves sanctuary at Westminster to join his brother, Edward V, at the Tower of London.
		22 June. Dr. Ralph Shaw delivers a public sermon at Paul's Cross in London setting forth Richard of Gloucester's claim to the throne
		26 June. At an assembly of political notables at Baynard's Castle in London, Henry Stafford, Duke of Buckingham, presents Richard of Gloucester with a petition requesting him to take the throne.
		6 July. Coronation of Richard III and Anne.

TIMELINE

21 July. Richard III leaves Windsor Castle for a Royal tour of his realm.
End of July. John Cheyne's rebellion
Early August. John Welles' rebellion from Maxey, Northants.
30 August. Death of Louis XI of France; accession of Charles VIII.
24 September. Buckingham writes to Henry asking for support.
10 October. The men of Kent launch their rebellion.
18 October. Buckingham's rebellion begins.
19 October. Richard hears of Buckingham's rebellion whilst at Lincoln and orders his army to meet at Leicester on 21 October
31 October. Henry sails from Brittany to England.
2 November. Buckingham is executed at Salisbury.
2 or 3 November. Henry arrives of the coast of England but fearing a trap returns to Brittany.
25 December. Henry Tudor, Earl of Richmond, takes oath to marry Elizabeth of York, eldest daughter of Edward IV.

1484 15 January. First meeting of the three Estates in Tours, France.
22 January. Richard holds his one and only Parliament.
20 February. Parliament is dissolved.
1 March. Elizabeth Woodville, widow of Edward IV, and her daughters leave sanctuary at Westminster.
13 March. Renewal of the Auld Alliance between France and Scotland.
7 April. Attempted abduction or murder of Pierre Landais in Brittany.
18 April. Louis of Orléans, the Duke of Alençon and the Count of Dunois arrive in Brittany seeking support from Landais against the Beaujeus.
April. Richard's son, Prince Edward, dies at Middleham castle.
30 May. Charles VIII's coronation at Reims.
8 June. Richard, whilst at Pontefract, agrees to a truce between Brittany and England.
June. In France, the Duke of Orléans rebels but is arrested, it is the beginning of the 'Mad War.'
June and July. Richard personally directs naval operations from Scarborough against both the Scots and French.
July. Colyngbourne's rebellion. Colyngbourne is captured and executed.
July? An alliance between Burgundy, England and Brittany against France is proposed.
11 August. Richard prohibits piracy against all nations, except France.
September. Henry escapes from Brittany into France.
September. Three-year peace treaty between England and Scotland.
October. Hammes Castle defects to Henry Tudor. John de Vere, earl of Oxford escapes and joins Tudor.

2 November. Sir William Brandon leads an armed revolt in Colchester which spreads into Hertfordshire.

6 December. Richard denounces how the French 'by many and sundry ways, conspire and study the means to the subversion of this our realm.'

8 December. Richard issues a general Commission of Array.

1485 January. Maximillian invades Flanders

17 March. Death of Anne Neville, wife of Richard III.

23 March. Orléans is forced to capitulate and submit to Madame at Evreux.

30 March. Richard III is forced to publicly deny any intention of marrying his niece Elizabeth of York, eldest daughter of Edward IV.

14 April. King Charles makes his formal entry into Rouen for the opening of the Norman Estates, accompanied by Henry Tudor.

Early May. Henry is given the support he needs to launch another invasion.

27 May. French army enters Ghent.

16 June. Richard moves the court to Nottingham and prepares for invasion.

22 June. Letters sent to Richard's sheriffs and commissioners of array instructing them to be ready to defend the realm against rebels and traitors.

June. Breton dissidents invade Brittany from France. Pierre Landais is arrested.

19 July. Landais hanged.

24 July. Richard orders that the Great Seal should be brought to him at Nottingham.

1 August. Henry sails from Harfleur to Wales.

7 August. Henry and his army land at Dale near Milford Haven in Wales.

9 August. A peace treaty is concluded between France and Brittany.

11 August. Richard hears of the landing and mobilises his army.

14 August. Henry reaches Machynlleth in Wales.

17 August. Henry is at Shrewsbury.

19 August. Henry meets Sir William Stanley at Stafford.

19 August. Richard leaves Nottingham for Leicester where he will meet his army.

20 August. Henry reaches Tamworth in the evening.

21 August. Morning: Richard and his assembled army leave Leicester.

21 August. Henry meets with the Stanleys at Atherstone.

22 August. Battle of Bosworth. Death of Richard III.

25 August. Richard III is buried in the Church of the Greyfriars, Leicester.

Sept–Oct. Rebellions against Henry Tudor.

30 October. Henry VII's coronation.

7 November. Henry VII's first Parliament opens at Westminster.

TIMELINE

	18 January. Henry VII marries Elizabeth of York, daughter of Edward IV.
1486	19 September. Birth of Prince Arthur, first child of Henry VII.
	24 May. A boy who is claimed to be Edward Plantagenet, Earl of Warwick, son of George, Duke of Clarence, and nephew of Edward IV, is crowned king of England in Dublin. Later named as Lambert Simnel by Henry VII.
1487	16 June. Battle of Stoke – Henry VII defeats Yorkist army led by 'Lambert Simnel'.
	28 June. Birth of Prince Henry, future Henry VIII.
1489	November. A man claiming to be Richard Duke of York, son of Edward IV, appears in Ireland. Later named by Henry VII as Perkin Warbeck.
	8 June. Death of Elizabeth Woodville, widow of Edward IV, at Bermondsey Abbey.
1492	3 November. Treaty of Étaples concluded between England and France, forcing 'Warbeck' to leave France for Burgundy. Warbeck spends most of 1492 in France and Burgundy, where he is supported by Margaret, Duchess of Burgundy and sister of Edward IV.
	23 July–3 August. 'Warbeck' launches unsuccessful invasion of Kent
1495	Henry VII authorises a tomb to be built over Richard III's grave in Leicester.
	10 July. Execution of William Stanley for his involvement in the 'Perkin Warbeck' conspiracy.
	November. 'Warbeck' is given shelter in Scotland by James IV.
	21 December. Death of Jasper Tudor, Duke of Bedford and uncle of Henry VII.
1497	17 June. Henry VII crushes Cornish rebels at the Battle of Black Heath.
	7 September. 'Warbeck' lands in Cornwall.
	30 September. The truce leading to the Treaty of Ayton is concluded with Scotland, ending Scottish support for 'Warbeck'.
	5 October. 'Warbeck' surrenders.
	16 November. Execution of 'Warbeck.'
1499	29 November. Execution of Edward Plantagenet Earl of Warwick, son of George, Duke of Clarence, and nephew of Edward IV.
	2 April. Death of Prince Arthur.
1502	6 May. Execution of Sir James Tyrell.
	11 February. Death of Elizabeth of York, wife of Henry VII and daughter of Edward IV.
1503	30 April. The treaty Intercursus Malus is concluded with Duke Philip of Burgundy; the treaty leads to the expulsion of leading Yorkist, Edmund de la Pole, Earl of Suffolk, from the Netherlands.
1504	29 July. Thomas Stanley dies at Lathom.
1506	21 April. Death of Henry VII; uncontested accession of Henry VIII as second king of the House of Tudor.
1509	29 June. Death of Margaret Beaufort, mother of Henry VII.

1525	24 February. Battle of Pavia and death of Richard de la Pole.	
1536	October–February 1537. The Pilgrimage of Grace.	
1541	27 May. Execution of the last Yorkist, Lady Margaret Pole, aged 68, daughter of George Duke of Clarence and niece of Richard III.	
2005	August. The Battlefields Trust begins the search for the Bosworth battlefield, on behalf of Leicestershire County Council.	
2009	February. Launch of the 'Looking for Richard Project'.	
2010	19 February. Site of the actual Battle of Bosworth is announced to the public.	
2012	24 August. Investigation of the likely site of Greyfriars Priory in Leicester begins.	
	12 September. The discovery of Richard III's remains are made public.	
2015	26 March. Richard III's remains are reinterred in Leicester Cathedral.	

1

The Wars of the Roses

*Ye shall hear of wars and rumours of war;
see that ye be not troubled, for all these things
must come to pass, but the end is not yet.*
                                    Matthew 26:6

The so-called Wars of the Roses were like no other wars in medieval England. Like the civil war between Stephen and Matilda now called the Anarchy (1135 to 1153), they were not fought for land, wealth or religious ideals but the right to rule the country. Exactly when the wars started has been debated by historians for many years. The first fighting began with Jack Cade's rebellion against Henry VI in 1450 and lasted for 37 more years. During this time there were five kings (Henry VI, Edward IV, Edward V, Richard III and Henry VII) and seven reigns, 10 *Coups d'etats*, 15 invasions (of which five were successful) and 16 battles, starting with the First Battle of St. Albans and ending with Stoke in 1487. There were also numerous sieges, failed rebellions and several private battles such as that between the Nevilles and Percys at Stamford Bridge in October 1454 and Thomas Talbot, 2nd Viscount Lisle and William Berkeley, 2nd Baron Berkeley at Nibley Green in March 1469. As the name suggests, the Wars of the Roses, rather than one long war, was a series of interconnected rebellions in four distinct phases:

    1450–9. Descent into War
    1460–5. The war of succession
    1469–71. The destruction of the Nevilles and Lancaster
    1483–7. Buckingham's rebellion and the rise of Henry Tudor

For the majority of the time, it was relatively peaceful, most of the war being fought with words and political manoeuvring within the Royal Court.

    At the time, there appears to have been no collective name and the fighting was simply referred to as York's rebellion, Warwick's rebellion etc. In 1646, Sir John Oglander published a pamphlet entitled *The Quarrel of the Warring Roses*. Then in 1762, David Hume wrote of 'the Wars of the Two Roses' in his *History of England*. The actual phrase 'The Wars of the Roses' is usually credited to Sir Walter Scott in his 1829 novel *Anne of Geierstein*. Some modern historians have since used the term 'Cousins' Wars' to describe the period, there is however no contemporary evidence to support that this was used at the time.

Whilst the White Rose was one of the badges of the house of York, probably coming from either the 1st Duke of York or the Mortimer line, the earliest association linking a red rose with the House of Lancaster was Edward I's brother, the Earl of Lancaster, using a red rose device. It was also used by Henry Bolingbroke – the future Henry IV, and the first king of the House of Lancaster – when he had red roses decorating his pavilion at a joust in 1398. However, the red rose was not used as a badge of the house of Lancaster again until after Henry Tudor had taken the throne, when he combined the so-called Lancastrian red rose with the White Rose of York to create his most famous heraldic device, the Tudor Rose. This floral union symbolised the restoration of peace and harmony and his marriage to Elizabeth of York in January 1486.

A Family Divided

The wars may have started in 1450, but we have to go back 100 years to the reign of Edward III to find its roots. Edward III, unlike his father Edward II, was a strong and energetic king. During his reign, he succeeded in regaining royal authority and transformed England into one of the most formidable military powers in Europe. When in 1337, Edward declared himself rightful heir to the French throne, war with the French was inevitable. What followed, known today as the Hundred Years War, ravaged France and the south coast of England until 1453. Within a few years the English controlled huge parts of France, prompting the contemporary chronicler Jean Froissart to write of Edward, 'His like had not been seen since the days of King Arthur.'

To prosecute a war of this scale, Edward needed huge amounts of manpower but soon found that the old feudal system of obligatory service was not effective. Instead, he created a system of recruitment by contract, with the nobles acting as recruiting agents. The nobles recruited lesser nobles, who in turn would each recruit a set number of men, or even lesser nobles and so on. In return for a fixed period in the army a soldier could expect to receive pay, clothing and the support from the noble, and all this would be laid out in a written contract. In effect, this created private armies for the nobles. With a strong king and a common cause it was very effective, but as we shall see, in different circumstances, open to abuse.

Edward had five sons that reached maturity: Edward of Woodstock, Prince of Wales (the name Black Prince came long after his death); Lionel of Antwerp, 1st Duke of Clarence; John of Gaunt, 1st Duke of Lancaster; Edmund of Langley, 1st Duke of York; and Thomas of Woodstock, 1st Duke of Gloucester. Edward as the eldest was heir to the throne and appeared to be following in his father's footsteps after the stunning victories over the French at Crécy and Poitiers.

Edward's second son Lionel had been betrothed as a child to Elizabeth de Burgh, 4th Countess of Ulster (died 1363), daughter and heiress of William de

Burgh, 3rd Earl of Ulster. He was called Earl of Ulster from 1347. He married her in 1352, but before this date he had entered into possession of her great Irish inheritance. Their daughter Philippa was born at Eltham Palace in Kent on 16 August 1355. On 13 November 1362, he received the title the 1st Duke of Clarence. The following year Lionel's wife died. In 1366 it was proposed that Lionel should marry Violante daughter of the Visconti of Milan. After two years' negotiations a settlement was arranged. Violante brought with her a dower of two million florins of gold and many Piedmontese towns and castles, including Alba. According to *Hardyng's Chronicle*, there was talk in England of how the princes and towns of Italy had promised to do homage to Lionel, and how in time he might become emperor or king of Italy. After the marriage of his 12-year-old daughter Philippa to Edmund Mortimer, 3rd Earl of March, in the Queen's Chapel at Reading Abbey, Lionel then left for Italy. His marriage to Violante was celebrated before the door of Milan Cathedral on 5 June. Five months of continuous feasts, jousts, and revels followed, but early in October Lionel was taken by a sudden and violent sickness at Alba and died on 7 October 1368.

Edward's third son, John of Gaunt, aged 19, married his third-cousin Blanche at Reading Abbey on 19 May 1359. Blanche was daughter and ultimately sole heiress of Henry of Grosmont, Duke of Lancaster. When his father-in-law died in 1361, Gaunt received half of Henry's lands, the title Earl of Lancaster, as well as the Palatinate of Lancaster and became the greatest landowner in the north of England. The following year John inherited the rest of the Lancaster property when Blanche's sister Maud, Countess of Leicester, died without issue. On 13 November 1362, John received the title Duke of Lancaster from his father.

On 6 August 1385, Edward's fourth son, Edmund of Langley, was elevated to Duke of York. Langley's first wife, Isabella, was a daughter of King Peter of Castile and María de Padilla. She was also the sister of the Infanta Constance of Castile, the second wife of Langley's brother John of Gaunt. They had two sons and a daughter: Edward of Norwich (*c.*1373–25 October 1415), Constance of York (*c.*1374–28 November 1416) and Richard of Conisburgh, 3rd Earl of Cambridge (*c.*20 July 1375–5 August 1415). The contemporary chronicler Thomas Walsingham considered Isabella to have somewhat loose morals. Richard, his youngest son received no lands from his father and was mentioned neither in his father's will nor his brother's will (although his brother's will might not have been made until after Richard's execution). Because of this, it has been suggested that Richard's father and brother did not recognise him as a full blood relative, and that he may have been the child of an illicit liaison between his mother and the King's half-brother John Holland.

It may also be the source of the now often vaunted false paternity suggested by the intensive investigation into Richard III's DNA. DNA samples were taken from the descendants of Henry Somerset, 5th Duke of Beaufort, who descended from Richard's 2nd great-grandfather Edward III. However, although the Mitochondrial DNA (which is passed from mother to child) extracted from Richard matches that taken from descendants of his sister Anne of York, the Y-chromosomal DNA (which is passed from father to son) extracted from the skeleton apparently doesn't. This means that somewhere along the line at least one false paternity occurred. These could have occurred anywhere between Edward III and Henry Somerset, the 5th Duke of Beaufort (1744–1803).

Tragedy struck in 1376 when the Black Prince died after an illness. Edward III died a year later and in accordance with the rules of succession, the Black Prince's 10-year-old son, Richard, succeeded to the throne. Richard II's reign was a troubled one, and plots and revolts continually plagued him. He did not enjoy war as his father and grandfather had done and negotiated a 28-year truce with the French, losing much of the previously won territory in the process. As the years passed, Richard II became more tyrannical. As he had not produced an heir, he named his cousin Roger Mortimer, 4th Earl of March, as his successor. The Earls of March (the March was the borderlands between England and Wales) were the chief Anglo-Norman lords in Ireland and the second most senior line of descent in succession to the throne, through Roger's mother Philippa, the only daughter of Lionel of Antwerp.

During King Richard II's minority, Gaunt effectively ruled the country and had become the wealthiest and most powerful man in England after the King. He also had an eye for the ladies, marrying three times. His third wife was his long-time mistress Katherine Swynford and they already had three sons by the time they were married, who were legitimised by Parliament in 1397. The children took the family name of Beaufort and were eventually known as the Dukes of Somerset.

On Gaunt's death in 1399, Richard II confiscated all his land and exiled his son and heir Henry of Bolingbroke for life. Henry returned to England with an army. The entire project was, according to both Froissart and Henry IV's first biographer, John Capgrave, writing in the 1440s, engineered by Archbishop Arundel, not by Henry himself. It seems clear that plans were put in place for Henry's usurpation of the throne by his father long before his death. During the preceding months complex planning and plotting had been taking place on Lancastrian estates in England. And on a tide of popular support, aided by disaffected nobles, Henry was soon in control of the kingdom. On 13 October 1399, he was proclaimed King Henry IV, bypassing the descendants of Edward III's second surviving son, Lionel of Antwerp, 1st Duke of Clarence. Richard meanwhile was held captive in Pontefract Castle where he eventually died, probably from starvation, in February 1400. The house of Lancaster now ruled England.

Henry IV's reign, like Richard's before him, was plagued by rebellions, instigated in part by the Mortimers, rightful heirs to the throne: Edward, 2nd Duke of York, and his sister Constance. In September 1400 Owain Glyndŵr began a rebellion in Wales. A separate series of rebellions were led by Henry Percy, Earl of Northumberland with his son Harry Hotspur.

In 1402, Edward III's last surviving son, Edmund of Langley, 1st Duke of York, died at the age of 61. Although a competent military commander during the Hundred Years War he was retiring and unambitious, playing little part in the politics of the time. His son, Edward, inherited the dukedom and made Fotheringhay in Northamptonshire his home, repairing the castle, and where he began the building of the nearby Collegiate Church. Early in 1408, aged 32, Edward's brother Richard of Conisburgh, 3rd Earl of Cambridge, secretly married his cousin twice-removed, Anne Mortimer, the daughter of Roger Mortimer, 4th Earl of March and elder sister of Edmund, the 5th earl. Anne brought Richard no financial benefit and it seems as though theirs was a marriage of love. Their marriage was validated by papal dispensation on 23 May 1408.

Henry IV survived all the rebellions against him, and in 1413 his son Henry V peacefully succeeded to the throne. Henry V was the epitome of medieval kingship and an outstanding military commander. He renewed the war against France with vigour, conquering much of northern France, and his famous victory at the Battle of Agincourt has long since entered national mythology. In May 1420, the Treaty of Troyes was signed by Henry V of England and Charles VI of France. It recognised Henry V as Charles' successor, and stipulated that Henry's heirs would succeed him on the throne of France, thereby disinheriting the 17-year-old Dauphin of France. The treaty also betrothed Charles VI's daughter, Catherine of Valois, to Henry V, further strengthening his claim to France's throne. His successes intensified English pride in the King and his dynasty, ending the uprisings that marked his father's and the beginning of his own reign.

Richard of Conisbrough, grandfather of Richard III. Executed in the aftermath of the Southampton Plot of 1415. Stained glass window in St. Laurence's Church, Ludlow. (Author)

Richard Plantagenet, 3rd Duke of York

Richard Plantagenet, 3rd Duke of York, was born on 21 September 1411, the son of Richard of Conisburgh, 3rd Earl of Cambridge, by his wife Anne Mortimer, who was said to have died giving birth to him. She was buried at Kings Langley, Hertfordshire, once the site of Kings Langley Palace, perhaps in the conventual church which houses the tombs of her husband's father Edmund and his first wife Isabella of Castile. Through his mother, Anne, Richard had a claim to the English throne that was arguably superior to that of the reigning House of Lancaster.

On 31 July 1415, the day before Henry V and his army planned to sail to France, Edmund Mortimer, 5th Earl of March arrived at Portchester from

Southampton with news of a plot to usurp Henry. Richard of Cambridge, Sir Thomas Grey of Hetton, and Lord Scrope of Masham were named as the main conspirators. Although Cambridge pleaded with the King for clemency, he was beheaded on 5 August 1415 and buried in the chapel of God's House at Southampton. Although the Earl's title was forfeited, he was not attainted, and the four-year-old orphan Richard became his father's heir. Within weeks of his father's death, Richard's childless uncle, Edward of Norwich, 2nd Duke of York, died at the Battle of Agincourt on 25 October 1415. After some hesitation, King Henry V allowed Richard to inherit his uncle's title and (at his majority age of 21) the lands of the Duchy of York.

The wheel of fortune turned again in August 1422 when Henry V died, probably from dysentery. He was succeeded by his only son, Henry, who was just nine months old. Once again, the country found itself ruled by a child. During the King's minority, the longest in English history, England was governed by a council that included the King's younger uncle, Humphrey, Duke of Gloucester, and his great-uncle Henry Beaufort, Bishop of Winchester. English territories in France, which by this time amounted to almost a third of the country, were governed by Henry's eldest paternal uncle, John, Duke of Bedford. Henry VI was crowned at Westminster in 1429 and under the terms of the Treaty of Troyes proclaimed King of France on the death of Charles VI.

Richard, 3rd Duke of York, stained glass window in St. Laurence's Church, Ludlow. (Author)

In October 1417 Richard Duke of York's wardship was granted to Ralph Neville, 1st Earl of Westmorland, with the young Richard under the guardianship of Robert Waterton. Ralph Neville had fathered 23 children, 20 of whom survived infancy, through two wives and had many daughters needing husbands. So, in 1424 he betrothed the 13-year-old Richard to his daughter Cecily Neville, then aged nine. On the death of his maternal uncle Edmund Mortimer, 5th Earl of March, on 18 January 1425, Richard inherited the Earldom of March and Mortimer estates in Wales, and in the Welsh borders around Ludlow, as well as the Earldom of Ulster. In October 1425, when Ralph Neville died, he bequeathed the wardship of York to his widow, Joan Beaufort. By now the wardship was even more valuable. Little is recorded of Richard's early life. In May 1426 the so-called 'Parliament of Bats' was held at Leicester, so named because although weapons such as swords were banned, people brought clubs, sticks and bats. It was during this parliament that the Duke of Bedford knighted the four-year-old Henry VI in St.

Mary de Castro Church, who in turn knighted 36 others. One of them was the then 14-year-old Richard, 3rd Duke of York. In October 1429 (or earlier) York, aged 18, married Cecily Neville. They would have 13 children together and are listed on the Clare Roll of 1456:

> After the time of long barrenness,
> God first sent Anne, which signifyeth grace,
> In token that at her heart's heaviness,
> He as for barrenness would from them chase.
> Harry, Edward, Edmund, each in his place
> Succeeded; and after twain daughters came
> Elizabeth and Margaret, and afterwards William.
> John after William next born was,
> Which both be passed to God's grace:
> George was next, and after Thomas
> Born was, which son after did pace
> By the path of death into the heavenly place.
> Richard liveth yet: but last of all
> Was Ursula, to Him who God list call.

Richard, Cecily and his surviving children undoubtedly intended the Collegiate Church of St. Mary and All Saints at Fotheringhay to be the mausoleum of the House of York. It already housed the tomb of his uncle, Edward the second duke, and all the children who died young were buried there (although where has now been lost). In time, Richard, Cecily and their son Edmund, would also be buried in the Church.

St. Mary and All Saints Church Fotheringhay, Northants. Construction started under Edward 2nd Duke of York and continued under Richard, the 3rd Duke. (Author)

Richard became the wealthiest and most powerful noble in England, second only to the King himself, and had a greater claim to the throne. In 1448 he adopted the surname 'Plantagenet' which would serve to emphasise his royal lineage. The House of York was finally going to step into the limelight.

Burgundy and France

The English army's use of *chevauchée* raids ('scorched earth' tactics) had devastated the French economy and the French army had not achieved any major victories for a generation. French failures in the war were made worse as Charles VI, who became the French king in 1380, suffered from frequent bouts of insanity including at one point believing he was made of glass, and was often unable to rule. The King's brother Louis, Duke of Orléans, and the King's cousin John the Fearless, Duke of Burgundy, quarrelled over the regency of France and the guardianship of the royal children. This dispute included accusations that Louis was having an extramarital affair with the Queen, Isabeau of Bavaria, and allegations that John the Fearless kidnapped the royal children. The conflict climaxed with the assassination of the Duke of Orléans in 1407 on the orders of the Duke of Burgundy.

The Duke of Orléans was succeeded by his young son Charles and was placed in the custody of his father-in-law, the Count of Armagnac. Their faction became known as the 'Armagnacs' and the opposing party led by the Duke of Burgundy was called the 'Burgundian faction'. In 1418 Paris was seized by the Burgundians, who massacred the Count of Armagnac and about 2,500 of his followers. After all four of his older brothers had died in succession, the future French king, the 14-year-old Charles VII, assumed the title of Dauphin (heir to the throne). His first significant official act was to conclude a peace treaty with John the Fearless, the Duke of Burgundy, in 1419. This ended in disaster when Armagnac partisans assassinated John during a meeting under Charles's guarantee of protection. The new Duke of Burgundy, Philip the Good, blamed Charles for the murder and entered into an alliance with the English. Soon, nearly all of northern France and some parts of the south-west were under Anglo-Burgundian control with the English controlling Paris and Rouen whilst the Burgundian faction controlled Reims, which had served as the traditional coronation site for French kings since 816.

Charles VI died on 21 October 1422 in Paris, at the Hôtel Saint-Pol. He was interred in Saint Denis Basilica. The Dauphin Charles failed to make any attempts to expel the English from northern France out of indecision and a sense of hopelessness. Instead, he remained south of the Loire River, where he was still able to exert power, and maintained an itinerant court in the Loire Valley at castles such as Chinon. He was still customarily known as 'Dauphin', or derisively as 'King of Bourges', after the town where he generally lived.

A dramatic change of French fortunes began in 1429 after the 17-year-old Joan of Arc met with Charles at the Royal Court in the town of Chinon. On 29 April 1429, she arrived at the city of Orléans which had been besieged by the English for five months. The lifting of the siege on 8 May was interpreted by many of the French to be a sign of God, and it gained her the support of prominent clergy such as the Archbishop of Embrun and the theologian Jean Gerson, both of whom wrote supportive treatises immediately following this event. To the English, the ability of this peasant girl to defeat their armies was regarded as proof that she was possessed by the Devil. French victory followed victory. After pushing further into English and Burgundian-controlled territory, Charles was crowned King Charles VII of France in Reims Cathedral on 17 July 1429. On 23 May 1430, Jean was captured by the Burgundians north of Compiègne. She was handed over to the English for the sum of 10,000 livres tournois and put on trial for heresy on 9 January 1431 at Rouen, the seat of the English occupation government. Joan was executed by burning on 30 May 1431.

In the summer of 1435 representatives of England, France, and Burgundy which was virtually an independent state, met for the Congress of Arras. English negotiators believed it to be a peace negotiation between England and France and proposed an extended truce and a marriage between King Henry VI of England and a daughter of French king Charles VII of France. However, the English were unwilling to renounce their claim to the crown of France. When in mid-session the English delegation broke off from the congress to put down a raid by French captains Xaintrailles and La Hire, the French delegation and the leading clergy took the opportunity to urge Philip the Good to reconcile with Charles VII.

When the English delegation returned they found that their ally had switched sides. They walked away without an agreement. A week later the French and Burgundians agreed to the second Treaty of Arras. The treaty reconciled the longstanding feud between King Charles VII of France and Duke Philip III of Burgundy (Philip the Good). Philip recognised Charles VII as King of France and, in return, Philip was exempted from homage to the crown and received the Counties of Auxerre and Boulogne, the cities on the Somme and Péronne, Ponthieu and Vermandois, with its capital Saint-Quentin. By breaking the alliance between Burgundy and England, Charles VII consolidated his position as King of France against the rival English claim, isolating it. On 13 April 1436 the Parisians opened the gates of Paris to Jean de Dunois the illegitimate son of Louis I, Duke of Orléans, and Arthur de Richemont, the Constable of France. On 12 November 1437, Charles VII and his son Louis rode into Paris in triumph.

Henry VI: King of England

In 1437, Henry, aged 15, was declared old enough to rule. He sadly lacked the charisma and strength of his father. Pope Pius II would describe him as 'a man more timorous than a woman, utterly devoid of wit or spirit.' In November 1437 Piero da Monteita papal tax collector reported that Henry avoided the sight of women, affirming them to be the work of the Devil and quoted from the gospel, 'He who casts his eyes on a woman so as to lust after her has already committed adultery.' The *Hardyng Chronicle* described him as having 'great innocence, simplicity and inability to distinguish between good and evil.' Henry was an exceptionally pious man, with no interest in war, and spent his time on projects such as the foundation of Eton College and King's College, Cambridge, and to which he diverted funds that were urgently needed elsewhere. A French embassy in 1445 reported it was received by the King on three days, and all he said was '*Saint Jehan grant mercis*'. He had little understanding of the workings of government and much of the day-to-day running of the country was carried out by the Royal Council. These were advisors selected by the King to give counsel on questions of foreign and domestic policy and raising finance, as well as conducting daily administration and helping to dispense justice. Unsurprisingly, the great nobles considered themselves his natural advisors. Weak-willed, Henry was easily persuaded by the self-interested nobles and frequently granted titles, lands, offices, pardons, and monetary rewards without any thought to the merits or the consequences of their requests.

By 1430, Richard Duke of York was Constable of England, and two years later was appointed Guardian of the Coast of Normandy. In 1436, he was appointed to the most prestigious post in the royal court, the King's Lieutenant in France. Due to the poor state of the royal finances, largely due to Henry's spending (in one year alone, he spent the entire royal income on his court), York financed most of his campaigns himself.

Preferring to pursue a policy of peace between the two countries, Henry allowed England's military position in France to deteriorate. In 1444, a truce was negotiated with France and marriage between the 23-year-old Henry and King Charles's 16-year-old niece, Margaret of Anjou was arranged. Once crowned, it would not take long for the formidable Margaret to establish herself as the power behind the throne, and like her husband, she had her favourites. Writing in the 1450s, Thomas Gascoine said that, 'Almost all the affairs of the realm were conducted according to the Queen's will by fair means or foul.' According to the *English Chronicle*, 'The Queen, with such as were her affinity, ruled the realm as she liked. The officers of the realm especially the Earl of Wiltshire, Treasurer of England enriches himself, fleeced the poor people, disinherited rightful heirs and did many wrongs.'

Henry, anxious to achieve a final settlement in France, soon fulfilled a rash promise to surrender Maine and Anjou. The decision to sue for peace was not popular with the English people or the Duke of York, who openly opposed it in court. This led to York being replaced in France by one of Henry's favourites, his cousin Edmund Beaufort, Duke of Somerset in 1446. And to add insult to injury, York was made Lieutenant of Ireland for the next 10 years, effectively sending him into exile, although this may have been a position he wanted.

Whilst King Henry enjoyed the peace, the French prepared for war and in 1449 marched into Normandy with three armies. Edmund Beaufort, Duke of Somerset, failed to gather in his garrisons to form a substantial field force to oppose them. During October 1449, the French laid siege to Rouen, the English capital of Normandy. Somerset surrendered it almost without a fight. Within a year Normandy itself had fallen. As a consequence, Somerset became distinctly unpopular. However, because he retained the King's favour, he maintained his prestigious position at court. This just added to the unrest at home.

Descent into War

In June 1450, 3,000 men of Kent and Sussex rose in revolt and marched on London led by a mysterious figure known as Jack Cade. Unlike the Peasants' Revolt almost 70 years earlier, their number included lords, landowners and merchants. Their demands were simple: remove from power those they considered traitors (such as Somerset), restore justice to the counties, and put men of royal blood (such as York) in key positions. As with so many other protests of this type, it began peacefully but soon turned ugly. After presenting their complaints the rebels began to return home. However, the King's men began to harry the rebels and attacked the county of Kent as well, threatening to turn it into a 'deer forest'. The rebels returned to London, dragging members of Henry's council into the street and executing them. An orgy of violence and looting followed and only ended when the citizens of London drove them out after vicious street fighting that left hundreds dead.

Within weeks, York returned to England without permission, and after evading an attempt by Henry to intercept him, arrived in London on 27 September. By this time, the unrest in London was such that Somerset had to be put in the Tower of London for his own safety. In April 1451, Somerset was released from the Tower and appointed Captain of Calais. When one of York's councillors, Thomas Young, the MP for Bristol, proposed that York be recognised as heir to the throne, he was sent to the Tower and Parliament was dissolved. Frustrated by his lack of political power, York retired to Ludlow. In 1452 York, declaring that his sole object was to rid Henry of Somerset and other evil counsellors, raised a force and marched to London. Henry and a royal army met him at Dartford, and York laid before him a bill of accusation against Somerset, at the same time swearing fealty to the king. However, York still lacked any real support outside Parliament and his own retainers. Then, a bitter feud between the Nevilles and Percys boiled over into armed conflict with Somerset supporting the Percys' cause. The Nevilles, although related to York, had up to this point been Lancastrian supporters but with Somerset against them, they sided with York.

During the summer of 1453, everything changed. Firstly, Margaret of Anjou found herself pregnant. Then, in August, an attempt to regain lost territory in France ended in disaster when an English army in Gascony was ripped to shreds by French artillery at the Battle of Castillon. The defeat spelt the end of English rule in France, and soon afterwards Henry VI suffered a catastrophic mental breakdown. He became completely unresponsive, unable to speak, and had to be led from room to room. Modern analysis of his symptoms have led experts to agree that it was a form of schizophrenia, probably inherited from his grandfather, Charles VI of France. With no sign of Henry recovering, a Great Council was called, and despite attempts by Somerset to prevent him attending and the protestations of Margaret of Anjou, York was appointed Protector of the Realm and Chief Councillor.

York wasted no time in committing Somerset to the Tower and appointing his brother-in-law, Richard Neville, 5th Earl of Salisbury, as Chancellor. When Henry recovered his reason in January 1455 York was quickly dismissed and Somerset released. York, Salisbury and Salisbury's eldest son, Richard Neville, Earl of Warwick (who would be known to future generations as 'The Kingmaker'), returned to their estates and gathered their armies. York's dispute with Somerset would have to be settled by force. On one side, the House of York with their powerful Neville supporters, on the other, the House of Lancaster supported by Somerset and the Percys, Earls of Northumberland.

On 21 April, the King and his advisors decided to hold a council at Leicester the following month. York, Salisbury and Warwick were invited of course, but they suspected it was a trap and instead decided to intercept the King and take him into their 'protection'. The two sides collided at St. Albans on 22 May. The fighting that followed was closer to an armed brawl than a battle. But significantly, among the dead were Somerset, Henry Percy, 2nd Earl of Northumberland and Thomas Clifford, 8th Baron de Clifford. The King was effectively York's prisoner.

Henry once again went into decline and York was again made Protector. His Protectorate lasted until February the next year when the King began to recover. With the birth of her son, Edward, Margaret began to get more involved in the affairs of state and court politics. She began by removing Yorkist sympathisers from positions of the royal office including Warwick, who was now Captain of Calais, starving him of funds in an attempt to force him out. However, Warwick turned to what was effectively piracy to pay his troops. With all attempts to stop York and his supporters ending in failure, Margaret played her last card in June 1459.

The War of Succession

The Royal army, now under command of the Queen's new favourite, Henry Stafford, Duke of Buckingham and a great-grandson of Edward III through Thomas of Woodstock, marched on Ludlow, York's powerbase in the Welsh Marches. Salisbury, en route for Ludlow was ambushed by a Lancastrian army at Blore Heath on 23 September 1459. However, Salisbury turned the tables by feigning retreat in his centre. The Lancastrian cavalry under Lord Audley charged and were cut to pieces. A second attack on foot by Lord Dudley was also destroyed.

York was ready for the Lancastrians and formed a defensive position at Ludford Bridge, just outside Ludlow, on 12 October 1459, but disaster struck when Andrew Trollop and a contingent of men from Calais defected to the King's cause. The Yorkists fled. York and Edmund, his second son, to Ireland, Warwick and Edward, York's eldest son, to Calais. In 1460, the Yorkist lords planned a return to England. Warwick and Edward, the 'Calais Lords' as they were known, landed at Sandwich and marched north. The Lancastrians who were now based at Coventry marched south. The two sides met at Northampton on 10 July 1460. Mid-battle, Lord Grey came over to the Yorkist side and in the ensuing rout all the Lancastrian commanders were killed and the King taken into custody.

Aged 18, it was Edward's first battle. His skeleton, exhumed in 1789, measured six feet 3–3/4 inches, nearly a foot taller than the average fifteenth-century man. *The Croyland Chronicle* described Edward as 'a person of most elegant appearance and remarkable beyond all others for the attractions of his person.' Other contemporary writers described Edward in superlatives, 'the tallest', 'the fairest', 'the strongest.' He did, however, have a weakness for the ladies. Mancini wrote, 'he was licentious in the extreme … he pursued with no discrimination the married and the unmarried, the noble and the lowly: however, he took none by force.'

York returned to England soon after Northampton, and for the first time asserted his claim to the throne. After a long discussion, a compromise was effected, by which Henry was to retain the crown during his lifetime, after which it was to revert to York and his heirs. However, Queen Margaret refused to recognise this arrangement and gathered an army in the north. The two sides clashed again at Wakefield (30 December 1460), but this time both York and his son Edmund were killed. The Yorkist claim to the throne then passed to his son Edward who went on to defeat the Lancastrians at Mortimer's Cross (2 February 1461). As dawn broke, a meteorological phenomenon known as a parhelion (sun dog) occurred: three suns were seen to be rising. The appearance of the parhelion so soon before the battle seems to have frightened his troops, but Edward of York appears to have convinced them that it represented the Holy Trinity and that therefore God was on their side.

However, the tables were turned when Warwick was defeated, and Henry VI was recovered by a Lancastrian army led by Queen Margaret at the Second Battle of St. Albans on 17 February. Despite this setback, Edward was formally declared king in London on 4 March 1461. Friend and foe could see his inspiring leadership in the front line of battle, using his great height to advantage. Edward would go on to prove himself to be an outstanding battlefield commander and never lost a battle. His skill frequently gained tactical advantages and his ability to 'read' a battlefield meant he could position his forces favourably.

Once crowned, Edward and Warwick went on to virtually wipe out the Lancastrian army 25 days later at the Battle of Towton on Palm Sunday, 29 March 1461. It is still known today as the bloodiest battle in English history. Lancastrian resistance continued in the north and was finally extinguished by Warwick's brother, John Neville, in the Battle of Hexham on 15 May 1464. Henry VI had escaped into the Pennines, where he spent a year in hiding, but was finally caught by Edward's men in July 1465 and imprisoned in the Tower of London. Queen Margaret fled to France with her son, the young Prince Edward, and many of their leading supporters.

On becoming king, Edward met and secretly married Elizabeth Woodville (at the time called Widville or Wydville), the widow of Sir John Grey of Groby, a Lancastrian knight who had been killed in the Second Battle of St. Albans in 1461. Elizabeth had two sons from her marriage, Thomas, later created Marquess of Dorset, and Richard Grey. Elizabeth was the eldest child of Sir Richard Woodville, created Baron Rivers by Henry VI on 9 May 1448. Two years later, as Sir Richard, he was invested as a Knight of the Garter in 1450. He was appointed Warden of the Cinque Ports in 1459. Her mother was Jacquetta of Luxembourg, whose first husband was John of Lancaster,

Duke of Bedford, the brother of Henry V. Elizabeth first met Edward when she came to petition him for the restoration of her son's estates. The King had wanted her to become his mistress, but she refused. Bewitched by her beauty, he finally proposed, and they were supposedly married in secret at the Woodville's manor of Grafton in Northamptonshire on 1 May 1464. It was the first royal match with an Englishwoman since the thirteenth century. When he announced the marriage, a horrified Privy Council told him 'that he must know that she was no wife for a prince such as himself, for she was not the daughter of a duke or earl … but a simple knight.'

Elizabeth was a strong-willed woman and brought her large and ambitious family to court. The Woodvilles proved to be avaricious and grasping and they were soon occupying key government positions. Richard Woodville was created Earl Rivers in 1466 and appointed Lord Treasurer in March 1466, then Constable of England on 24 August 1467. They also gained advantageous and prestigious marriages for their other 12 surviving children amongst the nobility. This included Catherine, their eighth daughter, to Henry Stafford, 2nd Duke of Buckingham and Richard III's future supporter. Their rapid rise alienated the overmighty subject Warwick, turning him from Edward's supporter into his relentless enemy.

The Destruction of the Nevilles and Lancaster

In 1469, Warwick, his influence in court waning, instigated a rebellion. Edward's brother, George, Duke of Clarence also heartily disliked the new Queen. Warwick, who possessed influence over George and with whom he had been brought up, wished to arrange a marriage between him and his eldest daughter and co-heiress, Isabel Neville. The King refused to sanction the match, but in defiance of his brother Clarence married Isabel at the Église Notre-Dame de Calais.

An army led by 'Robin of Redesdale' marching south was met by a largely Welsh army led by William Herbert, Earl of Pembroke, sent by Edward to suppress them. The ensuing battle which took place at Edgcote in Northamptonshire on 24 July was a disaster for the Yorkists, the flower of Welsh nobility either cut down or executed. Edward himself was taken prisoner at Honiley in Warwickshire by Warwick's brother George, whilst in bed. Soon after, the senior Woodvilles, Earl Rivers and Sir John Woodville, were captured and executed. However, with the political tide still against him, Warwick was forced to release Edward in October.

Despite attempts at reconciliation on Edward's part and although pardoned, Warwick with Clarence tried again, inciting a rebellion in Lincolnshire under the leadership of Robert Welles, Viscount Welles, which was crushed by Edward at the Battle of Empingham (Losecote Field) on 12 March 1470. Warwick and Clarence promptly took a ship for Calais with the Countess of Warwick, and her daughters Anne Neville and the heavily pregnant Isabel, Duchess of Clarence, fleeing the country. Isabel's child was stillborn and buried at sea. Denied access to Calais, they sought refuge with King Louis XI of France.

Warwick entered into an alliance with Margaret of Anjou who had been in exile in France for nine years, agreeing to restore the deposed Henry VI in exchange for French support. This alliance was sealed by the betrothal of Warwick's younger daughter, Anne Neville, to Edward, the Lancastrian Prince of Wales, at the Château d'Amboise in France. On 9 September 1470, Warwick, Clarence and Jasper Tudor landed in Devon. His army reached Coventry where it was joined by the Earl of Shrewsbury and Thomas Stanley. Warwick's powerful brother, John Neville, 1st Marquess of Montagu, also switched his allegiance to the Lancastrians and with a large army converged on Edward who was at Doncaster. Trapped between two armies, Edward fled to King's Lynn and then to Burgundy with Hastings, Rivers, Worcester, Norfolk, and Saye.

Henry VI was briefly restored to the throne (an act now known as the Readeption) but was in reality little more than the puppet of the ambitious Warwick. During Henry VI's restoration, Queen Elizabeth took sanctuary at Westminster Abbey where she gave birth to the Yorkist Prince of Wales, also named Edward. Warwick and Clarence had Parliament disinherit Edward IV and his heirs, claiming the King was not the true son of the Duke of York, but the product of Duchess Cecily's liaison with an archer named Blaybourne, who was in the employ of the Duke of York when he was stationed in France.

In November 1470 French ambassadors arrived in England to finalise an agreement between Warwick and King Louis XI to make war on Burgundy. On 6 February 1471 the Bishop of Bayeux wrote to his king to confirm that the alliance between Warwick and France against King Edward and Charles, Duke of Burgundy, was now agreed. The same day Warwick wrote to the Calais garrison ordering them to begin the war. Charles of Burgundy, fearing the new-found Anglo-French alliance, met with Edward in early January 1471 and provided the necessary resources for King Edward to return to England and regain his throne.

On 14 March 1471, Edward and his brother Richard returned to England with an army. They first marched to York and then to Coventry. Clarence promptly switched sides and joined Edward's forces. The three brothers and their army were heading out of London when they found the way barred by Warwick's army at Barnet on 14 April. It was to be Warwick's last battle and the 18-year-old Richard of Gloucester's first. A thick morning fog hampered both sides, but eventually Warwick's troops were routed, and Warwick was himself cut down trying to make his escape.

As Edward's army was battling Warwick's, a new threat appeared when Margaret of Anjou landed at Weymouth with another army. Margaret was heading for the Welsh border regions where she could join with Jasper Tudor. Edward marched to meet them, and the two sides clashed at Tewkesbury on 4 May. It was a decisive victory for the Yorkists, with the last of the Lancastrians, including the 17-year-old Prince Edward, Margaret's son, killed or executed. The handful of Lancastrian supporters that remained escaped to France, including Jasper Tudor and his young nephew Henry.

At the beginning of May 1471, Thomas Neville, an illegitimate son of William Neville and cousin of Warwick, sometimes called the Bastard of Fauconberg, landed at Sandwich. He advanced towards London, gathering troops as he went, and received notable support from Canterbury. On 14 May, he wrote to London's aldermen, asking to be allowed to bring his men into the city. When they refused, he burnt Southwark and laid siege to the city with an estimated 20,000 men. When London resisted, Thomas and 600 horsemen rode to Sandwich via Rochester, where he learned that the Lancastrian cause was lost. Edward IV marched on Sandwich and captured most of the Bastard's followers, although Thomas and some of his fleet escaped. Thomas fled to Southampton, where Edward took him prisoner. On 22 September 1471, he was executed at Middleham. His head was set on London Bridge, 'looking into Kentward'.

Edward was once again king, and Henry a prisoner in the Tower of London. By the end of the May Henry VI was dead, the circumstances shrouded in mystery. It was the end of the struggle between the Houses of York and Lancaster. Or so it was thought.

War broke out between France and Burgundy in 1472. Duke Charles laid siege to Beauvais and other towns. However, these sieges proved unsuccessful; the Siege of Beauvais was lifted on 22 July 1472, and Charles finally sued for peace.

On 28 May 1473, Lancastrian John de Vere, 13th Earl of Oxford, landed at St. Osyth in Essex. However, he fled when faced by an army led by Henry Bourchier, 1st Earl of Essex, Lord Dinham and the Gascon, Gaillard Durfort, Lord Duras. Oxford had escaped to France after the Battle of Barnet and gathered support at the French court who funded a number of raids on Calais. After St. Osyth he returned to France where a Milanese source stated that early in July, Lord Oxford, asking for money to start the war, sent the King of France 24 'seals of knights and lords and a duke' as proof of their determination to rise against Edward but Louis refused to help. Oxford turned to piracy and according to Warkworth, he acquired plenty of booty and 'riches.' That October, Oxford with 80 men invaded the coast of Cornwall and occupied St. Michael's Mount. Edward IV sent John Fortescue in December with pardons for all except Oxford, his two brothers, and Lord Beaumont. They surrendered on 1 February 1474. The Earl was then imprisoned at Hammes, which was the period's maximum-security gaol, joining Archbishop Neville who had been arrested for treason after Barnet.

Edward put an alliance with Burgundy and Brittany together. Then in 1475, he declared war on France. His army, said to be the largest assembled, landed at Calais in June. However, his ally Charles the Bold, Duke of Burgundy, failed to provide any significant military assistance, which led Edward to undertake negotiations with the French. He came to terms with the Treaty of Picquigny, which provided him with an immediate payment of 75,000 crowns and a yearly pension of 50,000 crowns, thus allowing him to 'recoup his finances'. The English renounced their claim to French lands such as Normandy, and the Hundred Years' War could be said to be finally over. Louis bragged that although his father had driven the English out by force of arms, he had driven them out by force of pâté, venison, and good French wine.

The same year, Clarence's wife Isabel gave birth to a son, Edward, later Earl of Warwick. They already had a daughter, Margaret, born on 14 August

1473. Isabel died on 22 December 1476, two months after giving birth to a short-lived son named Richard (6 October 1476–1 January 1477), and they were possibly buried together at Tewkesbury Abbey in Gloucestershire. Their surviving children were cared for by their aunt, Anne Neville, until she died in 1485. Clarence was convinced Isabel had been poisoned by one of her ladies-in-waiting, Ankarette Twynyho, whom, as a consequence, he had judicially murdered in April 1477, by summarily arresting her and bullying a jury at Warwick into convicting her of murder by poisoning. She was hanged immediately after the trial. Clarence's mental state, never stable, deteriorated from that point and led to his involvement in yet another rebellion against his brother Edward.

The arrest and committal to the Tower of London of one of Clarence's retainers, an Oxford astronomer named Dr John Stacey, led to his confession under torture that he had used the black arts and had 'imagined and compassed' the death of the King. Stacey implicated Thomas Blake, a chaplain at Stacey's College (Merton College, Oxford) and Thomas Burdett. All three were tried for treason, convicted, and condemned to be drawn to Tyburn and hanged. Blake was saved at the eleventh hour by a plea for his life by James Goldwell, Bishop of Norwich, but the other two were put to death as ordered. Edward summoned Clarence to Windsor and accused him of treason, before ordering his immediate arrest on 10 June 1477. Mancini writing after the death of Edward IV, made it clear that he thought the Woodvilles were behind Clarence's arrest because 'according to established usage, she was not the legitimate wife of the king,' and that her children would never come to the throne – unless Clarence was removed.

Clarence was imprisoned in the Tower of London and put on trial for treason against his brother Edward IV. Clarence was not present whilst Edward himself prosecuted his brother before demanding that Parliament pass a Bill of Attainder against him. Edward declared that Clarence was guilty of 'unnatural, loathly treasons' which were aggravated by the fact that he was his brother, who, if anyone did, owed him loyalty and love. Following his conviction, he was 'privately executed' at the Tower on 18 February 1478, by tradition in the Bowyer Tower, and soon after the event, the rumour circulated that he had been drowned in a butt of Malmsey, a fortified wine.

Charles the Bold, Duke of Burgundy, had been killed fighting against René II, Duke of Lorraine, and the Swiss Confederacy at the Siege of Nancy on 5 January 1477. Consequently, his only daughter Mary had inherited all the large Burgundian domains in France and the Low Countries. She had married Maximilian Habsburg, son of Frederick III, the future Holy Roman Emperor on 16 August 1477, and he claimed the territories by right of his wife. The Duchy of Burgundy was also claimed by Louis XI, King of France under Salic Law and vigorously contested the Habsburg claim, threatening war. Maximilian undertook the defence of his wife's dominions from an attack by Louis and envoys, including Edward's sister, Margaret, the Dowager Duchess of Burgundy, were sent to England asking for support. Edward eventually sent 1,500 archers and 30 men-at-arms under Sir John Milton, Sir Thomas Everingham and Sir John Dichefeld in August 1480, which he described as an appetiser for the dowry for Anne of York.

Edward IV was disappointed by the failure of his 1474 treaty with James III of Scotland who had promised that his son, Prince James would marry Cecily of York. The betrothal was made in October 1474 with a 45-year truce to last until 1519. However, border conflict had restarted in 1480, perhaps due to Scotland's 'Auld Alliance' with France. According to one chronicle, the Earl of Angus had attacked Bamburgh Castle, and the Earl of Northumberland had raided in Scotland. By October 1480, James III had written to Louis XI of France asking for guns and artillerymen to repulse further attacks. Eleven ships were put on war-footing for Scotland in February 1481 and Sir Robert Ratcliffe was commanded to arm a fleet with guns and gunners on 8 July. These ships commanded by John Howard made raids in Forth, attacking Blackness Castle and harassing shipping in the spring and autumn of 1481.

In 1482, Edward backed an attempt by Alexander Stewart, 1st Duke of Albany, brother of King James, to take the Scottish throne. Albany fled by sea to Paris, where in September 1479 he was welcomed by King Louis XI and received royal favour by his marriage to Anne de la Tour. Louis, however, would not assist him to attack his brother the king, and crossing to England he made a treaty with King Edward IV at Fotheringhay in June 1482. Edward reached Fotheringhay Castle to plan strategy with Richard of Gloucester later in 1482, but returned to London, perhaps with failing health and energy, never joining the campaign. Gloucester led an invasion of Scotland that resulted in the capture of Edinburgh and the King of Scots himself. However, once the English left, the Scottish nobles freed the King. Albany fled to Dunbar between Christmas and the New Year. On 2 January 1483 Albany made an abortive second attempt to seize James III. Edward IV was offered the restoration of the dowry, so far as paid, of the Princess Cecilia; but this was never carried out, and negotiations for the marriage of Princess Margaret of Scotland with Anthony, Lord Rivers took place. On 11 February 1483 Edward entered into a new treaty with Albany to aid him in acquiring the Scottish crown, and promised him one of his daughters in marriage. On 19 March Albany managed to force James III into a humiliating indenture. by which, among other provisions, James granted Albany a full remission for all 'treason and other misdeeds.'

Edward himself fell fatally ill at Easter 1483. In the small hours of 9 April, King Edward IV died, a few days short of his 41st birthday. It is not known what actually caused Edward's death. After his exile in Europe, he ate and drank excessively. Mancini reported that he used emetics, but still appeared grand and regal. Commines saw Edward in 1475 during the French Campaign and noted Edward was 'beginning to get fat and I had seen him on previous occasions looking more handsome.' Household records in 1478 state that Edward had health officers 'including the doctor of physic, who held consultation with the cook and stood much in the king's presence at his meals, counselling or answering to the king's grace which diet is best according, and to tell the nature and operations of all the meats.'

The Croyland Chronicle reported that the court was baffled, saying: 'The king took to his bed neither worn out with old age nor yet seized with any known kind of malady, the cure of which would not have appeared easy in the case of a person of more humble rank.'

Mancini wrote that:

> Edward fell into the greatest melancholy, lamenting that by his inactivity the Flemings, ancient friends, had been permanently estranged from him … so as to mitigate or disguise this sorrow, yet was he never able altogether to hide it … they say there was another reason for his death was, that he being a tall man and very fat though not to the point of deformity allowed the cold damp to strike his vitals, when one day he was taken in a small boat, with those whom he had bidden go fishing and watched their sport too eagerly. He there contracted the illness from which he never recovered.

Commines echoed Mancini and thought he was depressed following the Treaty of Arras, but twice states that apoplexy caused death. Vergil, however, wrote that he died of an unknown disease, but it was rumoured poison was the cause.

Edward was buried in St. George's Chapel, Windsor Castle. He was succeeded by his 12-year-old son, Edward V. However, before his death, Edward seems to have added some codicils to his will (although no evidence of this survives), the most important being to name his brother Richard, Duke of Gloucester as Protector after his death. It would have far-reaching effects.

2

Weapons and Warfare in the Reign of Richard III

The English are all good archers and soldiers...
This nation is cruel and bloodthirsty and they
even fight among themselves in the same way,
waging great battles.
                    Gilles de Bouvier c.1450

The English had built a fearsome reputation as soldiers during the Hundred Years War. Victories such as Crécy, Poitiers, Agincourt and Verneuil were celebrated throughout the kingdom. Many of the men who fought in the Wars of the Roses would have had fathers, grandfathers and uncles who would have taken part in these great battles. All, from the king down to the humblest archer, would have had something to prove. By the time of Bosworth, after many years of relative peace under Edward IV, the number of experienced soldiers and commanders was dwindling. Those that had experience usually learned their trade from fighting the Swiss and French in the service of Burgundy.

The social structure of fifteenth century England was still based on the feudal system that began in Anglo-Saxon times and was built upon by William the Conqueror. It created a strict pecking order where everyone knew his or her place. Society was, in theory, divided into three classes of people. Those who fight (the nobility and gentry), those who pray (the church) and those who work (everyone else). At the top was the King, followed by the nobility who considered themselves the King's natural advisors and were expected to fight and lead men on his behalf. There was a strict order of precedence within the nobility with Dukes being the highest, and there was also an order of precedence within each rank. In 1455 there were (in order) six dukes, one marquis, 12 earls, one viscount, then the baronage, of which there were over a hundred. Not all were able to fight as some were either too young or old, others simply chose to stay out of the fighting. Numbers would also fluctuate during the wars as new titles were created, men died, or titles combined.

According to T.B. Pugh, the 'gentry' of fifteenth century England comprised of all the landowners between the baronage and the yeoman farmers. Most counties seem to have contained between 50 and 70 'county gentry' families so that in overall terms it is likely that the county gentry of England consisted of between 2,300 and 2,500 families. The Knights Banneret were first created by Edward I. During times of war they led a company of troops under their own banner (which was square-shaped, in contrast to the tapering standard or the pennon flown by the lower-ranking knights). Then came the ordinary knights of which there was around 750 (not to be confused with the Knights of the Shire who sat in the House of Commons). In addition to the knights, there were around another 800–1,200 esquires who were of roughly equivalent wealth and status to the knights but who for various reasons had not assumed knighthood. The steady decline in the number of knights through the fifteenth century led to a corresponding rise in the status of the esquires, so that little distinction was drawn between them in social terms. Below these came the gentlemen of which by 1500, there were 5,000 entitled to a coat of arms.

Command

Fifteenth-century commanders were expected to personally lead their men into battle and to inspire them with deeds of valour and personal bravery. The military experience, and reputation of a commander, whether a king or nobleman, could boost the morale of a force, and give an army the edge in hand-to-hand combat. Unlike today, a commander did not have a birds-eye view of events as they unfolded, instead, they only had the height advantage of a horse or, if they were very lucky higher ground. Consequently, they would have seen little more than the enemy front line, or if they were in the thickest of the fighting, virtually nothing at all. Nobles learned to fight from an early age, so by the time they reached maturity, using a sword or poll-axe was second nature. Being given their first suit of armour whilst they were very young, meant that as an adult, providing it was made especially for them, it was like a second, very hard, skin. Many English nobles and captains also served military apprenticeships with the Burgundians, probably the most advanced military society in the west, taking part in the battles against the French and Swiss. One example is in 1466 when Thomas Howard, son of the Duke of Norfolk, was sent by Edward IV to Burgundy along with a considerable band of young gentlemen of Yorkist families. He served for two years with Burgundy, and returned home at the close of 1468 when he was at once made esquire of the body to Edward IV. This experience must have set him in good stead, as he fought for Richard III at Bosworth and in the subsequent regimes became recognised as a skilled commander, eventually leading the English to victory at Flodden in 1513. This means that for the later stages of the Wars of the Roses there would have been a pool of experienced men, captains and commanders used to fighting within the Burgundian organisational system.

Each division or battle in an army would be commanded by one or two nobles. A letter from George Neville to Francesco Coppini, a papal legate written after the Battle of Towton describes their role:

> I prefer you should learn from others than myself how manfully our King, the Duke of Norfolk, and my brother and uncle bore themselves in this battle, first fighting like common soldiers, then commanding, encouraging and rallying their squadrons like the greatest captains.

Controlling an army in the field was difficult at best, drums could beat time for a march or attack, and trumpets sounded commands, but it was a noble's or a town's standard or banner that kept a force together. It not only identified where a particular unit was on the battlefield. It also served as the rallying point, and to keep men together in the confusion of a medieval battle. The most commonly depicted is the standard, which was a long tapering flag with either a rounded or swallow-tailed end and showed the colours, badge, crest and motto of its owner. Its length was dependant on the status of the noble with the king having the largest at 8–9 yards long whilst a knight's banner was just four yards long. Some, called company standards, were no more than two yards long and two feet deep. Probably more common on the battlefield was the square standard or banner. This was stiffened and had a batten along the top to keep it unfurled. These could show a heraldic symbol or badge on the livery colours, although this was not always the case, as it is recorded that one of Henry's banners at Bosworth was a Dun Cow on *tarlatan*, which was a silk, tabby-woven (usually striped) textile. It is probable that a noble would bring more than one standard and banner to a battle and may have had variations to denote archers and billmen for example. Towns too would have their own badges emblazoning a banner. Although, in theory, a banner should prevent two units on the same side from attacking one another, similarities could cause horrendous errors. At the Battle of Barnet, for example, Oxford's star and streamer badge was mistaken for Edward IV's sun in splendour by John Neville, Marquess Montagu's archers, who shot a volley arrows at their own side. Thinking that Montagu had changed sides, Oxford's men retreated, leading to the collapse of the whole army.

Identifying the enemy and its movements were as critical then as it is today. Both sides would have used light cavalry as *scouriers*, the medieval equivalent of scouts. However, their skills left a lot to be desired, and at the time of Blore Heath, Somerset's and Warwick's armies passed within a few miles of each other without spotting one another. Warwick's scourers also failed to detect the Queen's army as it descended on St. Albans in 1461. By the time of Bosworth they would have been experts at observation and liaison, shadowing enemy troops and securing advance positions. They could also be used to spread false rumours as to which way an army was heading. Although there is no earlier evidence of the light cavalry in the role, on Richard's march to Bosworth, scouriers acted as flank protection for the columns of men and wagons. Both sides also had intricate webs of spies, although because of the number of Henry's supporters that chose to remain secret, he was probably better informed of events in England than Richard was of events in France.

Recruitment

Since the Assize of Arms of 1181, which was updated by Edward I as the Statute of Winchester in 1285, all the free people of England were required by law to carry weapons commensurate with their wealth. There were six different classes, the wealthiest expected to provide a *hauberk*, a helmet of iron, a sword, a knife and a horse, whilst the poorest providing a bow and arrows. To ensure they were kept in good condition weapons were inspected twice a year by a constable or sheriff. By 1388 everyone was encouraged to practice archery and it became law that all artisans and labourers should practice archery at the butts (a target) every Sunday. Most would start as young children on small bows and increase the strength of the bow as they grew, so by the time they had matured they could use a powerful warbow. However, by the time of the Wars of the Roses archery practice was in decline, forcing Edward IV to issue a new statute commanding that 'every town should have a pair of butts for shooting, within the town or near it and every man at the same town between the ages of 60 and 16 shall muster at the said butts and shoot up and down three times every feast day.'

Archers practising at the butts from a contemporary illustration. (Author's collection)

The young would also practice for war on holidays during Richard's reign as Dominic Mancini noted in 1483: 'it is a particular delight of this race that on holidays, their youths should fight up and down the streets clashing on their shields with blunted swords or stout staves in place of swords.' In 1450, Gilles le Bouvier wrote: 'The English are all good archers and soldiers … This nation is cruel and bloodthirsty, and they even fight among themselves in the same way, waging great battles.' These men with massive upper body strength from working in the fields since childhood and highly developed muscles from years of archery practice meant that there was a large pool of fighting-fit men that the nobles could call on.

The recruitment of troops under contract for pay instigated by Edward I had grown into 'Livery and Maintenance', the expression deriving from the French word *livrée*, meaning delivered. Livery referred to the coat in the noble's colours, usually with his badge or emblem. given to a retainer (employee). Maintenance referred to the Lord's duty to 'maintain' or support his retainers, by word or action, in any lawsuit in which they were involved. It was common to have a document drawn up that detailed an individual's military and civil obligations to his lord in return for pay, protection, land or other benefits. This document would be sealed with wax and then perforated or indented and torn in two, the lord retaining one half and the individual keeping the other. From this, we get the phrase 'indentured retainer'. A group of such men were therefore known as a lord's retainers. The closest to a noble would normally act as his bodyguards, both during normal duties and on the battlefield and were referred to as his household. Naturally, a lord would recruit his best, most experienced men as his retainers and it was not uncommon for an individual to be retained by more than one lord. The lords also built up increasingly larger networks of 'fee'd' retainers who were paid a fee for fealty and service rather than those of the household who were given food and clothing. Monetary payments were replaced by 'Good Lordship' – aid, favour, support and preferment – and magnates developed affinities of those who had sworn to serve them, usually for life. In return for which the lord would give his livery. The size and strength of such affinities relied on perceptions of the lord's demonstrable power which was directly proportional to his access at court to the King.

The other common method of raising an army was through a Commission of Array. This was a written grant of authority from the king to appoint commissioners in towns or shires, who were normally members of the gentry, to gather all able-bodied men for military service. Notices would be pinned on church doors, but as few could read, they would be read out in town squares and in the churches. A Commission of Array divided men into companies of between 50 and 100 men under the leadership of a captain. As early as the Welsh Wars of Edward I, the companies were subdivided into groups of 20 men led by a *vintner* (from the French '*vingt*' meaning twenty). In July 1468, the commission for Cornwall specified 'hobelars' (light cavalry) and archers which were to be arrayed in companies of 1,000, subdivided into hundreds and twenties.

The town was expected to supply and pay the men and twice each year and royal commissioners were given authority under their Commissions of Array to inspect and report on the military readiness of the county or town in their charge. The problem came when a man who was expected to be part of an array was also part of a retinue, especially if it was for the opposing side.

Organisation

There were four main types of troops in an army, the man-at-arms, the archer, the spearman, armed with a variety of staff weapons and the light cavalry, equipped much the same as a foot soldier and performing a variety of roles. In addition, there would have been handgunners and artillery, possibly operated by mercenaries. The majority of the infantry would have been on foot, although there are accounts of mounted archers and of footmen riding to the battle but dismounting to fight.

Sadly, there are no detailed descriptions of how an English army was organised in the middle and late fifteenth century. We know that they normally split into three divisions or 'battles'. These were called the vanward or vanguard (sometimes just the van), the mainward or mainguard and the rearward or rearguard. The terms can be somewhat deceiving as the vanward could mean either the front or right-hand battle. It could also mean the battle with the best troops. Similarly, the mainward could be the centre battle and rearward the left-hand battle.

Another thing we do not know is how the retinue and arrayed men were combined, if at all. Evidence suggests that arrayed men were divided into twenties, hundreds and thousands. This implies that they all fought together in one body, being the least experienced, although there is nothing to collaborate this. Being organised in this manner would have had its advantages, as it would have helped morale and allowed them to be controlled easier. We can get an idea of the organisation of a militia army, their battle formation and what they wore from the contemporary records of the City of London known as *London Journal IX*. As London prepared for Henry Tudor's invasion in July 1485, the aldermen mustered 3,178 men at Leadenhall from 73 livery companies. They seem to be grouped by role and the type of personal protection, as bowmen on foot came first, followed by the 'Bregandynes', then the armed men with the *Jakkes* taking up the rear (see below for details).

It is impossible to say how many arrayed men were at Bosworth or where they were positioned. Richard would have probably been unsure if they would stand and fight and would have wanted his best troops at the front. The organisation of the retained men is equally elusive. However, we do have some clues from Europe.

Firstly, Burgundy and England were closely allied, particularly as its ruler Charles the Bold was married to Richard's sister, and Edward IV had pursued a Burgundian alliance as part of his foreign policy. We hear from Commines that their tactics were heavily influenced by the English. Like the English, archers were placed together in one block and men-at-arms and infantry in another. The Burgundian organisation, was based on a unit known as the *lance*. This was a man-at-arms supported by a swordsman, a spearman, three archers, a handgunner and a squire. They would then be grouped into *ordonnance* companies of 100 lances. The main difference between the English and Burgundian (and French) armies was that both Burgundy and France had permanent, fully trained, standing armies whereas most of the English were part-time, only called for in a time of need. Charles the Bold, made a number of ordinances prescribing the organisation of his forces in the 1460s and 1470s. In the first ordinance of 1468, the army is clearly organised in three man lances; a man-at-arms, a *coutilier* (also *coutillier*, *coustillier*) and a valet. In *The Ordinance of Abbeville* of 31 July 1471, a company was divided into units of 10 lances commanded by a *Desenier* (possibly from the French *dessiner*, to draw up, designate). This 10-lance unit was again split into a group of six lances commanded by the *Desenier* himself, and a four lance unit commanded by a *Chef de Chambre* (Head of the Barracks). Charles recruited 1,250 lances and set each lance at one man-at-arms, one mounted valet, one *coutilier*, three mounted archers, one crossbowman, one handgunner and one longspear.

The lance as a tactical unit was also common practice throughout Europe. In France, *les Compagnies d'ordenance* were introduced in the *Grande Ordonnance* of 1445, in the name of King Charles VII. There was not a single *Grande Ordonnance*, but rather two dozen or more, published simultaneously across France. Each company was made up of anywhere from 30 to 100 lances In *Les Lances fournies pour les Compagnies d'ordonnance du Roi* (The lances furnished for the Companies ordered by the King), each *lance fournie* ('furnished' or 'equipped lance') was made up of six men, each with a horse, but only four of them were counted as combat personnel. The senior member was a fully armoured man-at-arms (*gen d'armes*, or *gendarmerie*). This man was supported by a squire or serjeant-at-arms known as a *écuyer* or *coutilier* (literally 'dagger man,' a contemporary term for mounted bandits and brigands) who was a lighter horseman and helped him handle the 16- to 19-foot lance when they fought on foot. The man-at-arms and the *coutilier* were further assisted by a page, or *valet de guerre*, who was responsible for caring for their armour, equipment, and horses. The lance also contained two archers, who were at first considered mounted infantrymen, provided with horses for mobility alone. Some were apparently equipped with bows and arrows, others with crossbows, and all also carried swords or axes and some armour.

The Duchy of Brittany also ordered the equivalent of the lance in an ordinance of 1450. While the basic lance was the familiar three man structure of man-at-arms, *coutilier* and page, dependent on the wealth of the man-at-arms, additional archers or *juzarmiers* (that is, men equipped with a *guisarme*) could be present. In Germany, the three-man lance (*gleve*) may have existed in the early fourteenth century, with a knight supported by two sergeants. The English knight Sir John Hawkwood is credited with introducing the lance to Italy during the 1360s, although they were probably in use earlier. By the 1380s Italian accounts mention *gros valets* and *flanking esquires*, and in the fourteenth and fifteenth centuries, mercenary soldiers were recruited in units known variously as *barbuta, lance* or *corazza*, consisting of two to six men. The three man lance consisted of two combatants, a men-at-arms and an armed squire, plus a page. The *kopia* (Polish for lance) was the basic military formation in medieval Poland, identical to the lance unit employed elsewhere in Western Europe. A *kopia* was composed of a knight and his retinue (of 3–12 soldiers). On campaign, several *kopias* were combined to form a larger unit, the *chorągiew*. From the fifteenth century the term *kopia* was replaced by *Poczet*.

So was the lance used as a tactical unit in England? We have a clue from the feudal muster of 1378, where two or three, even as many as five, troopers appear with each knight, when the Earl of Lincoln registered the names of himself, five knights, and three troopers as satisfying his *servitium de bitum* of seven and a half knights. Two of the knights and one trooper occur in each retinue and it seems that 30 lances formed his normal strength. Even Chaucer's Knight in the *Canterbury Tales*, with his son the Squire and his Yeoman archer suggests similarities to a lance. An indenture dated 1388 for Sir Thomas Gerberge also says that the lord agrees to provide maintenance for the knight, his squire and significantly, two yeomen. Both Cosneau's *Le connétable de Richemont (Artur de Bretagne) (1393–1458)* and Luce's *Chronique du Mont-Saint-Michel* when discussing the *Lances Fournies* note that in 1425, the French lance only had two archers whilst at the same time in the English military system, there were three archers per man-at-arms, and that every man had a *coutilier* and a *serviteur*.

Another clue comes from details of Lord Hastings' retinue as he prepared to invade France with Edward IV in 1475 with what contemporaries described as the largest army to invade France. This document lists a number of his senior retainers and the forces they would be bringing. Beside each one is a number of lances and a number of archers. There is no mention of billmen on this list, although it is inconceivable that none were taken on such an important expedition. So, where were they? Some historians have suggested that in this instance a lance means one man and that 'archers' is a catch-all for all the other infantry. However, the list says Hastings was only taking 40 lances and 300 archers and Lord Grey of Codnor, 10 lances and 155 archers. This gives an average ratio of 7:1 archers to men-at-arms, which seems very high, considering at the height of the Hundred Years War a ratio of 3:1 was the norm and by this time the hand gun was beginning to replace the archer. We only have to compare the number of men Hastings took to France with the 3,000 he reputedly brought to Leicester when Edward IV returned to England four years earlier to see there is a huge disparity. And we only have to look to the likes of the Duke of Buckingham, who boasted of a personal retinue of over 1,000, and that William Stanley mustered an apparent 3,000 men at Bosworth, to see that if a lance is a single man for the French campaign then they are exceptionally small retinues for such high-ranking nobles. In 1509, Henry supplemented his Yeoman of the Guard with 'The Band of Pensioners and Spears'. Hall says that 'This year the King ordained fifty gentlemen to be spears, every of them to have an archer, a demi-lance and a costrel, and every spear to have three great horses.' With all this in mind, the English lance was most likely a unit of men, comprising of a man-at-arms and perhaps a squire and two footmen, similar to the Burgundians, and common practice throughout the rest of Europe.

Horses

Horses in the Middle Ages were rarely differentiated by breed, but rather by use. One of the best-known of the medieval horses was the warhorse or destrier, renowned for its capabilities in war. As such it was required to be strong, fast and agile and was usually well trained. Analysis of existing horse armour located in the Royal Armouries indicates the equipment was originally worn by warhorses and suggests a size of 15 to 16 hands (60 to 64 inches or 152 to 163 cm), or about the size and build of a modern field hunter or ordinary riding horse. Research undertaken at the Museum of London, using literary, pictorial and archaeological sources, supports military horses of 14 to 15 hands (56 to 60 inches or 142 to 152 cm). Coursers were generally preferred for hard battle as they were light, fast and strong and therefore frequently used for hunting. They were valuable, but not as costly as the destrier. A more general-purpose horse was the 'rouncey' commonly used by squires, men-at-arms or poorer knights which could be kept as a riding horse, trained for war or sometimes used as pack horses. Sometimes the expected nature of warfare dictated the choice of horse. In 1327 when a summons to war was sent out in England, it expressly requested rounceys, for swift pursuit, rather than destriers.

The well-bred palfrey could equal a destrier in price and was popular with nobles and highly ranked knights for riding, hunting and ceremonial use.

Ambling was a desirable trait in a palfrey, as the smooth gait allowed the rider to cover long distances quickly in relative comfort. The hobby, a lightweight horse, about 13 to 14 hands (52 to 56 inches or 132 to 142 cm) was developed in Ireland from Spanish or Libyan (Barb) bloodstock. It was a quick and agile horse, popular for skirmishing and was often ridden by light cavalry known as Hobelars. Another type was the jennet, a small horse first bred in Spain from Barb and Arabian bloodstock. Their quiet and dependable nature, as well as size, made them popular as riding horses for ladies.

The sumpter (or pack horse) carried equipment and belongings. Common riding horses, often called 'hackneys', could be used as pack horses. Cart horses pulled wagons on campaign. These draught horses were smaller than their modern counterparts; pictorial and archaeological evidence suggests that they were stout but short, approximately 13 to 14 hands (52 to 56 inches or 132 to 142 cm), and capable of drawing a load of 500 to 600 pounds (230 to 270 kg) per horse. Four-wheeled wagons and two-wheeled carts were more common in towns, such as London and, depending on type of vehicle and weight of the load, were usually pulled by teams of two, three, or four horses harnessed in tandem. Starting in the 12th century, in England the use of oxen to pull carts was gradually superseded by the use of horses.

Tactics

Warfare in the fifteenth century followed classical Roman thought, and no self-respecting commander would be without his copy of Vegetius' *De re Militari* (Concerning Military Matters) written in the fifth century. An updated version, *Le Livre des Faites d'Armes et de Chevalerie* (The Book of Deeds of Arms and of Chivalry) was written by Christine de Pizan in 1410. Another updated version written in ballad form, commissioned by Lord Beaumont, called *Knyghthode and Bataile* was presented to Henry VI shortly before the Battle of Northampton in 1460. Richard III had an English translation of *De re Militari* made either for himself or possibly his son. He also was known to have copies of both Ramon Lull's *Order of Chivalry* (translated and printed by Caxton) as well as William Worcester's *The Boke of Noblesse*. Soon after Bosworth, Henry VII ordered William Caxton to make copies of *Le Livre des Faites d'Armes et de Chevalerie* so that 'every gentylman born to armes& all manere men of were, captains, souldiours, vytayllers & all other should haue knowlege how they ought to behaue theym in the fayttes of warre & of batayles.' This shows that they were not just books of interest but military manuals to be studied and used.

Fighting in three battles left few tactical options during the medieval period. With so many archers on both sides, the tactical supremacy of the archers during the Hundred Years War was largely negated. However, to leave them behind could have devastating consequences, as the Welsh discovered at the Battle of Edgcote in 1469. Here, separated from their archers, the Welsh infantry had to endure an arrow storm with no way of replying. They were forced to charge the rebel army and were cut to pieces when outflanked. Archers could be placed either with their battles or, as at

WEAPONS AND WARFARE IN THE REIGN OF RICHARD III

Towton and Bosworth, in a long line at the front of the army. After the initial archery duel, the archers would revert to their light infantry role and fight with sword and buckler. At the end of the day, all battles would have to be decided by hand strokes.

This does not mean there was no room for ingenuity though, and surprise flank attacks were common. At Wakefield, after sallying out from Sandal Castle to confront a Lancastrian army, Richard of York was killed by just such an attack. Edward IV expected an assault on his flank at Tewkesbury and hid 200 'spears' in a wood to protect it, but seeing there was no threat, they then charged into the Lancastrians themselves. The final phase of the Battle of Edgcote was likewise determined by the timely arrival of reserves who fell upon the flank of the Welsh army. However, because of the effectiveness of the longbow, successful cavalry charges were few and far between in the Wars, as the French discovered at Crécy and Agincourt, and Lord Audley found out to his cost at Blore Heath in 1459. The only time a cavalry charge could be effective would be if all the archers and infantry were engaged in hand-to-hand fighting.

Several modern commentators have suggested that the English army of 1485 was old fashioned compared to the rest of Europe. This is almost certainly not the case. There was a rich pool of English soldiers and captains who had fought in Europe and were experienced in Continental warfare. As well as the nobles already mentioned fighting with the Burgundians, the Twenty-first Ordonnance Company of the Burgundian Army of Charles the Bold was composed entirely of English and Welsh. They were formed in 1475 under Sir John Middleton and were composed of 100 men-at-arms and 1,600 archers. They fought at Neuss, Grandson and Morat but were destroyed at Nancy on 5 January 1477. According to Commines, there were another 300 Englishmen from Guynes at the Battle of Nancy led by a low-born man named as Colpin. The English had not only faced longspears as early as 1444 but had them available themselves before Bosworth. If they did not use them *en masse*, it was through choice not ignorance.

Personal Protection

Full plate armour, or as it was called at the time, harness or *cap-à-pie* (head to toe), was normally the preserve of the wealthy and noble class. A complete set of plate armour made from well-tempered steel would weigh around 15–25 kg (33–55 lbs). In comparison, according to a report in Jane's *Defence*, in Afghanistan the modern British soldier carries in excess of 65 kg (145 lbs). When in armour, the medieval knight remained highly agile and could jump, run and otherwise move freely as the weight of the armour was spread evenly around the body. The armour was articulated and covered a man's entire body completely from neck to toe. The price of a complete harness could cost anything from £2 10s to over £7 for highest quality. Therefore the best could cost as much as a third of the annual income of an esquire or a high-performance car today. At the same time, an archer would have earned just 6d per day. Therefore, very few, probably no more than 10 percent, would have worn full armour at Bosworth.

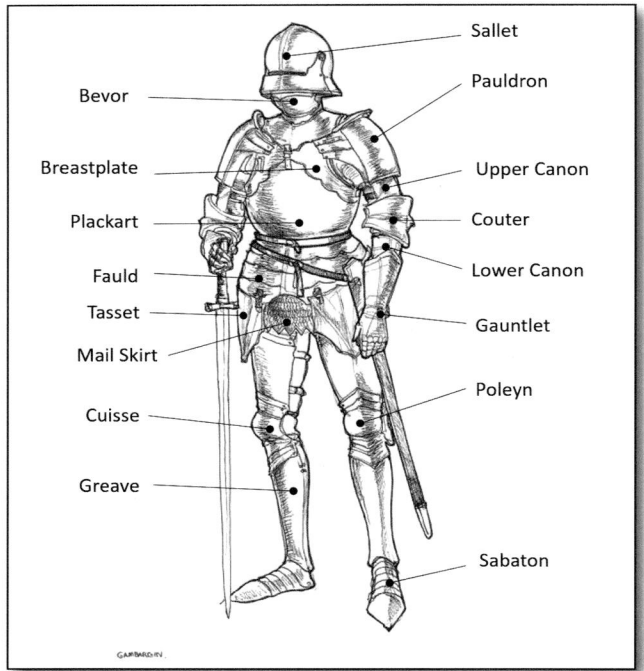

Typical late fifteenth century armour showing all the main parts. Illustration drawn by and © Gambargain.

By the 1430s two very distinct centres of armour production had emerged in Europe. The first was Italian and mainly from Milan and Brescia, with the most famous being made by the Missaglia family of Milan, now generally termed 'Milanese'. By 1425, having discovered how to harden armour, the Italians were making considerable improvements to their designs. Smooth round surfaces, limiting where a sword might bite, and two-part breastplates, with the lower one overlapping the upper one to give double the protection, became features of their armour. They also added a smaller right elbow protector (*couter*), with the upper wing larger than the lower, and a larger reinforced *couter* on the left arm as well as asymmetrical shoulder guards (*pauldrons*).

The second, came from southern Germany, especially Augsburg, Nuremberg and Landshut, with armour made by the Helmschmied dynasty of Augsburg the most famous. In the 1420s and 1430s, their breastplate was more angular with the upper part flared out and the lower back angled into the waist, giving the armour its characteristic 'box' shape. In the 1420s a small arm defence covering the shoulder, known as a *spaudler*, came into use, and by the 1450s this was attached to the *rerebrace* (sometimes known as an upper cannon). The leg harness was very similar to that of the Italian style, although with smaller side wings on the *poleyns* and *sabatons* made of horizontal plates in the shape of contemporary footwear. However, it was not until the 1460s that it developed into a more slender, elongated form, often with fluting that we recognise today as the 'Gothic' style.

Armour was also made in England, although little survives today other than that depicted on alabaster tombs. There was a workshop making armour for the nobility in the Tower of London before 1450, and in 1453 Henry VI granted a charter to the London Armourers Company. This type seems to have been developed to suit fighting on foot, whereas European armour was designed for mounted warfare and reinforced on the right side. Flanders and France also had their own armour industries and, among other pieces, seem to have made cheaper copies of Milanese and Gothic designs. As well as the quality armour there were probably cheaper, massed produced and more affordable sets of armour that would not have given the same level of protection.

An 'arming doublet' was worn beneath the armour. This was usually made from *fustian* (a type of cloth, often described as being made of cotton, flax or wool, of various textures and qualities), often with a velvet lining and with gussets of mail at the most vulnerable parts of the body such as the

WEAPONS AND WARFARE IN THE REIGN OF RICHARD III

armpits. The arming doublet also had waxed cords attached called arming points, onto which the armour was attached. A mail collar and a mail skirt or pair of shorts (*fauld*) was also sometimes worn.

Another type of armour was the brigandine. This first appeared towards the end of the fourteenth century and came into wide use in the fifteenth century. Contemporary art suggests that it was far more common than plate armour. They were generally front-opening garments with small armour plates, sometimes riveted between two layers of stout cloth, or just to an outer layer, the richest being of velvet. Many brigandines appear to have had larger, somewhat 'L-shaped' plates over the central chest area. The rivets, or nails, attaching the plates to the fabric usually in threes were often gilt, or of latten, and sometimes embossed with a design. In more expensive brigandines, the outer layer of cloth was usually of velvet. Being made from small plates meant that the brigandine was far more flexible, giving a greater degree of movement than full plate and therefore probably why it was a popular type of armour along with its relative cheapness.

Reconstruction of English-style helmet based on the effigy of William Martyn in the Athelhampton Chantry of Puddletown Church, Dorchester. (Armour Services Historical)

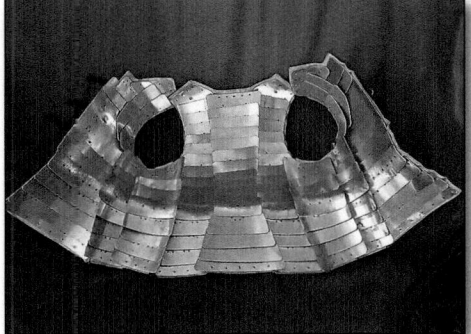

The inside of a brigandine showing the individual plates. (Armour Services Historical)

A standard brigandine. The brass rivets hold the individual plates in place. (Armour Services Historical)

The ordinary medieval soldier would have worn his everyday clothes on a campaign which usually consisted of a shirt, doublet, woollen hose and boots. The 1457 'Bridport Muster Roll' lists 201 names (four of which are women) and of these, 119 have some form of protection. It lists 74 sallets (see below), although some have more than one, and seven men had a sallet, but no other form of protection. Two had full sets of harness, but are likely to be of an earlier period, and another two had brigandines. The most common personal defence was the *jakke* (or jack), with 67 being listed, two of which were worn with mail shirts. Another brought a mail shirt only. There was also one set of leg armour and one set of breast and backplate. Most would have worn a

57

A modern reconstruction of a heavily padded jakke made from layers of canvas or linen and stuffed with straw or similar. (Author)

German tipping sallet. (Armour Services Historical)

padded *jakke* for protection, made from layers of canvas or linen stuffed with tow, wool, straw or even scraps of mail. They were normally fastened down the front with laces and came either with or without sleeves, which were attached to the body by cords. The Duke of Norfolk's accounts describe his *jakkes* as being made from 18 folds of white fustian and four folds of linen, whilst Falstolf's inventory of 1459 has *jakkes* filled with mail and horn.

The most common helmet during the wars was usually called the *sallet*, worn by both the rich and poor, with and without full plate armour. There were numerous variations on the style but was generally a close-fitting helmet with a 'tail' at the rear covering the neck. The front was cut out around the face and closed with a visor, fastened to the sides of the helmet, which could then be lifted to provide extra ventilation. A slit between the top of the visor and the helmet bowl provided vision when the visor was down. The type known as a German sallet also had a long tail over the neck, but was often formed of several plates, and a deep skull fitted to the shape of the head. It had either a visor pivoted at the sides, the eye slot formed between the lower edge of the skull and the upper edge of the visor or was in one piece with eye slots cut in the front.

The first references to the sallet in Italian sources date to 1407, although it was not popular until after 1430. The German sallet seems to have first appeared in the 1420s but seems to have been rare until the 1460s.

By the mid fifteenth century, a regional variety of sallet had evolved in England and the Netherlands, termed the 'English–Burgundian style'. It was usually worn with a *bevor* (a plate gorget that extended over the chin) and had very similar facial protection and frontal appearance to the German sallet. However, it was more curvaceous and possessed a less extreme projection to the rear. French sallets were very similar to the English–Burgundian type and all have been classed as *short-tailed sallets*.

Another variation on the sallet is what is now known as an *archer's sallet* and frequently seen in contemporary art. This was a single piece, close-fitting helmet without face protection, in a number of styles from a simple skull cap, to those that have either a rounded or short-tailed back. An Italian equivalent was the *barbute*, which closely resembled classical Greek helmets. It is not clear how much they were worn in England, although John Paston enquired about a set of armour from Bruges, including a barbute in 1473. However, by the time of Bosworth, they may have gone out of fashion as the open face was resulting in too many casualties, particularly from arrows.

The *armet* was another type of helmet, but its use seems to have been restricted to men-at-arms. The earliest surviving example dates to 1420 and was made in Milan but appears to have not become common until the end of the century and into the next. The typical armet consisted of four pieces: the skull, the two large hinged cheek-pieces which locked at the front over the chin, and a visor which had a double pivot, one either side of the skull. The cheek-pieces opened laterally; when closed they overlapped at the chin, fastening by means of a spring-pin which engaged in a corresponding hole, or by a swivel-hook and pierced staple. A multi-part reinforcement for the bottom half of the face, known as a wrapper, was sometimes added, its straps were protected by a metal disc at the base of the skull piece called a rondel.

Detail of a reconstructed sallet and bevor with mail underneath. (Author)

Dominic Mancini observed Richard III's men in London during 1483 and described them as:

> Hardly any without a helmet ... just as their bodies are stronger than other peoples', for they seem to have hands and arms of iron ... They do not wear any metal armour on their breast or any other part of the body, except for the better sort who have breastplates and suits of armour. Indeed, the common soldiery has more comfortable tunics that reach down below the loins and are stuffed with tow or some other soft material. They say that the softer the tunics the better do they withstand the blows of arrows and swords, and beside in summer they are lighter and in summer more serviceable than iron.

Household and retinue troops would have been better protected than the common footman, with some wearing additional armour such as brigandines. This meant that at Bosworth few men would have looked the same on the battlefield except for their livery. Very few would have worn the latest armour, and some would have still worn older styles. However, the vast majority would have worn little more than a jack and sallet.

Although the shield was no longer required by the knights and men-at-arms due to the protection that was given by armour, lighter troops would often carry a small, round, iron or steel shield called a 'buckler'. Some would have a large, man-sized shield called a pavise that provided protection for

RICHARD III AND THE BATTLE OF BOSWORTH

Contemporary image of a soldier with poll-axe, sword and buckler. Note the method of hanging the sword. From the *Chroniques Sire Jehan Froissart*. Mid fifteenth century, Bibliothèque Nationale Paris, 2644. (Image: Matthew Ryan)

Effigy of Sir Richard Vernon (d. 1517) in St Bartholomew's Church Tong, in Shropshire, showing his Esses collar.

archers, crossbowmen and gunners, particularly whilst reloading. Some had slits to fire through, and others were studded with nails to act as an obstruction when thrown on the ground. Falstolf lists several of these shields in his inventory, and the Bridport Muster Roll lists two.

Various forms of livery were used in the Middle Ages to denote attachment to a great person by friends, servants, and political supporters. The livery collar, usually of precious metal, was the highest form of these, usually given by the king to his closest or most important associates. From the collar hung a badge or device indicating the person the livery related to. The collar of Esses was a royal badge of the Lancastrian house, the white swan, as in the Dunstable Swan Jewel, usually being its pendant. Henry VII brought back the collar of Esses either with a portcullis or a Tudor rose hanging from it. The kings of the House of York and their chief followers wore the Yorkist collar of suns and roses, with the white lion of March, the Clare bull, or Richard's white boar for a pendant device.

Throughout the Wars of the Roses, soldiers often wore a bend (sash), tabard or coat in the colours of their lord or town. They would also wear their lord's badge and these together were called a lord's livery and were a mark of affinity. However, both Edward IV and Richard III tried to ban the wearing of livery coats. On several occasions, Richard sent out instructions that only his colours should be worn or else the transgressor would face severe penalties. So by the time of Bosworth, it is possible Richard's army was wearing one colour, his colours being azure (blue) and murrey (purplish red), although instructions sent out by the Duke of Norfolk before the Battle of Bosworth, tells his men to wear his own red livery. The *Ballad of Ladye Bessiye* on the other hand, tells us that William Stanley's men wore red with a white hart badge and Thomas Stanley, tawny and green with a yellow Eagle's claw badge. We know that the French clothed Henry's men

WEAPONS AND WARFARE IN THE REIGN OF RICHARD III

whilst he was still in France, so they probably wore Henry's colours of vert (green) and argent (white). We do not know whether the French troops wore the colours of their old unit or Henry's. As to those who joined him en route, they probably stayed with their own colours. Towns would also have their own colours and badges, and these would also be emblazoned on a banner. In 1455 Coventry equipped 100 archers giving them bends (sashes) of red and green, a new multi-coloured coat for its captain and a new 'Black Ram' banner. The chamberlain's accounts for Nottingham in 1464 lists payments for red cloth for their soldiers' jackets and fine red cloth for their captain. In addition, white fustian was purchased to make letters, and to have the letters cut out and sewn on to the jackets. *The Rose of Rouen*, a poem about the Battle of Towton, lists some of the badges for other towns; for example, the 'Griffon' for Leicester, the 'Harrow' for Canterbury, the 'Wolf' for Worcester and the 'George' for Nottingham.

Reconstruction of a Yorkist livery collar with the sun in splendour and white rose badges. Hanging from it is Richard III's boar badge.

Contemporary image of a civilian with sword. (Matthew Ryan)

Weapons

In Henry VII's Act of Attainder against Richard during his first Parliament in 1485, it was said that Richard's army 'kept the said host in being with banners displayed, strongly armed and equipped with all kinds of weapons, such as guns, bows, arrows, spears, glaives, axes and all other weaponry suitable or necessary for giving and advancing a mighty battle against our sovereign lord.' Although this seems to be a generic description for weapons at the time, it does show the variety that was available.

The sword was still the main weapon of the knight throughout the Wars of the Roses and could vary from the short and broad arming swords to the narrow and long hand-and-a-half sword (bastard sword). Contemporary illustrations and effigies suggest that some carried both.

Another type of sword was the single-edged falchion, which had a short, heavy blade with the combined weight and power of an axe but had the versatility of a sword. They were found in two different forms from the 11th century onwards. The first one was the cleaver type, which looked very similar to a large meat cleaver, but was rare if used at all, in the fifteenth century. The second was a cusped type, characterised by a straight blade with flare-clipped or cusped tips. A variation similar to the falchion was the hanger. This was also a short, single-edged short sword, but with an S-shaped cross guard that formed a simple knuckle guard to protect the hand. This type was more likely a foot soldier's or archer's sword; although in the Bridport Roll, 69 swords are listed; only one is described as a hanger.

RICHARD III AND THE BATTLE OF BOSWORTH

Contemporary image of an archer. Note falchion type sword and the method of wearing. Based on an illustration in Jean Wavrin's Recueil des cronicques d'Engleterre c.1470–c.1480. (Matthew Ryan)

Another weapon popular with the nobility and footman alike was the poll-axe. The head, mounted on a pole around six feet long, had an axe on one side and a form of hammer on the opposite side. A square section spike protruded out the top of the head. Some had iron strips called *langets* running down the shaft for a variable length, others a circular iron hand-guard. They would be used two-handed, probably like an axe, the hammer cracking armour and locking joints, the point to stab. Ten such weapons are mentioned in the Bridport Muster Roll, and there are many shown in the hands of the nobility and gentry in contemporary illustrations too. The 1481 inventory of Calais garrison lists 60 'gylt' and 172 'ungylt' ones.

The majority of ordinary footmen (except archers) carried staff weapons. The most common one listed in the Bridport Muster Roll was the glaive, a knife-like blade mounted on a six foot pole, primarily for cutting, of which 11 are listed on the roll. However, if contemporary images and inventories are to be believed, the most common was the simple spear. It was also the weapon of the commoners listed in the earlier statutes. Almost 45 percent of the soldiers illustrated in *The Beauchamp Pageant*, which was probably commissioned in the mid 1480s, are armed with spears, whilst less than 23 percent have bills. The mid-fifteenth century *The Maire of Bristow is Kalendar* shows spears and glaives as the main weapons. The Bridport Muster Roll, on the other hand, only lists five out of the 210 people equipped with spears, and only three with bills. A rare painted panel found in Grafton Regis church called 'The Kiss of Judas' and dated to around 1460, also shows mainly spears. Contemporary accounts also mention 'long debeofes' which appears to be an attempt to anglicise the staff weapon or spear known as the *langue-de-boeuf*, better known as the *langdebeve* (oxtongue), an early form of partisan, but one without lugs at the base of the head.

A modern reconstruction of a poll-axe. (Author)

The bill seems to have been based on the common agricultural billhook used for chopping branches from hedges and trees. It would have been used much in the same way in battle as it would have been used in the fields and, therefore, required no training. This is supported by contemporary European paintings which invariably show them being used over-hand. It had a pronounced forward curving blade, sometimes with a hook or spike on the back and often with a spike on top, mounted on a pole approximately 1.5–1.8m (5–6ft) long. It was a simple, practical weapon, unlike the longer, more ornate versions often seen today, which are based on guards' weapons from the time of Henry VIII.

WEAPONS AND WARFARE IN THE REIGN OF RICHARD III

Out of the 40 or so bills in the Royal Armouries at Leeds, only two are tentatively classified 'English Military, 15th century.' A socketed bill head was found at Desford which is situated between Bosworth battlefield and Leicester. It is 610 mm long and the blade 141 mm at its widest, with a 64 mm spike on the back. Although it is believed to be late medieval, as there is no context, we cannot say if it was connected to the battle or not. The 1475 muster roll of the Ewelme half-hundred detailed in *The Stonor Papers* describes most of the footmen having bills, but we do not know whether this is an actual description or generic term.

In 1481, there were there were 84 'white' bills and 119 'black' bills in the Calais armoury. What the difference between the two types is unknown but may refer to one being polished and the other as forged. However, George Silver, writing in his *Paradoxes of Defence* just over 100 years after Bosworth, wrote:

> The Black Bill, or Hedging bill, is an instrument of warre, and also in domestick affaires, by Labourers and husbandmen, and by reason thereof, is generally known as an hedging bill: It hath a cutter and a putter from her as the country man terms it and to such the staffe or handle is a yard and halfe long or thereabouts, because it is used with both hands, and in warre is termed, a black bill.

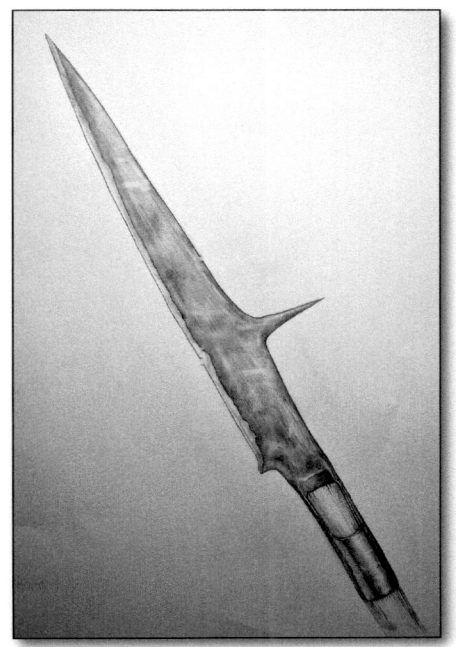

Reconstruction of a fifteenth century glaive based on a rare example in the Royal Armouries. (Matthew Ryan)

Reconstruction of a fifteenth century bill based on a rare example in the Royal Armouries. (Matthew Ryan)

He goes on to say bills are less effective in single combat (though he claims they still hold the advantage over the two-handed sword) however, their weight and shortness makes them far more effective and that they are the perfect length at delivering blows in a battle among multitudes of men. Another type of bill listed by Silver is the 'Welch hook or forest bill' which he says was eight or nine feet long and has advantage against all manner of weapons. This is probably the same weapon as the 2,000 'Welsh bills' that Richard ordered his usher of the chamber to procure in 1483, so it is likely some of his troops would have been equipped with them at Bosworth.

The European equivalent of the bill was the halberd and is generally believed to be the type of weapon that killed Richard at Bosworth. Although halberd-type weapons had existed since the bronze age, the type seen at Bosworth was based on the Danish Axe and developed by the Swiss. The first mention of the word 'halberd' is in a text by the poet Konrad of Würzburg, who died in 1287. In 1348 the Franciscan, John of Winterthur, described in his chronicles the Battle of Morgarten in 1315, commenting on the effectiveness of the halberd: 'The Swiss had in their hands a terrible sort of weapon called a halberd in the vernacular, with which they cut through their enemy's armour as though with a razor, and reduced them to pieces.'

63

Reconstruction of a fifteenth century bill. (Matthew Ryan)

In a separate account, John recounts a description by the king of Bohemia of Swiss mercenaries from the Canton of Glarus serving in the army of Duke Ludwig of Austria in 1330: 'As the King of Bohemia passed through the camp of the Duke and reached the battle lines of the men of Glarus, he saw their fighting equipment and the murderous weapons, the Gesa, in dialect called halberds, and said with amazement: "What a terrible sight this wedge formation is, with its horrible and frightening instruments of death".'

Unlike the bill, the halberd blade was rectangular, although by the mid fifteenth century the edge of the blade became oblique to facilitate a slicing rather than a chopping action. This shape lasted through most of the fifteenth century and into the sixteenth. Initially, the spike was little more than an extension of the blade, but gradually became narrower and longer. As it became longer and more vulnerable to breakage, so, at the start of the fifteenth century a median ridge appeared to strengthen it.

The earliest halberds had two eyes at the back of the blade to fasten it more securely to the shaft and to lessen the chance of breaking the shaft at the junction of the wood and metal. It also had a separate beak between the two eyes or fastened onto the upper eye. Eventually, the two eyes and the beak were forged into a single socket. The shaft was almost always ash. Initially, the socket for the shaft was behind the axis of the spearpoint but was gradually moved forward and for a short time was in front of the axis. However, by the time of Bosworth, it was in line with the spear. *Langets*, integral with the head, first appeared early in the 1400s, strengthening the shaft and helping to prevent the head from being cut off.

It is not known whether the halberd was used in England, although 11 percent of weapons shown in *The Beauchamp Pageant* are of this type. Comparing the bill to the halberd, Sir Roger Williams in his *A briefe discourse of warre* published in 1590 mentions that he thinks the halberd is overall the better weapon so long as the head is made from good steel. Humfrey Barwick writing in 1592, claimed that the difference was a matter of skill and that halberds were better for officers who were well-practised in their use 'But for our common countrie men, not vsed to handle a halbard as aforesaid: I woulde wish him to have a good strong black Bill.' He continues that 'Halbards are not to be put in the hands of an ignorant person', suggesting much more skill and training was needed to wield one.

Other weapons used on the battlefield includes axes (10 are mentioned on the Bridport Muster Roll), the *mass de plumbo* (lead maul) and its noble equivalent, the mace. If mounted, the main weapons for the heavy cavalry were the lance, and for the light cavalry the spear. Another weapon primarily for the cavalry was the warhammer, which had a small hammer on one side and a beak on the other, mounted on a short shaft. There was also a long-shafted version for fighting on foot, often referred to as the *bec-de-corbin*.

Just about everyone carried a dagger of some kind. There were three main types available in the fifteenth century, with the Rondel the most common.

WEAPONS AND WARFARE IN THE REIGN OF RICHARD III

These were single-edged blades up to 10 inches long, with large circular roundels for the handguard and pommel to give a secure grip and to assist in hammering the blade home. The ballock dagger (called a kidney dagger by the Victorians), as the name suggests, had a distinctively shaped handle, with two oval swellings at the guard resembling male genitalia and were often hung at the front. The *Misericorde* was similar to a stiletto and had a straight and narrow blade often triangular in section. It was frequently used to deliver a final 'mercy' blow to the mortally wounded.

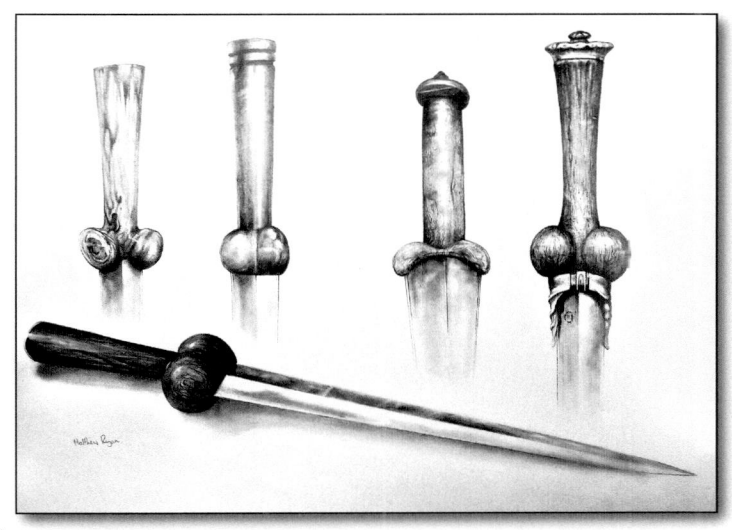

Variations of the Ballock Dagger. (Matthew Ryan)

The Archers

The English archer was famed throughout Europe for his skill and effectiveness in battle and remained the backbone of armies during the Wars of the Roses. Indentures suggest a ratio of archers to footmen as 2 or 3:1, sometimes more, and in some instances, towns such as Coventry only supplied archers. Contemporary Burgundian chronicler, Phillipe de Commines, wrote that 'in my opinion archers are the most necessary thing in the world for an army; but they should be counted in thousands, for in small numbers they are worthless'. The archer's D-shaped longbow was typically made from yew, imported from Italy and Spain, and was over 1.8 m (6 ft) long. A statute issued in the fifth year of Edward IV's reign insisted that 'Every Englishman, and Irishman, that dwell with Englishmen and speak English, that be betwixt sixteen and sixty in age, shall have an English bow of his own length, and one fistmele, [handful] at the least, betwixt the nocks [where the string was affixed], with 12 Shafts of the length of three quarters of the Standard.' The string was made from flax/linen or hemp. Bows were measured by the strength it took to pull one, and if we go by the bows found on the *Mary Rose*, the strongest could pull 81 kg (180 lb).

A line of archers at the annual Bosworth festival.

65

RICHARD III AND THE BATTLE OF BOSWORTH

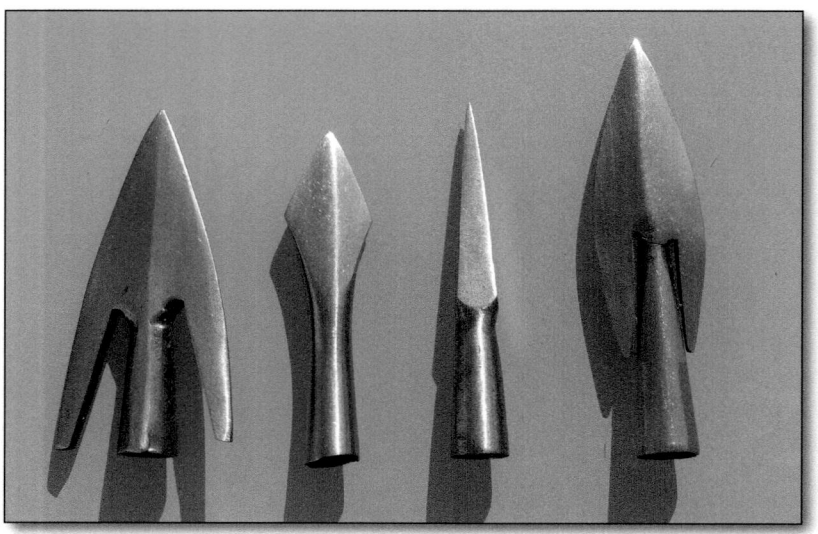

Arrowheads. Left to right: curved broad head, quarrel (crossbow), Type 10 War Bodkin, Stafford Castle type 16.

Medieval Archer from the *Beauchamp Pageant* which was published around 1485. He is wearing an archer's open-face sallet and what appears to be a brigandine over a mail shirt. (Author's collection)

Between 1434 and 1436 the Calais victualler sold 1,705 bows to soldiers, and in 1460–61 the victualler brought 380 more and sold 147 of them to the men. Arrows were a cloth yard, around 30 inches (762 mm) long and made from ash, apse (poplar) or birch. The fletchings (feathers) were made from the primary feathers of a goose, and were 7–12 inches (177–304 mm) long. There were several different arrowheads available, although archaeological evidence suggests the most common type in this period was a barbed, dual-purpose arrowhead (now known as the 'type 16') which was effective against most targets.

A petition by the Fletchers for the better regulation of their craft is recorded in the *Calendar of Letter-Books of the City of London: L*, during the reign of Richard III, and gives an interesting insight into their manufacture:

> That all suche persones as ben admitted allowes wtin the said craft shall have and take from hensfurth for their labour for the werkmanship and makyng of thise thinges underwriten after the Rate ensuyng that is to sey for the makyng of c beryngshaftes [heavy shafts, used for long distance]. of seasonable Tymber well and clenly made wt cros nokked skynned [peeled?] and sered [varnished]. xiiijd.; for makyng of c of the best beryng shaftes well and clenly crosnokked after the best maner and skynned and sered as is aforesaid xvjd.; for the makyng of c merke arrowe shaftes [lighter shafts for shooting at a mark] well and clenly made after the forme aforesaid xxd.; and for the makyng of c boltes well and clenly made after the best forme and after the maner above rehersed.

The archer would have worn either a simple skull cap or a close-fitting sallet with no visor, so he could pull the string back to his cheek and take aim. There are also numerous accounts of archers taking off their boots in battle, to get a better purchase with their feet. An archer carried 48 arrows and could shoot between 12 and 15 arrows per minute at a range of 250 yards (228 metres), shooting in high arcs down on to the opponents.

Furthermore, once an opponent was within 100 yards (90 metres) the archers could shoot direct into faces and weak points in armour with considerable accuracy. As well as his longbow, most archers carried some form of sword and a buckler. Of the 112 possessing bows and arrows in the Bridport Muster Roll (one has three bows, along with four staff weapons, two jacks and two sallets), 33 wore a jack and sallet, with a sword and dagger or another side arm. Twenty-three of the archers also possessed various staff weapons.

Black Powder Weapons

Cannons and 'handgonnes' were first used *en masse* in England at the Battle of Northampton in 1460. The Lancastrians had built a large protective camp for their guns, much in the same way as the French had done at Castillon seven years earlier. However, either through poor mixing of gunpowder or through damp, the guns proved to be ineffective.

They were not used again in large numbers until the Battle of Barnet, where Warwick positioned them on his right flank when the battle started. In Europe, guns were sometimes placed in front of the infantry, but more often, in prepared defensive positions on the flank. It had long been established that the most effective way to deploy artillery was in enfilade, that is to say across its longest axis or at an angle to the enemy's line, rather than head-on. With armies only several ranks deep, this would then reap maximum destruction. Christine de Pizan in her military manual, says that firepower should be placed on the wings. The French had done this at the Battle of Castillon, cutting an English/Gascon army to pieces. Also, Charles the Bold's plan for the Battle of Morat in 1476, placed his artillery on the left flank almost at a right angle to his battle-line in an attempt to destroy the Swiss before they reached his army. In Europe, artillery continued to be positioned behind ditches and banks throughout the next century. We do not know what part black powder (gunpowder) weapons played at Bosworth, although we do know Richard brought an artillery train with him. *The Ballad of Bosworth Fielde* only gives two types of cannon, 'bombards' and 'serpentines'; however, there were many different sizes and calibre (bore) all with different names such as 'crapedeaux', 'crapaudines', 'courtaulds', 'faucons' and 'sakers' as well as serpentines. The bombard was primarily a siege weapon of very large calibre, its purpose being to hurl huge stones at town and castle walls. Richard was not expecting to fight a siege, so it is much more likely that what is meant is one of the larger calibres of field guns.

It is not known with any degree of certainty when guns were first used in England although they seem to be common by the 1320s and the word 'canonys' (cannons) first appears in England around 1378. These early guns were cumbersome and difficult to use, but in the mid fifteenth century there seems to have been a revolution in their design and use. Firstly, with the

Lead cannonball from the 1460 Battle of Northampton. (Author)

Reconstruction of a fifteenth century breech-loading cannon. (Author)

invention of the wheeled carriage, which made them more portable and secondly with the improvements made to black powder.

Black powder was a mixture of saltpetre, sulphur and charcoal. The saltpetre was imported from India via Venice and by the time of Bosworth was probably made at Frankfurt in Germany and possibly in England as well. Sulphur was also imported, coming from two sources in medieval Europe – Sicily and Iceland. The mixture was confusingly known as serpentine powder and was very fine and unreliable due to high water absorption of the saltpetre. How much was mixed in England, and how much was imported ready mixed is not known, although there was a 'powder house' at the Tower of London in 1461. Medieval guns took great skill to load, if rammed in too tight the powder would not explode, and too loose, it would just belch and the ball would roll out of the barrel. If the mix was wrong it would produce coloured smoke, fizzle and bang without firing, or even explode, killing or maiming the crew. It would not travel well either, and if shaken its constituent parts would separate, forcing it to be mixed again before use. However, in the 1420s a new process called 'corning' was developed. Gunpowder was first made into a paste (often with the urine of a wine drinker) and then dried into balls and loaves which were then ground to a powder. This not only made it more stable but far more

Reconstruction of a ribauldequin, also known as a rabauld, ribault, ribaudkin or organ gun. This was a late medieval volley gun with many small-calibre iron barrels set up parallel on a platform, in use during the 14th and 15th centuries. When the gun was fired in a volley, it created a shower of iron shot. (Author)

Looking down the barrel of a reconstructed medieval cannon showing the staves that give cannonballs their distinctive shape. (Author)

powerful. It also meant different types of powder (sorted by grain size and by the ratio of its constituents) could be produced for different types of weapons. Both types of powder were still in use at the time of Bosworth, but corned powder may have been regarded as a black art, so it is not known how much Richard would have had.

There were also two designs of gun in common use. The cast bronze gun, which was muzzle loaded, had been in use since the beginning of the century, although the cost had made their use prohibitive until the middle of the century when the price of bronze dropped dramatically. Also, trunnions could be cast into the barrels which meant they could be elevated much easier. The other type, which had been in use much longer was made from around 10 wrought iron bars arranged in a cylinder and held in place by iron hoops. These were breech loaders with separate chambers into which the powder and ball were loaded. The chambers were sealed with a wooden plug, to prevent the powder separating, and then positioned at the back of the barrel. To ensure a good seal, a wooden wedge was hammered in behind the chamber. However, corned powder may have been too powerful for iron cannons, so serpentine powder was probably used.

Cast lead balls were more suited to the iron cannon because the softer metal would deform to the shape of the barrel. However, when the cannon was fired, the wooden plug would also burst out, flattening the back of the ball. This necessitated an iron or stone cube being cast into the ball, to limit the deformation. Cast iron cannonballs were also common, although to be effective they needed a smoother, rounded barrel, so were more likely used with cast bronze guns. Only lead balls (mostly 60 mm diameter) were found during the recent archaeological investigations at Bosworth, although this does not mean there were no cast iron ones used, just that few probably survived in the soil (although some may yet be discovered). It must be remembered that medieval cannonballs did not explode, instead relying on their energy to smash through enemy lines. Recent experiments with a 60 mm lead ball have shown that with a flat trajectory (no elevation), they first impacted the ground at around 109 yards (100 metres) then bounced up to 10 times to a distance of 874 yards (800 metres). However, these tests were in ideal conditions, that is to say on flat, dry ground. At Bosworth, much of the ground was soggy from the marsh (which would have absorbed some, if not all their energy), and rose upwards from Richard's position, so his guns would have had limited range, with cannonballs burying themselves in the ground rather than bouncing.

Margaret of Anjou had increased the royal arsenal to over 100 guns by 1460. Edward IV had instituted a gun foundry at Calais before 1473 and by the early 1480s the royal artillery train amounted to around 233 guns, with names like the *Great Edward of Calais*, the *Great Brazen Gun*, the *Messenger*, the *Fowler of Chester* and *Little Edward*. Many of these guns were brought to England for Richard's campaigns in Scotland in 1481 and 1482 and some must have been taken to Bosworth. For the Scottish campaign, Edward also ordered a potgun (a short, wide cannon akin to a mortar) of brass and another of iron, as well as 100 'hakeguns' (hook guns) of brass and 150 handguns. Before he became king, Louis XI sent Richard a gift of a great bombard, possibly to help persuade him to support the Treaty of Picquigny. In his letter of thanks, Richard remarked 'I have always taken and still take in artillery … I assure you it will be a special treasure to me.' In December 1483, Richard recruited William Clowke of Gelderland as gunmaker and on 18 January made an agreement with John Bramburgh to make gunpowder. On 27 February 1484, Richard ordered seven serpentines on carts and 28 'hacbushes' (see below) with frames. As the threat of invasion grew, Richard appointed Roger Bykeley to commandeer all necessary workmen and weapons for the defence of the realm on 5 March. Six days later he appointed Patrick de la Motte as Chief Cannoneer or Master Founder at a daily wage of 18d and three *gunnoures* at 6d per day for making cannons in the Tower of London and elsewhere. Then on 16 June ordered two serpentines, two guns to 'lye on walls' and 12 more hacbushes.

Reconstruction of a medieval handgunner. (Author)

Handguns were known by many different names in England during the fifteenth century. These include 'handcannons', 'arquebus', 'hakeguns', 'hagbusshes', 'hackbuts' and 'handgonnes'. By the time of Bosworth, handgonnes had become commonplace. Duke John the Fearless could equip 4,000 by 1411 in Burgundy and in Charles the Bold's army of May 1471 it is recorded that there were 1,200 crossbowmen, and 1,250 handgonners. To start with, the English seem to have preferred to employ mercenaries as 'handgonners'. The *Great Chronicle of London* says Edward IV had 500 'black and smoky sort of Flemish gunners' when he entered London in April 1471. Although he continued to use mercenary handgonners throughout his reign, he did employ his own, and in readiness for his Scottish campaign, ordered 250 new brass handguns.

These were first called a 'harquebus', *hakenbüchse* in Germany, 'hackbut' by the English, and *arquebus* by the French. These had a simple S-shaped trigger, called a serpentine, fastened to the side of the gun stock. This pivoted in the middle and had a set of adjustable jaws, or dogs, on the upper end that held the smouldering end of a length of match that had been soaked in saltpetre. Pulling up on the bottom of the serpentine brought the tip of the match down into contact with powder in the flashpan, a small, saucer-shaped depression surrounding the touchhole atop the barrel. After 1440, aiming from the cheek, or with a shortened stock propped against the shoulder, or over the shoulder, became popular. Gunmakers realised that a heavier shorter stock was as effective means of absorbing recoil. Although there had been attempts to standardise sizes, they still varied greatly, with barrels typically between 20–40 inches (500 and 1,000 mm) long and calibres between 0.50 and 0.65 inches (12.5 and 16 mm).

Towards the end of the fifteenth century the serpentine had started to be replaced by a mechanism, enclosed within the gunstock, that consisted of a trigger, an arm holding the match with its adjustable jaws at the end, a sear connecting trigger and arm, and a mechanical linkage opening the flashpan cover as the match descended. This was what would become known as the

Detail of a reconstructed medieval handgun firing mechanism. (Author)

matchlock, and it changed very little until the flintlock musket replaced it in the final years of the seventeenth century. In 1482, the Milanese fielded 1,250 handgonners, and 233 crossbowmen as well as 352 arquebusiers, which possibly refers to weapons with a matchlock mechanism. Another innovation at the end of the century was the pre-measured charge that could be poured into the gun, which greatly speeded up loading. It is unclear exactly when it first came into use, although some may have been in use by Bosworth.

Communications

Communications between armies and centres of power were very slow and were normally by letter or word of mouth. A message, depending on the urgency, could take several days to travel one hundred miles, even by horse. So he could keep in touch with his Scottish campaign in 1482, Edward introduced a system of couriers, an idea borrowed from France. He appointed 10 men to be stationed equally along the 335 mile (539 km) route to Berwick. Each was expected to ride the 33 miles (53 km) to the next station flat out with any news, for which they were paid 12 pence a day. This meant news could travel over 100 miles each day. It was the first attempt at a postal system and not unlike the American pony express. Richard revived the system when he came to the throne, but had only 20 miles between posts. News for the general public would normally be a lot slower. Important information or royal edicts were passed from the Government or Royal Council to the sheriffs of counties and towns. Handbills could then be posted on church doors etc. or read out from the pulpit. The traditional place for handbills to be first posted was on the door of St. Paul's in London. Subversive bills and newsletters would also be posted in exactly the same way.

Logistics and the Army on the March

Writing in 1498, Venetian envoy Andrea Trevisan said: 'that when war is raging most furiously, they [the English] will seek for good eating, and all their other comforts, without thinking of what might befall them.' Therefore, a good supply of food was essential in maintaining the morale and fighting capacity of the army. An army would typically march 15 miles per day, although Edward IV, en route to Tewkesbury in May 1471, force-marched his men 35 miles in one day. Men were expected to carry their own weapons, equipment and supplies with them. Some, especially the men-at-arms, would have carried their equipment in carts. A treatise written around 1450, known as the 'Hastings MS', lists what each man-at-arms should take in the field and include; a tent, a chair, a basin, a board and a pair of trestles to set his meat and drink on, a board cloth, a knife for cutting his meat, a cup to drink from, and a hammer and nails. Recommended food includes six loaves of bread, two gallons of wine and a mess of meaty flesh or fish.

Although medieval man had no knowledge of the science of diet as we understand it today, or caloric requirements, we can make educated guesses as to what supplies a medieval army needed. Studies of the Roman military diet before AD 200 suggest soldiers having a diet of approx. 3,400 calories per day from wine, meat and grain with a wine/vinegar mix, hard-baked biscuits and dried fish or meat when on campaign. In 1327, King Charles IV of France provided his troops with an estimated 3,250 calories per day. On campaign during the First World War, western armies received rations of between 3,200 and 3,800 calories per day. Today, soldiers require around 3,000 calories. Evidence from the ancient, medieval and early modern periods all suggest that most calories came from grain products. One kg (2.2 lbs) of bread made from medieval wheat or rye or 750 grams (1.65 lbs) of biscuit can provide approximately 2,000 calories. Dried beans provide 1,250 calories per kg; fresh meat, 2,500 calories per kg; and dried meat 3,200 calories per kg.

Michael Prestwich in his *Armies and Warfare in the Middle Ages: The English Experience*, suggests that 1000 men would require roughly 167 quarters (6.35 metric tons) of cereals per week. A bushel of wheat (25.4kg), could normally provide 30 loaves. C. Given-Wilson in his *The royal household and the king's affinity*, suggests that a quarter of grain could feed up to 270 men. Bakers of the royal household were also expected to bake 40 superior simnels, 140–150 salt simnels, or 260 bakers' loaves from a quarter of corn. A simnel was originally a yeast-leavened bread made from the highest quality flour possible (*simnel* derives from the Latin *simila* – the whitest and finest of flours). A superior simnel would feed four men, the salt simnel would feed two, and one loaf would be sufficient for one man. Based on all this, Bachrach and Bachrach (*Warfare in Medieval Europe*) suggest 2,500 kg (2.5 metric tons) of food supplies were required for 1,000 men per day.

Water was probably the most logistically challenging item to provide, due in part to the amounts required. Your body is about 60 percent water. Lose even 1.5 percent of that and mild dehydration will occur, causing dizziness or light-headedness, headaches and a loss of strength and stamina, even cramps, spasms, and soreness, all symptoms that can be ill afforded on the battlefield. Armour with padding or just a padded jack is the perfect insulator which would lead to increased sweating and therefore dehydration. Once again, the science of hydration was not known, although people would have been aware of the need to drink plenty. However, to stop and take a drink during a battle had its own inherent risks. There are numerous accounts of fully armoured men, such as Lord Dacre fighting at Towton in 1461, raising their visors to drink, only to be hit in the face by an arrow. We also read of wine and beer being taken on campaign. Alcohol decreases the production of anti-diuretic hormone used by the body to reabsorb water so that the body loses more fluids than normal through increased urination. Whilst the minimum intake of water is still debated, modern military manuals suggest for a 68 kg (150 lbs), active person a minimum of 4.27 litres (7.5 pints) per day to maintain optimum performance. So, for 1,000 soldiers, that equates to 4,270 litres, 1,128 gallons or 4.2 metric tons of water per day.

Far more physically fragile than humans, horses also require large amounts of food and water on campaign. The quantity of food needed generally depended on the animal's weight, most horses requiring between 10 and 15 kg (22 to 33 lbs) of fodder and grain per day, and because they are likely to reject brackish water, up to 45 litres or 10 gallons of fresh water per day. This necessitated armies on the move to stay close to rivers and streams where fresh water was readily available. Mules need around 7.5 kg (16.5 lbs) of fodder and grain and oxen, although rarely used for transport during the Wars of the Roses, require around 20 kg (44 lbs) of fodder each day most of which could be obtained from grazing.

Although a man was expected to carry his own food with him on the march, it was likely that it would soon run out. *Knyghthode and Bataile* warns of the importance of adequate supplies when its author wrote:

> Have purveyance of forage and victual
> For man and horse; for iron smiteth not
> So sore as hunger doth if food fail.

The king or commander of the army would be expected to pay for what supplies were needed, although this did not always happen in practice, and occasionally towns were expected to hand over supplies free of charge. Sir John Fortescue wrote around 1460 that:

> And for that his highness nor his said company in no wise should be destitute or wanting of victuals for man or horse: He strictly chargeth and commandeth every victualler, and all other his subjects dwelling in every town or place where his said highness and his said company shall come, to provide and make ready plenty of bread and ale, and other victuals, as well for horse as for man, at reasonable price in ready money therefor to them.

Victuallers would therefore normally ride ahead and secure what supplies they could; harbingers would look for billets and sites to make camps and foragers would also be sent out for extra supplies and fodder. *Knyghthode and Bataile* describes the role of the harbinger as:

> A Mesurer, that is our Herbagere,
> For pavilion and tent assigneth he
> The ground, and saith 'Be ye there, be ye here!'
> Each hostel eek, in castle and city,
> Assigneth he, each after a degree.

However, Gregory writes that it was a matter of contention that the mounted infantry would ride ahead and take all the best billets, then eat and drink all the supplies before the footmen arrived.

Richard III would have been able to draw on local supplies and the night before Bosworth, received them from Coventry. One of the reasons that Henry probably chose late August to invade was that most of the harvest would have been gathered and provided ample food for his men. Even a small army such as Henry's could consume vast amounts. In the 15 days it took his army to march from Milford Haven to Bosworth they would have needed more than 97 tonnes of food as well as 135 tonnes of fodder for the horses, plus thousands of gallons of water. Most of this would have had to be foraged or donated by towns. Soon after Bosworth, Henry VII granted 100 marks to the abbey at Merevale in compensation for 'right gret hurtes, charges and lossis by occasioun of the gret repayre and resorte that oure people commyng toward oure late feld made, as welle unto the house of Mira valle aforesaide as in going over his ground, to the destruction of his cornes and pastures.'

A royal warrant, issued by Henry VII on 29 November 1485, gave compensation to a number of villages near the battlefield for sustained losses of their 'corn and grain by us and our company at our late victorious field.' Atherstone received £24 13s 4d, (in two payments of £20 and £4 13s 4d), Mancetter, £5 19s; Fenny Drayton, £20; Witherley, £13; and Atterton £8 10s.

As well as the men and food supplies, an army needed to take huge supplies of arrows and equipment, such as bridges. They also took all the associated trades needed to maintain them in the field, such as blacksmiths, coopers, farriers, carpenters, masons, arrow makers etc., and all their equipment. We can get an idea of the size of a small artillery train from Burgundian documents relating to the transportation of five medium serpentines, four small serpentines, a bombard and two *courtaux* from Luxembourg to Dijon in 1474. Each medium serpentine needed three horses to pull it, the small ones, two. They took 30 casks of powder, five casks per cart with four horses to pull each cart. Another one and a half carts were needed for the unspecified number of lead shot, and five for the stone shot. Sixteen horses were needed to pull the two *courtaux* and five carts for 200 stone shot for them. Another 24 horses were required to pull the bombard with 10 carts to carry its mantlet and 10 carts to carry the 100 stone shot taken for it. They also took 2,500 bows, 2,700 arrows and 6,000 strings in 11 carts. Four carts were needed for the saddler, cooper, carpenters and tools, two carts were needed for the gunners and their equipment. So, in total, this train alone needed 50 carts and 257 horses, just for 12 guns.

An army on the march could, therefore, be of considerable length and as much as one day's march from one end to the other, and that is without the women, tradesmen etc., that would inevitably follow the army. *Knyghthode and Bataile* warns of how cumbersome moving three divisions as one body was, saying it was preferable to take a smaller one. It was, therefore, not uncommon for armies to march in separate battles along different routes. Even then, the mounted troops had to stop to wait for the slower moving parts to catch up.

Light horse, referred to as scourers, aforeriders or prickers, protected the flanks of the slower moving infantry and baggage on the march. There were also behind-riders, which were light cavalry and archers to protect the rear.

The Transformation of Warfare in Europe

Warfare in Europe had followed a different path, with mounted charges much more common. As a result, the Swiss had developed the use of the longspear and halberd to counter the ferocious charges by Burgundian heavy cavalry. The longspear (*Pique longue* in French), was a 15 to 22 foot (5 to 7 metre) pole tipped with a narrow, square section pointed head. It was also known as a marespike or Moorish pike, and is often incorrectly called a pike in modern writing (a later term), The Swiss usually formed up in a *Gewalthaufen* (battle), a rectangular or square block often with a *keil* (wedge) at its head. Along its edges, four ranks deep were men armed with the longspear, whilst at its centre were a mass of halberdiers and men with giant two-handed swords. Against cavalry, they would form a hedgehog with all the longspears pointing outwards, but against infantry, they would use the longspears to break up a formation, then the halberdiers and swordsmen would rush out to attack the disorganised enemy. The *Gewalthaufen* would be preceded by a screen of crossbowmen and handgunners that could retreat under the longspears for protection, should the need arise. And like the English, the Swiss favoured a flank attack where the *Gewalthaufen* proved very effective. These tactics were copied by the French in their wars with Burgundy, and were used to great effect, especially at Bosworth. The use of the longspear was not as simple as it sounds. The Swiss chronicler Müller-Hickler, wrote sometime before 1496 that:

> The most unfavorable aspect was the vibrating of the long shaft. I have personally learned from fighting with the longspear that it is almost impossible to hit the target, because with a strong thrust the point quivers so much. This is particularly true when one makes energetic jabs and most apparent when the full length of the lance is used, and it is thrust out far by stretching the right arm.

There was also a more certain, relatively slower thrust to be used when the opportunity offered itself if the person fighting with the armoured 'double-pay mercenary' wanted to aim the desired thrust at the neck and the lower body in such a way as to strike the joint of the harness.

The first time the English encountered the longspear was in 1444 when Richard's father, Richard of York was Lieutenant of France. Although England and France were still at war, there was a long period of peace between the two sides. Since the Treaty of Arras of 1435, which marked the end of hostilities between Charles VII, and Philip the Good, large multinational bands of unemployed mercenaries known as *Écorcheurs* (lit. Flayers) had terrorised France including Normandy. York was also keeping diplomatic channels open with the French, and it appears that Charles contacted him requesting support for an expedition into Alsace under the Dauphin. York must have agreed, as he rounded up around 8,000 of these unemployed soldiers and masked marauders also known as *Faulxvisaiges* from Normandy and sent them to support the Dauphin under Matthew Gough. The Old Zürich War between the seven cantons of the Old Swiss Confederacy and the canton of Zürich had been going on since 1440, and in 1444, Frederick III, Holy Roman Emperor, appealed to Charles VII of France to send an army to relieve the siege of Zürich. Charles sent the Dauphin with an army of around 20,000 mercenaries including the English into Switzerland. The Swiss sent an advance force of 1,300 men armed with longspears to meet them. The French vanguard was surprised and routed at Pratteln and Muttenz. Then, buoyed by their success, the Swiss crossed the Birs to meet the main French army at the Battle of St. Jakob an der Birs on 26 August 1444. The Swiss, joined by

200 locals, formed into three squares each of 500 men. Time and time again, the French cavalry charged the squares only to be repulsed. Aeneas Silvius Piccolomini (later Pope Pius II), described the battle in detail, telling how the Swiss ripped bloody crossbow bolts from their bodies and charged the enemy even after they had been pierced by spears or had lost their hands, charging the Armagnacs to avenge their [own] deaths. After several hours, the Swiss retreated into the small hospital of St. Jakob. The French bombarded the hospital with their artillery but the Swiss refused to surrender and when the French charged into the hospital the remaining Swiss were forced back to the hospital's garden and killed to the last man within half an hour. The clash showed the effectiveness of the longspear against heavy cavalry but also exposed their weakness to artillery.

The successes of the longspear over cavalry reverberated throughout Europe. The costs of raising mounted troops were also increasing due to economic pressures and political status of the European nobility. Soon, most countries were copying them. In Burgundy, Charles the Bold's ordinance of 1471 included the recruitment of 1,250 longspear men. The following year the Burgundian Chancellor ordered urgent recruitment of another 2,000 for the ordnance companies. These were to be 'most expert in war' and 'of an age and physical strength to endure and undertake the hardships, duties and operations required and necessary in waging war.' They were also to be equipped with 'haubergeon jackets with stiffened sleeves and on the right arm metal strips over the mail guard.' The Burgundian Wars of 1476–7 had again shown that cavalry was virtually useless against any well-trained longspear formations.

In Italy longspears were being used before 1432 when an agreement between Florence and the condotta of Micheletto Degli Attendoli included 100 foot, all armed with long lances. By the last quarter of the fifteenth century, the Picchieri (infantry armed with longspears) was a part of most Italian armies. Meanwhile, in Spain during the struggle for Granada in 1483, King Ferdinand of Aragon reportedly hired a Swiss unit that was to serve as a model for the formation of a similar infantry.

We do not know to what extent longspears were used by English armies in the late fifteenth century. However, in 1481, the inventory of the Calais garrison, the closest England had to a professional army, listed 941 spearheads awaiting shafts, 144 marespikes and another 360 unheaded in its inventory. In May 1483, Maximilian's receiver of artillery placed an order with a weapons manufacturer in Malines for 1,200 longspears to be delivered to the King of England. At the time of Bosworth, Guînes castle held 67. And, just seven years after Bosworth, an indenture between Henry VII and Rhys ap Thomas included the provision for 200 footmen armed with longspears.

France

In France, the military organisation was based on the *compagnies d'ordonnance* and the francs-archers and as early as 1448, the latter included longspears. The French foot was traditionally called the *gens à pied* or *piétons* (literally pedestrians), but by the late fifteenth century had begun to be called *infanterie* (from the Italian *la fantaria*), *aventurier* and *soldat*. Louis XI abolished the francs-archers after their failure at Guinegate in 1479, and in their place sought a force of 14,000 volunteers with longspears from Normandy and Picardy based on the Swiss model. According to Commines he added 2,500 pioneers, who were to be called the *Gens du Champ* and 1,500 men-at-arms, of his old standing forces, who were to fight on foot with longspear and halberd (the men-at-arms did not want to fight with the *infanterie* and were disbanded in 1483). Sometime before 1486, they also had companies of Gascon arbalestriers, presumably crossbow men or hand gunners. The new army was to be ready at any moment for mobile operations beyond the borders of the kingdom and were to be France's first professional army, paid quarterly in three-monthly instalments. According to *Les Rosier des Guerre*, written by Pierre Choisnet for Louis XI around 1482, they were organised in units of 1,000 men commanded by a Royal Lieutenant. Below them were 10 Captains, who each commanded 10 *Dizainers*, who in turn were in charge of 10 footmen.

The army was assembled at a mobile encampment (*coups de manoeuvre*) similar to a Hussite wagon lager and again, according to Commines, in imitation of Burgundy's army. Initially, the army assembled near Hedin in Picardy. The following year, 4,000 Normans and 6,000 Picards assembled at Pont de l'Arche near Rouen in Normandy. To form the basis of the camp Louis ordered 700 tents and 700 carts. As for life in a camp, it was decided to house 20 men per tent, and the carts to move all their equipment including artillery.

Six thousand Swiss were brought in as demonstration troops and Swiss instructors reportedly remained there for over a year. Louis also ordered 18,500 long daggers, 14,500 halberds and 5,500 longspears, which suggests a ratio of two or three halberds to one longspear. These developments concerned Melchior Russ, a Swiss official, who reported back home that Louis XI was having a large number of longspears and halberds fabricated in the German style, adding if he were also able to train men who could wield them, he would no longer need the services of anybody else.

The new army also caused concern in England as it was thought that the French were planning to attack Calais. Louis wrote to Lord Hastings, saying '… I beg you to be so good as to tell my cousin your king, that I have no such thought, nor will I do or suffer any damage to the smallest village in the territory of Calais…'

When Henry Tudor returned to England in 1485, it was these troops that he would bring with him. According to the *Ballad of Bosworth Fielde* armed with:

10,000 more spikes with all
And harquebusyers, throw lye can théth ringe

As well as these troops, Louis had an elite company of Scottish bodyguard, the *Garde Écossaise* which formed part of the *archiers du corps* or *gardes de la manche*. From the outset of the Hundred Years War, there were Scottish companies officially fighting for Philip IV of France. At the Battle of Poitiers, the 1st Earl of Douglas and the future 3rd Earl of Douglas fought for John II, where the future 3rd Earl was captured along with many Scottish knights. In the 1360s there were Scotsmen to be found in the army of Bertrand du Guesclin. In 1418 Robert Stewart, Duke of Albany appointed his son, John Stewart, 2nd Earl of Buchan, Chamberlain of Scotland to command the Scottish expeditionary force, the largest army that medieval Scotland had ever sent abroad. 7,000–8,000 men arrived at La Rochelle in October 1419 and made their way to Tours. The Scottish leadership sent another 4,000–5,000 reinforcements in 1420. The Dauphin picked one hundred of the best to be his personal bodyguard. The Scots were shattered at the Battle of Verneuil in 1424, when they lost 6,000 men. They then fragmented into free companies, and also joined *Compagnies d'ordonnance* within the French Army.

After Louis XI came to power his company of Scottish bodyguard formed part of the *archiers du corps* or *gardes de la manche*. The company was made up of 25 bodyguards and 75 archers and each bodyguard had four men-at-arms under his command. A detachment of 25 Scottish bodyguards equipped with *guisarmes* and bows, acted as 24-hour close protection for the French King and accompanied him wherever he went, posted guards on his sleeping quarters and even escorted his food from kitchen to table. The bodyguard, as well as the captain of the guard, was always Scottish. First, Guillaume Stuyer (1461–64), then his brother Thomas (1465–72) and after him Robert Conyngham (1473–78), and Jean Conyngham, Bailly of Chartres, councillor and chamberlain to the king (1479–1492). The Scottish *Compagnie d'ordonnance* was initially made up of 50 *Lances fournies* but later divided into two separate 50-lance companies under Conyngham (plus a Spanish and an Italian company, each of 100 lances).

Battlefield Wounds and Their Treatment

There are very few contemporary accounts of battles in any detail, and even less in the first person and even fewer that describe injuries in detail. One rare account that describes the horrors of medieval warfare is *The Unconquered Knight: A Chronicle of the Deeds of Don Pero Niño, Count of Buelna*, written by the head of Niño's military household, Gutierre Diaz de Gamez. He began a chronicle of his master's deeds in about 1431. The chronicle recounts that at the Battle of Ponteverdra in 1397. Niño first faced Gomez Domao but after trading blows to each other's head he was stuck in the neck by an arrow which pinned his gorget to him. However, the account tells us that he did not feel the wound, although it restricted the movement in his upper body. He was then hit in the nostrils by a crossbow bolt which although dazing him did not stop him. He soon found himself in the press of his enemies who sometimes hit his nose causing him great pain. When he returned to his camp after the battle, he found his shield shattered, sword hilt broken and the blade toothed like a saw and covered in blood. As well as the arrow and crossbow bolt wounds, he found he had many flesh wounds all of which went on to heal. In fact, he lived another 56 years and took part in several more battles.

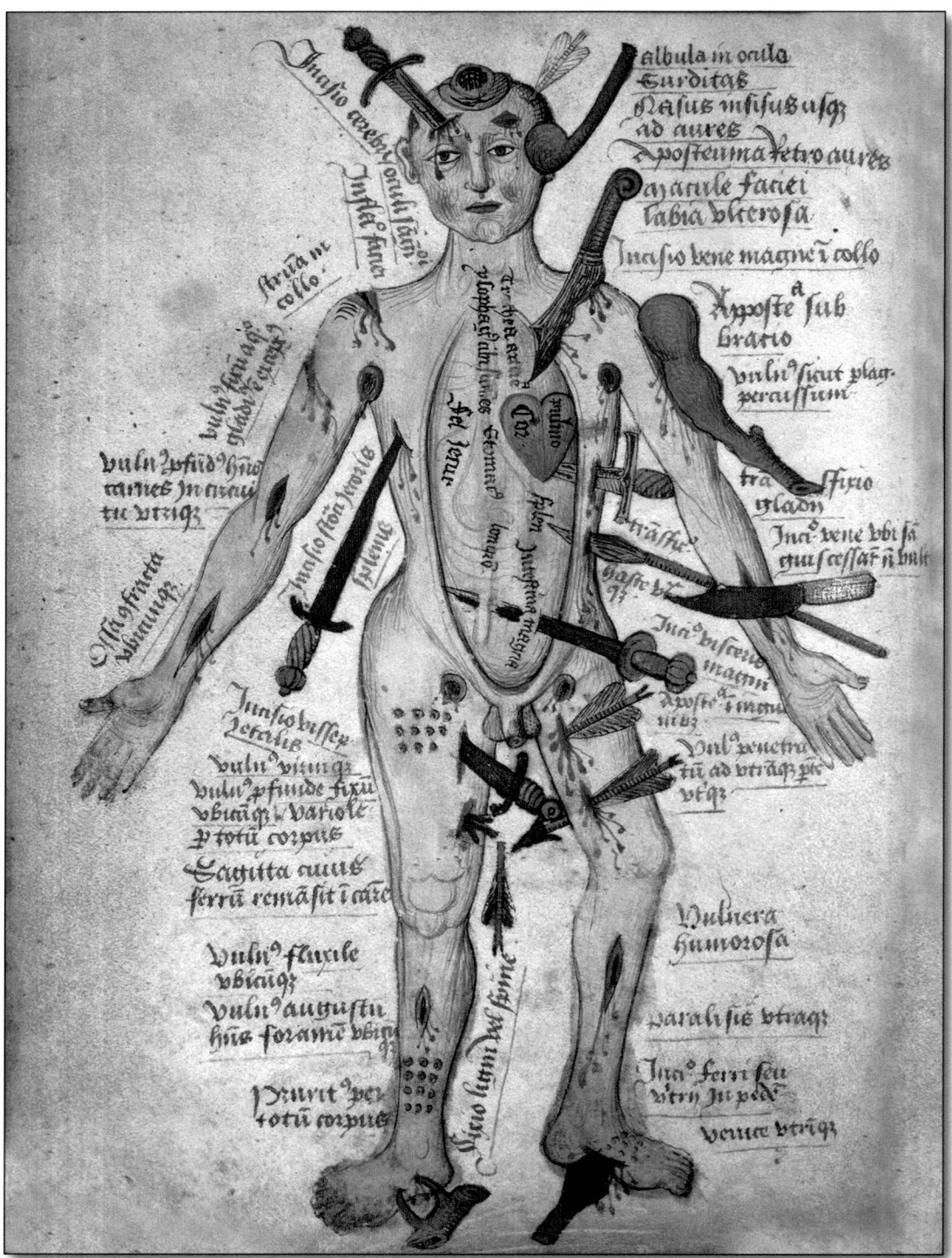

The 'Wound man' from an English anatomical treatise. The 'wound man' is a figure found in a number of manuscripts and printed books produced in the 15th and 16th centuries. Pseudo-Galen, *Anathomia*; WMS 290. (Wellcome Collection. CC BY 4.0)

Gerhard von Wessel writing in a newsletter of 17 April 1471 on the condition of soldiers in the immediate aftermath of the Battle of Barnet tells of how many followers were wounded 'mostly in the face and lower half of the body, a very pitiable sight … Those who set out on good horses and sound bodies returned home with sorry nags and bandaged faces, some without noses etc. and preferred to stay indoors.'

Very few mass war graves from the medieval period have been discovered. Those that have been unearthed obviously do not show the flesh wounds but they give valuable insights into trauma and injuries sustained during medieval warfare through the damage evident on the skeletons. One such group of graves from the Battle of Visby on the Island of Gotland, fought in July 1361, was discovered by Dr. Oscar Wennersten in 1905. He exhumed one of the graves and found 300 bodies complete with their armour and weapons. Archaeologists Bengt Thordeman and Poul Nørlund discovered more bodies during excavations of two further mass graves at Visby between 1912 and 1928, bringing the total bodies recovered to 1,185.

There were 456 perimortem injuries (trauma that occurred around the time of death) with visible evidence of cutting weapons, such as swords and axes. The cutting wounds can be split into two groups, those which showed hacking evidence but finished at the bone and those which actually severed the bone. Some had evidence of multiple blows before the death blow. Heads also seem to have been a target and several took many blows. Many of the skulls still have their mail hoods, and although the hoods did provide some protection, many of the blows cut through the mail and into the bone. One of the skulls had received a blow to the bridge of the nose that cut right through the upper jaw. The use of war hammers was also suggested by square section holes in skulls. One skull had three crossbow bolt heads in it, as well as two holes where it appears that the beak of a polearm or a hammer had been used.

There were another 126 wounds from piercing weapons such as arrows and lances as well as a number of crushing injuries. Approximately 70 percent of the blows identified at Visby were aimed at the lower leg. There were also several skeletons where a foot has been severed. One poor unfortunate seems to have had both legs severed with a single blow that landed on the outside of right leg below the knee then struck the inside of the left leg.

In 1996, construction workers stumbled across a mass grave with a number of casualties under the floor of Towton Hall presumably from the Battle of Towton. The grave was excavated by archaeologists from the University of Bradford and the West Yorkshire Archaeology Service. It was and is the only mass grave of a known medieval battle found in England to date. The remains of 38 individuals, including 28 complete skeletons, were recovered. The bodies belonged to men who ranged in ages from 17 to 50 years old and were between five and six feet tall. A greatly increased bone mass on the left forearm and the right upper arm of nine of the bodies suggests that they may have been archers. The transformation of cartilage (ossification) of the broad, thick, radiating muscle, situated on the outer surface of the pelvis (gluteus medius) to bone indicates that at least one skeleton, known as 'Towton 16', may have also been a horseman.

Like Visby, many of the skeletons had perimortem injuries mostly to the head and none of them seem to have been wearing helmets at the time of death. There were 113 wounds on the 27 recovered skulls, including six blows to 'Towton 10' and at least 13 blows to 'Towton 32'. An osteological examination of the skull wounds suggests that 73 were caused by sharp force trauma, 28 were produced by blunt force trauma, and 12 were the result of puncture wounds, possibly from a poll-axe. There was also a total of 43 postcranial (the bones below the skull) injuries on all 38 bodies, many of which were what appears to be defensive wounds to the arms.

The body with some of the most severe injuries is known today as 'Towton 25'. He was between 36 and 45 years old at the time of his death and sustained nine wounds to his head. Because of the direction and pattern of his skull fractures, osteologists can identify the order in which 'Towton 25' received his injuries. The first five blows were by a bladed weapon to the left side of his head and would not have been immediately fatal. He then received another blow to the back of his head that opened a large horizontal gash, causing other radiating fractures down the base and sides of his skull. The bone fragments embedded in his brain would have most probably been fatal. 'Towton 25' received another wound that cut through his face from his left eye to the right side of his mandible (jaw). Another separate grave of a high-status male aged between 36 and 45 and 6 ft 1 inches (1.85 metres) tall was also found nearby. He has a stab wound to his left foot, which shattered one of the bones and cut two more. There was also a cut to the lower jaw and blunt force trauma to the base of the skull.

Most Wars of the Roses armies retained surgeons, despite wound treatment being rudimentary, and even the most severe of injury was not necessarily fatal. An ossuary from the 1385 Battle of Aljubarrota in Portugal excavated in 1958 held the bones of 400 individuals aged 20 to 60. An examination of the bones revealed many had healed lesions probably caused by slicing weapons. One showed signs of a right arm amputation and another had his left upper leg amputated, both had healed sometime before the battle.

Nine of the Towton bodies showed signs of well-healed trauma to the skull ranging from superficial cuts to deep penetrating wounds. 'Towton 16', aged 46 to 50 years (the oldest of the group), had received a blade wound to the left side of his face, through his mouth, splitting his jaw bone and causing a secondary fracture to his chin. The fact that this had happened around 10 years before Towton, and that there were no signs of infection, is testament to the surgeon's skill and also 'Towton 16's good fortune. Contemporary medical textbooks give instructions for such an injury, saying that wax was first put on the place where the bone was cut, followed by a double layer of dressing with a splint or a piece of leather the length of the jaw. This would then be carefully sewn onto a skull cap.

The skill of some medieval surgeons can also be seen in the treatment of Prince Henry, the future King Henry V, who had been wounded in the face by an arrow at the Battle of Shrewsbury in 1401. The surgeon, John Bradmore, who had been in the service of the crown since at least 1399, recounted how other had tried to remove the arrowhead with potions and other cures but had no success. According to Bradmore, the arrow had penetrated on the left side of his nose and entered at an angle (*ex traverso*), to a depth of six inches. After he successfully removed the arrowhead with a purpose-designed tool, he began healing and closing the wound. The doctor squirted white wine and put into the wound a probe made of barley, flour, honey and flax fibres. For the next 20 days he repeated the process, cleaning the wound and making the probes smaller and smaller. This allowed the wound to heal naturally and eventually close.

Although it appears that many survived their wounds, infection and the dangers of sepsis, tetanus and peritonitis after a battle was ever present. Margaret Beaufort's third husband, Sir Henry Stafford, possibly died from an infection almost six months after he was wounded at Barnet. John Paston was wounded in the left forearm at the same battle. Concerned over possible infection, he wrote to his family to ask for money to pay a surgeon to attend his wound with 'leechcraft' and 'physic'. So, as accounts of battles, for the most part, only record deaths on the battlefield, the total number of deaths attributable to combat could in reality, have been substantially larger than listed.

The State of the Kingdom

When Henry Tudor landed in England in 1485, the chronicler Molinet noted at the time how the nobility was unwilling to prepare for war, some deciding to turn their backs, others were prepared but instead of helping the King they came to settle their debts with him and to avenge the bad deeds he had done. Since then, some authors have suggested that the limited number of men that came to Richard's aid was due to his bad deeds whilst others remained neutral. This may have been the case for some of course, but for the vast majority, the reality was probably somewhat different. The experienced soldiers of the Hundred Years War had long gone. The typical fighting age at the time was 18 to 35 years old, so the vast majority of those under 32 years old were still children the last time any major fighting took place in England 14 years earlier. Apart from the nobility, who in theory at least, should have trained in the art of war from an early age, there was a small pool of experienced fighting men, some learning their craft in Flanders, Brittany and Burgundy. Others had fought against the Scottish under Richard, however a large number of those had fought under Stanley, and probably did so again in 1485. Some had experience in the tournament and although its original purpose had been to train for war, by this time it had become a relatively sterile and safe environment. This shortage of fighting men was echoed by William Caxton in 1484 when he translated Raymond Lull's *Order of Chivalry* for Richard. He asked where was the custom and usage of noble chivalry and noted that instead of practising military exercises, knights now go to the baths and play at dice. It was not just a problem at the upper echelons of society either, as in May 1485 Richard complained to the bailiff and constable of Ware that instead of archery practice, the inhabitants were playing cards, dicing, bowling, and other 'unlawful and inhibited disports.' So, in reality one of the possible reasons Richard did not have enough fighting men at Bosworth was simply because they did not know how to fight.

3

Richard: Duke of Gloucester

Build me a son, O Lord, who will be strong enough to know when he is weak, and brave enough to face himself when he is afraid, one who will be proud and unbending in honest defeat, and humble and gentle in victory.

Douglas MacArthur

Richard Plantagenet was born on 2 October 1452, at Fotheringhay Castle in Northamptonshire, the twelfth of 13 children and the fourth surviving son of Richard Plantagenet, Duke of York, and Cecily Neville. The Duke of York and Cecily had moved to Fotheringhay, his mother's favourite castle, that August, after York's failed rebellion. For the next few years, Richard lived predominantly at Fotheringhay with his brother George and sister Margaret. He would have also visited his elder brothers Edward and Edmund at Ludlow as well as Berkhamsted and Baynard's Castle in London. Little is known of his formative years, but it is possible that he was destined for the church as he had a high level of learning including Latin.

Although we know little of his life, the discovery of his remains has allowed us to gain a little knowledge about him and his lifestyle. A DNA analysis of Richard's remains suggests that he is likely to have had blue eyes and to have been born with blonde hair, although it probably darkened as he got older. Samples were taken from two of his teeth, a thigh bone and a rib. Teeth mineralise between age 0–15, depending on the tooth, and don't regenerate, so their composition remains fixed for the rest of a person's life. Leg bones regenerate slowly, recording the last 10–15 years of our life, while ribs turn over relatively quickly and record the last 2–5 years. Changes in carbon and nitrogen isotopes found in both his teeth and bones suggest he had a varied, protein-rich diet which included large amounts of marine fish and seafood from around the age of three. These levels dropped off considerably around the age of five when family fortunes took a dramatic downturn. Analysis of oxygen and strontium in Richard's tooth enamel also suggest that he lived at Fotheringhay until about the age of seven or eight when he moved to be with his father and brothers at Ludlow. However, he did not stay there long enough to enjoy it.

After his father and elder brothers fled from Ludlow on 12 October 1459, Cecily, Margaret, George and the seven-year-old Richard were taken to

RICHARD: DUKE OF GLOUCESTER

The site of Fotheringhay Castle, Northants, where Richard III was born and lived until he was around eight years old. (Author)

Coventry where they were put into the care of Cecily's sister, the Duchess of Buckingham, and moved to Tonbridge Castle in Kent. Here, according to a contemporary account, they received 'many a great rebuke'. In 1460, in the aftermath of the Battle of Northampton, the Yorkist wheel of fortune turned again, and Cecily and her children were released. By September, whilst their mother went to meet the Duke on his triumphal return from Ireland, the children stayed at John Falstolf's mansion in Tooley Street, Southwark opposite the Tower. Soon after, Richard was reunited with all his family at York's London house of Baynard's Castle, where he spent his eighth birthday.

Tragedy struck again two months later when Richard's father, the Duke, and elder brother Edmund were killed at the Battle of Wakefield. The Lancastrian army descended on London, according to *The Croyland Chronicle*, like locusts who swept onwards like a whirlwind. At first, Richard and George were hidden in the home of an Alice Martyn (now lost to time). Then, for greater safety, they were then sent to Utrecht in the care of Bishop David, an illegitimate son of the Duke of Burgundy. They were probably treated with indifference, but as soon as news of Edward's stunning victory at Towton reached Burgundy, they were treated as Princes of the Royal Blood. Around 9 April they were taken to Sluys accompanied by 23 people, where they were entertained as royalty for a week. From there, they were taken to the ducal court of Philip III, now known as 'the Good' at Bruges. A banquet was held in the children's honour in the alderman's hall and where the Duke's council, all the ladies of the city and many noble lords were invited. The Milanese ambassador noted that 'The Duke, who is most kind in everything, has been

George Duke of Clarence's Black Bull of Clare, Edward IV's arms and Richard's white boar badge on the pulpit of Fotheringhay church. (Author)

to visit them in their lodgings, and showed them great reverence.' Then on 22 April, they were escorted to English-held Calais where they stayed until the 28th when they crossed the Channel. The Mayor and aldermen of London formally received them at Billingsgate on 2 June, and when Edward returned from the north 10 days later, they knelt before him.

Richard was now aged nine and second in line to the throne after his brother George. On 26 June he was dubbed a Knight of the Bath, then on 1 November 1461, soon after his ninth birthday, Richard was created Duke of Gloucester. He was given his own household that included four high-born boys of his own age, a full range of servants, an income of £1,000 per year from his brother and probably lived at the Placentia (now Greenwich Park). It is also possible he spent some time studying under the Archbishop of Canterbury around this time, although exactly when is unknown, as Edward's recompense came 10 years later and is somewhat vague. His next accolade came on his tenth birthday when he was created Admiral of England, Ireland and Aquitaine. Life for Richard improved considerably, shown by a rise in his protein levels again, reaching the maximum at about the age of 14.

Sometime before 1465, Richard left for the north and Warwick's power base of Middleham Castle, where he became a page and where he would learn to be a knight. It was here that Richard would have learned the arts of chivalry and warfare, as well as literature and law. King Edward granted the earl £1,000 for the expenses of his younger brother's tutelage. Richard would have spent time at all the Neville manors especially the castle of Sheriff Hutton, which would have also brought him into regular contact with all the other great northern families. His companions at the time included the Earl's daughters, Isabel and Anne. It was here that he would also meet his lifelong friend, Francis Lovell, who would continue to support Richard's cause long after his death, and where he first met Thomas Parr and Thomas Huddleston who would die fighting for him at Barnet (and were commemorated later at Queens' College, Cambridge on his request).

On 11 May 1461, the Nevilles founded the college of St. William at York Minster with 36 canons, 30 vicars choral and 20 chantry priests. It was the largest foundation in the north of England and remained so until Richard became King. On 22 September 1465, George Neville was invested as Archbishop of York. To celebrate the Nevilles held an enormous feast

Middleham Castle. It was here that Richard spent a considerable amount of time training to be a knight and it later became his home. (Author)

at Cawood Castle. It would be an ostentatious public demonstration and a reminder of the Nevilles' unbridled power in the north. Richard sat at the main table in the *cheefe chamber* with the Duchess of Suffolk and the countesses of Northumberland and Westmorland and both of Warwick's daughters. Amongst the food and drink consumed at the feast was: 1,000 muttons; 104 oxen; 400 swans; 12 porpoises and seals; 4,000 mallards and teals; 2,000 geese; 2,000 hot custards; 100 tuns of wine and 300 tuns of ale.

It was around this time that Richard began to develop a rare form of idiopathic adolescent-onset scoliosis. This is not the same as kyphosis where its sufferers are commonly called hunchbacks. What caused the scoliosis remains unknown, but it may have genetic connections. Based on a 3D reconstruction of Richard's spinal column, scientists have concluded that his scoliosis was spiral shaped with a Cobb angle (the measure of the curvature of the spine in degrees) of 70–90 degrees during life. A Cobb angle of 10 degrees is regarded as a minimum angulation to define scoliosis and today over 40 degrees would require surgery. Whilst Richard's Cobb angle is classed as severe, the upper and lower spine was still aligned correctly and the S-shaped curve well balanced. Once his spine began to twist, it put additional stresses on the vertebrae in the middle of his spine and some grew wedge-shaped. With the spinal column bent to the side and the vertebrae rotating, it would have pulled the rib cage round to produce a protrusion on the back. By the time he was fully grown, he would have been slightly taller than average at about 1.73 m (5ft 8 in), although would have looked 5–10 cm (2–3 ins) shorter because of the scoliosis. Richard was a gracile and delicate man; but his hips and leg bones were well formed, so he would not have not walked with a limp, and there was no evidence of a withered hand or arm. His right shoulder was slightly higher than his left, and right clavicle misshaped from the extra work it needed to do, but would have been very easy to disguise under the layers of medieval clothes.

This meant that only the immediate members of his family, his tailor, armourer and intimate circle such as the esquires of the body would have known of the condition. This matches the only surviving description of him given by Nicholas von Poppelau, a Silesian who spent time at Richard's court in 1484 which described the King as 'three fingers taller than I, but a bit slimmer and not as thickset as I am, and much more lightly built; he has quite slender arms and thighs, and also a great heart.' So, the discovery of Richard's remains showed unequivocally that the later writers including More and Shakespeare got it very wrong. However, when he was slung naked over the horse after he was killed, his ribs would have risen up on one side, creating a bulge or 'rib hump' for all to see, probably giving rise to the fable that became part of our collective consciousness until now.

There is a debate as to whether his twisted ribcage would have squeezed his lung, causing shortness of breath during his knightly training. However, it is probable that Richard's scoliosis was not disabling, as back pain, breathing, or heart problems are rare, even in severe cases. The Olympian Usain Bolt has a similar condition and reports that as long as core strength is maintained there are no adverse effects. Dominic Smee, a young man with almost identical scoliosis, did not experience any pain during his teens, and only gets muscle cramps in cold weather conditions or when lifting something heavy, though not enough to need painkillers. He described the pain from a trapped nerve as 10–20 times worse. Dominic was put through his paces for a Channel 4 TV documentary *Richard III: The New Evidence*, shown in 2014. It not only showed that a 70–90 degree Cobb angle can be easily disguised by loose clothing but more importantly that Dominic (and therefore Richard) could wear and fight in full plate armour.

His armour was made especially for him from CK45 spring steel, the closest modern equivalent to medieval armour steel, by Swedish armourer Per Lillelund Jensen. Ordinary armour normally sits on the waist, however, because of the sideways curvature of his spine Dominic's rib cage rests on his hip, which caused his ribs to rub against the plate and restrict his breathing. Therefore, the armour was designed to accommodate the curvature of the spine and rest on his shoulders instead of his waist. This would have been something that fifteenth-century armourers could also easily achieve. At 62 pounds total weight his armour is also lighter than average to allow for greater agility and to minimise the impact of the asymmetrical weight distribution on his horse.

The programme followed his training in medieval horsemanship and martial arts. It proved that despite no previous training, Dominic had no problem wielding medieval long swords, lances and axes, and he could ride in and out of armour, fight, twist and bend more than they'd thought possible from the scans. The research team also found that the stiff back of a medieval war saddle would have actually helped Richard remain upright.

Little else is known of Richard's remaining time with Warwick's household, or even with any certainty when he returned to court. In February 1466, Richard was created the 198th Knight of the Garter. Two years later, Richard, aged 16, officially became of age and was given the lands of Thomas Hungerford in Somerset, Wiltshire and Dorset (although they would be taken back later). He was evidently firmly established at court by this time, and high in favour with his brother, the King. He (and Warwick) accompanied Margaret his sister, to Margate before she sailed to Burgundy and her marriage to the Duke, Charles the Bold, in June 1468. Richard's first official duty seems to have been when he sat on the Commission of Oyer and Terminer Edward set up at Salisbury in February 1469, that condemned Lancastrians Henry Courtenay and Thomas Hungerford to death.

We do not know of Richard's movements or actions at the time of Warwick's first rebellion, in 1469 other than he spent a week at Fotheringhay with his brother and the Queen gathering men before they headed towards Newark at the start of the uprising. Edward went on to Nottingham. Richard was not with him when he was captured outside Coventry, nor at the battle, so we can only guess that he went into Yorkshire or returned to London to lead its defence.

In the fallout of the rebellion, Richard, now 17, was created Lord High Constable of England on 17 October 1469. The Lord High Constable was the commander of the royal armies and the Master of the Horse. He was also, in conjunction with the Earl Marshal, president of the Court of Chivalry or Court of Honour. It was the highest military appointment in the realm and had previously been held by Earl Rivers. Edward also gave Richard the honours of Clitheroe and Halton, both held by the Stanleys. However, they refused to give them up and Edward had to intervene. It would be the first of many disputes with the powerful Stanley family. In addition, he was given the castles and honours of Sudbury and Gloucester which had previously belonged to the father of Edward's former mistress, Eleanor Talbot.

By this time Richard had discovered the opposite sex and had two acknowledged illegitimate children, although both their mothers remain unknown. John of Gloucester, also known as 'John of Pontefract', was knighted at York by his father on the 8th September 1483 as part of the celebrations to mark the investiture of Richard's legitimate son, Edward, as Prince of Wales. There was also a daughter, Katherine, who married William Herbert, Earl of Huntingdon, in 1484.

To fill the void left by the death of Pembroke after Edgcote, Richard was made Chief Justice of North Wales on 7 November, and 10 days later, chief steward of the Duchy of Lancaster's lordships in South Wales, followed by the earldom of March on 30 November. This in effect made him Edward's principal representative in Wales and the Marches. To support and advise him, Walter Devereux, Lord Ferrers of Chartley, a former servant of his father, was given positions in Wales. Ferrers was another of the gentry who would die fighting for Richard at Bosworth. Sir Roger Vaughan and John Donne were similarly given posts in Wales.

Taking advantage of the death of Pembroke, Thomas ap Gruffudd ap Nicholas' sons Morgan and Henry seized Carmarthen and Cardigan Castles. At the end of October, Richard was empowered to recover them. Armed with the Commission of Array to raise men from the Marches, an order to reduce both castles and authorisation to offer a pardon, he left London for Wales. On 6 January 1470, a commission headed by Richard was issued for South

Wales. Shortly after Richard and a young duke (possibly Henry Stafford, Duke of Buckingham) were at a Great Session at Carmarthen. According to the poet Lewis Glyn Cothi, here they met four of Thomas's sons, Morgan, Henry, Dafydd and Hopkin, together with their Basset, Rede and Mansel kinsmen. Their younger brother Rhys ap Thomas (who would go on to support Henry Tudor), whose biography was written in the 1620s by his descendant Henry Rice, suggests that had accompanied his father into exile at the Burgundian court after in 1461 and probably did not return until the early 1470s. There are no records of any fighting and it appears pardons were issued along with assurances of no further uprisings.

Whilst he was still in Wales, rebellion erupted in Lincolnshire. Richard was ordered to array the men of Gloucestershire and Hereford to assist in the pursuit of the rebels. He headed north and was at Hornby Castle in Lancashire, home of his family's long-time supporters the Harringtons. On 25 March 1470, Edward referred to a variance between Richard and Stanley. We know Richard was there the following day, when he signed a warrant. For some time, the Stanleys had been involved in a vicious feud with the Harrington family from Hornby for dominance over north Lancashire. After Thomas and his eldest son John were killed at the Battle of Wakefield in 1460, the inheritance was passed to John's two young daughters. The Stanleys gained their wardships in 1468, effectively taking control of all the Harrington lands. William Stanley then locked both girls up in his fortress at Holt. Stanley had the Harrington girls married to members of his own family; Anne to his son Edward Stanley, later Lord Mounteagle, Elizabeth, to John Stanley, thus securing title over their lands. James and Robert Harrington, John's younger brothers, refused to give up Hornby. It has been suggested that Lord Stanley, Warwick's brother-in-law, and his men were en route to join Warwick when they clashed with Richard and his men on the way to join his brother. The *Stanley Poem* gives details of an incident that appears to have taken place around this time although it cannot be collaborated from other sources:

> That was called Richard Duke of Glocester,
> For a fond fray had benne amongeste their tenantes,
> The melancholicke duke tooke to much grievaunce,
> And sware by cockesbludd, quod he, shortly I shall
> Kill the Earle of Darby and burne Lathum hall.
> He assembled many a man togeither,
> To Preston in Amaundernes brought them thether.
> And from Lathum hall xij. myles no further way,
> For honor the duke had better ben away.
> He sent to the earle that he would his house burne.
> And also kill him, or do him a worse turne.
> …At Preston was the duke with an army bigge,
> The earle cam to meete him hard at Riblebrigge,
> …There had beene a fray, but some rann from theire good,
> And yeat to this day is called Waltoun woodde.
> Jacke Moris of Wiggan brought the duke banner
> To Wiggan kirke [Wigan Church], yt served fourty yeares there.'

The poem continues that Stanley complained in person to King Edward who said that he would rebuke Richard. Richard, it appears from the poem, came to court three days later but the lesson was bittersweet as 'Yeat he studied still to put the earle [Stanley] to rebuke.' Although the poem does not give a date, a general pardon issued to Thomas Stanley on 2 June 1470 for 'all offences committed by him before 11 May last' probably for supporting the rebels, suggests it was around May 1470. There is a further possibility that it occurred as Edward was fleeing to Europe during Warwick's next rebellion. Whichever time it was, the animosity between Richard and Stanley was clearly there, and would only fester.

After Warwick and Clarence fled to France, Richard once again profited from a failed rebellion when on 26 August 1470, he was created warden of the West Marches, which had been held by the Nevilles since 1399. On 9 September 1470, Warwick, Clarence and Jasper Tudor returned with an army, landing in Devon. Warwick's Army reached Coventry where it was joined by the Earl of Shrewsbury and Thomas Stanley. Warwick's brother, John who had been made Earl of Northumberland by Edward, but then promptly stripped of the title, before being made Marquess Montagu, changed sides and marched to meet Warwick. Edward was at Doncaster at the time and now trapped between two armies. He had no alternative but to flee to King's Lynn and then to Holland with Hastings, Rivers, Worcester, Norfolk and Saye.

By 11 October, Edward and his supporters were at Louis of Grunthuyse's house in The Hague. It is possible that Richard did not join them until later, as there is no mention of him in any initial correspondence. There is however, a chronicle written by a Cistercian monk Adam le But, at Les Dunes Abbey which says that 'the younger brother of the now fugitive King Edward … put up as much resistance as he could' and later that 'the Duke of Gloucester came to him from England with many men.'

Meanwhile, back in England, Henry VI was returned to the throne (the Readeption). Edward was declared a usurper and Richard a traitor whilst both were attainted by Parliament. Stanley, with Hornby Castle still holding out against him, also saw his opportunity. On or about 5 March 1471, he rented a cannon to bombard the castle, as on that day, *The Patent Roll* records:

> the Appointment of Thomas Maynwaryng, esquire, Thomas Corewen, Thomas Aghton, Thomas Colbrond and Edmund Selonge to take carriage for the transport of a cannon called 'Mile Ende' from Bristol to the castle of Horneby for delivery to Thomas Stanley of Stanley, knight, for the siege of the castle.

Edward returned with 2,000 men including Flemish hand gunners in 36 ships, landing at Ravenspur on 14 March. Richard landed four miles away with another 300 men. The city of Hull refused to open its gates to the Yorkists, so they marched on to York. The King's reception in Yorkshire was generally cool, so rather than proclaim that he had returned to reclaim his kingdom, he told the Yorkshiremen that he was only claiming his rights as Duke of York, echoing Henry IV's claim in 1399. Whilst Edward negotiated his entry into York, Richard remained outside in command of the army. The

Milanese Ambassador noted at the time that 'It's a difficult matter to go out by the door and come in through the window.' Edward and Richard left York on 19 March and marched to Leicester via Wakefield and Nottingham. At Leicester they were joined by a force of 3,000 men under the command of Sir William Norris, raised from the estates of William Hastings. Edward bypassed the city of Coventry and the Kingmaker with a small army, who refused his challenges to meet and fight. Clarence decided to change sides again and three miles outside Warwick the three brothers were reconciled. Via Daventry and Northampton, they entered London on Thursday 10 April, where Edward was briefly reunited with his wife and saw his son and heir for the first time.

They left London two days later, heading towards St. Albans, the last reported sighting of Warwick. Warwick had reached Barnet and had taken up a defensive position across the St. Albans road, in the area now known as Hadley Green. The two sides clashed at Barnet on 14 April 1471. Details of the battle are scant, but it appears that the 18-year-old Richard and his division were on the right flank and facing the division of Sir Henry Holland, Duke of Exeter. He immediately encountered difficulties when, on a fog-shrouded battlefield, he could not properly align with the opposite division. Eventually, he found Exeter's men and marching uphill, collided with it at an angle, hitting the battle in the flank. During the hand-to-hand fighting that followed Richard was slightly wounded and Exeter's men chased from the battlefield. It would be an overwhelming victory for the Yorkists and resulted in the death of Warwick. It would also be Richard's first encounter with John de Vere, Earl of Oxford.

As Edward and Richard were fighting at Barnet, Margaret of Anjou and her son Edward, Prince of Wales was landing at Weymouth, with Sir John Langstrother, the Prior of St. John of Jerusalem, and a small army of Frenchman. On hearing the news that Margaret had landed and was marching north, Edward, who by then had returned to London, marched out again to cut them off before they could reach Wales.

On the night of 3 May King Edward, after a superhuman forced march, was at Tredington, three miles from Tewkesbury. At dawn the next day, he broke camp and moved towards the Lancastrians, deploying his own army into three divisions led by Richard on the left, Edward and Clarence in the centre, and Lord Hastings on the right. *The Arrivall Of Edward IV* describes the Lancastrians as deploying themselves on the outskirts of Tewkesbury:

> in a close even at the townes ende; the towne, and the abbey, at theyr backs; afore them, and upon every hand of them, fowle lanes, and depe dikes, and many hedges, with hylls, and valleys, a ryght evill place to approche, as cowlde well have bene devysed.

Edmund Beaufort, 4th Duke of Somerset faced Richard, Lord Wenlock, with Prince Edward of Westminster, Henry VI's heir, were in the centre and on the opposite wing, John Courtenay, 15th Earl of Devon.

The battle was fierce, and close run. Somerset charged Richard's division, however, they held their ground and Somerset's men were routed. *The Arrivall* records that Somerset's men were pursued by Richard's division, whilst:

the Kynge coragiously set upon that othar felde, were was chefe Edward, called Prince, and, in short while, put hym to discomfiture and flyght; and so fell in the chase of them that many of them were slayne, and, namely at a mylene, in the medowe fast by the town, were many drownyd; many rann towards the towne; many to the churche; to the abbey; and els where; as they best myght.

Somerset and many of his men took sanctuary in the Abbey. Many Lancastrians were killed trying to flee the field. Shortly after the battle, King Edward attended prayers at the Abbey. He had Somerset and the Lancastrian survivors within the Abbey removed and tried before Richard, as Constable of England, the next day. They were beheaded on a makeshift scaffold in the town.

One of the earliest atrocities committed by Richard according to Shakespeare was Richard plotting the murder, and revelling in the death of, the 17-year-old Prince Edward during the battle. *Holinshed's Chronicles*, published in 1577, on which Shakespeare partly based his play, claims that Richard struck the first blow against Edward. Polydore Vergil, in his *Anglica Historia* wrote that William, Lord Hastings, George, Duke of Clarence and Richard, Duke of Gloucester killed Edward after they captured him. The near contemporary *Warkworth Chronicle* had Prince Edward captured by his brother-in-law George, Duke of Clarence whilst fleeing the field after the battle was lost. It describes how Prince Edward cried out for mercy. However, Clarence refused to listen and had him executed on a makeshift block in the field. The most contemporary source, *The Arrivall*, on the other hand, has Edward being 'slayne in the field.'

Thomas Neville, the Bastard of Fauconberg, after his failed siege of London, escaped to Southampton but surrendered himself and his fleet to Richard, Duke of Gloucester. Pardoned by the King, Neville went into the north to serve under Gloucester. However, for reasons unknown he was executed at Middleham Castle on 22 September 1471.

With Warwick dead, the Percys were restored, Edward IV began to deliberately make his brother Richard 'the greatest landowner as well as the most important official north of the Trent', starting on 18 May 1471, when Richard aged 20, was created Great Chamberlain of England. Soon after, he was granted the manors and lordships of Middleham, Sheriff Hutton (Yorkshire) and Penrith (Cumberland) with all attached fees and holdings. On 4 July 1471, he was appointed chief steward of the Duchy of Lancaster including the lordships of Tickhill, Pontefract, Pickering, Easingwold, and Huby, as well as the Forest of Lancaster and Bowland and appointed surveyor of the Forest of Galtres (Yorkshire). The appointments did not stop there and four days later he was appointed co-administrator of the Principality of Wales, County of Chester and Duchy of Cornwall for the Prince of Wales, the future Edward V, until he reached age 14. The following week he was granted all the lands held by Richard Neville, late Earl of Warwick, in Yorkshire and Cumberland.

Anne Neville, Warwick's younger daughter was taken prisoner after Tewkesbury. We don't know what Anne looked like but the chronicler Rous, who knew her personally, described her as beautiful, amiable, virtuous and gracious. Anne was first taken to Coventry and then to the house of her brother-in-law, George of Clarence, at Coldharbour House, London. By this time, Richard was indicating he wanted to marry Anne and she became the subject of a dispute between Clarence and Richard. Both Anne and her sister were heiresses to their parents' vast estates. As he was anxious to secure the entire inheritance, Clarence opposed her getting married to Richard and treated her as his ward. There are various accounts of what happened subsequently, including a story that Clarence hid her in a London cookshop, disguised as a servant, so that his brother would not know where she was. Richard is said to have tracked her down and escorted her into the sanctuary of the Church of St. Martin le Grand.

The exact date of the wedding of Anne Neville and Richard is not known. The first real reference we have to them being married comes from May 1474, although many have speculated that it must have occurred during or before March 1472. Anne and Richard resided mainly in the north as Duke and Duchess of Gloucester. By identifying with Anne's kin and subjects in the north, Richard gained their support and loyalty.

Richard had a residence and a priory at Pontefract Castle by virtue of his office as Chief Seneschal of the Duchy of Lancaster in the northern parts. He is shown by contemporary papers in the *Plumpton Correspondence* to have spent time there in great state during 1472. Once he was enthroned, Richard gave the town a Charter of Incorporation. Barnard Castle also became a personal possession of Richard by right of his wife. His badge of a white boar can still be seen carved on the soffit of an oriel window projecting from the west wall of the Inner Ward, and the rectangular tower on the east side of the Town Ward is named Brackenbury's Tower after Richard's retainer Sir Robert Brackenbury of Selaby. Brackenbury was a younger son of Thomas Brackenbury of Denton, County Durham and was one of Richard's close associates. He was treasurer of Richard's household when he was Duke of Gloucester and when King Edward died, Brackenbury was almost certainly one of the Northerners who accompanied Richard to London. Shortly after Richard took the throne Brackenbury received several new appointments, including Constable of the Tower of London.

Edward continued to heap lands in the north on Richard, making him Keeper of all the forests beyond the River Trent in May and Steward of lordship, town, and manor of Ripon in August, as well as Justiciar of Wales. On 20 May 1472, it seems that Richard resigned the office of Great Chamberlain into his brother Clarence's hands, although it would be returned to him after Clarence's execution. It was also at this time that Edward IV created the Council of the North as a base for royal authority in the north, with permission to issue letters in the King's name. The council was based at Sandal in Yorkshire and its main responsibilities were to keep the peace and punish lawbreakers. Edward gave the council a budget of 2,000 marks per annum and issued regulations which meant that councillors had to act impartially and declare any vested interests, and meet at least every three months. It was essentially an autonomous branch of the King's Council and its jurisdiction and procedure remained largely intact until 1641. Richard was made the first Lord President of the Council, until his accession to the throne. In June 1484, he visited Sandal and authorised the building of a new tower in the castle, and the following October a new bakery and brewhouse.

Elsewhere the dispute between the Harringtons and Stanley was still ongoing, and the Harringtons had clearly had not vacated the castle, as on 21 June 1473 Edward had to step in, ordering:

> [A] Commission to the king's brother Richard, Duke of Gloucester, the king's kinsmen Henry, Earl of Northumberland, and John, Earl of Shrewsbury … to take into the king's hands all castles, lordships, manors, lands, rents and services with knight's fees and advowsons late of Thomas belonging to the king by reason of the minority of Anne and Elizabeth, daughters and heiresses of the said John and kinswomen and heiresses of the said Thomas, and to remove James Haryngton, knight, and Robert Haryngton, knight, and others who have taken possession.

Stanley refused to allow Robert Harrington, to exercise his hereditary offices of bailiff in Blackburn and Amounderness, which he had acquired by marriage. Stanley falsely indicted the Harringtons, packed the juries and attempted to imprison them. Soon after, Edward gave the castle and Harrington lands back to the Stanleys yet both James and Robert remained loyal to Richard, even fighting for his cause after his death.

Ever since he returned from exile in 1471, Edward had been planning to invade France with his brother-in-law Charles the Bold, Duke of Burgundy, and share the kingdom between them. Initially, Burgundy was unwilling to support England's plans and an attempt to reach an agreement at Bruges in August 1473 proved unsuccessful. However on 25 July 1474, the Treaty of London was signed ensuring Burgundian support for the English invasion of France. Edward agreed that Burgundy could retain all of its sovereign territory along with some territorial claims in France as long as it would recognise him as King of France and support the invasion which was to happen before 1 July 1475. Preparations began soon after, and took until the summer of the following year until they were ready. Ships were commandeered and hired. Soldiers, particularly archers, and craftsmen had to be found and impressed, and weapons collected. At least 13 great cannons with names like *Messenger*, the *Edward*, *Fowler of Chester* and the *Megge* were gathered. An Italian observer noted that Edward's artillery train was more impressive than even the Duke of Burgundy's. Before they had even left England, Louis XI, King of France had already sent Hastings '*a tresgrande et beau present*' to smooth the way to peace. Norfolk and Stanley received similar. Heralds and pursuivants were also given generous gifts at secret meetings. Louis' army had also marched into Picardy and laid waste to it, to deny the English supplies. He was not known as *l'universelle aragne* – the Universal Spider – for nothing, as he continued to spin his webs of plots and conspiracies against England.

The exact size of the army that crossed the sea on 4 July 1475 is not known, but it was at least 13,000 men and included most of the nobility. Richard promised 110 men-at-arms and 1,000 archers but brought more. This huge army crossed to Calais, where it waited for Charles the Bold, many anticipating a dramatic march to Paris and a decisive battle. The Duke, however, was occupied besieging the town of Neuss and when he eventually arrived, instead of an army, he only brought a small retinue. Charles was full of praise and empty promises. In the end, the King and his army marched slowly into France, the Duke accompanying them for part of the way. According to one source, Stanley and Norfolk pressed money into a French prisoner's hand in order to be commended to the French king in anticipation of a catastrophic defeat.

Most English lords were recommending that the invasion should be given up. Richard and a few others are said by Continental chroniclers to have disagreed. However, as soon as Charles had ridden back to Neuss, Edward started negotiations with the French. By 27 July, they were at Beauvais. Louis offered Edward 75,000 crowns immediately and 25,000 annually for as long as they both lived, plus the marriage of his eldest son to one of Edward's daughters. A seven-year truce that accompanied the proposed treaty would allow trade to flourish again between the two countries. Richard refused to attend the negotiations and was not present at the signing of the Treaty in protest at what he saw as a dishonourable surrender. He argued that the King had a force strong enough to win at least one battle against the French while they still mustered their full strength. Then, the King could negotiate the same peace, if he so desired, from a position of greater strength and return home having won the field on French soil and forced them to negotiate possibly an even better settlement. Richard was in the minority on the council, each of whom were to receive a hefty pension from France too. Richard refused his, though he was later to meet with Louis XI and accept gifts from him. A speedy conclusion was reached when the two kings met on a specially constructed bridge at the town of Picquigny, just west of Amiens, on 29 August. Each king was followed by his army in battle array as far as Amiens to satisfy the honour of both. The invasion had been brought to a bloodless and inglorious end.

Both Richard and Clarence went to visit Louis XI soon after, and a German eyewitness recorded that 'on the Thursday, 31 August, the two brothers of the king of England came to Amiens and dined with the king in the morning.' Commines wrote that Louis was able to 'bribe the war-mongering Duke of Gloucester into compliance, with gifts of horses and costly tableware.' Rotherham, the chancellor was to receive a pension of 1,000 crowns per year from the French, John Morton, 600 crowns, Norfolk 1,200 crowns. Dorset, the Queen's son from her first marriage, Sir John Cheyne and Thomas St. Ledger were all promised pensions too. Hastings was already in receipt of 1,000 crowns a year from the French but was given an additional 2,000 per year. When it was delivered, it was noted by the French ambassador that Hastings refused to sign for it. By the beginning of September, the English army was on its way home, although Edward stayed in France until the end of the month. However, behind the scenes, the Universal Spider was living up to his name and had made separate peace treaties with Burgundy and Brittany.

Once home from France, Richard used his authority to bring additional benefits to the north. For example, Hull and Beverly were given financial concessions and Pontefract was made into a borough. Scarborough was made a shire incorporate, which was a dignity usually only given to far larger towns such as London and Bristol. He also extended his local prominence through making gifts to local religious institutions. In February 1475 Richard was appointed as sheriff of Cumberland for life, which entitled him to the profits of the shrievalty, the demesne lands of Carlisle Castle and the city's fee farm. Sometime between 1473 and 1476, Anne gave birth to a son, probably in the round Nursery Tower at Middleham Castle. They named him Edward.

There is evidence of Richard's influence in York as early as 1475 when the city made presents to him and his servants. The mayor wrote letters to him, and Anne wrote letters to the mayor. Next year the city enlisted Richard's support when its dismissed common clerk appealed to Percy for backing, and he also intervened with Edward to recognise the right of the city to freely elect a successor. He intervened, too, in a war of the civic factions that had developed, and which had driven one old alderman, William Holbek, into sanctuary at the Dominican friary. Richard, accompanied by Percy and a large following, appeared at Bootham Bar and solemnly warned the citizens to keep the peace. On the other hand, he successfully persuaded Edward not to withdraw the city's liberties.

The next time Richard and Anne left the north appears to have been for the reinterment of his father Richard, Duke of York and brother Edmund at Fotheringhay. It is probable that they had been interred at the Priory of St. John the Evangelist at Pontefract after their executions. On or about Sunday 21 July 1476, the bodies were exhumed, and the coffins placed in hearses in the choir of the church of the Priory. In the evening, a dirge was sung, and Vigil of the Dead said, attended by many Bishops, including those of Durham, Hereford and Chester, with abbots and other clergy. Several choirs sang, including that of the Chapel Royal which later accompanied the bodies on the journey and sang at every service on the way. Next morning, Monday 22nd July, a requiem mass was said, and a sermon delivered, probably by the Bishop of Durham before the procession left Pontefract. Richard was the chief mourner during the journey and rode at the head of his father's effigy, followed by the Earl of Northumberland, Lord Stanley and Lord Welles and the lords. They were to stay with the body throughout, attend all the services and masses *en route*, and have the privilege of standing and kneeling within the barriers of the hearse. All the mourners were dressed in black with black hoods, the officers of arms wearing their colourful coats over their mourning habits. There was, according to one source, 400 poor accompanying the procession. They were also in mourning habits but with worn-out shoes and hose and carried large torches. The procession reached Fotheringhay on the afternoon of 29 July and was met by King Edward dressed in a dark blue hooded mourning habit trimmed with fur. The King 'very humbly did his obeisance to the body, laid his hand on it and kissed it, weeping.' Also waiting to escort the body were the King's brothers and numerous earls, dukes and barons including the Earls of Essex and Kent, all dressed in mourning. The next day, the funeral services were held with three masses, one for Our Lady, one for the Trinity and a requiem mass, then a sermon was given by Thomas Rotherham, Bishop of Lincoln and Chancellor of England. A herald recorded that over 20,000 people came to Fotheringhay on that day, and 5,000 were given alms of a penny each. Over 1,500 people were accommodated in

The tomb of Richard's parents, Richard Duke of York and Cecily Neville, St. Mary and All Saints Church Fotheringhay, Northants. (Author)

pavilions and tents specially constructed under the supervision of the King's pavilioner, Richard Garnet. The accounts mention 31 tuns of ale (a tun is 250 gallons!), 49 beef cattle, 90 calves, 210 sheep, 200 piglets, and large quantities of fish including pike, salmon and shellfish, and poultry including hens, capons and cygnets were all consumed at the feast that followed. Forty pipes (barrels) of wine, provided by the royal cellar, were also drunk.

By this time, Richard was being accepted as the natural heir to the Nevilles. He even secured the support of the ageing Ralph, Second Earl of Westmorland, and his nephew, another Ralph, who came from the senior branch of the family (those descending from Ralph's first marriage). Both John, Lord Scrope of Bolton, and Ralph, Lord Greystoke, had become members of his council as early as 1475, and by the time he took the throne were joined by Thomas, Lord Dacre of Gilsland, and Thomas, Lord Scrope of Masham. Richard also continued to accumulate lands in the north including the forfeited barony and estates of Skipton Castle which he exchanged with Sir William Stanley for his interest in Chirk, in the Welsh Marches. He gave £20 towards rebuilding Coverham Abbey near Middleham, recovered lands taken by Edward IV from Pontefract priory, and gave lands to found a chantry at Wilberfoss to pray for the souls of the royal family.

His associations with York continued to grow and during December 1476, the York City Records state that :

> …by the mayor and council it was wholly agreed and assented that the Duke of Gloucester shall, for his great labour … made to the king's good grace for the conservation of the liberties of this city, presented at his coming to the city six swans and six pikes.

The following year, both Richard and Anne became members of York's Corpus Christi Guild and gave extensive gifts to the citizens of York and York Minster.

Richard's connections with Cambridge University started around 1475–76 when he gave 20 marks to the university. Richard made numerous grants to Queens' College, and his wife, Queen Anne, was considered a founder. On 1 April 1477, he gave the property of Fowlmere, Cambridgeshire, to the college, with the aim to fund four priests, fellows of the college, to say prayers for his living relatives and for the souls of the departed. Among the people to be commemorated in the prayers were friends who had fallen in the battles of Barnet and Tewkesbury. Prayers were also to be said for John de Vere, the 12th Earl of Oxford, who had been executed by Edward IV in 1462 and to whom the manor of Fowlmere had once belonged. In 1478–79, Richard gave £20 for the rebuilding of the university church, Great St. Mary. On 7 April 1481, the congregation of the University wrote to Richard proclaiming their gratitude for the many favours he had shown them, and that they would 'ask every Cambridge doctor or bachelor or theology who preached to mention Richard by name, to commend him to their listeners, and ask for prayers for his wellbeing.' In early 1480 or 1481 two representatives of the University travelled to London to see Richard and in 1482 they staged a procession to celebrate his victory against the Scots. Ten years after Richard's death, his master of the rolls and keeper of the great seal, Thomas Barowe, gave £240 for the rebuilding of Great St. Mary and for 'masses, prayers and ceremonies in honour of King Richard III and Dr Thomas Barowe – who were to be enrolled in the list of the university's benefactors.'

York Minster. (Author)

After the arrest of his brother Clarence, Richard may have believed that he was next to be targeted by the Woodvilles as he demanded that all his tenants in the Bishopric of Durham swore loyalty to him and they should be prepared to fight on his behalf. In February 1478, Richard travelled south to attend the parliament in which his brother Clarence was attainted for treason and privately executed. According to Mancini, Richard was 'so overcome with grief that he could not dissimulate so well, but he was overheard that he would one day avenge his brother's death.' He also attended the marriage of Edward's younger son, the four-year-old Prince Richard of Shrewsbury, to five-year-old Anne Mowbray, the Duke of Norfolk's heiress, in St. Stephen's Chapel, Westminster. Anne was the daughter of John de Mowbray, 4th Duke of Norfolk, who had died on 14 January 1476, making her an extremely wealthy heiress. It was a magnificent occasion and Richard cast among the common people a 'great number of gold and silver coins … brought in basins of gold.' Anne died around 19 November 1481, shortly before her ninth birthday. Her eight-year-old husband would inherit all her lands and money. Someone clearly wanted her money because shortly before he died Edward instigated an Act of Parliament giving the rights to the Mowbray fortune to his son with reversion to his descendants. Failing that, to the descendants of Edward himself.

On 21 February 1478, whilst he was still in London, Richard procured royal licences to establish two colleges, one at Middleham and one at Barnard

RICHARD III AND THE BATTLE OF BOSWORTH

Richard III's boar badge on a misericord now in St. Peter and St. Paul Church, Hemington, Northants formerly from Fotheringhay Church. (Author)

Castle. The college at Middleham was to consist of a dean, six chaplains, four clerks and six choristers. One of the clerks was charged with offering perpetual masses for the good of Richard's living family and the souls of all the faithful departed. The statutes for the college were drawn up on 4 July 1478, in English rather than the usual Latin. It states that the dean should be chosen from among the six priests. Should none of them be suitable, he should be one of the priests and fellows for whose education Richard had made provision at Queens' College, Cambridge. The stalls were to be named after a number of saints:

> Also that the said Sir William Beverley, Dean, and his successors, have the principall place and stall of the right side of the high quere of my said Collage which I wil be called Oure Lady stall; and Sir Laurence Squier … the first prest that shalbe admitted thereto occupie the principall place and stall to be called Saint George stall; and Sir William Symson, second prest, in the next stall to the Deane on the said right side, and that stall to be named Seynt Kateryn stall; and … Sir Richard Cutler, therdprest the secund stall on the said left side, that stall to be called Saint Ninian stall; and Sir William Buntyng … the fourtprest, the third stall on the said right side, the same to be called Seint Cuthbert stall; and Sir Hugh Leverhede, the fiftprest, the third stall on the said left side, the said stall to be called Seint Antony stall; and Sir John Bell … the sext prest the fourt stall on the said right side, and that to be called Seint Barbara stall; and two of the…clerks on the said right side, and the other two clerks and the clerk sacristanebeneth theme on the left side, at the assignacion of the said Dean; and the sex queresters there places accordingly as the said Deane shalassigne theme…

William Beverley was made the first dean of the college. When Richard became king in 1483, Beverley was promoted to dean of the college of St.

George's in Windsor. He is also thought to have been a royal councillor. The establishment at Barnard Castle was to consist of a dean, 12 chaplains, 10 clerks, six choristers, and one clerk (sic), to celebrate divine offices in the castle chapel. It was to be dedicated to Christ, the Blessed Virgin, St. Margaret, and St. Ninian. However, only the licence exists, so it is likely that it was not founded.

Skirmishing on the Scottish border had restarted in 1480, possibly at Louis XI's request. The Earl of Angus had attacked Bamburgh Castle, and in retaliation, the Earl of Northumberland had raided in Scotland. By October 1480, James III of Scotland had written to Louis asking for guns and gunners to repulse further attacks, although the request fell on deaf ears. There were three more raids into England by the Scots. In reply, Edward IV began making preparations for an invasion of Scotland. Anthony Woodville, Earl Rivers, agreed to send 3,300 men, his nephew the Marquess of Dorset another 600 and Lord Stanley 3,000 archers. Eleven ships were put on war-footing for Scotland in February 1481 and Sir Robert Ratcliffe was commanded to arm a fleet with guns and gunners on 8 July. These ships then made raids in the Forth, attacking Blackness Castle and harassing shipping. In the summer, Richard led another raid into south-west Scotland burning Dumfries and other towns. His force included 120 archers from York under the command of Alderman Wrangwissh, which had been given in return for remission of taxation. Following the fresh news of Scottish incursions into England Richard returned to the front, laying siege to the town and citadel of Berwick, which he failed to take.

On 12 March 1482, York City Records noted that 'It is agreed that for great labour, good and benevolent lordship that the right high and mighty prince the Duke of Gloucester has at all times done for the welfare of this city praise and thanks.'

At the same time, there was another outbreak of civil unrest in York, and Richard sent back one of their number who had been sheltered by a member of his household after committing an unknown offence. The city reciprocated by taking prompt action against a saddler who was alleged to have slandered the Duke, and by raising 80 men for his service in Scotland in June and a further 100 men in July.

Edward's invasion plans received a huge boost when in May 1481 Alexander Stewart, Duke of Albany, the brother of King James III of Scotland landed in England at

Micklegate Bar was the most important of York's four main medieval gateways. Richard's father's head was placed here after he was killed at the battle of Wakefield in 1460. (Author)

Southampton from France. Edward IV, Albany and Richard made a formal treaty at Fotheringhay Castle that in return for helping take the throne, Albany would do homage to Edward IV and break the Auld Alliance with France. He would also give Edward Berwick, which had been given to James by Margaret of Anjou 20 years earlier, Lochmaben Castle with land in Annandale, Liddesdale, Eskdale and Ewesdale. The treaty was sealed on 11 June 1482 and Albany signed it 'Alexander R' for Alexander, King. Edward began preparing an army of 20,000 men to invade Scotland by sea and land at once. On 12 June 1482, Richard was made commander. Ten days later, John Elrington was appointed war treasurer. Richard used Scarborough Castle, which was granted to him in 1472, as a base for naval preparations against the Scots. New handguns were made and hundreds of lead shot were cast in the Tower. Bombards and cannon, from the Tower and Calais with names like the *Great Brazen Gun*, the *Great Edward of Calais* and the *Messenger*, some which had been part of the 1475 French expedition, were gathered at Barnard Castle and then transported by sea to Newcastle.

The army mustered at Alnwick at the start of July. It was bolstered by 1,800 mercenaries along with hundreds of gunners and ordinance experts from Germany, Switzerland and Burgundy. Two thousand sheaves of arrows were also brought from Newcastle upon Tyne by 120 cart horses. According to Edward Hall's *Chronicle*, published in 1542, there were three battles (or divisions). The vanguard was commanded by the Earl of Northumberland with Lord Scrope of Bolton, Sir John Middleton, Sir John Ditchfield, and 6,700 soldiers. Richard led the middle guard, with Albany, Francis Lovell, Lord Greystoke, Sir Edward Woodville, and 5,800 men. Lord Neville led the rearward with 3,000 men, Thomas, Lord Stanley on his right with 4,000, whilst Lord Fitzhugh, Sir William Parr and Sir James Harrington were on the left with 2,000. Another 1,000 men guarded the carriage of the ordnance.

The only surviving piece of wall at Fotheringhay Castle with a plaque in memory of Richard III. (Author)

Berwicktown was held by David Lindsay, Earl of Crawford and Andrew, Lord Gray and surrendered by negotiation. Stow noted that the keeper of Berwick Castle, Patrick Hepburn, would not give up the castle, so Stanley, Parr, and Sir John Elrington with 4,000 troops were left to besiege it. *The Stanley Poem* claims that Richard, Northumberland and their men left without warning, hoping that Stanley would be caught and killed by the advancing Scottish army. The English army moved west and divided into two, with Richard heading for Edinburgh. Both Richard and Northumberland carried out *chevauchées* in the same way their forbears had done in France at the height of the Hundred Years War. Hall's *Chronicle* gives a list of some 29 places destroyed by Richard en route to Edinburgh and another 28 places were burned by the Earl of Northumberland (who carried out a parallel campaign in the borders). Richard Grafton in his *Chronicle* published in 1569 copying Hall, has the same detail of the army, although states a total of 44 towns were burnt.

The Scottish army of James III had reached Lauder Bridge, to the west of Richard, where there was some kind of coup involving Archibald, Earl of Angus. The exact details of the events at Lauder are unclear, but chronicles suggest that some of the king's favourites were hanged from the bridge. James III was taken back to Edinburgh on 22 July. There were now three separate factions in Scotland; Albany's party, the loyalists, and the Lauder mutineers. At the beginning of August, Richard's army entered Edinburgh but with James safe in Edinburgh Castle, he could not establish Albany as King.

Once the details of the Fotheringhay treaty were revealed, Scottish support for Albany evaporated. Consequently, Albany, his brother's party, and the keepers of the castle were all reconciled. On 2 August, Albany and Gloucester signed a bond with Colin, Earl of Argyll, Archbishop Scheves, Lord Avandale, and James Livingstone Bishop of Dunkeld which promised a pardon for Albany. Richard then took the surprising decision to leave Edinburgh. The English army made a truce on 4 August 1482 then withdrew to Berwick where he disbanded all but 1,700 men. Berwick Castle fell on 22 August after a two-week siege and was delivered to Stanley. Richard may have returned to Newcastle, however, at the time of the ending of the siege, an impressive total of 70 knights and bannerets were made. Richard is said to have made James Tyrell, Richard Radcliff, Thomas Molyneux, Robert Harrington, Edward Stanley of Haughton and Sir Ralph Assheton of Middleton and 36 more men bannerets, most of whom not only came from the north of England but would play a prominent part in his future government.

Edward IV wrote to Pope Sixtus IV on 25 August, (the day after hostilities ended, but probably before news could reach him) describing the campaign in Scotland, explaining that Richard had spared all the citizens of Edinburgh, helped by the intercession of Albany, who was restored to his estates by the power of the English army. He also wrote that the taking of Berwick was the chief advantage he had gained and was taken on the army's return, not without slaughter and bloodshed. He also extolled his younger brother 'Thank God, the giver of all good gifts for the support received from our most loving brother, whose success is so proven that he alone would suffice to chastise the whole kingdom of Scotland.'

The Croyland chronicler was dismissive of the campaign, noting that it cost too much for too little gain and that King Edward was grieved at the 'frivolous expenditure'. Not everyone in York was so enamoured of Richard either. The *York House Book* notes on 30 December, that John Lam was alleged to have said that the men sent to Richard for Scotland 'deserved no wages, for they had done nothing but make whips of their bowstrings with which to drive carriages.'

Richard initially returned to Sheriff Hutton but was back in London by the middle of January the following year for, unbeknown to everyone, what would be Edward's last Parliament. Edward took the unusual step of granting Richard a brand new palatine lordship consisting of Cumberland, Westmorland, and any parts of south-west Scotland he conquered. The parliament publicly congratulated Richard, Northumberland and Stanley for 'their noble deeds, acts and services done and to be done for the lord king in defence of the realm in the Scottish war.' The Scottish campaign had cemented Richard's military reputation. Even Mancini, who was not his greatest fan, wrote: 'Such was his renown in warfare that whenever a difficult and dangerous policy had to be undertaken, it would be entrusted to his discretion and generalship.'

Richard had shown that he was courageous on the battlefield and not afraid of taking risks. He took an interest in the art of war and the latest military trends. He had demonstrated he was extremely pious in establishing a number of chantries. His concern for even the lowest soldier was shown when he commemorated the fallen long after their deaths. Above all, Richard had proved his loyalty to his brother and his men, living up to his personal motto *Loyaulté me Lie*.

But by April, Edward was dead! The wheel of fortune was turning again.

4

Henry Tudor

Beware of Wales, Christ Jesu must us keep
That it make not our child's child to weep,
Nor us also, if so it go his way
By unawareness; since that many a day
Men have been feared of their rebellion
Look well about, for God wot we have need.
The Libell of English Policye c.1436

The Tudurs of Penmynydd

The Tudur family could trace their line of descent back to Cadwaladr and the oldest ruling families in Welsh history. Ednyfed Fychan (d. 1246) a son of Cynfrig ab Iorwerth, was a servant to Llywelyn ap Iorwerth – 'the Great' – from 1215 to 1240, becoming the Prince's lord steward (one of the most important offices in the administration). In his capacity as steward, Ednyfed represented his Prince in negotiations with Henry III, King of England, as well as other lords and princes. As a reward for his services, Ednyfed was granted land in Caernarfonshire and on Anglesey including Penmynydd and Trecastell. Ednyfed then married South Walian Princess Gwenllian, daughter of Lord Rhys. They had six or seven sons, each of whom followed their father into the service of the Princes of Gwynedd. Goronwy ap Ednyfed (son of Ednyfed), became the steward of Llywelyn ap Gruffudd (also known as Llywelyn the Last), the King of Gwynedd by 1258. Then, after Goronwy's death, his brother Tudur ab Ednyfed became a steward, despite having pledged an oath of fealty to King Henry III. Because of their service to the Welsh princes, the family gained additional lands and became one of the wealthiest in North Wales.

His sons Tudur ap Goronwy otherwise known as Tudur Hen ('the Elder') and his brother Goronwy ap Goronwy known as Goronwy Fychan (Goronwy the Younger), joined the rebellion of Madog ap Llywelyn. The rebellion failed, and the remaining family members swore their allegiance to Edward I and on his death, to Edward II. His son Goronwy ap Tudur Hen, became a soldier in the English army and took part in King Edward I of England's invasion

RICHARD III AND THE BATTLE OF BOSWORTH

of Scotland. He stood by Edward II in his war against the barons and was part of the army that prepared to invade Scotland in 1314. When Tudur died in 1311, his large land holdings passed to his son Goronwy ap Tudur Hen. Goronwy had two sons: Hywel, who gained a position in the Church as a canon of Bangor Cathedral and later Archdeacon of Anglesey; the other son was Tudur ap Goronwy, who became a royal officer on Anglesey and may have served Edward III in France after 1337.

Tudur ap Goronwy married Margedferch Tomos, the daughter of Thomas ap Llywelyn whose sister was the mother of Owain Glyndŵr. They had five sons: Goronwy, Ednyfed, Rhys, Gwilym and Maredudd. All held important positions in North Wales, several holding positions as *rhaglaw* (bailiff). Ednyfed and Goronwy ap Tudur both drowned in 1382. At some point between 1387 and 1395, Maredudd was made *rhaglaw* of the commote at Malltraeth. Maredudd also became a burgess in Newborough, a part of Anglesey and was named escheator of Anglesey between 1388 and 1391, a role normally reserved by the crown for Englishmen. His brothers Rhys and Goronwy held similar roles in the commote of Dindaethwy. The brothers were loyal servants of Richard II and Rhys and Gwilym accompanied the King on his campaign in Ireland. However, when their cousin Owain Glyndŵr led a revolt against Henry IV, the surviving Tudur brothers openly sided with him.

Rhys and Gwilym captured Conwy Castle on Good Friday 1401, and the youngest, Maredudd led the rebels in north-east Wales. When the rebellion collapsed in 1406, all three brothers were outlawed, and their lands confiscated. There are conflicting accounts of Rhys' death: one states that he was captured and executed in 1412, another says that he died at his home in Anglesey. Gwilym was pardoned in 1413. Maredudd ap Tudur's final fate is unclear. Nevertheless, we do know that at some point, he married a lady named Marged from Anglesey and they had at least one child born around 1400. His name was Owain ap Maredudd ap Tudur.

Almost nothing is known of Owain's early life. It is possible that he and, or his father, was one of several Welshmen that secured positions at court after the Glyndŵr Rising. He may be the 'Owen Meredith' that is recorded as joining the retinue of Sir Walter Hungerford, 1st Baron Hungerford, the steward of the King's Household in May 1421. The sixteenth-century Welsh chronicler Elis Gruffydd also writes that he was a *sewer* (someone who places dishes on the table and tastes them) and servant of Catherine of Valois, wife of Henry V.

Catherine of Valois was the youngest daughter of Charles VI of France and Isabeau of Bavaria. When Henry V died in 1422, Queen Catherine was left a widow aged 20 and was the first foreign-

Contemporary image of a soldier wearing a hood over his helmet. From *Chroniques Sire Jehan Froissart*. Mid fifteenth century, Bibliothèque Nationale, Paris, 2644. (Matthew Ryan)

born Queen to outlive her husband and remain in England, no doubt to care for the six-month-old King, Henry VI. According to the *Incertiscriptoris Chronicon Angliæ* (also known as *Giles Chronicle*) she 'was unable fully to curb her carnal passions', and at some point, she possibly had a relationship with Edmund Beaufort, future Duke of Somerset. The Beauforts were the illegitimate offspring of John of Gaunt, third surviving son of Edward III. Although later legitimised, they were prevented from making any claim to the throne first by Richard II and then Henry IV – John of Gaunt's legitimate son and heir. It was possibly the rumour that he intended to marry her that prompted Parliament to introduce a bill that stated that if the Queen married, it should only be with the King's permission, which would only be given once he came of age. Otherwise, the new husband would forfeit all his lands and possessions.

How Catherine met Owain ap Maredudd ap Tudur, and when the relationship started is unknown. A later poem by poet Robin Ddu of Anglesey written in 1461, says that it began when he fell into the Queen's lap while dancing. Another, by Elis Gruffydd, a sixteenth-century chronicler from Flintshire, says that he caught the Queen's eye when swimming. They seemed to have married in secret at an unknown date. She would be the first widowed queen of England to remarry for 300 years. The fifteenth-century *Chronicle of London* states that '… Oweyn [Tudor] hadde prevyly wedded the quene Katerine, and hadde iij or iiij children be here.' Polydore Vergil also wrote:

> this woman after the death of her husband…being but young in years and therefore of less discretion to judge what was decent for her estate, married one Owen Tyder, a gentleman of Wales, adorned with wonderful gifts of body and minde, who derived his pedigree from Cadwalleder, the last King of the Britons.

The relationship began when Catherine lived at Windsor Castle, and where she became pregnant with their first child. By 1430, she had stopped living in the King's Household and Edmund was born around that time, either at Much Hadham Palace in Hertfordshire or at Hadham in Bedfordshire. Contemporary rumour claimed that this first child was fathered by Edmund Beaufort. Rumour was a potent political weapon at this time, so it may have been an attempt by the King's uncle, Humphrey of Lancaster, the Duke of Gloucester, to discredit the Beauforts. Some modern historians have suggested that his name, the fact that their arms are similar, and that it was possibly Henry VIII who saved his tomb, as sufficient proof to say his true father was Edmund Beaufort. A proclamation about Henry Tudor from Richard, once king, written on 23 June 1485, stated:

> for he is descended from bastard blood both on his father's side and on his mother side; for Owen, his grandfather, was born a bastard, and his mother was daughter of John, Duke of Somerset, who was son of John, Earl of Somerset, son of Dame Katherine Swynford, and begotten in their double adultery, and so it is quite evident that no title can, nor may be, attributed to him, in him who fully intends to enter this Realm, with the purpose of a conquest…

True or not, it did not stop Edmund from marrying Edmund Beaufort's niece, Margaret Beaufort in 1455 without seeking papal dispensation for consanguinity. However, if Edmund Beaufort was the father, then Edmund Tudor was not Welsh, and the future Henry VII was Beaufort on both sides.

The second son, Jasper, was born at Hatfield probably in 1431. There was also a possible third son although very little is known of his life. Polydore Vergil stated this child, whom he did not name, became 'a monke of the order of St. Benet, and lived not longe after.' The historian William Camden referred to the child as Edward Tudor and suggested that he is buried in the chapel of St. Blaise in Westminster Abbey near the tomb of Abbot Nicholas Litlington. Vergil also mentions a daughter who became a nun, though no other source corroborates this. These children were not only the half-brothers of King Henry VI but also, through their mother, first cousins of the King of France, Louis XI, and second cousins of Duke François II of Brittany. In 1432, Owain ap Maredudd ap Tudur was naturalised as English. His petition to the Commons names him as Owen ap Meredith, and in his pardon of 1439, he is named as Owen Meredith. He was also sometimes called Owen fitz Maredudd, but from 1459, he became known as Owen Tudor Esquire.

In 1436, Catherine retired to Bermondsey Abbey. Whether it was enforced when her secret marriage was discovered, or whether she was genuinely ill at the time is not known. In her will of 1 January 1437, she wrote: 'a long grievous malady, in the which I have been long, and yet am, troubled and vexed by the visitations of God.' Two days later she was dead. She did not mention Owen or their children in her will but made her son, King Henry VI, her executor.

Edmund and Jasper were sent to the Abbess of Barking to be brought up and educated. Soon after Catherine's death, the Duke of Gloucester called Owen to appear before the council for violating the law of the remarriage of the Dowager Queen. However, he sought sanctuary in Westminster Abbey where he remained for some time. Owen finally appeared before the council maintaining his innocence. He was cleared and allowed to return to Wales. Despite his safe conduct, he was captured by Lord Beaumont, his possessions were seized, and he was committed to Newgate jail. In 1438 he escaped but was later recaptured and held in the custody of Edmund Beaufort who was at the time, the Constable of Windsor Castle. In 1439 Henry VI of England granted him a general pardon, restoring his goods and lands. In addition, Henry VI granted him a pension of £40 per annum, which was increased to £100 in 1459, provided him with a position at court, and appointed him the Keeper of the King's Parks in Denbigh.

Henry VI began to take an interest in his two half-brothers and welcomed Edmund and Jasper to court, and on 23 November 1452 Edmund was created Earl of Richmond and Jasper Earl of Pembroke, with a public acknowledgement they were the king's uterine brothers. They were also given the distinct honour of having precedence over all other nobles below the rank of Duke. Edmund was granted Baynard's Castle and Jasper a house in Brook Street, Stepney, as well as land in their respective earldoms. The Tudors had risen from nothing to become one of the most important families in England.

Margaret Beaufort

Befitting his new-found status, the 24-year-old Edmund needed a suitable bride. They found the 12-year-old Margaret Beaufort, the daughter and sole heiress of the late John Beaufort, 1st Duke of Somerset, grandson of John of Gaunt. Margaret was born at Bletsoe Castle, Bedfordshire, on 31 May 1443. Around the time of her first birthday, according to the French chronicler Thomas Basin, the Bishop of Lisieux, in his *Histoire de Charles VII*, Somerset died of illness, but *The Croyland Chronicle* reported that his death was suicide, after a disastrous campaign in France. The infant Margaret became the ward of William de la Pole, later Duke of Suffolk, and his wife Alice Chaucer, granddaughter of the poet Geoffrey Chaucer. Before his death, William de la Pole managed to arrange the marriage of his young ward to his son, John de la Pole. This was the first of Margaret's four marriages. The wedding may have been held between 28 January and 7 February 1444, when she was perhaps a year old but certainly no more than three. However, it is more likely that they were married in 1450. Because of the consanguinity, papal dispensation was granted on 18 August 1450. Sometime after Suffolk's death, Henry VI dissolved the marriage and he granted custody of Margaret to Edmund and Jasper. Margaret was not bound by the marriage contract as she had entered into the marriage before reaching the age of 12. Even before the annulment of her first marriage, Henry VI chose Margaret as a bride for his half-brother, Edmund. Margaret was 12 when she married the 24-year-old Edmund Tudor on 1 November 1455 at Bletsoe Castle. In her will, made in 1472, Margaret refers to Edmund Tudor as her first husband. Canon law, following Gratian, the Italian monk and scholar, in the 12th century, set the lower limit on marriage at 12 for girls, 14 for boys, and it was not unusual for members of the aristocracy to marry young. However, soon after the marriage, Margaret was pregnant. It is possible that Edmund raped Margaret as it was unusual for marriages to be consummated before a girl reached the age of 14 because of the risk to her health and wellbeing.

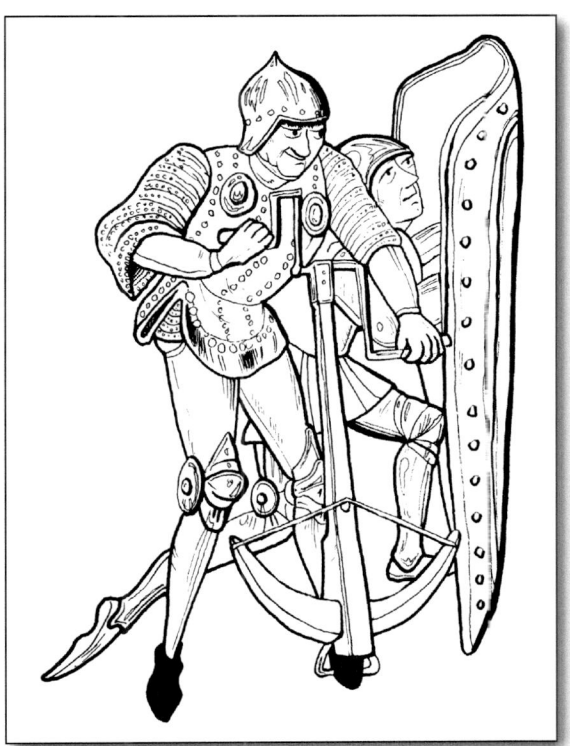

Contemporary image of a crossbowman with another protecting him with a large pavise whilst he reloads. Note what appears to be a brigandine over mail. Based on an illustration in the *Chroniques Sire Jehan Froissart*. Mid fifteenth century, Bibliothèque Nationale, Paris, 2644. (Matthew Ryan.)

Both brothers attended the Parliament of 1455 where Richard, Duke of York was once again named Protector of England. While York cancelled the majority of the grants Henry had made during his reign, those to Edmund and Jasper were not included. In 1456, Edmund was sent to Wales after Gruffydd ap Nicholas had rebelled and captured Aberystwyth, Carmarthen and Carreg Cennen castles. Although skirmishing continued for several months, all the castles had been recaptured by August 1456.

In April 1456 York's men, Sir Walter Devereux and his son-in-law Sir William Herbert, gathered a force of about 2000 men from around Herefordshire. Herbert, known as 'Black William', was a Welsh nobleman, politician, and courtier, son of William ap Thomas, 'the Blue Knight of Gwent', founder of Raglan Castle, and grandson of Dafydd Gam, who died fighting at Agincourt for Henry V. They arrived at Carmarthen Castle, which they quickly took and captured Edmund Tudor. Edmund was held prisoner at the castle whilst his attackers moved on to Aberystwyth. It was there on 1 November 1456, that he died leaving a 13-year-old widow who was seven months pregnant with their child. What he died of is not clear. Plague is most likely, although there were rumours at the time that Edmund had been poisoned or had died from injuries sustained during fighting. Both Devereux and Herbert were tried at Hereford by King Henry VI, Queen Margaret and the Duke of Buckingham. Herbert was offered a pardon, but Devereux was imprisoned until February 1458.

Margaret Beaufort was taken into the care of her brother-in-law Jasper at Pembroke Castle. It was here that she gave birth to a boy on 28 January 1457. Margaret's spiritual adviser, John Fisher, wrote that the birth was a very painful one, because of her small build and young age, and Margaret was almost certainly physically damaged by it. She would never bear another child. The Welsh chronicler Elis Gruffydd claimed that the baby was baptised Ywain (Owain) but his mother stopped the ceremony immediately, insisting that he should be named Henry Tudor.

Two months later Jasper Tudor and Margaret visited the Duke of Buckingham at Greenfield, near Newport. It was here that Margaret entered into an agreement to marry the Duke of Buckingham's second son, Sir Henry Stafford, to gain his protection and avoid having another husband forced on her. As they were second cousins, papal dispensation was required and this was granted on 6 April 1457. The 14-year-old Margaret married the 33-year-old Henry on 3 January 1458 at Maxstoke Castle in Warwickshire. The couple first went to live at Bourne Castle in Lincolnshire. The castle was close to both Croyland Abbey (where they became members of their confraternity) and Margaret's mother and her stepfather, Lionel de Welles, 6th Baron Welles, at Maxey Castle (then in Northamptonshire but now in Cambridgeshire). Welles and Margaret's mother had also had a son, John, born around 1450 and Margaret's half-brother.

As conflict with the Yorkists approached, Jasper became one of Queen Margaret of Anjou's closest supporters. It was him who she fled to after the Lancastrian defeat and capture of the King at Northampton in 1460. Jasper and the Earl of Wiltshire raised a new army in Wales which included Jasper's father, Owen. Their army was defeated by Yorkists led by Edward, Earl of March at Mortimer's Cross on 2 February 1461. Although Jasper managed to escape the carnage, Owen was captured and taken to Hereford for execution. According to *Gregory's Chronicle*, just before he died, he murmured 'that hede shalle ly on the stocke that wass wonte to ly on Quene Katheryns lappe.' His head was placed on the market cross, then 'a madde woman kem by dhys here and wysche a way the blode of hys face,' and placed 100 candles about it. William Herbert took control of South Wales whilst Jasper continued to support the Lancastrian cause, fighting another battle at Twt Hill, just outside Caernarfon. Virtually nothing is known about the battle except it was another defeat for Jasper and afterwards, he joined the Queen in Scotland.

Once Edward became king, one of his first moves was to grant the wardship of the five-year-old Henry Tudor to William Lord Herbert for £1,000. Margaret and her son were separated, and Henry was raised at Herbert's stronghold at Raglan Castle as the Earl of Richmond. According to Polydore Vergil, he was 'kept as prisoner, but honourably brought up with the wife of William Herbert.' Also with Herbert was the young son of the 3rd Earl of Northumberland, Henry Percy. Percy would eventually become the Fourth Earl and fight for Richard at Bosworth. They were educated by Edward Haseley and Andrew Scot, two Oxford graduates, and Sir Hugh Johns.

In *The Life of Henry VII*, Bernard André later wrote 'he was handed over to the best and most upright instructors to be taught the first principles of literature. He was endowed with such sharp mental powers and such great natural vigour and comprehension that even as a young boy he learned everything pertaining to religious instruction rapidly and thoroughly, with little effort from his teachers.' He continued that the young Henry had 'great mental quickness and capacity for learning. He possessed such becoming noble manners, such charmful grace of royal expression, and such great beauty that, like a peacemaking Solomon, he increased his stature before all mortals of his time.'

All three tutors were amply rewarded once Henry was King. During his time at Raglan, his mother was allowed to write to him and visited him at least once.

In the meantime, Jasper, acting as Queen Margaret's envoy, had sailed to Brittany seeking support before returning to Scotland. Across England it was rumoured that there was to be a large-scale invasion in support of Henry VI. Concern grew when a captured Lancastrian divulged that the Duke of Somerset with 60,000 Spanish was going to land in East Anglia. More Spanish and French were to land at Sandwich, whilst Jasper Tudor and the Duke of Exeter were to land on Anglesey. John de Vere, 12th Earl of Oxford, seems to have been close to the centre of the plot, however in February 1462 after letters sent from the Earl to Margaret of Anjou were intercepted and taken to the King, Oxford was arrested, together with his son Aubrey and Sir Thomas Tuddenham. They were convicted of high treason before the Constable of England, John Tiptoft, Earl of Worcester. He was beheaded on Tower Hill on 26 February 1462, His son Aubrey had been beheaded on the same scaffold six days earlier. Despite being allowed to succeed his father, the Earl's second son, also named John, never forgave the Yorkists.

On 16 April 1462, Queen Margaret sailed to Brittany, travelling to Angers. In June 1462, King Louis and Margaret of Anjou were at the French palace at Chinon in Touraine. They were soon joined by Jasper Tudor and together they agreed on a secret alliance. On 24 June, Louis agreed to lend Margaret 20,000 livres tournois and in return, if Henry VI recovered Calais, Jasper was to be made its captain who would then hand it over to the French for a payment of 40,000 crowns. Four days later all three were at Tours where a public treaty between Louis XI and Henry VI, promising not to support the enemies of the other, which would last 100 years was signed. By late October Queen Margaret and Jasper were back in Northumberland but after

Reconstruction of civilian dress with livery coat, fifteenth century. (Author)

Bamburgh Castle fell on Christmas Eve 1462, they returned to Louis court. It would be another seven years before Queen Margaret returned to England.

Duke François of Brittany, sympathetic to King Henry's plight, sent Guillaume de Cousinot to England. He reported back to François the danger King Henry was in and his need for men and *materiel*. Jasper followed soon after, stopping in France and collecting a letter from Louis urging François to aid Jasper in his return to Wales. It is possible that Jasper returned again, this time with a small army after Duke François placed a fleet of ships under vice-admiral Alain de Morte at his disposal on 26 March 1464. A number of his men were arrested for insurrection, but there is no mention of Jasper himself. It appears that Louis was spinning another web, for less than three months later, he sent François another letter, this time criticising him for supporting Jasper. François replied that he only thought he was carrying out Louis' wishes. It appears that Jasper spent at least some of the next three years in France. In the spring of 1468, Edward IV signed an alliance with both Burgundy and Brittany. On 1 June, Louis gave Jasper three ships to return to Wales. He landed near Harlech, which had been under siege by Yorkists since 1461, and headed for Denbigh, burning the land and gathering men as he went.

Edward decided that Harlech could no longer remain under Lancastrian control. Lord Herbert was issued with Commissions of Array to raise an army in the border counties, and probably gathered around 9,000 men. It is possible that he even took the 11-year-old Henry Tudor with him. He split this army in two. One half, under Herbert, attacked from the south, whilst his brother Richard approached from the north. The siege lasted for another month before the castle finally surrendered. A Welsh tradition tells of a mother on Anglesey whose seven sons were all involved in the rebellion. She pleaded with Herbert to leave her one of the seven, but they were all executed. All of Wales was now under Yorkist control and as a reward, Edward created Herbert Earl of Pembroke, Jasper's title. Jasper went into hiding then possibly returned to Brittany before continuing to France.

In July the following year, Warwick finally rebelled against Edward. The northern army under 'Robin of Redesdale' marched south. Edward sent the new Earl of Pembroke to deal with the rebels, and the two sides met at Edgcote in Northamptonshire. It was a disaster. Over 150 Yorkist Welsh nobles were killed fighting for Herbert. In the long term, it would mean that there were few Yorkists left in Wales to oppose Henry Tudor in 1485. The Welsh poet Guto'r Glyn lamented 'Let us hasten to the north to avenge our country. My nation is destroyed, now that the earl is slain.' Lewis Glyn Cothi also wrote, 'The greatest of battles was lost by treachery; at Banbury dire vengeance fell upon Wales.' Herbert and his brother were captured and executed at Northampton by Warwick. It is possible that as a ward of Herbert, 12-year-old Henry Tudor was watching the carnage. Accounts suggest he was rescued from the slaughter by Sir Richard Corbet. Corbet was the brother-in-law of Herbert's wife, Anne, and had been the ward of Lord Ferrers before he married his daughter, Elizabeth. Corbet took the young Henry to the home of his father-in-law, Lord Ferrers, at Weobley in Herefordshire. What happened next to Henry is confused.

According to a petition that Corbet gave to Henry when he was king (later printed in Owen and Blakeway's 1825 *History of Shrewsbury*), Corbet said 'after the death of Lord Herbert after the field of Banbury, hee was one of them that brought your grace out of danger of your enemys, and conveyed your grace unto your town of Hereford, and there delivered you in safety to your greate Uncle.'

The *Westminster Abbey Muniments* show that when Lady Margaret and her husband heard of the battle, fearing her son was a prisoner of Warwick, she sent John Bray and seven servants to find him. Bray was probably a brother of Reginald Bray, receiver-general and master of the household to Sir Henry Stafford, and who would go on to play a leading role in Lady Margaret's intrigues. They eventually found Henry at the home of Lord Ferrers at Weobley sheltering with Anne Devereux, Herbert's widow. Young Henry probably stayed in the household for some time, as it is recorded that payments were sent for two of Ferrer's servants and for Henry to buy him a '*bowe and shafts*'. In August Lady Margaret went alone for the first of several meetings with Clarence, who now held the honour of Richmond, at his London house, no doubt to discuss Henry's future. In the meantime, the legal councils of Stafford and Lady Pembroke met at the Bell in Fleet Street on 21 October 1469, to try to come to an agreement over Henry's wardship. Henry Parker, Lord Morley, who served as Lady Margaret's cupbearer during his youth in the 1490s, described her dinner table conversation as 'joyous,' loving merry tales as well as talk of godly matters. Her later confessor John Fisher, Bishop of Rochester, described her as having a 'holding memory' where anything 'of weight and substance wherein she might profit, she would not let for any pain or labour to take upon hand.' Fisher himself would later be executed by Margaret's grandson Henry VIII on Tower Hill on 22 June 1535, for his religious beliefs after he had been created a cardinal.

Lionel de Welles, 6th Baron Welles, Lady Margaret's stepfather, was killed fighting for the Lancastrians at Towton. His son Richard then became the 7th Baron Welles. Lady Margaret, her mother, Margaret Beauchamp, and her son, his half-brother, John Welles, laid claim to his estates. They were finally settled on Baron Welles by Edward in 1468, but it appears that John Welles and his mother continued to live at Maxey. In February 1470, rebellion broke out in Lincolnshire. Lord Welles' son Sir Robert, set himself up as a 'great captain' of the people of Lincolnshire and openly declared for Warwick and Clarence. Edward lured Lord Welles to London under the pretext of a pardon, then took him prisoner. Edward then marched an army to meet the rebels at Empingham. Edward then ruthlessly executed Welles in front

RICHARD III AND THE BATTLE OF BOSWORTH

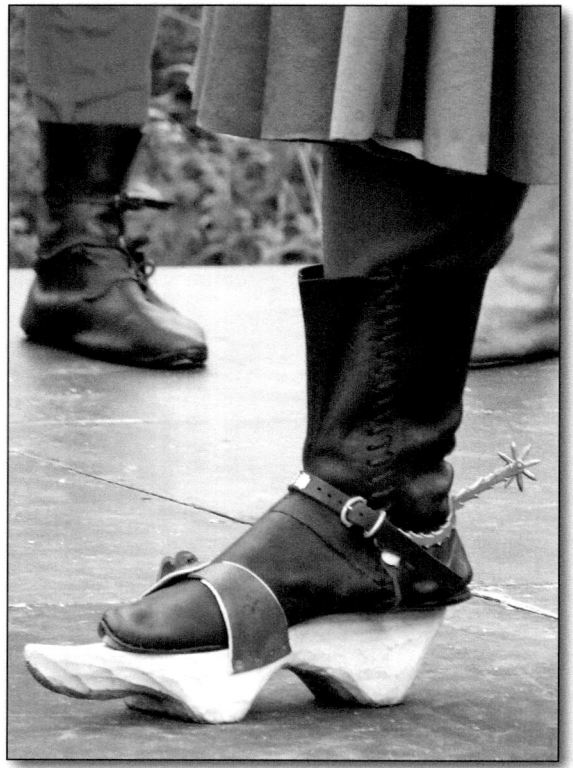

Reconstruction of civilian boots with clogs. (Author)

of the rebel army. The rebels were slaughtered. Sir Robert Welles and his commander of foot, Richard Warren, were captured during the rout and were executed a week later on 19 March. Welles confessed his treason and named Warwick and Clarence as the 'partners and chief provokers' of the rebellion. Documents were also found proving the complicity of Warwick and Clarence, who were forced to flee to France.

Louis met with Warwick and Clarence at the Château d'Amboise overlooking the River Loire. Sforza de Bettini, the Milanese ambassador, reported that Louis was 'greatly rejoiced about it, considering it good news, and he is devoting himself more than ever to preparations for war.' If his plans came to fruition, he could now make war on Burgundy without the threat of interference by England. They were soon joined by Margaret of Anjou and her son. Jasper was probably already with the French court. An alliance was eventually forged between Warwick, Clarence, Jasper Tudor and Margaret of Anjou. Warwick, Clarence and Jasper returned to England in 60 French ships on 13 September 1470, landing at Dartmouth and Plymouth. Whilst Warwick and Clarence were forcing Edward to flee England and putting Henry VI back on the throne, Jasper returned to Wales and gathered his forces. It is probably at this point that Corbet returned to Weobley to collect young Henry and take him to his uncle.

By this time, Lady Margaret and her husband were living in the palace at Woking in Surrey. She appears to have been in good favour with King Edward, however, at the same time she was in close communication with her Lancastrian cousin Edmund, Duke of Somerset. She met with him at least in October 1470 and again in March 1471. Somerset visited her several times at Woking around this time too, and it appears that he tried to persuade Stafford back to the Lancastrian cause.

In October 1470, Jasper and Henry returned to London, visiting both King Henry and Margaret Beaufort. Vergil, somewhat fancifully, later wrote of young Henry's first meeting with the returned King Henry VI:

> It is said that the king, seeing the boy, held his silence for a while, studying his character, and then said to the nobles who were present This indeed is the one to whom we and our adversaries must yield our power.

Bernard André agreed, writing that:

> Summoning the earl of Richmond into his presence as he was washing his hands, the king prophesised that some day the boy would undertake the governance of the kingdom and would have all things under his own power.

On 28 October, Jasper and Henry Stafford met to discuss Henry's future. Two days later, Lady Margaret, Stafford and Henry travelled to Woking, where they spent a week together. From there they spent a further week visiting Guildford, Maidenhead, Windsor and Henley-on-Thames before Henry was returned to the care of Jasper. It would be another 15 years before Henry would meet his mother again.

On 6 February 1471, the Bishop of Bayeux wrote to his king to confirm that the alliance between Warwick and France against King Edward and Charles, Duke of Burgundy, was now agreed. The same day Warwick wrote to the Calais garrison ordering them to begin the war.

A few weeks later, Edward returned to England and regained control of his Kingdom. When Louis XI was told of Edward's success, he told the Milanese ambassador 'I am busy with new schemes. It is impossible to fight against fortune.' Jasper failed to join up with Margaret of Anjou and her army at Tewkesbury. Roger Vaughan of Tretower (who had executed Jasper's father, Owen) was sent by King Edward to capture Jasper and Henry at Chepstow. However, Roger fell into Jasper's hands and was beheaded by him at Chepstow. The two fugitives made it to Pembroke, where they were besieged by a force under the command of Morgan ap Thomas, who had been pardoned by Richard whilst he was still Duke of Gloucester after he had seized Carmarthen and Cardigan Castles. As Morgan's men began digging trenches and ditches around the castle, a relief force led by Morgan's brother Dafydd, 'with hooks, prongs and glaives, and other rustic weapons' scattered the army. Considering all his family was still Lancastrian, perhaps Morgan's heart was not in the fighting, if he even fought at all. Jasper and Henry escaped yet again, this time to Tenby. They were sheltered by the mayor, Thomas White, a wine merchant. Tradition has it that they hid in White's cellar in Tenby High Street for four days. From there, the Tudors made their way through the tunnels beneath the town, and to the seashore where White's small boat was waiting. From there they sailed for France with a few close friends and servants. It was 2 June 1471, and their 14-year exile had just begun.

Contemporary image of a crossbow man with a windlass to draw the crossbow hanging from his belt. Based on an illustration in the *Chroniques Sire Jehan Froissart*. Mid fifteenth century, Bibliothèque Nationale, Paris, 2644. (Matthew Ryan)

5

France, Brittany and Henry Tudor

Men are so simple and so much inclined to obey immediate needs that a deceiver will never lack victims for his deceptions.

Niccolo Machiavelli

He was known as Louis the Prudent to his friends. However, Louis XI's taste for intrigue and his intense diplomatic activity also earned him the nicknames 'the Cunning' (Middle French: *le rusé*) and 'the Universal Spider' (Middle French: *l'universelle aragne*), as his enemies accused him of spinning webs of plots and conspiracies. Vergil also described him as 'being an hard and froward man of nature was injuryous and spytefull both to frind and foe'. He was born in Bourges on 3 July 1423, the son of King Charles VII of France and Marie of Anjou. At the time, the Hundred Years War was still raging with the English and Burgundians were controlling most of northern France, including the city of Paris.

Louis grew up in the castle of Loches in Touraine, isolated from his parents. From the age of six he studied history, rhetoric, Latin grammar, mathematics and music. When he was not studying, he would practice horseback riding, and how to handle weapons such as the bow and arrow, lance and sword. Away from the court, he learned to live as a simple man. In 1433, Louis went to live with his mother and sisters at Amboise where he was treated according to his rank as Dauphin of France. On the afternoon of 25 June 1436, the 13-year-old Louis married 11-year-old Margaret of Scotland, daughter of King James I who was said to resemble a beautiful doll. The wedding ceremony took place in the chapel of the castle of Tours, and was presided over by Renaud of Chartres, the Archbishop of Reims. His father came to the wedding in riding clothes complete with spurs. Following the ceremony, 'doctors advised against consummation' because of the relative immaturity of the bride and bridegroom. Margaret continued her studies, and Louis went on tour with his father to loyal areas of the kingdom. The beautiful and cultured Margaret was popular at the court of France, but her marriage to Louis was not a happy one, in part because of his strained relations with her father-in-law, who was very attached to her. She died childless at the age of 20 in 1445.

Louis grew up aware of the continuing weakness of the French nation. He regarded his father as a weakling, whose inability to harness the power of the French nobles added to the instability in France. Louis despised him for this. Even at this time, Charles was taken aback by the intelligence and temper of his son.

In 1440, aged 16, Louis came under the influence of Charles I, Duke of Bourbon and took part in an uprising known as the *Praguerie*, which sought to neutralise Charles and install Louis as regent of France. The uprising failed, and Louis was forced to submit to his father, who chose to forgive him. The following year he was fighting the English, and in 1443 aided his father to suppress the revolt of the Count of Armagnac. In 1444 Louis gathered an army of between 15,000 to 20,000 *Écorcheurs* against the Swiss of the canton of Basel cumulating in the Battle of St. Jakob an der Birs on 26 August 1444 (see pp.76–77). The heroism of the Swiss made a great impression on the young prince, and once king, Louis set about building an army in the Swiss fashion. Louis led his *Écorcheurs* into the Alsace to ravage the countryside. The Dauphin formally made peace with the Swiss Confederacy and with Basel in a treaty signed at his headquarters at Ensisheim on 28 October, and withdrew his troops from the Alsace in the spring of 1445.

When Louis returned to the court at Nancy he continued to quarrel with his father. Louis sent agents into Agenais in an attempt to incite its cities of into treason but the plot was immediately reported to the King. He then launched a political campaign to remove Pierre de Brezé his father's chief minister, but Antoine de Chabannes, revealed the plot to Charles. He also berated his father's mistress Agnès Sorel in public and according to Aeneas Sylvius Piccolomini (later Pope Pius II) he chased her to the King's bed. Louis was ordered out of court to Dauphinéa province in south-eastern France. Despite frequent summonses by the king, the two would never meet again.

Louis lived mainly in Grenoble, in the tour de la Trésorerie. From there he led his own political establishment and married Charlotte of Savoy, daughter of Louis, Duke of Savoy, against his father's wishes, and continued to plot and scheme. Charles VII sent numerous letters to Louis ordering him back to court. They were ignored. Eventually Charles snapped and sent an army to compel his son to his will. On 30 August 1456 Louis fled to Burgundy, where he was hosted by his uncle, Philip the Good, the Duke of Burgundy and Charles' greatest enemy.

Louis continued to spread his webs across Europe, forging close links with Francesco Sforza, Duke of Milan, and to counter his father's support for Queen Margaret of Anjou in England, entered into a secret agreement with Richard Neville, Earl of Warwick. In 1459 Francesco Coppini, a papal legate, was sent to England by the Pope to stop the fighting between the Yorkists and Lancastrians. He was also on a secret mission from the Duke of Milan to promote an English attack on France in order to divert Charles VII away from his assault on Italy. It was Louis who put Coppini in touch with Warwick. Coppini joined with Warwick and the future King Edward IV for their invasion of England in June 1460. After the death of Richard of York and Warwick's father Salisbury at Wakefield, the Duke of Burgundy sent a force of handgunners in support. At the same time Louis sent Jean de

Lannoy, Lord de La Barde, to Warwick with a banner bearing an image of the Virgin. Louis also began to meddle in Burgundian politics and by mid 1461 relations between Louis and his uncle had reached breaking point. Prospero da Camogli, Sforza's ambassador to Louis who was at Genappe, reported 'Every day the danger grows that this hostility will uncover itself. On the side of the Dauphin, only his need holds it hidden; on the side of the Duke, only the opportunity offered by the Dauphin's presence if war with France should break out.' However, everything changed on 22 July 1461, when King Charles VII died. Louis rushed to Reims to be crowned, in case his younger brother, Charles Duke of Berry, should try to do the same. Three days later he was crowned Louis XI, King of France aged 38. He rode into Paris in triumph on 31 August.

Once King, Louis pursued many of the same goals that his father had, such as limiting the powers of the dukes and barons of France. Among other initiatives, Louis instituted reforms to make the tax system more efficient. He suppressed many of his former co-conspirators, who had thought him their friend, and appointed 'new men' who had shown promising talent to senior positions within the government. Continuing his father's policy, Louis turned his back on his uncle, the Duke of Burgundy. He developed a series of anti-Burgundian alliances, and encouraged a group of pro-French councillors in the Burgundian court. His ultimate aim: the total destruction of the Burgundian state. When the Duke of Burgundy needed funds to launch a crusade, Louis gave him 400,000 gold crowns in exchange for the territories along the Somme ceded as part of the 1435 Treaty of Arras.

At this time, Brittany was still an independent duchy ruled by Duke François II. Six years earlier, François had joined the League of the Public Weal, an alliance of nobles organised by the new Duke of Burgundy, Charles the Bold, with Louis' teenage brother Charles Duke of Berry as a figurehead. Their aim was to stop Louis enlarging French royal domains by annexing all of the remaining independent duchies, which as well as Burgundy included Berry, Normandy, Orléans, and Brittany. In the War of Public Weal that followed, the Burgundians met Louis' forces at the Battle of Montlhéry on 16 July 1465 near Longpont-sur-Orge. The Bretons were prevented from joining the battle when Louis' uncle, Charles Comte du Maine, attacked them from two sides. The battle itself was inconclusive. Eventually, Brittany's army and other members of the League of the Public Weal rejoined the Burgundian forces and together they besieged Paris starting on 19 August 1465. Louis XI pretended to yield, and a truce was signed on 3 September.

In April 1468, Duke François agreed to a 30-year alliance with Edward IV at a conference in Greenwich. As well as agreeing a commercial treaty England was to supply 3,000 archers to Brittany at two months' notice, should it be threatened. However, in July 1468, whilst Charles the Bold was occupied celebrating his wedding to Edward IV's sister Margaret in Burgundy, and before Edward could gather men to support them, Louis invaded Brittany. He then forced the Bretons to agree to the Treaty of Ancenis and to abandon their allies, before withdrawing. In December 1470, Charles the Bold accused Louis of plotting his assassination. A new anti-French alliance with England, Burgundy and Brittany was beginning to take shape. Although

Louis' attention was focused on Burgundy and their alliance with England, he always kept an eye on Brittany.

When Jasper and Henry fled from Tenby on 2 June 1471 their intended destination was France and the court of Jasper's first cousin, Louis XI. However, fate once again intervened and strong winds blew them off course. Tradition has it that they were forced to shelter on Jersey. Other sources suggest that they were either shipwrecked or captured by the Bretons and came ashore in Brittany at the fishing ports of either Camarat or Le Conquet near Brest in north-west Finistère. Another source says they were captured at St. Malo.

Henry and Jasper were escorted to Nantes, the Breton capital, and then to François II's court at the Château de l'Hermine near the fortified hill-top town of Vannes. The welcome speech was later turned into a verse and published in 1562. They were treated with all the courtesy due to English nobles of the royal blood and welcomed by Duke François. He promised to protect them and assured them they could move freely throughout the Duchy. However Commines, who was at the court noted, 'the duke treated them very gently as prisoners.'

Edward was alarmed when he heard the news and immediately sent a message to François requesting that Henry and Jasper be handed over. Vergil wrote that: 'indede he tooke very grevously, and thowgh hys mynd gave him that soome evell wold coome therby.' Edward's biggest fear was that they would fall into the hands of Louis. On 28 September, John Paston wrote that 'some say that the king of France will see him safe and set him at liberty again.' Others believed that Louis 'would have easily crowned him [Henry] King of England.'

Edward's attempt to recover the two guests only served to reiterate their significance to Duke François, who replaced their servants with his own men 'to wait upon and guard them'. François wrote back to Edward that he could not return them to England by reason of his promise and fidelity. Edward wrote again, calling on Francois, on his honour, good fame and constancy to keep Henry and Jasper under arrest, promising to send aid, money and huge gifts if he agreed. François seems to have looked after them well, as a record in his wardrobe accounts for early in 1472 shows a gift to Henry of a long black velour robe with a changeable taffeta lining and a short padded robe of damask.

On 4 October 1471 Margaret Beaufort's husband, Henry Stafford, died, probably from injuries he sustained at Barnet. In June 1472, instead of waiting for the end of the customary year of mourning, Lady Margaret quickly married her fourth husband, Thomas Stanley. Stanley's own wife, Eleanor Neville, sister of Warwick, had died around the same time and despite his past, Stanley had recently been appointed Steward of the King's Household by Edward, and as such he had become a regular member of the Royal Council. This gave Lady Margaret unbridled access to the King and a place in the Royal Court. She attended all the royal events such as the funeral of Richard, Duke of York, at Fotheringhay and was even chosen by Queen Elizabeth to be godmother to one of her daughters. Just before her marriage, Margaret placed her Beaufort estates in Somerset and Devon in trust with a separate estate for her son.

At the start of 1472 Louis, becoming increasing concerned over the new coalition, decided to make a pre-emptive strike against its weakest link – Brittany. This time, as well as his own men, he had persuaded King James of Scotland to invade with an additional 6,000 men. In March 1472 Duke François II of Brittany asked Edward for 6,000 archers. It was not until April that Edward allowed any men to go, and even then, decided that 'Anthony Woodville, Earl of Rivers may take 1,000 men-at-arms and archers to Brittany and other parts beyond the sea at his own expense'. Rivers' 14-year-old brother, Edward Woodville, was to join him on the expedition and was knighted just before they left. On 6 June 1472, Charles the Bold revived his claim that Louis had tried to have him assassinated and then invaded France. Charles rampaged through Normandy, hoping to meet up with François and the Bretons. However, with Louis threatening the Breton borders, François could not join him. Charles' invasion proved an anti-climax when, in June, his army ground to a halt laying siege to Beauvais. In response Louis sent 3,000 men under Anthoine de Chabannes into Hainault, burning all before them. Louis' Scottish allies failed to arrive, possibly due to the expense of mounting such a campaign. However, in July, he personally led an army of over 5,000 men into Brittany, capturing Ancenis on 7 July, with Chantocé and Machecoul falling soon after. On 20 July, La Guerche was captured, and on the following day Pouancé was taken. What part the English played in the defence of Brittany is not known, however John Paston wrote in November that many had been lost to 'fflyxe' and dysentery.

On 23 July, Edward sent his secretary, William Slefeld, and John Sapcote to negotiate a treaty with François that would enable him to invade France through Brittany. Edward authorised an additional 1,000 archers and 20 lances for Brittany under the exiled Gascon Gaillard IV de Durfort, Lord Duras, which left England in early August. Louis was still at La Guerche on 11 August, when he moved through the Laval, arriving at the castle of Ponts-de-Cé which controlled the crossing of the Loire into Brittany on 29 August.

On 4 September, Charles the Bold wrote to François saying:

> I have pitched camp here between Rouen and Neufchâtel with the intention, still, of returning towards Rouen, unless I pursue the war somewhere else more damaging to the enemy. I shall do everything in my power to compel them to retreat from your frontiers ... I have burned and ravaged the whole land of Caux so that it won't cause any trouble either to you or to us for a long time.

With the help of Rivers, the Anglo-Breton Treaty of Châteaugiron was agreed on 11 September but not ratified by Edward until 24 October. The treaty promised that the English would invade France by 1 April 1473, assisted by the Bretons. When Edward opened parliament on 6 October Louis XI was described as 'the principal ground, root and provoker of the King's let and trouble, and by subtle and crafty means endeavoured to disturb the realm of England.' He had good grounds, for at the same time, with Louis still threatening his borders, François II was negotiating a separate treaty with the French. As soon as it was concluded on 15 October, François sent emissaries to England requesting that Edward postponed any invasion of France until

November 1473 (after the treaty with the French expired). Louis also put pressure on Burgundy and they too concluded a peace treaty with France on 3 November. Edward began to bring his troops in Brittany back home during October and November. Even Edward succumbed, and signed a treaty with France on 22 March the following year. However, he kept it secret, not even telling Parliament. Despite the treaties, behind the scenes, Edward was still negotiating with his European allies to invade France at the first opportunity.

With rumours that the English envoys had been ordered to kill Henry if they were unable to secure his extradition, and the French threatening the borders, sometime before October 1472 Henry and Jasper were moved to the Château de Suscinio. The thirteenth-century château was the Breton dukes' summer palace near St. Gildas Abbey on the Rhys Peninsula, where they were placed in the care of Jean du Quélennec, Vicomte du Faou and Admiral of Brittany since 1432. It seems that once the immediate threat had passed, Henry and Jasper were back at François' court at Nantes by late 1473. Their whereabouts over the next year are not known.

Louis XI was also determined to get his hands on the pair and in 1474 demanded that Henry and Jasper should be freed frankly and swiftly and sent to his court. He sent detailed instructions to Guillaume Compaing, dean of St. Pierre en Pont, his ambassador to the Breton court. In his instructions, he wrote how Jasper was part of his household and in his service going 'from place to place with the King [Louis] to serve him and accompany him.' After Tewkesbury, they continue, the two were 'advised to go to the King as their lord and single refuge, and that it would be his pleasure to welcome them as humble servants.' Louis instructions considered all possible arguments that François may give for keeping Henry and Jasper and how to respond. For example, if François could give examples of the two's subjects waging war against him, then Louis would offer suitable reparations. Compaing was also told to directly threaten the Bretons and to say '…it would seem therefore that the Lord of Brittany would want to lead a war against him, which the King does not think that is what the Lord of Brittany wants…' The instructions concluded with 'If the Lord of Brittany refuses to free Pembroke and Richmond with their people and goods it shall be asked of him that he should neither take nor move them from his hands.'

Concerned that there would be further attempts by either the English or French to take his guests they were split up and removed to more secure locations. Jasper was sent to the Château de Josselin, the seat of the Vicomte de Rohan. Rohan would later be arrested for murder and would flee to France. Young Henry was sent into the care of Jean IV, lord of Rieux, at the remote Château de Largoët near Elven. Rieux was the Marshal of Brittany and would become the guardian of Duchess Anne of Brittany, future Queen of France. He too had close connections to the French court and would later rebel against Duke François. Henry was kept in the seven-storey, octagonal 'Tour d'Elven', one of the highest donjons (keeps) in France. Local legend says that he stayed in a small room on the second floor, whilst other French sources suggest that he was kept on the sixth or seventh floors. Although still a prisoner, Henry would have been held in comparative luxury and although many have translated donjon as a dungeon, it was a residence for the Marshal and his family.

Papers in the National Library of Wales suggest the possibility that around this time, the 18- or 19-year-old Henry Tudor fathered a son, 'by a Breton lady' who was named as Roland Velville. Welsh poet Dafydd Alaw described Velville as 'A man of kingly line and of earl's blood.' After taking the throne, Henry knighted Velville and he is recorded as being Henry's 'companion' and a champion jouster. However, S.B. Chrimes has suggested he was little more than a close companion during his exile.

There has been some suggestion that also around this time Edward proposed that Henry could marry his daughter Elizabeth of York. However, as Edward considered Henry to be 'the only impe now left of King Henry the sixth's blood' he was unlikely to have made such promises except, perhaps as a ploy to persuade Henry to return to England. Not only that, Elizabeth was part of a bigger game. One of the clauses of the Treaty of Picquigny was that as soon as he become of age, the Dauphin Charles should marry Elizabeth. However, Louis continued to toy with Edward and had no intention of allowing the marriage to take place. Each time ambassadors were despatched to France they were never given definite answers, only that Louis would send envoys to England. They were also given large presents, so they went home satisfied. Weeks became months, and nothing was resolved.

In November 1476, Edward sent a delegation to Brittany led by Thomas Whiting, the Chester Herald. They told François that Edward wished to arrange a marriage for Henry with one of his affinity and that they would take him back with them. Eventually 'wearied with prayer and vanquished with price', François consented. Henry was taken from Largoët to the port of St. Malo by the ambassadors. When they arrived, Henry 'fell by into a fever'. Whether feigned or genuine, his illness delayed their departure.

When Jean du Quélennec discovered that Henry was on his way back to England, he rushed to the court. Du Quélennec told François that he had forgotten the promise he made and that he was consigning 'that most innocent imp, to be torn to pieces by bloody butchers, to be miserably tormented, and finally to be slain.' On hearing this, François had a change of heart and sent his Treasurer, Pierre Landais, to stop the ship from sailing. Landais arranged for Henry to escape to sanctuary either in one of the port's chapels or St. Vincent's Cathedral in the centre of the town. The ambassadors tried to lure him out but were met by hostile townspeople who surrounded the chapel. The ambassadors were furious that Henry had escaped from their grasp, but Landais said that it was their own negligence that allowed Henry to enter into sanctuary. He also assured them that Henry would be either kept in sanctuary or returned to the Duke's care 'so there should be no cause to fear him.' As soon as the delegation left, Henry returned to Duke François' court. He was placed into the care of Vincent de la Landelle at the Château de l'Hermine within the secure walls of Vannes. Jasper was also brought back to Vannes and kept in the household of Bertrand du Parc, probably spending at least some of the time at the frontier castle of Fougères on the Norman border.

When Louis discovered how close Henry had been to being taken back to England he sent a delegation to Brittany led by Guillaume de Souplainville, Admiral of Guinne, demanding Henry and Jasper be handed over to them. François flatly refused.

FRANCE, BRITTANY AND HENRY TUDOR

In March 1477, Edward sent Morton and Sir John Donne to negotiate with Louis. They told him that François had told Edward that Louis hated him and longed for his undoing because of his friendship with England, but Edward would be glad to find an excuse for breaking their treaty. However, Louis knew the real truth – that they had been negotiating in secret for months. Morice Gourmel, who had been François and Edward's confidential messenger, had copied every letter that had passed between them and had sold them to Louis. Soon after the English left Guillaume Chauvin the Breton Chancellor arrived at the French court with a delegation saying that they desired peace and a good understanding with Louis. The temptation was too great for Louis to resist, and he read out loud the letters he had obtained. Chauvin, who had not been party to the negotiations with the English (perhaps because he could not be trusted) was shocked. Louis then sent the letters back to François with a note saying he did not want to hear any more protestations of friendship until François cast off the king of England for good. François mobilised his army and waited for a possible French invasion.

After the death of Charles the Bold, Edward renewed the commercial treaty with Burgundy on 18 December 1478. He also made a secret alliance with Mary of Burgundy and Maximilian. In early 1479, Morton warned the French ambassador, the Bishop of Elne, that if France would not agree to

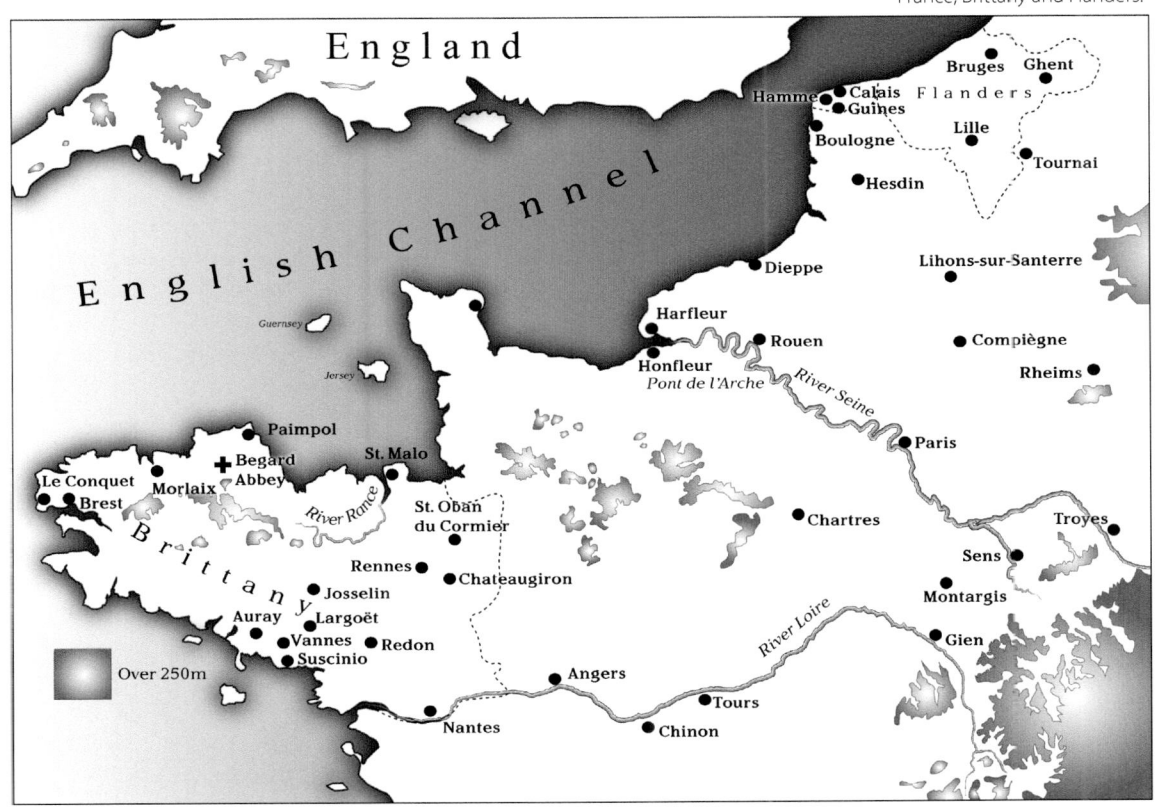

Map showing key places in France, Brittany and Flanders.

extend the truce, England would break relations and make a formal alliance with Maximilian. Elne signed, but Louis would later renounce the agreement. According to Flemish sources, in June the same year the Flemings captured a French ship and on it found gifts for Lord Howard and letters from Louis exhorting him to ensure that 10,000 Englishmen joined his army to invade Flanders. According to the report, Edward arrested Howard and 11 unnamed associates, but nothing more is known. However, this does show what Louis expected from his 'pensioners'.

In the meantime, Louis had refused to extend a truce with Maximilian and turned on Burgundy, once again using harassment and attrition. However, in response, Maximilian marched into Artois and attacked the French near the village of Guinegate on 7 August 1479. It was the first time that longspears had been used in large numbers by an army other than the Swiss. Maximilian formed his infantry into two large squares, one commanded by the Count Engelbert of Nassau, who had also fought under the Archduke's father-in-law at Nancy. The other square was commanded by the Count of Romont. These large, deep squares were not to be the only innovation employed in the Archduke's army. The Archduke himself, instead of joining the cavalry arm as was the European tradition, joined the infantry square with 200 of his nobles. While it was not unheard of for some poorer nobles to do this, the fact that such a prominent official as the Archduke himself doing this was unheard of. What is more, there were over 300 English led by Sir Thomas Everingham on Maximilian's side. At the beginning of the battle The French commander, Philippe de Crèvecoeur, forced back the knights within the left infantry square and captured the Burgundian artillery drawn up on their flank and turned it on the square. However, instead of following up their advantage on the left flank, the French knights chased after the Burgundian knights who were fleeing from the field. Meanwhile, on the other flank, the Burgundians held fast and slowly fought their way forward and defeated the remaining French. Commines reported that Louis was deeply troubled as he was not accustomed to losing. In the immediate aftermath of the battle, due to their poor performance, he disbanded the Franc-Archers and converted his army to a rapid reaction force equipped with longspears.

In the spring of 1480, public opinion was pushing Edward IV to act against Louis. Edward sent Louis a letter insisting on an immediate cessation of his war with Maximilian, offering to be arbiter. Louis dismissed the offer out of hand and recalled the Bishop of Elne, his permanent ambassador in England. In June, Edward sent Lord Howard to Paris with the message that if Louis did not accept arbitration, he would side with Maximilian. Louis told Howard that he meant to force Maximilian to accept his peace terms at any cost. He then gave Howard more plate and coin, and (as a Breton spy put it) left him to pound the pavements of Paris. In early August 1480, Maximilian and Edward agreed on a new treaty which included sending archers to Burgundy and in return Maximilian promised to pay Edward his annual pension of 50,000 crowns if Louis refused to do so.

Louis took the threat of another English invasion seriously and in a letter of November 1480 wrote that his defence preparations included stationing his rapid reaction force in Normandy and Scottish ships at Dieppe. Louis had also extended his web into Italy, where he persuaded Lorenzo de Medici of Florence, controller of the largest bank in Europe, to prevent Maximilian and his wife Mary, Duchess of Burgundy, from borrowing money, and to withdraw his banking interests from England. Then, to keep Edward occupied and stop him interfering with his plans, Louis convinced James III, King of Scotland, to invade England. Forced to defend his own border and short of funds, Edward was powerless to send aid to the Burgundians – and he would have known who was behind it. With all hope of military aid gone, Maximilian was forced into a truce with Louis.

To remind Edward who had the power in Europe, Louis treated one of Edward's heralds to a public piece of play acting where Louis told the Bishop of Elne, 'I was assured that you were a better deceiver than any of the English. I believed it and I am the one deceived!' The bishop was then publicly charged with compromising the interests of France. Once the herald had left, the Bishop quietly slipped back to his own diocese. English envoys in Paris were mocked and told that Edward would not get his next payment. Louis then gloated that he enjoyed very good relations with the Burgundian envoys and that he knew all about the archers Edward was going to send to Burgundy, describing it as an act of hostility towards France. Where Louis obtained the information from was never disclosed. England was full of French spies at the time, although it is possible that the source may have been one of his English 'pensioners'. Louis was not paying them huge sums of money for doing nothing!

During the summer of 1480, Edward began to negotiate for his eldest son Edward to marry Anne, the daughter and heiress of François of Brittany, and by November had reached an agreement. By the following June they had drawn up an agreement whereby the two would be married, but if Anne would die before that time came then Prince Edward would marry her younger sister. Conversely, if Prince Edward died, then Anne would marry his younger brother Richard. There was also a treaty of mutual aid where Edward would provide Brittany with 3,000 archers at his own expense if France attacked Brittany.

It was during this time of intense political manoeuvring that François moved Henry into the custody of Jean Guillemet. He was transferred again in 1481, this time to Louis de Kermené, one of the Duke's bodyguard. It is possible that Guillemet and de Kermené had joint custody, as both were paid 2,000 livres for Henry's expenses in 1481–2. By 1 October 1482, Henry was in the custody of Jean de Robichen. Why these moves took place or even exactly where Henry was living during this time is not known. These changes of custody may have been connected to the power struggle between Pierre Landais, the Treasurer, and his rival Guillaume Chauvin, the Chancellor. Landais was the son of rich clothiers from Vitré. He entered the service of Duke François as a *valet de garde-robe*. His ambition and acumen soon brought him favour with the Duke, and he rose to become Treasurer and Receiver-General of Brittany. He promoted the interests of the bourgeoisie, and encouraged trade and enterprise. Landais was in favour of continuing Breton independence whilst Chauvin was pro-French and, if Landais' accusations at the time were correct, was another one of Louis XI's pensioners. Chauvin was eventually arrested and imprisoned by Landais, thereby securing his own position as *de facto* prime minister of Brittany.

By June 1481, Louis had forced Edward to terms too. The treaty was ratified in secret by Edward in November 1481 after he had received another instalment of his pension. Maximilian's envoys frantically appealed to Edward to save them from the clutches of Louis. Edward simply informed them that the war with Scotland prevented him from giving aid and suggested they sought another truce with France. To remind Edward to stay out of his war with Burgundy, Louis made him wait for his next payment. In May 1481, desperate for funds for his Scottish war, he wrote to Louis asking for his next payment which had been due at Easter. It finally arrived in August.

When Mary of Burgundy died after a riding accident Flanders and Brabant revolted against Maximilian. In September 1482, Louis published his secret agreement with Edward, destroying any chance of aid coming from England. Without English support, Maximilian was forced to sign the Treaty of Arras on 23 December 1482. It included the marriage of Maximilian's daughter to the Dauphin of France and delivered Artois, the county which surrounded the Pale of Calais, and Picardy, into French hands. England and Brittany were excluded from the peace. According to *The Croyland Chronicle*, Edward 'thought nothing else but taking vengeance' on the French. Not only did it mean the end of his marriage hopes for Princess Elizabeth but as Louis no longer needed him, the end of his lucrative pension, too.

Mary's four-year-old son, Philip the Fair, inherited her lands in the Netherlands, and Maximilian retained Flanders, claiming a right to rule as Philip's guardian. The French openly supported Flemish 'particularism' against the Burgundians. Several Flemish cities challenged Maximilian's guardianship of Philip, fearing centralisation of power in the combined Habsburg lands. On 5 June 1483, the Flemish cities formed their own regency council for the young prince and were backed by Louis, spinning another web. This, however, was to unravel, when Louis died on 30 August the same year. His heir, King Charles VIII, was only 13 and his regency council renounced the Parliament of Paris' claim of jurisdiction over the Flemish towns and withdrew its armies in spite of earlier French promises to support them.

By February 1483, Edward was becoming increasingly concerned that like Maximilian, François might give in to French demands. He wrote to François offering 4,000 archers for three months service at his own expense, to be ready at one month's notice. Within weeks, however, Edward was dead.

6

Richard: The King

There is nothing more difficult to take in hand, more perilous to conduct, or more uncertain in its success, than to take the lead in the introduction of a new order of things.

Niccolo Machiavelli

Most descriptions of Richard have been tainted by later Tudor black propaganda. For example, More described him as 'little of stature, ill fetured of limmes, croke backed, his left shoulder much higher than his right, hard favoured of visage … he came into the worlde with the feete forwarde … and also not untothed.' Vergil writes along the same lines saying, 'He was lyttle of stature, deformyd of body, thone showlder being higher than thother, a short and sowre cowntenance, which semyd to savor of mischief and utter evydently craft and deceyt.'

As we now know, there was no 'croke back' and no withered arm. To the medieval mind, physical deformity and illness were seen as divine retribution for sin and showed an evil mind. Belief in the Chain of Being meant that monarchy was ordained by God and inherent in the very structure of the universe. Rebellion was a sin not only against the state, but against heaven itself. Conversely, the King has a moral responsibility to God and his people. In return for his absolute power, he is expected to rule his subjects with love, wisdom, and justice. To do otherwise was to abandon those natural qualities that made a noble fit to rule in the first place. Misusing regal authority was seen as a perversion of divine order. It is therefore possible that the descriptions either in words or art should not be taken as literal, in a time where literacy levels were low they were to convey his character. Although Richard's right shoulder had been slightly higher than his left, it was probably not visible under his voluminous gowns or armour. It has already been noted that the scoliosis would have probably only been visible after his death when his body was taken back to Leicester.

The three surviving paintings of Richard have not helped. One of the oldest, in the Royal Collection, was probably painted sometime during the years around 1515–20, but probably based on an older, now lost portrait. Richard is dressed in a gown of black velvet, lined and trimmed with spotted lynx fur. Round his neck is a large and elaborate gold collar studded with diamonds, rubies and pearls, whilst on his hat, is a brooch in the form of a Greek cross. He is shown as playing with the ring on the little finger of his right hand. The significance of the ring is uncertain, but may be a symbol of authority, or a symbol of marriage. However, X-rays have revealed that soon after it was completed, it was subtly changed. It has been suggested that the artist may have thinned the lips and turned the corners of the sitter's mouth downwards to make the facial expression seem more menacing, whilst his right shoulder was made a little higher.

Another early portrait, and copy dated to around the same time, is in the collection of the Society of Antiquaries of London. The arch-topped painting shows Richard dressed very similar to another portrait of his brother, Edward IV, which had been painted on a panel from the same tree, felled around 1510. It shows a long sharp-featured face with light brown hair and grey-blue eyes. There is a slight unevenness to Richard's shoulders, but unlike the Royal Collection portrait, the shoulders do not seem to have been altered. Restoration work undertaken in 2007 revealed that the central horizontal line of the mouth was moved to a slightly higher position in order to make the jaw look more tightly set. Who painted the original is unknown, although the inscription on the frame, 'Richard Rex tertius', is in a humanist script typical of the Flemish painters, and his hands are delicately rendered in the style of the Flemish painter, Rogier van der Weyden, who also painted Charles the Bold. Based on her DNA work, Dr Turi King, a geneticist at the University of Leicester, has suggested that this portrait is most like his actual appearance.

A third portrait now known as the *Richard III with the Broken Sword* painting, which dates from 1520–1550, portrays all the negative traits from the writings of More, Vergil etc. with a prodigious humpback, and a shortened left arm that sprung unnaturally from the left shoulder. At some point before 1787, as Richard's reputation began to be rehabilitated, radical alterations were made to correct these abnormalities. The shoulder line was altered so that it receded into the background and there was an attempt to reduce the severity of the hunchback and 'withered' hand.

In 2012, the Richard III Society commissioned a reconstruction of Richard's head and face based on his skull. The face was reconstructed from detailed scans of the skull by Caroline Wilkinson, professor of craniofacial identification at Dundee University, who has worked on many modern forensic cases. She did the initial work blind, without any knowledge of who it was. The skin colour and texture, eyes and hair were then added by Janice Aitken, of the University's art college, using the portraits for the final details. Whilst the reconstruction, now on display at the King Richard III Visitor Centre at Leicester, is undoubtedly the closest we are going to get to looking into his actual face, it is not a photographic reconstruction. We do not know if he looked thinner or fatter, the size of his ears, how many wrinkles he had, if he had bags under his eyes, or whether he smiled or habitually wore a frown.

In his *Historic Doubts on the Life and Reign of King Richard III*, Horace Walpole wrote that: 'the old Countess of Desmond [Katherine FitzGerald] who had danced with Richard declared that he was the handsomest man in the room except for his brother Edward, and was very well made.' However, this would have made her at least 135 years old at the time of her death. Nicholas von Poppelau, who visited England in 1484 and was entertained by Richard on several occasions, said: 'King Richard is … a high-born prince, three fingers taller than I, but a bit slimmer and not as thickset as I am, and much more lightly built; he has quite slender arms and thighs, and also a great heart.' George Buck's *The History of King Richard the Third*, quoted a speech by Archibald Whitelaw, the Archdeacon of Lothian, who came to Richard's court with an embassy from James III of Scotland in 1484, as saying 'Never has so much spirit or greater virtue reigned in such a small body.'

Despite this, ridiculous claims such as the one by Richard's contemporary John Rous saying that 'Richard was born after two years of pregnancy, with teeth and hair to his shoulders, and as an adult he was small of stature, with unequal shoulders, the right higher than the left,' heavily influenced Shakespeare and remains in the minds of some today.

An analysis of carbon and nitrogen isotopes from Richard's ribs show that his diet had changed dramatically around this time. No longer campaigning on the borders and in Scotland, his diet changed to high-status food that included pork, wildfowl and freshwater fish. A substantial change in oxygen isotopes shows that he also began to drink more wine. All this was in keeping with his new role as King. A soil sample from the pelvic area of his remains suggests that Richard also suffered from roundworm in his later years. This could have been contracted whilst he was on campaign, where personal hygiene would have been far from ideal, but could have equally come from crops where human faeces was used as fertiliser, or from the hands of his cooks.

On Edward's death, the crown passed to his 12-year-old son Edward. At the time, the new King was in the Welsh Marches at Ludlow, under the care of his uncle, Anthony Woodville, Lord Rivers, and his half-brother, Sir Richard Grey. In 1473, Anthony Woodville had been appointed as governor to the three-year-old Edward V. John Alcock, Bishop of Worcester, was President of his Council and teacher. There he had a substantial household befitting his status as Prince of Wales with Thomas Vaughan, who was over 70 years old, as his Chamberlain and Treasurer.

The Woodvilles' had long since taken control of the King and country. A hostile Mancini wrote that the Queen: 'attracted to her party many strangers and introduced them to court so that they alone should manage the private and public business of the crown, surround the King, and have bands of retainers, give or sell offices, and finally rule the very King himself.'

In February 1483, King Edward issued ordinances for his son's household at Ludlow. They were to be overseen:

> by the said Bishop [John Alcock, Bishop of Worcester], lord Richard [Sir Richard Grey, the Queen's younger son from her first marriage], and Earle Rivieres his Governo[ur], and Sir Thomas Vaghaun to occupy as Chamberleine, Sir will[ia]m Stanley, as Steward of household Sir Richard Croft as Tresorer and Richard Hant as Countroler and also they to bee of my said Sonnes Counceil.

The ordinances gave instructions on everything from meal times to his education. It also made provision for a physician or surgeon 'sufficient & cunnynge' to be continually in the household. Edward clearly intended that they should keep a tight leash on his son. Another states that he could not 'Give, write or send commands without the advice of the Bishop of Winchester, Lord Richard [Grey] and Earl Rivers', another, that he was to be always accompanied by two people.

The following month Rivers wrote to Andrew Dymmock, his attorney, saying he had agreed that his nephew Dorset would take over Anthony's position as deputy constable of the Tower, and that Anthony and his sureties would be discharged from the bond they had entered into with the constable of the Tower, John, Lord Dudley. He also added 'Send me by some sure man the patent of mine authority about the lord prince, and also a patent that the king gave me touching power to raise people if need be in the march of Wales.' What this meant can only be guessed at.

It took four days for the news of his father's death to reach the new king. Back in London, according to *The Croyland Chronicle*, 'farsighted members of the council thought that the uncles and brothers on the mother's side should be absolutely forbidden to have control of the person of the young man until he came of age.' Lord William Hastings, the old King's close friend was in fear of his life and that the Woodvilles 'would sharply avenge the alleged injuries done to them by that lord.' He threatened to withdraw to Calais unless the King's escort was limited. Hastings and the Dowager Queen's elder son, Thomas Grey, the Marquis of Dorset, contested for mistresses and the King's favour and were both the object of court gossip. It was, however, Anthony Woodville and Hastings' quarrel over the Captaincy of Calais that caused all the difficulties. Rivers wanted the position, but Edward IV awarded it instead to Hastings. In August 1482, Hastings had expelled Rivers' ally Robert Ratcliffe's servants from Calais. In an attempt to limit any disturbance, the Dowager Queen Elizabeth wrote to the new King that he should not bring more than 2,000 men to London with him. Hastings then sent word of Edward's death to Richard, who was on his estates in the North, urging him to come with a well-armed retinue. Richard wrote to the Dowager Queen, promising 'submission, fealty and all that was due from him to his lord and King Edward V.' Then according to *The Croyland Chronicle*, at York Minster a tearful Richard held a Requiem Mass for his brother and the city swore an oath of allegiance to the new King with Richard 'setting them an example by swearing the first of all.'

On 24 April, Anthony Woodville and the new king left Ludlow for London. Their party also included Sir Richard Grey, Sir Thomas Vaughan and 2,000 men probably raised by Rivers by the patent given by King Edward to 'raise people if need be in the march of Wales'. The whereabouts of William Stanley, the Steward of the Princes' household at this time, are unknown. Around the same time, Richard left York with 600 'gentlemen of the north'. It was planned that the two groups were to meet at Northampton. According to Mancini, around 27 April, the new King's council in London set the coronation for 4 May, only a week later. The Woodvilles, who were travelling down Watling Street from Wales, stopped 17 miles from Northampton at Stony Stratford,

RICHARD: THE KING

close to their powerbase and home at Grafton Regis. Then Rivers and possibly Grey rode to Northampton to meet Richard on 29 April. At some point, Richard was joined at Northampton by Henry Stafford, Duke of Buckingham, and 300 men. Stafford was a descendant of Edward III through Thomas of Woodstock, his youngest son. His father had died of the plague in 1458, and his grandfather was killed at the Battle of Northampton in 1460 where the five-year-old Henry was also knighted by Henry VI. His mother was another Margaret Beaufort, daughter of Edmund Beaufort, 2nd Duke of Somerset and a cousin of the other Margaret Beaufort who was the mother of Henry Tudor. In 1465, aged 11, he was created duke and the following year he was married to Katherine Woodville, Elizabeth Woodville's sister, which according to Mancini, he highly resented. On reaching his majority in 1474, he was made a Knight of the Garter, and in 1478 was the high steward at the trial of George, Duke of Clarence, but seems to have played no other part in the government, possibly because of his strong Lancastrian connections.

According to *The Croyland Chronicle*, at Northampton, Rivers was 'greeted with a particularly cheerful and merry face and, sitting at the Duke's table for dinner, they passed the time in pleasant conversation.' However, the next morning Rivers was arrested by armed retainers. The heavily outnumbered Richard and Buckingham moved to Stony Stratford, dismissed Edward's household and arrested Vaughan, Richard Haute (another Woodville relative and the controller of the household at Ludlow), along with Grey (if he had not already been arrested), and sent all four to Pontefract Castle. Mancini claims that the Woodvilles were planning to assassinate Richard by preparing ambushes 'both in the capital and on the road, which had been revealed to him by their accomplices'. He continued that 'it was common knowledge that they had attempted to deprive him of the office of Regent conferred on him by his brother'. According to *The Croyland Chronicle*, Richard asserted that 'his only care was for the protection of his own person, as he knew for certain that there were men in attendance upon the king who had conspired against his own honour and his very existence.'

On hearing the news of her family's arrest, the Queen tried to persuade other lords to oppose Richard. According to Mancini:

> The queen and the marquess, who held the royal treasure, began collecting an army, to defend themselves and to set free the young king from the clutches of the dukes. But when they had exhorted certain nobles who had come to the city, and

The eldest of the two Princes, Edward V. Stained glass window in St. Laurence's Church, Ludlow. (Author)

others, to take up arms, they perceived that men's minds were not only irresolute but also hostile to themselves. Some even said openly that it was more just and profitable that the youthful sovereign should be with his paternal uncle than with his maternal uncles and uterine brothers.

On 31 April the Queen and her younger son Richard Duke of York, along with Thomas Grey, the Marquis of Dorset, her son from her first marriage and her brother Lionel, Bishop of Salisbury, sought sanctuary at Westminster Abbey. It is thought that they stayed in College Hall, the abbot's dining hall, and in order to get her furniture, chests and other items in, her servants broke down the Abbey walls.

At the time, Marshal of France, Philippe de Crèvecoeur, Seigneur d'Esquerdes, known to the English as Lord Cordes, had taken advantage of Edward IV's death to raid English ships on the grounds that he had been unable to get restitution for ships and goods seized from him by the English. He had long advocated capturing Calais from the English and had said he would gladly live seven years in hell to achieve this end. Mancini noted that, 'in the face of threatening hostilities, a council, held in the absence of the Duke of Gloucester, had appointed Edward Woodville' to deal with the French threat and given 2,000 men with another 1,000 given to the Marquis of Dorset to keep the sea. On April 30, he took to sea with his fleet of 20 ships, seizing £10,250 in English gold coins from a vessel possibly moored at Southampton, claiming that it was forfeit to the Crown. The amount of coin was substantial, equating to more than 15 percent of the total royal revenue. Where it came from and where it was going is unknown, but it could have been funds for Henry Tudor or more likely pensions from the French, being not dissimilar to Edward's and Hastings' pensions combined. Mancini recorded that on the day before Elizabeth Woodville and her family went into sanctuary, 'it was commonly believed that the late King's treasure, which had taken such years and such pains to gather, was divided between the queen, the marquess, and Edward.' This is echoed by More who wrote 'the lord marquess had entered into the Tower of London, and thence taken out the King's treasure, and sent men to the sea.' However, this is unlikely as Edward IV's cash reserves had been almost totally exhausted by the Scottish campaign.

The new King must have been brought back to Northampton, for on 2 May, a letter written from town and signed by him asked the Archbishop of Canterbury to see to the safekeeping of the Great Seal, the royal treasure and the Tower of London. The next day Richard, King Edward V and their entourage set out for London, spending the night at St. Albans.

On 4 May, the day of the proposed coronation, the new king, Richard, Buckingham and their men all dressed in mourning attire arrived in London via Barnet. The Mayor and aldermen dressed in scarlet, with 500 citizens dressed in violet, welcomed the royal party at Hornsey Park. Dominic Mancini, who wrote one of the few eyewitness accounts of events, noted that:

> … ahead of the procession they sent four wagons loaded with weapons bearing the devices of the queen's brothers and sons, besides criers to make generally

known throughout the crowded places by whatsoever way they passed, that these arms had been collected by the duke's enemies and stored at convenient spots outside the capital, so as to attack and slay the Duke of Gloucester coming from the country.

However, Mancini continues:

… many knew these charges to be false, because the arms in question had been placed there long before the late king's death … when war was being waged against the Scots.

His source for this explanation was not revealed.

Prince Edward was escorted to the Bishop of London's palace. Richard summoned the magnates and citizens to swear fealty to Edward, which according to the Croyland Chronicler, was done 'with the greatest pleasure and delight'.

At a council meeting on 10 May Richard, now aged 31, was officially appointed Protector and the coronation was postponed until 22 June. At the same meeting, Richard asked that those arrested at Northampton and Stony Stratford should be declared traitors, but the request was refused. John Russell, Bishop of Lincoln, replaced Archbishop Rotherham as Chancellor of England. At the same time, Buckingham was made Chief Justice and Chamberlain of both North and South Wales for life, and Constable and Steward of all the castles and lordships of Wales.

Richard had not forgotten the potential threat posed by Edward Woodville. On 9 May he put William Berkeley in charge of the Isle of Wight and ordered Edward Woodville's castle at Portchester to be delivered to William Ovedale. At the council meeting the next day he ordered Sir Thomas Fulford and John Halewell to sea with all haste 'to go to the Downs among Sir Edward and his company'. He sent letters to officials in Calais about the restitution of ships and goods between England and France, and then on 14 May gave orders for Edward Brampton, John Welles and Thomas Greyson 'to go to the sea with ships to take Edward Wodevile.' William Berkeley, William Ovedale and Roger Kelsdale were authorised to receive all those prepared to make their peace with Richard with the exceptions of Edward Woodville, Dorset and Robert Ratcliffe as well as responsible for victualling ships. According to Mancini, the Genoese captains of two of Woodville's ships, fearing reprisals against their countrymen in England if they disobeyed Richard's orders, encouraged the English soldiers on board to drink heavily, then bound the befuddled men with ropes and chains. With the

Contemporary image of a soldier carrying a glaive. From *Chroniques Sire Jehan Froissart*. Bibliothèque Nationale, Paris, 2644. (Matthew Ryan)

Englishmen immobilised, the Genoese announced their intent to return to England. All but two of the ships, *The Trinity* and *The Falcon*, those under the command of Edward Woodville himself, followed suit. Edward Woodville and his two ships managed to escape and fled to Brittany, where he joined the exiled Henry Tudor. There, he received a pension of 100 livres a month from Duke François of Brittany.

It was around this time that Thomas, the Marquis of Dorset, had possibly escaped from sanctuary at Westminster. Mancini reported that when Richard learned he had escaped, 'supposing that he was hiding in the adjacent neighbourhood, he surrounded with troops and dogs the already grown crops and the cultivated and woody places, and sought for him, after the manner of huntsmen, by a very close encirclement, but he was never found.' He may have joined Edward at sea, but it is also possible he remained closer to home, as we next hear of him in Yorkshire during Buckingham's rebellion.

Around 15 May Prince Edward was moved to the Tower, but this was not as sinister as it sounds, as at this time it was another Royal Palace and the traditional place kings stayed before their coronation. It looked as if Edward's coronation was going according to plan.

However, everything changed. Richard must have become aware of plots against him, for on 10 June, a letter was sent to the City of York, despatched by his trusted servant Sir Richard Ratcliffe, asking for as many men as they could gather to assist against the Queen, who intended to murder him. Ratcliffe came from a gentry family in the Lake District and was one of Richard's trustees in the lordship of Richmond and the steward of Barnard Castle. He had been knighted at Tewkesbury and created a knight banneret during the siege of Berwick. York replied soon after that it would send 200 horsemen defensibly arrayed under Thomas Wrangwysh and that they would meet with Northumberland en route at Pontefract.

Three days later, whilst most of the Council met at Westminster to complete the arrangements for Edward V's coronation, Richard, Buckingham, Lord Hastings, Lord Stanley and his new wife Margaret Beaufort, Bishop Morton and Bishop Rotherham gathered at the Tower for unstated business. According to Thomas More, Richard left the meeting, but quickly returned with armed guards crying 'treason, treason'. A scuffle broke out as guards entered the room, Stanley is recorded as being wounded in the face and according to More 'shrunk at the stroke and fell under the table, or else his head had been cleft to the teeth: for as shortly as he shrank, yet ran the blood about his ears.' However, out of all the contemporary accounts, it is only More that mentions Stanley as being present, and the anonymous author of the *Historical notes of a London Citizen* adds Oliver King, Edward IV's secretary (but only that he was arrested at the same time). William Lord Hastings was immediately arrested, dragged outside and beheaded in the Tower grounds with a log used as a makeshift block.

Thomas More claimed that William Catesby had gone to Richard and that his 'account of the Lord Hastings's words and discourse, which he so represented to him, as if he had wished and contrived his death.' Polydore Vergil wrote that even before Richard arrived in London, Lord Hastings 'called together unto Paul's church such friends as he knew to be right careful for the life, dignity, and estate of Prince Edward, and conferred with them what best was to be done.' Grafton wrote that 'Lord Stanley sent to him [Hastings] a trusty and secret messenger at midnight in all the haste, requiring him to rise and ride away with him.'

Catesby was the son of Sir William Catesby of Ashby St. Ledgers, Northamptonshire, and Philippa, daughter and heiress of Sir William Bishopston. His father was sheriff of Northamptonshire in 1442–3 and 1451–2, and sometime before May 1453, was made an Esquire of the Body to Henry VI. His son was trained for the law in the Inner Temple and we first hear of him as 'W. Catysby, lectorem', discoursing on the nature of the Magna Carta. As an aspiring lawyer, Catesby initially progressed in the service of Hastings but acted for many others too. He married Margaret, daughter of William La Zouche, 6th Baron Zouche of Harringworth, and the couple would go on to have three sons. Catesby's mother-in-law, Zouche's second wife, was Elizabeth St. John, the maternal half-sister of Margaret Beaufort and a close friend of the Woodvilles. She was godmother to the new King Edward and entered sanctuary with the Dowager Queen. After Zouche's death, Elizabeth St. John married John Scrope, 5th Baron Scrope of Bolton, who was a prominent northern Yorkist and took part in Richard's expedition to Scotland. Scrope was also father-in-law to another of Richard's key councillors, Richard Ratcliffe. Upon the death of his father, Catesby inherited a large number of estates in the Midlands. These included Welton, Harlestone and Heyford, Watford, Creaton, Hinton, Braunston, Ashby, Stanford, Stormsworth, and Yelvertoft, Hellidon and Hinton all in Northamptonshire. He was also land-agent for many others. It is probable that William Catesby junior sat as Knight of the Shire for Northamptonshire in Edward IV's last Parliament and where his uncle, John Catesby of Whiston in Northants, was knighted. He had already come to Richard's attention before 14 May 1483 when he was granted for life the office of Chancellor of the Earldom of March. Following Hastings' execution, Catesby was made Chancellor of the Exchequer, Chamberlain of the Receipts and Constable of the Castle and Master Forester of Rockingham, as well as being named steward of certain Crown lands in Northamptonshire. All were offices previously held by Hastings. Richard then made Catesby an esquire of the Body and a full member of his Council.

According to Grafton, immediately after the execution Richard gathered the aldermen of London together and provided them with evidence 'that the Lord Hastings and other of his conspiracy had contrived to have

The tomb of William Catesby, Ashby St. Ledgers Church, Northants. Catesby was the only noble to be executed by Henry Tudor after Bosworth. (Author)

suddenly destroyed him and the Duke of Buckingham there the same day in council', which seems to have satisfied them. What that evidence was has not survived. It is far from clear why Richard took this unprecedented and sudden step, especially as Hastings had proved himself a valuable ally to Richard, particularly against the Woodvilles. Whatever it was, it must have been incredibly serious.

Richard's actions have been taken by many as a pre-emptive strike against his enemies and those who blocked his path to the throne. However, that is based on the assumption that it was connected to his taking the throne. What if it was not connected, and instead related to something else? Richard's justification for the execution, whatever it was, was accepted by a council still heavily laden with Woodville and the old king's supporters, so points towards something more than factional politics. Richard had confirmed Hastings as Master of the Mint and the prestigious role of Captain of Calais before 13th June, so was acknowledging his importance. We must therefore look to Europe for possible answers. It cannot be a coincidence that all those in the room (except Margaret) were in receipt of pensions from Louis XI. And, as we have already seen, Louis expected something in return for the pensions he handed out. The only other main recipient of a French pension was John de Mowbray, 4th Duke of Norfolk, but he had died very suddenly a year after Edward's invasion. Then there is the substantial sum of money recovered by Edward Woodville just over a month earlier. The discovery of the money was around the same time Stanley had warned Hastings they should flee together. Was there more evidence that showed Stanley's and Hastings' complicity in something found on the ship?

It is suspicious that Hastings not only received the largest pension, but had refused to sign for it. Commines claims that Hastings told Pierre Clairet, a steward of Louis' household, in a private meeting in London, that 'If it pleases you that I should take it you can put it here in my sleeve, but you'll get neither letter or quittance from me because I don't want people to say of me "The Lord Chamberlain of England was the King of France's pensioner"'. The Count of Castres had also reported Hastings' 'friendly feelings' towards Louis, and soon afterwards Hastings was assuring Louis that he would do everything in his power to be of service and sending him horses and dogs. Thomas More also notes that Hastings was accused by Rivers of something not recorded 'in such wise that he was for a while far fallen into the King's [Edward IV] indignation and stood in great fear of himself.' It may be no more than part of their ongoing feud, but at the same time, it may have been more than mere rumour. Perhaps Edward had heard of his continuing close relationship with France? Another interesting point is that out of all of Hastings' considerable retinue, John Harcourt is the only one known to have joined the rebels in Brittany. If, as suggested in later accounts, Hastings was part of the wider conspiracy, why didn't more of his men join Henry in Brittany?

Stanley was kept a prisoner in the Tower for some time after Hastings' execution, but after Richard was proclaimed King, he released him and reappointed him Steward of the Royal Household. Richard then summoned him and the Countess of Richmond to attend his coronation. Why he

RICHARD: THE KING

The brick-built Kirby Muxloe Castle near Leicester. William, Lord Hastings, probably financed by French gold, began work on the castle in 1480 but after his execution by Richard it was left unfinished. (Author)

was arrested or released has never been explained, especially knowing the continuing hostility between the two, and that Stanley was arrested for a crime that warranted Hastings' execution. It may have been due to the same dilemma that Edward faced when Warwick was killed. Both controlled great swathes of the country and commanded large armies. To take further action would have risked the Stanley forces descending on him, particularly Stanley's eldest son Sir George Stanley, 9th Baron Strange, who commanded a considerable force of his own. Strange was related maternally to both Anne Neville and Richard, and at the same time had strong Woodville connections, as he was married to Jacquetta le Strange, who was one of the Dowager Queen's sisters. The difference between 1471 and 1483 was that then Edward had Richard to fill the void they would leave. At this stage, Richard had no one except perhaps his old friend Lovell who could do the same.

Morton was committed to prison, first to the Tower, then later to Brecknock Castle, near the centre of Brecon, in the custody of the Duke of Buckingham. Rotherham joined him but was freed soon after. Morton, whom Mancini later described as 'a man of great resource and cunning, long trained in party intrigue', had been a confirmed Lancastrian from the beginning. After Towton he fled to Scotland but was captured and imprisoned in the Tower. He was also named in the bill of attainder that followed. However, he escaped and fled to France until 1470, where he lived with the exiled court of Margaret of Anjou at Bar. He then took an active part in the negotiations that led to the coalition of Warwick and Clarence with the Lancastrians and Louis XI and landed with Warwick at Dartmouth, but after Tewkesbury he seems to have been reconciled with Edward. In 1472, he became Master of the Rolls, was sent on a mission to Hungary in 1474, and was one of the negotiators of the Treaty of Picquigny in 1475. In 1479, after several minor ecclesiastical promotions, he was elected Bishop of Ely.

According to More and Vergil, Richard accused Elizabeth Shore, often called Jane, alongside Hastings, and that she was 'of counsel with the lord chamberlein to destroy him.' James Gardiner's nineteenth century book on Richard speculated that Jane was the go-between for the Dowager Queen and Hastings. Although this has since entered the national consciousness, there is no evidence to support it. Jane had probably been the lover of Edward IV, whom he described as the merriest of his concubines, then Dorset, and then at the time of his execution, Hastings. She may have even stayed at his new castle being constructed at Kirby Muxloe. More's account of these events has to be treated with extreme caution, however, as he also stated that Richard accused Jane of sorcery and witchcraft, 'and, as he spoke, he bared his left arm and showed it to the council, shrunk and withered', something that we now know from the examination of his remains could not have been the case. Why was *The Croyland Chronicler* silent on this? It is the sort of scandal he loved to write about.

Jane was, however, punished for immorality. She was called to account for some of Hastings' goods after his death and Dorset was accused of holding 'the unshameful and mischievous woman called Shore's wife in adultery'. Jane's punishment included open penance at Paul's Cross for her promiscuous behaviour by Richard. Not unlike the 'walk of shame' scene from the modern *Game of Thrones*, to atone for her sins Jane was then condemned to walk through the capital on a Sunday with a taper in her hand, while crowds of people watched. She wore nothing but a kirtle, a thin shift of linen meant to be worn only as an undergarment. Other sources say she wore a plain white sheet. This act in itself was not unusual, and a frequent punishment for such so-called crimes.

Richard requested that the Royal Council ask Elizabeth Woodville and her children to leave sanctuary. The council agreed with Buckingham, who argued that since the children had done no wrong they had no need of sanctuary. On 16 June, a delegation from the council, headed by Thomas Bourchier, the Archbishop of Canterbury, went to Westminster and persuaded the Queen to give up her son. Prince Richard then joined his brother in the Tower.

On 8 or 9 June, Robert Stillington, Bishop of Bath and Wells, announced to Richard and some members of the council that prior to his marriage to Elizabeth Woodville, the late King had made a pre-contract of marriage with Dame Eleanor Butler, daughter of the Earl of Shrewsbury. This made the Woodville marriage invalid under certain interpretations of canon law and made the children of the marriage illegitimate. *The Croyland Chronicle* tells us that 'It was set forth, by way of prayer, in an address in a certain roll of parchment, that the sons of King Edward were bastards, on the ground that he had contracted a marriage with one lady Eleanor Boteler, before his marriage to Queen Elizabeth.' In 1478, Stillington spent some weeks in prison, apparently as a result of some association with the disgraced George, Duke of Clarence. It has been suggested that he gave Clarence information about the king's prior association with Lady Butler, and in order to protect their position Clarence was executed at the insistence of the Woodvilles. It is unknown what evidence, if any, Stillington produced to prove his claim, and Eleanor had died in 1468, before the age of 34. However, it seems Richard was more than happy to believe the story.

Another possibility is that the information came from the Catesbys. William Catesby Snr was also a cousin of Eleanor Butler, and the younger William acted as a witness to several documents relating to her, including deeds of gift, and had previously acted extensively on behalf of John Talbot, Eleanor Butler's father. The fact that the younger Catesby was so well connected with the Talbots and many others, suggests the possibility that it was Catesby who was the original source of the information of the pre-contract. Although he was already well placed, after the announcement his rise was meteoric.

A letter to Sir William Stonor from Simon Stallworth notes that it was his thought that 'there shall be 20,000 of my lord protector's and my lord of Buckingham's men in London this week: to what intent I know not but to keep the peace.' The next day, 22 June, according to the *Great Chronicle*, the theologian and half-brother of Edmund Shaa the Lord Mayor of London, Dr Ralph Shaa Canon of St. Paul's, gave a sermon from St. Paul's Cross it was entitled 'Bastard slips shall not take root' alleging that Edward's children were illegitimate and that Richard was the only true heir to the throne. Mancini suggests that it went so far as to question the legitimacy of Edward IV himself, claiming that he had been fathered by an archer named Blaybourne in Rouen. This accusation had been made years before by Warwick and Clarence, but there is no evidence to show that Richard supported this attack on his mother's reputation. Cecily strenuously denied the allegation and the fact that Richard was staying at his mother's house at this time tends to suggest the opposite. It was at this point that the date of Edward V's coronation was indefinitely postponed by Richard.

According to Mancini at this time, 'After Hastings was removed, all the attendants who had waited on the King (i.e. Edward V) were debarred access to him. He and his brother were withdrawn into the inner apartments of the Tower proper ... began to be seen more rarely.' Richard must have been expecting trouble (either that or he was clearing the streets ahead of his coup) because he proclaimed that:

> ... no man, under pain of imprisonment, should take any lodging in the city or suburbs, except by appointment of the king's harbingers; every one was to be in his lodging by ten o'clock at night; and the carrying of glaives, bills, long and short swords and bucklers was prohibited.

Fifteenth century London from a contemporary illustration. (Author's collection)

On the Monday following Dr Shaa's sermon, the Duke of Buckingham addressed the assembled a gathering of Lords Temporal and Spiritual stating that because of the 'illegitimacy', the Crown belonged rightfully to Richard Duke of Gloucester. The next day, he said the same to the magistrates and chief citizens of London at the Guildhall. On Wednesday, June 25, with Richard's troops on the streets of London and all of his opponents barred from the City or from bearing arms, all parties met at Westminster and drew up a petition in which they reviewed the charges relating to the pre-contract and the illegitimacy of Edward's children and implored Richard to take the throne. It is difficult to believe that this was a spontaneous act, and that it came as a surprise to Richard. Their petition was unanimously approved and was formally presented to Richard at Baynard's Castle on the following day, 26 June. It is important to note at this point that although many have described Richard as a usurper, which is defined as 'to take possession of without a legal claim', he was in fact asked to take the crown by the three estates, the lords temporal and spiritual as well as the commons, although it could be argued that if the petition was made under duress then its legal validity is tenuous to say the least. It could therefore be argued that he did not usurp the throne. Richard accepted the crown after showing some reluctance, before riding to Westminster Hall where he took his seat on the white marble King's Bench. He was now King of England.

Around 23 June Anthony Woodville was brought from Sheriff Hutton, whilst Richard Grey, the new king's half-brother was brought from Middleham to join Thomas Vaughan, Edward V's Chamberlain, at Pontefract. On 25 June 1483 the three men were executed at Pontefract Castle. The execution was presided over by the Earl of Northumberland and Sir Richard Ratcliffe, and witnessed by troops making their way toward London. *The Croyland Chronicle* refers to their deaths as 'the second shedding of innocent blood,' and that the men 'were beheaded without any form of trial'. However, John Rous refers to the Earl of Northumberland as their principal judge, which may imply some form of judicial proceeding, no matter how brief.

On 28 June 1483 Richard created the 58-year-old John, Lord Howard, as the Duke of Norfolk. The title had previously been held by Edward IV's second son, Richard of York, after the death of John, the 4th Duke of Norfolk in 1476. However, the title was invalidated by his bastardisation leaving Howard as heir to the Duchy. Richard also made the new duke the Lord High Steward, as well as Earl Marshal, and Lord Admiral of all England, Ireland, and Aquitaine.

Howard was descended from English royalty through both sides of his family. On his father's side from Richard, 1st Earl of Cornwall, the second son of King John, whilst on his mother's side, Howard was descended from Thomas of Brotherton, 1st Earl of Norfolk, the elder son of Edward I of England by his second wife, Margaret of France, and from Edward I's younger brother, Edmund Crouchback. During his youth Howard had been in the household of his cousin, John Mowbray, 3rd Duke of Norfolk, and had been drawn into Norfolk's conflicts with William de la Pole, Duke of Suffolk. It is thought that Howard was with Lord Lisle on the ill-fated expedition to Guyenne, which ended at the Battle of Castillon in 1452. He took part in the Battle of Towton, probably in the 4th Duke of Norfolk's retinue, and was afterwards knighted by King Edward IV. He then became part of the Royal Household as one of the King's carvers. Over the next three years, he took part in the military campaigns against the Lancastrians. By 1467 he was a Knight of the Body, and in September 1468 was appointed Treasurer of the Royal Household. In the same year, he was one of three ambassadors sent to Burgundy to arrange the marriage of the King's sister, Margaret of York, to Charles, Duke of Burgundy. At about this time he was made a member of the King's council, and in 1468 he was among those who escorted Margaret to Burgundy for her wedding.

Sometime before 29 September 1442 Howard married Catherine, the daughter of Sir William Moleyns. They had two sons and four daughters, including Thomas who was born in 1443 and educated at Thetford Grammar School. Thomas took the King's side during the Robin of Redesdale rebellion in 1469, and sought sanctuary at Colchester when Edward fled to Holland in 1470, rejoining the royal forces on Edward's return to England. Soon after he was severely wounded at the Battle of Barnet on 14 April 1471. He was appointed an Esquire of the Body in 1473, and on 14 January 1478 was knighted by Edward IV at the marriage of his son Richard, the four-year-old Duke of York. Surviving Bosworth, he would go on to be 2nd Duke of Norfolk and Earl of Surrey.

Richard Duke of Gloucester began preparing for his own coronation. It was less than a week after his 'reluctant' acceptance of the petition from the three estates. On July 3 1483, Richard and his wife Anne Neville exchanged gifts. She gave him 20 yards of purple velvet adorned with garters and roses. He gave her 24 yards of purple cloth of gold and seven yards of purple velvet. They then spent the night in the Royal Apartments of the Tower of London, where, keeping with tradition, Richard created a number of new Knights of the Bath. The next day, Richard led the procession through the streets of London to Westminster beneath a red green and gold canopy held up by four knights. He wore blue cloth of gold, purple velvet and ermine, his clothes probably designed to conceal the increasing curvature of his spine, and rode a horse caparisoned in purple and gold cloth of gold. Anne followed behind Richard in an open litter draped in white damask and white cloth of gold between two palfreys. She wore a kirtle and mantle made of 27 yards of white cloth of gold trimmed with ermine and miniver along with lace and tassels of white silk and Venetian gold, with a train of crimson velvet. Her hair was down, with a golden circlet set with precious stones and pearls. A canopy of silk cloth was held over her throughout the journey. They were accompanied by Buckingham and Norfolk as well as many other nobles, the City aldermen, squires and yeoman of the Crown. Anne was attended by her servants and 12 noblewomen riding in three, four-wheeled horse-drawn carriages called *chares*.

The next day Richard and Anne made their way to Westminster Abbey. It was the first double Coronation since Edward II and Isabella on 25 February 1308. Traditionally, John Howard, Duke of Norfolk, as Earl Marshal and High Steward of England, should have overseen the Coronation. However, the role was given to Henry Stafford, Duke of Buckingham. Richard also broke with tradition and recited his Coronation vows in English instead of Latin, so his loyalty and duty to the country could be understood by all.

Entering the Abbey from the great west door, barefooted Richard wore a purple velvet gown, with a bishop at each shoulder, his train carried by the Duke of Buckingham. William FitzAlan, 16th Earl of Arundel and the Wardens of the Cinque Ports held the cloth of estate above the king's head. Henry Percy, Earl of Northumberland followed behind carrying Curtana, the Sword of Mercy. Thomas, Lord Stanley, bore the Lord High Constable's mace. Next came the Earl of Kent and Richard's closest friend Francis, Viscount Lovell, each carrying a pointed Sword of Justice. Richard's brother-in-law, the Duke of Suffolk, held the Sceptre and the King's nephew John de la Pole, Earl of Lincoln, the son of Richard's older sister Elizabeth, bore the Cross and Ball. Thomas Howard, Earl of Surrey, bore the sheathed sword of state held upright before him. Finally came Surrey's father, John Howard, Duke of Norfolk, carefully holding the crown in his hands. Richard's sister Elizabeth, Duchess of Suffolk, walked alone in state followed by a further 20 ladies of the nobility and a host of knights and squires. There was to be no place for his brother Edward's bastardised nephews, the one-time Edward V, to whom he had sworn a sacred oath in York, nor his younger brother, Richard.

Anne followed Richard into the Abbey. The Earl of Huntingdon bore her sceptre, Viscount Lisle the rod and dove, and the Earl of Wiltshire her crown. Over her head was borne a cloth of estate. On one side of her walked the Bishop of Exeter on the other the Bishop of Norwich. She too was barefoot, her hair loose, and she wore a purple velvet surcoat and mantle covered with rings and tassels of gold and a crimson gown trimmed with ermine. Margaret Beaufort bore her train behind her. The King and Queen took their seats of state whilst a number of hymns were sung. One at a time, they ascended to the high altar and prostrated themselves on the red-carpeted and cushioned floor. They were both anointed with holy oil by Thomas Bourchier, Archbishop of Canterbury and once they had been enrobed in cloth of gold, they took their places on two thrones set up on a stage. Anne held a sceptre and rod and a ring was placed on her right hand fourth finger. The Archbishop, assisted by the other bishops, then placed the crowns upon their heads. They were now King and Queen of England.

The banquet took place at four o'clock in Westminster Hall. The Duke of Norfolk entered first, riding a charger covered in cloth of gold to evict the gathered spectators and make room for the feast. A table on the dais was laid for the King and Queen. On the floor of the hall, four further tables were placed, one for the attending bishops, the second for the high-ranking nobility, a third for the barons and the fourth for the invited ladies. In all, over 3,000 people attended. Each filed in, pledging their loyalty to the King and Queen before taking their seat. The King and Queen were served their food on dishes of gold and silver. Lord Audley performed the office of state carver, Thomas Lord Scrope that of cupbearer. Lord Lovell, during the entertainment, stood before the King, 'two esquires lying under the board at the king's feet.' On each side of the Queen stood a countess with a plaisance or napkin for her use. Over the head of each was held a canopy supported by peers and peeresses.

RICHARD: THE KING

As the second course of the feast was being served, the King's Champion, Sir Robert Dymmock, rode into the hall on a destrier draped in red and white silk and wearing a bright white harness. He issued the traditional challenge to any who doubted King Richard's right to rule and the room rang to shouts of 'King Richard!' With no challenge forthcoming, the Champion was served a covered goblet of red wine. Taking a draught, he cast the rest upon the floor, keeping the cup as his reward, and rode from the room. Then the Garter King-at-Arms supported by 18 other heralds advanced before the King and solemnly proclaimed his style and titles. As darkness fell, the hall was lit by wax torches and cressets. It was the signal for the King and Queen to retire to their private apartments in the palace.

The initial response of the government of Brittany to Richard III's accession in June 1483 had been to regard it as an excellent opportunity to get some substantial English aid against France; especially as Edward IV had made such an offer just before his death in April 1483. In instructions given to Dr Thomas Hutton, who was sent to the Duke of Brittany to renew a commercial treaty, which 'by diverse folks of simple disposition' was supposed to have expired at the death of Edward IV, is the following passage:

Reconstruction of a noble's dress in the fifteenth century. (Author)

> Item, He shall seek and understand the mind and disposition of the duke, anenst Sir Edward Wydville and his retinue, practising by all means to him possible, to unsearch and know if there be intended any enterprise out of land, upon any part of this realm, certifying with all diligence all the views and depositions there from time to time.

On 21 July 1483, Richard III left Windsor Castle for a Royal tour of his realm. Richard's troubles were just beginning.

The 'Princes in the Tower'

Whilst a detailed examination of the fate of the Princes is outside the scope of this book, as the most controversial and contentious episode of Richard's short reign, it is worth briefly considering their fate.

Rumours of their death first appear at the time of Buckingham's rebellion in September 1483. *The Croyland Chronicle* noted that whilst Richard was in York:

> ... the two sons of king Edward before-named remained in the Tower of London, in the custody of certain persons appointed for that purpose. In order to deliver them from this captivity, the people of the southern and western parts of the kingdom began to murmur greatly, and to form meetings and confederacies.

He also says that around the same time,

> A rumour arose that King Edward's sons by some unknown manner of violent destruction, had met their fate.

The Cotton MS. Vitellius A XVI (probably the source for Fabyan's later chronicle) published in the *Chronicle of London* also recounted that, '...he also put to deth the ij childer of kyng Edward, for whiche cawse he lost the hertes of the people. And thereupon many Gentilmen entendid his distruccion.' However, late in 1483, Casper Weinrich from the Hanseatic League was reporting that Richard 'had his brother's children killed'. Yet around the same time, Mancini wrote: 'Whether, however, he has been taken by death, and by what manner of death, so far I have not discovered.' The French of course agreed with Weinrich, and Chancellor Guillaume de Rochefort reported in January 1484, that:

> ... without going farther for proofs of what I advance, examine what has lately passed in England. Edward, at his death, left two fair sons, the hopes of the nation; but instead of being suffered to ascend the throne of their ancestors, they have been basely massacred, and their assassin has been rewarded with the crown.

Another French chronicler, Commines, is confused, first saying it was Richard before being crowned, then after. He goes on to say, 'King Richard did not last long, nor did the Duke of Buckingham, who had put the two children to death.' *Holinshed's Chronicles*, written in the second half of the sixteenth century, also claim that the Princes were murdered by Richard. It was these chronicles that were one of the main sources used by William Shakespeare for his play *Richard III*. Henry Tudor, whom you would be expecting to be shouting from the rooftops about their murder to demonise Richard and strengthen his position at a time of opposition to his rule, is strangely silent and only has a vague reference to it, mentioning that Richard shed infant blood in his attainder.

The majority of the other accusations that Richard had murdered them come long after Bosworth. Robert Fabyan's *Chronicles of London* compiled around 30 years after the Princes' disappearance, names Richard as the murderer.

The Great Chronicle of London, written in 1512, and Polydore Vergil in 1516, both name Sir James Tyrell as the murderer but at Richard's request. Tyrell was the eldest son of William Tyrrell of Gipping, Suffolk and fought on the Yorkist side at the Battle of Tewkesbury, where he was knighted by Edward IV. A few months later he entered the service of Richard, who was then Duke of Gloucester. After Richard assumed power, Tyrrell was appointed High Sheriff of Cornwall in 1484. He seems to have played no

Unarmoured Burgundian handgunner. (Illustration by Bruno Mugnai © Helion & Company)
See Colour Plate Commentaries for further information

French longspear. (Illustration by Bruno Mugnai © Helion & Company)
See Colour Plate Commentaries for further information

John de Vere, 13th Earl of Oxford, Standard:

Francis Lovell, 9th Baron Lovell, 6th Baron Holand, later 1st Viscount Lovell, Conjectural Standard.

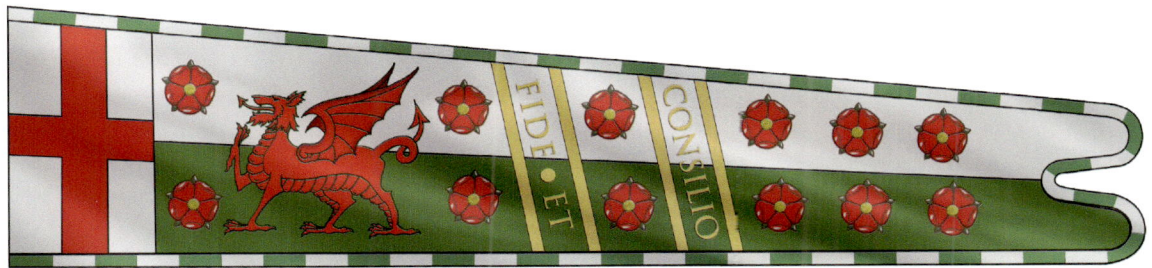

Henry Tudor, King Henry VII, Standard

Thomas Lord Stanley, Standard.

Artwork by Dr Lesley Prince © Helion & Company
See Colour Plate Commentaries for further information

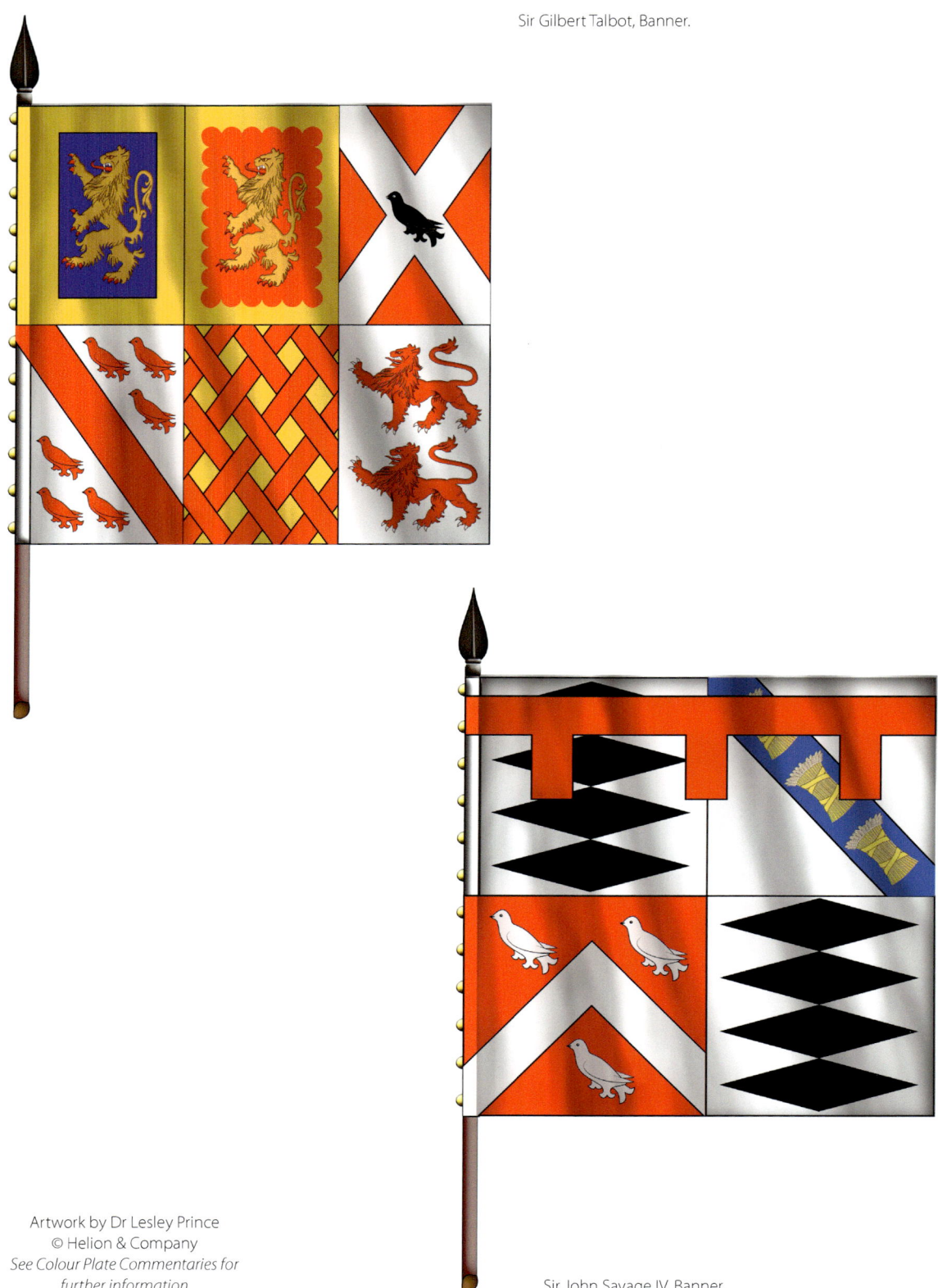

Sir Gilbert Talbot, Banner.

Sir John Savage IV, Banner.

Artwork by Dr Lesley Prince
© Helion & Company
See Colour Plate Commentaries for further information

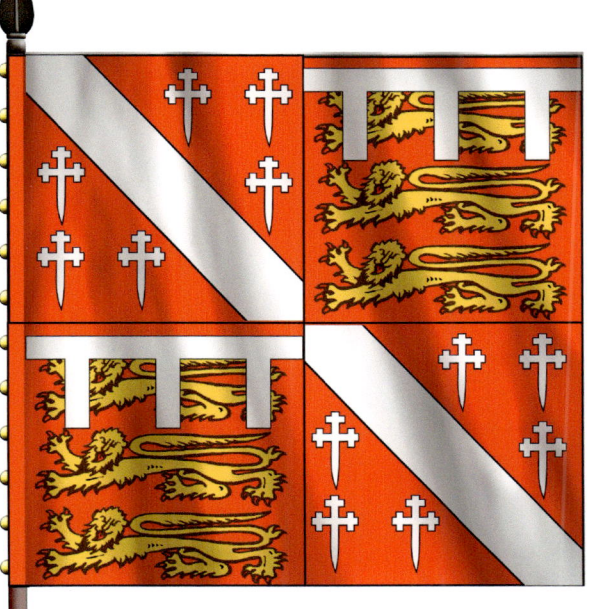

John Howard, 1st Duke of Norfolk Banner.

Rhys ap Thomas, Banner.

Artwork by Dr Lesley Prince
© Helion & Company
See Colour Plate Commentaries for further information

Richard III Royal Banner.

Richard III, Standard.

Artwork by Dr Lesley Prince © Helion & Company
See Colour Plate Commentaries for further information

William Catesby, Banner.

Artwork by Dr Lesley Prince
© Helion & Company
See Colour Plate Commentaries for further information

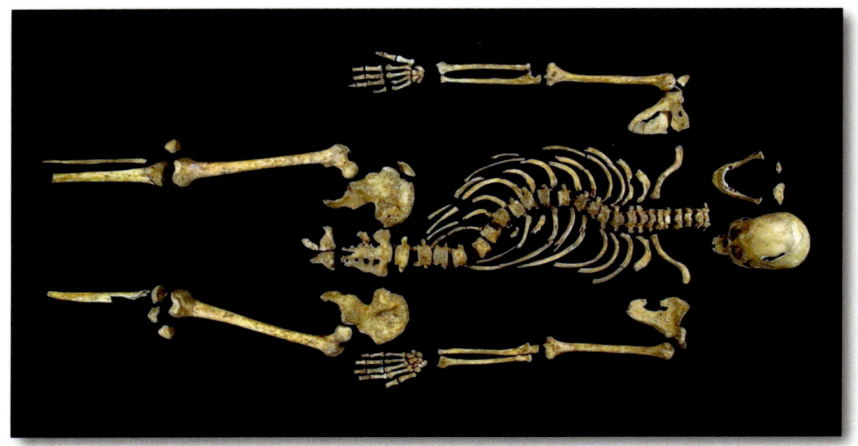

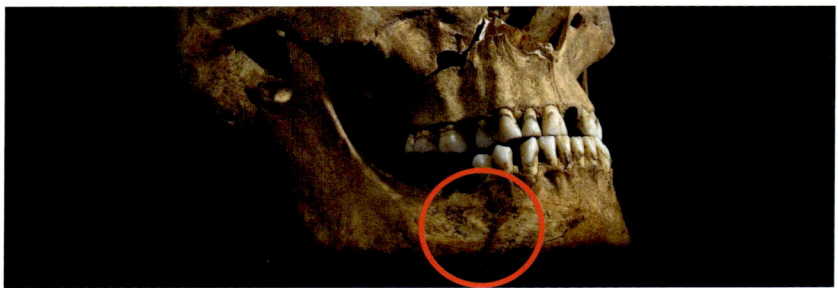

Richard III's skull and skeleton. (Images courtesy of University of Leicester)
See Colour Plate Commentaries for further information

part in the Battle of Bosworth as he was at Calais. It was around this time that Tyrell was given a huge sum of money at Guînes, although there is no surviving explanation as to why. The following year he returned to England and was pardoned by King Henry VII, who reappointed him governor of Guînes. However, in 1501, Tyrrell supported Edmund de la Pole, 3rd Duke of Suffolk, now the leading Yorkist claimant to the English throne, who was in voluntary exile. In the spring of 1501, Henry VII sent Thomas Lovell to Guînes to arrest Tyrrell. Tyrrell was tortured, tried and convicted of treason at the Guildhall in London on 2 May 1502 and executed four days later. He was not allowed to make the customary final speech. There was no mention of the children's murder by him at the time, although there is a reference to Henry VII suggesting blamed Tyrell when speaking to an ambassador, but when this was not well received, he dropped the subject. It was some years later that More wrote in his *History of King Richard III* that during his examination Tyrrell confessed to the murders of King Edward V of England and his brother Richard of Shrewsbury, 1st Duke of York. However, no copy of his confession has survived. *The Great Chronicle of London* says:

> … But howsoever they were put to death, certain it was that before that day they were departed from this world, of which cruel deed Sir James Tyrell was reported to be the doer, but others put that weight upon an old servant of King Richard's named _____.

Its author left the final name blank.

Polydore Vergil also identifies Sir James as the assassin, but an unwilling one, riding 'sorrowfully' into London to do the deed. But then he goes on to say, 'with what kind of death these sely [innocent] children were executed, it is not certainly known.'

However, not everyone blamed Richard. A manuscript in the College of Arms says they 'were put to death in the Tower by the advice of the Duke of Buckingham.' However, 'vyse' could be either 'advyse' – i.e. Buckingham was advising Richard III to do it, or 'devyse', that Buckingham was the prime mover in the decision, possibly without Richard's knowledge. Sir George Buck, in his *History of King Richard III*, published in 1646, on the other hand, says: 'I have read in an old manuscript book it was held for certain that Dr Morton and a certain countess, conspiring the deaths of the sons of King Edward, resolved that these treacheries should be executed by poison and sorcery.' Sadly, that manuscript is now lost.

Others have suggested that at least the elder of the brothers died of illness. Edward IV's ordinances for his son at Ludlow state that a physician or surgeon should always be with the household. This may have been Edward simply caring for his son, but it may also suggest that the Prince was ill and required continual medical attention. Mancini says that 'The Kings doctor John Argentine reported the prince sought remission of his sins by daily confession because he believed death was facing him.' This is often taken to mean that young Edward feared that his uncle was planning to murder him, but could equally mean that he feared the medical condition he was receiving treatment for. When Isabella and Ferdinand of Spain held a formal enquiry into Perkin Warbeck, Portuguese nobleman Rui de Souza stated that the Princes died from forced bleeding. The normally vehemently anti-Richard John Rous wrote in 1490, that after Buckingham's Rebellion, 'many great lords fled from the country, and shortly after the prince died a tragic death.' Rous took every opportunity to denigrate Richard, so if he thought Richard had murdered the Prince, this would have been his opportunity to say so.

There were others that believed at least Richard, the younger prince, survived. Molinet, writing in 1500, mentions Buckingham but is sceptical, believing only one Prince died, whilst the other was held prisoner. Nicholas von Poppelau, a Silesian ambassador to the Holy Roman Emperor Frederick III, wrote in 1484 that 'Many people say, and I agree that they are still alive.' Even Vergil wrote that there was 'Rumour that the boys had migrated secretly to some other country.' Francis Bacon, writing much later in 1621, noted that there were 'Whispers that at least one of the children were living.' Then we have the story of Perkin Warbeck. The majority of Europe appear to have believed he was Richard, Duke of York, the younger of the two princes and that is what he called himself too. It was only Henry who called him Perkin Warbeck.

However, we also have the story of the discovery of the Princes' remains. In 1674, some workmen remodelling the Tower of London dug up a wooden box containing two small human skeletons. The bones were found buried 10 feet under the staircase leading to the chapel of the White Tower. One anonymous report was that they were found with 'pieces of rag and velvet about them.' Four years after their discovery, the bones were placed in an urn and, on the orders of King Charles II, interred in Westminster Abbey, in the wall of the Henry VII Lady Chapel. A monument designed by Christopher Wren marks where the urn lies.

There is a major problem with the discovery. They were buried under the external staircase to the White Tower. That means that whoever buried them had to first dismantle a huge stone staircase, before digging down 10 feet and placing the bodies in the ground, then filling in the hole and rebuilding the staircase. They would have had to do this all in one night, without anyone seeing them. Even if it was possible to carry out this extraordinary feat of engineering in a night, to do it without being spotted in a place with up to 1,000 residents, would have been impossible. The Tower has been inhabited for over 1,000 years and bones that have been identified as Saxon or Roman have been found elsewhere on the site. It is therefore probable that the bones are a complete red herring, and more likely Saxon or Roman.

In 1933, the bones were removed and examined. It was concluded that the bones belonged to two children around the correct ages for the Princes but were not dated. They were found to have been interred carelessly along with chicken and other animal bones. There were also three very rusty nails. One skeleton was larger than the other, but many of the bones were missing. The examination has been criticised, on the grounds that it was conducted under the presumption that the bones were those of the Princes and concentrated only on whether the bones showed evidence of suffocation. No attempt was even made to determine whether the bones were male or female.

We therefore have a number of possibilities as to the fate of the Princes. The chroniclers of the time clearly state that it was only rumour that they had been murdered. Spreading just such a rumour was the perfect way to draw people into Buckingham's rebellion. However, Richard could have countered the rumours by bringing the Prince out of the Tower and showing him to the public. Nevertheless, if they were killed, Buckingham/Moreton and Margaret Beaufort must remain prime suspects as they had much to gain. Also, why didn't Henry VII make use of the knowledge they were dead to denounce Richard as their murderer? But then, some known sources also suggest the possibility that one of the Princes survived. Why didn't Henry use the knowledge of their death to denounce the man he named as Perkin Warbeck, who claimed to be Richard, the younger of the two princes? And why did William Stanley, who was Steward of the elder prince's household in Ludlow, then play a pivotal role in putting Henry VII on the throne, change sides and support Perkin Warbeck only to pay with his life? There are far more questions than answers. However, there are thousands of documents in archives all over England, France and the Hague that have not been investigated. One just might hold the answers.

7

Rebellions

The governments of the present day have to deal not merely with other governments, with emperors, kings and ministers, but also with the secret societies which have everywhere their unscrupulous agents and can at the last moment upset all the governments' plans.

Benjamin Disraeli

Flanders

Prince-Bishop David of Burgundy was the illegitimate son of Philip the Good, Duke of Burgundy and had been made Bishop of Utrecht by his father in an attempt to enforce more centralised Burgundian control over the Netherlands. When opposition to his rule flared up in 1481, he was forced to flee Utrecht and seek support from Maximilian. It was not until 21 April 1483 that David took back control of the city. Just over two weeks later, he was surprised in his old episcopal palace by a daring and stealthy night raid by dissidents and then imprisoned in Amersfoort. When Maximilian of Austria heard this news, he formed a large army under Joost de Lalaing to besiege Utrecht. Archduke Maximilian set up camp before the walls of Utrecht on 23 June and laid siege to the city. A bombardment of the city walls seriously weakened the city's defences and the defenders led by Viscount Jan of Montfoort, Engelbert of Cleves quickly requested a truce. During the negotiations a truce was declared, however, a group of Maximilian's troops broke the truce and the fighting began again with renewed vigour. Both sides suffered severe losses, and eventually, the defenders sued for peace.

England

On 21 July 1483, Richard III left Windsor castle for a Royal tour of his realm. Within days there was a plot to rescue Edward V and his brother, who were still believed to be held in the Tower of London. The plan was to set fire to parts of London as a distraction, then storm the Tower. According to John Stow's *Annales of England*, at its centre was Robert Ruffe, William Davy,

John Smith and Stephen Ireland. The plot was led by John Cheyne, Esquire of the Body and Master of the Bodyguard to Edward IV. He was also the half-cousin of Margaret Beaufort, their mothers being uterine half-sisters. Over 50 conspirators were arrested and they included men who had worked under Cheyne in the royal household. It was also reported that they had been in contact with Henry Tudor, inviting him to invade. However, Cheyney himself managed to escape as not long after, he appears to have been one of the leaders in the Duke of Buckingham's Rebellion in Salisbury.

Richard in the meantime was continuing with his tour. By 8 August he had reached Warwick, where he stayed for a week. It was around this time that another plot was being hatched against him. This time it was centred on John Welles, maternal half-brother of Margaret Beaufort, from the manor of Maxey in Northamptonshire, which he shared with his mother. However, the plot was soon uncovered, and Welles fled the country to join Henry in Brittany.

Soon after Richard received an extraordinary letter from Queen Isabella of Castile delivered by her ambassador Barnard de la Forssa. It began:

> the quene of Castelle was turned in hur hart fro England in tyme past for the unkyndeness the which she toke against the king last decessed, whom God pardon, for his refusing of her and taking to his wiff a wedowe of England; for the which cause also was mortalle werre betwixt him and the erle of Warrewyk, the which toke ever hur part to the tyme of his deth. And therfore she moved for thise cause against hur natur, the which was ever to love and favour England, as he said; she toke the Frenche kinges part, and made liges and confideracions with him.

It continued with a denunciation of the French, and now that Edward was dead, an offer of support. As to the French, she said: 'the Frenche king hath broken four principall articles appointed, concluded, and sealed betwixt him and the king of Castelle and hur.' She then offered Richard 10,000 'speres' (mounted troops) and 30,000 infantry to help him against the French. Richard, however, had more pressing problems.

Richard must have been growing concerned as to who else would turn against him. His intelligence network had probably alerted him to yet another rebellion, as whilst he was at Leicester on 17 August, he ordered '2,000 Welsh bills' from Nicholas Spicer, an usher of the Royal Chamber, 'in all haste to be purveyed and made for us'. He also authorised one of the officers of his household to impress as many smiths as were needed to complete the order. On the same day, he gave instructions for Buckingham to head a commission into treason in Kent, London, Surrey and Sussex. Little did he know Buckingham had already changed allegiance.

Relations with France were tense. Richard wrote to Louis telling him of his brother's death. According to Mancini almost immediately the French 'not only

The York window, St. Mary and All Saints Church, Fotheringhay, Northants. (Author)

made the seas unsafe but even bore off prizes from the English shore'. He also suggests that the originator of these raids was Lord Cordes, Seigneur d'Esquerdes, and that it was he who had 'made the beginning of the war between these two unfriendly nations.' Soon after, John Dynham, Lieutenant of Calais, wrote to d'Esquerdes, requesting the return of two English ships and prisoners taken. He replied:

> … in accordance with what I wrote to you, when our ships, losses, and injuries are restored to me, I shall be ready to remove my hand from all the arrests that I have caused to be made on this account and I will commission some one at Boulogne to have advice and communication with those whom you propose to send thither, in order to consider the means how this restitution of my said ships is to be made, and also the release of the said arrests.

When Louis XI finally replied to Richard's earlier letter on 21 July, it was curt to say the least:

> My lord and cousin, – I have seen the letters that you have written to me by your herald Blanc Sanglier, and thank you for the news of which you have apprised me. And if I can do you any service I will do it with very good will, for I desire to have your friendship. And farewell, my lord and cousin.

Richard wrote back to King Louis on 18 August. However, the letter was not carried by a herald, which was the norm, but a common groom of the stable, which in itself was probably a calculated insult.

> My lord, my cousin, … I understand that you wish to have my amity, of which I am very glad, in good form and manner; for I do not mean to break such truces as have hitherto been concluded between the late king of most noble memory, my brother deceased, and you, for the term of the same. Nevertheless, the merchants of this my kingdom of England, seeing the great occasions given them by your subjects by taking vessels and merchandise and otherwise, doubt greatly to adventure themselves to go to Bordeaux and elsewherein your obeisance, until they may be assured on your part that they may surely and safely exercise the feat of their said merchandise in all the places of your said obeisance according to the right of the said truces. Upon which matter, in order that my said subjects and merchants be not deceived under the shadow of the same, I pray you that by my servant, this bearer, one of the grooms of my stable, you will let me know by writing your full intention, and at the same time if you desire anything that I can do for you, that I may do it with good will.

It was not just French and Breton shipping that was being attacked by the English as at the beginning of August. Richard also received a letter in the name of the young Philip the Fair in Flanders complaining of English attacks on Flemish ships particularly herring fishermen and merchants:

> Most honored lord and cousin, that many complaints and grievances have been made to me by my subjects of this my country and earldom of Flanders of the

seizures daily made at sea by the subjects of your kingdom, wherein several of my said subjects, as well of my towns of Neuport, Ostende, Dunkirk, as others, have been very greatly and excessively wronged and injured, in as much as they have been taken and plundered by those of your realm, who keep always several vessels at sea; and their goods, merchandise, and ships, sold and plundered in that your realm, as goods of enemies. And, what is more, several of my said subjects have been thrown overboard and cruelly put to death. Which acts, being acts of war and of enemies, have already been continued for three months and more, in direct contravention of the treaty of merchandise which exists between your realm and subjects on the one side, and my countries, lordships, and subjects on the other.

It concluded:

> I request you as truly and affectionately as I can… you will stop, and cause to be removed the men-of-war of your said realm being on the sea from further doing any deeds of war against my subjects of my said country of Flanders.

Soon after proclamations were issued in England urging a cessation of hostilities and shortly afterwards Thomas Lye, sergeant-at-arms, was commissioned to make restitution for ships laden with fish taken from them.

Richard's ambassador had returned to England from Brittany around 26 August, for on that day Duke François' envoy to England, Georges de Mainbier, was given his instructions of what to say to Richard a few days later:

> he shall say to the said king that the duke thanks him most affectionately for the good will and affection which he exhibits towards him, of which he has been assured, both by Mr. Thomas Hutton, chaplain and ambassador of the said king, and by master Francis Dupon, the duke's secretary, lately returned towards him; begging him to continue and persevere. And he shall assure the said king that the duke has not less love and affection for him; in which he intends to persevere from good to better.

He was instructed to apologise for not sending ambassadors, but they would be sent later in September after the meeting of the estates. He was then to bring up the matter of English attacks on Breton shipping:

> Likewise he shall say to the said king how the duke has been advertised that a great number of vessels of the said kingdom of England put themselves in warlike array upon the sea, and have threatened to take and plunder the subjects of the duke. Wherefore he shall say to the said king that the duke requests him to prohibit his said subjects and others under heavy penalties from taking or plundering anything from the subjects of the duke, and to make provision that such seizures and robberies cease for the time to come. For the duke on his part wishes and means so to do.

Mainbier was then to bring up the subject of Henry Tudor and France. It very quickly sounded like a veiled threat:

he shall say to the said king, that king Lewis of France, since the decease of the late prince of good memory king Edward last deceased, has several times sent to the duke to pray and request him to deliver to him the lord of Richmond his cousin. And the said king Lewis has made the duke great offers; but the duke has given him no inducement, fearing that, the said king Lewis would thereby create annoyance and injury to some of the friends and well-willers of the duke. In consequence of which the said king Lewis gives great menaces to the duke of making war upon him, and the appearances of it are great. Also he shall represent to the said king the great power of men-of-war, artillery, and finances, which the said king of France has, and the nearness of the said kingdom to the duchy of Britanny [Pont de l'Arche].

And although the said duke should have good and abundant strength of men-of-war and artillery, nevertheless he would not be able long to support the war against such a power as that of the said king; Lewis without the aid and succour of the said king of England and of his other cousins and friends. Whereby of necessity the duke might be compelled to deliver to the said king Lewis the said lord of Richmond, and to do other things to which he would be very loth for the injury which he knows the said king Lewis would or might inflict upon the said king and kingdom of England.

To prevent this happening he was to demand that Richard sent troops to Brittany:

… against the said king Lewis if he commence war against the duke, and send him for part of his succours the number of 4,000 English archers, furnished with good captains and a good chief, and paid for six months at the expense of the said king of England, and to send the same within one month after the duke shall make request for them, as the said late king Edward had promised to do … and also to send to the duke, if he should require it, besides the said number of 4,000 archers, two or three other thousand archers within another month, furnished with good captains, at the pay and expense of the duke.

He was to then remind Richard of the consequences of not helping:

The duke will await the fortune of war, such as it shall please God to send him, rather than deliver into the hand of the said king Lewis the said lord of Richmond, or do anything prejudicial to the said king or kingdom of England.

However, this was little more than rhetoric. What Richard did not know was that Duke François was playing a double game and at the same time as the ambassador was threatening Richard, the Duke (or more likely Landais), was working with Henry who along with his supporters in England, were actively planning the invasion of England. The Bretons may have also had another plan in mind, as Breton chronicles suggest that not only did Landais want to bring about a revolution in England to place Henry Tudor on the throne, but afterwards Henry would marry François' daughter, Anne of Brittany, his only legitimate heir to reach adulthood, thereby securing the Breton succession.

REBELLIONS

Richard reached Pontefract on 27 August. He was joined by his son Prince Edward who had been at Middleham, and from there they travelled to York. The sheriffs met the king at Tadcaster, who then escorted Richard and his family to 'Brekles mills' (apparently not within the city) where they met the mayor and chief citizens. The cavalcade entered York by Micklegate Bar and was entertained by pageants as it passed through the streets. Preparations for his reception had been going on for a month. The wealthier citizens had contributed nearly £450 to buy presents for Richard and the Queen. Richard ordered 13,000 fabric boar badges to be distributed amongst its citizens. An official welcome was extended to the king by the mayor, and he was received by the dignitaries of the Minster at its West Door. Richard took up residence in the Archbishop's Palace, and a week of feasting and entertainment followed as the Vicars Choral Statute Book recounts:

> On the feast of the Nativity of the Blessed Virgin Mary, the King and the Queen both crowned, went in procession to the aforesaid church, the Prince and all other Lords, both spiritual and temporal being in attendance. The Bishop of Durham was the officiating prelate, and the High Altar was ornamented with silver and gilt figures of the 12 Apostles and many other relics given by the Lord King. These remained there until the sixth hour. After Mass they all returned to the Palace, and there before dinner, he [i.e. Edward of Middleham, Richard's nine-year-old son and heir] was created Prince by the Lord King, in the presence of all. And so they sat, crowned, for four hours, there being present the Dean, Robert Both, the Canons, that is Treasurer Portyngton, Archdeacon Potman of York and the Sub-Dean, and four other prebendaries, ten parsons and twelve Vicars with other ministers of the Church.

According to the *Crowland Chronicle*, 'He [i.e. Richard III] presented his only son, Edward, whom, that same day, he had created prince of Wales with the insignia of the golden wand and the wreath; and he arranged splendid and highly expensive feasts and entertainments to attract to himself the affection of many people.' Ten days later Richard gave practical expression of his gratitude to the city. He called the mayor, aldermen and others before him in the chapter house of the minster and promised a substantial reduction of their fee farm.

Much has been made of the fact that Richard planned to set up a 'college of an hundredth priests' in York Minster. A college is very different from a mausoleum where the dead are buried, especially a royal one. At this point, there were two Yorkist mausoleums – Fotheringhay, where Richard's uncle, father, mother and siblings were buried, and St. George's Chapel, where Edward was buried. The Neville College in York was still the largest in the north and the ghosts of the Nevilles were still strong in the city, so this could be seen as finally laying them to rest. Richard was in effect, creating something that would eclipse them, as well as to impress his own name on the city. There are several entries in the Privy Seal Register (Harleian Ms, 433) which probably date from between August 1484 and February 1485 that allude to the college. One of the early entries merely says that 'The Chirche of York hath a graunt for C prestes etc' but subsequent entries fill in some of

RICHARD III AND THE BATTLE OF BOSWORTH

St. William's College, York. The college was founded in 1460 by George Neville and the Earl of Warwick to house 23 priests and a provost. It was the largest college in the north of England. (Author)

the detail and make clear that Letters Patent setting up the college had been issued and that grants of income and property, (probably in the Duchy of Lancaster) had been made to the Minster. The Dean and Canons of York were given permission to collect the rents. Documentary evidence shows that by March 1485 the college was fully endowed. One hundred priests were an unheard of quantity – the wages would have been about £1,000 a year, and the plan required a £25,000 capital investment, about a third of the income of the English crown at the time. The Fabric Rolls of the Minster contain an entry showing that six altars for these priests had been erected, and the chantry priests had begun their daily round of prayers and masses on behalf of their royal founder and his family.

Probably whilst he was in the north, Richard planned a battlefield chapel at Towton. Richard set about exhuming the grave pits to give the bodies a decent Christian burial saying:

> Their bodies were notoriously left on the field ... and in other places nearby, thoroughly outside the ecclesiastical burial place in these hollows. Whereupon we, on account of affection, contriving the burial of these deceased men of this sort, caused the bones of these same men to be exhumed and left for an ecclesiastical burial in these coming months, partly in the parish church of Saxton in the said county of York and in the cemetery of the said place and partly in the chapel of Towton ... and the surroundings of this very place.

On 21 September, Richard left York and headed south, whilst Queen Anne and Prince Edward returned to Middleham. Meanwhile, in southern England, a full-scale rebellion involving the Woodvilles, Edward IV's displaced supporters, and the Tudors, was being planned. What Richard knew of the rebellion is unclear, as a month earlier Richard appointed Buckingham 'his dearest kinsman' as head of a commission of oyer and terminer to enquire into treasons and felonies in London and eight southern counties. However, it would soon set large swathes of southern England against him.

Richard reached Pontefract Castle on 21 September. The following day he probably became aware of another plot as he dismissed Robert Morton, Master of the Rolls and nephew of John Morton, from his office. At the same time, he wrote to the Sheriff of Southampton and no doubt other cities, outlawing retaining and the wearing of liveries. On 23 September, Bishop Lionel Woodville, the Queen's brother, had his 'worldly goods' seized. Richard probably suspected the Duke of Buckingham as well, as both the Crowland chronicler and Vergil say he ordered a close watch on him.

France

Louis XI, King of France died aged 60 on 30 August 1483. His son, Charles VIII, was only 13 years old and not in good health and, although he was regarded as possessing a pleasant disposition by his contemporaries, they considered him foolish and unsuited for the business of the state. The new King was placed in the care of his 22-year-old sister, Anne of Beaujeu, and her 43-year-old husband. Anne was almost 13 when on 3 November 1473 she married the 34-year-old Pierre Beaujeu de Bourbon. Anne was considered extremely intelligent, shrewd and energetic and known as 'Madame la Grande' or just 'Madame'. She was described as standing very erect and straight and as having clear and prominent brown eyes with a very direct gaze. She was dark haired with a high forehead, a widow's peak and finely-arched eyebrows. Like her father, she was described as having a proud nose but wasn't considered attractive. After her marriage, she became a part of her father's court at Plessis-les-Tours and spent much of the next 10 years in his company. It was here that she learned his policies, methods and approach to the governance of the kingdom, something she would continue as effective regent. Her father would describe her 'the least foolish woman in France'.

As soon as Madame took over management of the court, which was more formal than her father's, the expenses of the royal household were greatly increased and continued to go up steeply as long as she was in control. She quickly emerged as the power behind the throne and one of the most powerful women in the late fifteenth century. Although Anne and Pierre had custody of Charles and the loyalty of the civil service, they didn't have the support of the military, which was backed by the nobility.

King Louis did not specifically name a regent, however he left instructions that a royal council be formed that included Charlotte of Savoy, Louis d'Orléans, Duc Jean de Bourbon II and Madame's husband, Pierre. Louis d'Orléans was appointed the president of the royal council and lieutenant-general of the Île-de-France. The 22-year-old Orléans was the great-grandson of King Charles V, the First Prince of the Blood, and the most senior claimant as heir of Charles VIII. Louis XI had been highly distrustful of the close relationship between the Orléanists as they were known and the Burgundians and began to oppose the idea of an Orléanist ever coming to the throne of France. To this end he had compelled Orléans to be married to his disabled and supposedly sterile cousin Joan daughter of his second cousin. By doing so, Louis XI planned to extinguish the Orléans cadet branch of the House of Valois.

One of Madame's first acts was to send the 6,000 Swiss that had been employed by Louis at Pont de l'Arche back home and disband several companies of the army. During his reign, Louis having, on the slightest of suspicions, sentenced a great number of persons to imprisonment or exile. Madame, concerned that the people might be led to believe that she would continue the same principles of government which had been practised in the preceding reign, ordered the prison doors to be thrown open. She also recalled those who had been banished such as Philip of Savoy, and the Prince of Orange was restored to his estates.

England

Richard received news of Louis' death in a despatch from John Dynham in Calais saying:

> … knowe that I sent worde unto the kinges grace by Blanc-Rose of the dethe of the Frenshe king within ij. houres after the thidrnges come to me as I herd, howbeit I was not then in certain, as I am nowe. He died the xxv day of August at after none; on whose soule I pray God have mercy. And what direccion shalbe take therupon his decease with the dolphyn [i.e. the Dauphin, Louis' heir, Charles VIII] and that realme, it is not yit knowen. This I here say, the lord Disquerdes is in the handes of the gret lordes of Fraunce, the due of Orliaunce and other.

The letter continued that the garrison was anxious for a renewal of hostilities with France and asked if safe conducts should be granted to them. He said that Maximilian's capture of Utrecht was thought a so great a victory that even Ghent was awed, and they expected he would invade Picardy to add it to his dominions. According to Lord Dynham, the English looked with joy on his success, and he hoped for the safety of Calais, and that England would cultivate the friendship of such a powerful neighbour. Dynham also suggested that Richard should have a fleet in the channel:

> My Lord it is thought here that the king should have a navie upon the see, to shewe him selffe as a king to rule and kepe his stremes betwixt this and Dover, and that suchefolkes as shalbe sent unto the see may have a stract charge upon their lyves that they nether robbe ne spoille any of the kinges frendes, and namely, of the duke of Austriche contrees and Bretayne. For if they fall ennemys unto us, and no gretter suerte had betwixt the king our soverayn lord and theim, it shall not be good for this towne and marches.

On 10 October Richard III spent the night at Gainsborough Old Hall, home of Sir Thomas Burgh, a knight of the Garter. By the following day Richard had reached Lincoln. It was here that he received the news of what he seems to have suspected for some time; a new rebellion had broken out and the Duke of Buckingham was at its head. However, the truth of the rebellion is difficult to unravel as much is speculation or later Tudor propaganda. For example, Vergil even places it a year later in 1484.

Buckingham had everything going for him. Richard had tried to bribe him to back his regime and he had heaped titles and lands on him, making him one of the wealthiest men in the land, so it is difficult to understand what made him change sides unless he was truly outraged at what he knew Richard had done to take and hold of the Crown, and felt he was unable to trust his erstwhile benefactor. Vergil says that it was because Richard would not grant him lands formerly owned by the Duke of Hereford, but it is hard to believe greed was his only motive. After the 'Hastings' plot, John Morton, Bishop of Ely had been sent to Brecon Castle and into the custody of Buckingham. The silver-tongued Morton was a long-time ally of Margaret Beaufort, who as we have already seen played a significant part in the earlier plots, and it may have been him who turned Buckingham. More says that 'wisedom abused his pride' and Morton fed Buckingham with 'faire wordes and many pleasaunt praises', arousing his 'envy toward ye glory of ye king…' Perhaps whilst in his care Morton did play on Buckingham's vanities and told him all the conspirators wanted to see him on the throne? He did after all have a claim to the crown through Thomas Woodstock, the youngest son of Edward III, and according to More, Buckingham could not abide seeing Richard crowned. Perhaps it was a re-awakened desire for vengeance after the death of his father at the First Battle of St. Albans in 1458 and grandfather at Northampton in 1460? Or even his family ties to the Woodvilles, having married the Dowager Queen's sister, Katherine Woodville, over 18 years earlier. No doubt, the conspirators wanted him onboard as a high-ranking figurehead and for his military strength. Buckingham claimed that he could field 1,000 men and John Rous reported that he had boasted that not since Warwick had so many men worn a single badge. Hall writing 60 years later, suggests that Buckingham may have been involved in the plot even earlier, having met Margaret Beaufort, his second cousin, on the road between Worcester and Bridgnorth. According to this version of events, after she reminded Buckingham that her son had a better claim to the throne, he decided to promote the marriage of Elizabeth and Henry and to stir up a rebellion to place the crown on Henry's head. Whatever his motives, Buckingham was firmly on board by 24 September when he wrote to Henry asking him to return to England as soon as he could to marry Elizabeth, and with her, taking possession of the throne.

Henry Tudor had in fact been making plans for his return since August (see below). To inform her son of events in England Margaret had used Dr Christopher Urswick, her priest, as a messenger between those opposed to Richard and her son in Brittany. Vergil also suggests that 'before the duke all in a rage had begun to be alyenate in mynde (and) after the slaughter of king Edwardes children was known', a separate plot between Elizabeth Wydeville, who was still in sanctuary, and Margaret Beaufort to marry Elizabeth of York to Henry Tudor had been hatched. The Welsh physician, Lewis Caerleon, appears to have been the go-between for Margaret Beaufort and Queen Elizabeth, although what passed between them is no more than speculation. According to Vergil, Queen Elizabeth promised Margaret she 'would do her endeavour to procure all her husband King Edward's friends to take part with Henry her son, so that he might be sworn to take in marriage Elizabeth her daughter.' Vergil also says that Margaret 'apoynted Raynold Bray her servyteur … to be chief dealer in this conspyracy' and he gathered together Giles Dawbeney, Richerd Gylfoord and many more. He adds that Margaret was going to send Christopher Urswick to Henry Tudor, when 'behold she was suddenely advertysid of the same practyse purposyd by the duke of Buckingham' … so she sent Hugh Conwey with a 'good great sum of money'.

The date for the rebellion was set for 18 October 1483 (according to the later Attainder). *The Croyland Chronicle* tells us that:

> … the two sons of king Edward before-named remained in the Tower of London, in the custody of certain persons appointed for that purpose. In order to deliver

them from this captivity, the people of the southern and western parts of the kingdom began to murmur greatly, and to form meetings and confederacies … at last, it was determined by the people in the vicinity of the city of London (and southern counties) to avenge their grievances before stated; upon which, public proclamation was made, that Henry, duke of Buckingham, who at this time was living at Brecknock in Wales, had repented of his former conduct, and would be the chief mover in this attempt, while a rumour was spread that the sons of king Edward before-named had died a violent death, but it was uncertain how.

The Cotton MS. Vitellius A XVI noted that:

In this yere many knyghtes and gentilmen, of Kent and other places, gadred theym togider to have goon toward the Duke of Bokyngham, beyng then at Breknok in the March of Walis, which entended to have subdued kyng Richard; for anoon as the said kyng Richard had put to deth the lord Chamberleyn and other Gentilmen, … he also put to deth the ij childer of kyng Edward, for whiche cawse he lost the hertes of the people. And thereupon many Gentilmen entendid his distruccion.

It was planned that the men from Kent, Essex and Surrey would assemble at Maidstone, Gravesend and Guildford and march on London in a feint, hoping to keep the royal forces busy, whilst others would gather at Newbury and Salisbury. The Bishop of Exeter and his brother, Sir Edward Courtenay, would lead a rebellion in Devon and Cornwall centred on Exeter. Buckingham would lead an army from Brecon and meet with Courtenay and Henry Tudor who would land on the south-west coast with a large army. However, it appears that through either impetuosity, poor coordination or lack of communication, the men of Kent launched their rebellion on the 10th. Not only that, they announced that Buckingham was their leader, drawing attention to his involvement. The Duke of Norfolk, who was in London, wrote to John Paston the same day saying, 'with all diligence, ye make you ready and come hither, and bring with you six tall fellows in harness … (as) the Kentishmen be up in the Weald, and say that they will come and rob the city.' Norfolk immediately sent 100 of his own men to block the Thames crossing at Gravesend, preventing the men of Kent and Essex joining forces, and others to defend the capital. Hall's *Chronicle* notes that 'In Kent, Richard Gyldeforde and other gentlemen collected a great company of soldiers and openly began war.' Richard Guildford, besides being one of the four main organisers of the whole rebellion throughout England, was also the leader of the rising in Maidstone. His father, Sir John was a friend of the second Earl Rivers and is mentioned in his will.

Up to 5,000 men from Kent, Surrey and Sussex rallied their forces, probably on Penenden Heath, before marching through Rochester to Gravesend. There is only one short passage on the Kentish rebels which is found in Stow's *Annales*:

At the same time that the Duke of Buckingham was up in the West Country ther were many up in Kent; to wit Sir George Broune, Sir John Gilford and his sonne,

Foge, Scot and Hauts, after Clifford, Bonting, yeoman of the Crowne, with many other to the number of five thousand. These made a fray at Gravesend in the faire, where Bonting Slewe Master Mowbray with divers others.

The Croyland Chronicle noted that Richard acted 'in no drowsy manner, but with the greatest activity and vigilance.' He immediately wrote to York saying that Buckingham had turned traitor and requested as many mounted troops as they could muster to meet at Leicester on 21 October. On 12 October Richard dictated a letter to his chancellor, Bishop John Russell, saying 'we, by Godds grace entende briefly to avaunce Us towards our rebelle and traytour the Duc of Buckingham to resiste and withstande his maliciouse purpose.' He then asked for the Great Seal to be sent to him at Lincoln, since the Chancellor could not bring it himself on account of his 'infirmities and diseases'. Richard then added in his own hand:

> We would most gladly that ye came yourself if you may, and if ye may not, we pray you not to fail, but to accomplish in all diligence our said commandment, to send our seal incontinent upon the sight hereof, as we trust you, with such as you trust and the officers pertaining to attend with it, praying you to ascertain us of your news. Here, loved be God, is all well and truly determined, and for to resist the malice of him that had best cause to be true, the Duke of Buckingham, the most untrue creature living; whom with God's grace we shall not be long till that we will be in those parts, and subdue his malice. We assure you there was never false traitor better purveyed for, as this bearer, Gloucester, shall show you.

Richard remained at Lincoln for five or six days, making plans to crush the rebellion. Commissions of Array were sent throughout England. Richard's leading nobles, such as Lord Lovell, also summoned their own retinues, all to meet at Leicester. We are told that Lord Stanley's son George, Lord Strange, left Lathom in Lancashire with 10,000 men although his destination and which side he supported, remains unknown. Some of these Commissions would remain unanswered, however, as retainers such as William Stonor (a leading supporter of Lord Lovell), declared their support for the rebels. Edward Plumpton wrote to Sir Robert Plumpton at the time that:

> People in this country be so trobled, in such commandment as they have in the Kyngs name and otherwyse, marvellously, that they know not what to do ... The Duke of Buck: has so mony men, as yt is sayd here, that he is able to goe where he wyll; but I trust he shalbe right withstanded and all his mallice: and els were great pytty.

One of the biggest difficulties now was to know who was a friend and who was a foe.

On 18 October Buckingham unfurled his standard at Brecon Castle and marched on Weobley, the seat of Walter Devereux, Lord Ferrers, gathering men as he went. From here he rapidly marched through the Forest of Dean, to Gloucester, where he intended to cross the Severn and join with the Courtenays, who had raised their standard in the name of Henry Tudor and were marching from the West. However, 10 days of continual rain had caused the Severn to burst its banks, smashing bridges and making fords impassable. Cattle which were intended to provide food for the army, were drowned in their pastures, so the scarcity of supplies compounded his problems. Unable to communicate with, or join, Courtenay, Buckingham was forced to return to Weobley. Many of Buckingham's Welshmen viewed the failure to cross the Severn as an ill omen and despite promises and threats, his army began to melt away. Meanwhile, Sir Thomas Vaughan of Tretower, who had probably been tasked by Richard to watch Buckingham, was advancing on his rear after plundering Brecon Castle. Vaughan's father, Sir Roger, had been killed at Edgcote in 1469 supporting the Yorkist cause. Along with his two brothers and his followers, Vaughan positioned himself near Brecknock Castle, and closely guarded all the roads leading to the interior of Wales. Another of Richard's supporters, Humphrey Stafford, who was possibly a relation of Buckingham's, occupied all the Marches between Wales and England and destroyed the remaining bridges across the Severn. Buckingham fled. We are told that he sought shelter at Lacon in Shropshire with Ralph Bannaster, 'whom he above all men loved, favoured, and trusted'.

As Richard continued his journey south, warships were stationed in the Channel to keep a careful watch for any ships approaching or leaving the country. He arrived at Grantham on 19 October, where he received the Great Seal in the Angel Inn, in the presence of Sir Thomas Stanley and the Earls of Northumberland and Huntingdon. Richard then headed for Leicester, via Melton Mowbray, to meet his gathering army. By this time, the greater part of the South was in open rebellion. During his stay at Leicester, he put forth a proclamation offering 1,000 pounds or 100 pounds a year for life, for the capture of the Duke of Buckingham; 1,000 marks (approximately 660 pounds) for the Marquis of Dorset (who had escaped from sanctuary and possibly gathered an army in Yorkshire), or his uncle Lionel, Bishop of Salisbury, the son and brother of the widowed Queen; and 500 on the arrest of other leading insurgents. The following day a vice-constable was nominated, and invested with extraordinary powers to judge and execute, without delay, any rebels that were captured or delivered into his hands. Richard and his army left Leicester on 23 October and arrived at Coventry the next day. On receiving news that Buckingham and Henry Tudor were to join in the south, he marched towards Salisbury.

Around 29 October, no doubt lured by the huge reward offered by Richard, Bannaster handed Buckingham over to Thomas Mytton, Sheriff of Shropshire. On 1 November, Sir James Tyrell and Giles Wellesbourne escorted him to Salisbury. According to Grafton's *Chronicle*, once in custody Buckingham named many of his co-conspirators and requested an audience with Richard who had just arrived with his army. Richard refused. On 2 November 1483, Henry Stafford, Duke of Buckingham, was summarily executed in the Market Place, Salisbury.

Where he was buried has been subject to considerable debate. Local opinion was divided between St. Thomas's Church near Market Place and St. Peter's at nearby Britford. Both had high-status burials, the former beneath the centre arch, the latter on the north side of the chancel. In 1838 it was reported that a skeleton missing its head and right arm was found by workmen in a shallow grave, eight inches or so under a brick floor during renovations to the Saracen's Head Inn. The inn was located halfway along Blue Boar Row on the north side of the Market Place, and partially covered the old Blue Boar site (now Debenhams in the city centre). It was proudly announced that these were indeed the remains of Buckingham. However, in 1852 a near-contemporary source was published by Camden which put the site of Buckingham's burial beyond dispute. It was the Franciscan's own *Chronicle of the Grey Friars of London* and simply said 'This year the Duke of Buckingham was beheaded at Salisbury, and is buried at the Grey Friars.' The site is now lost but is believed to be close to the junction of Friary Lane and St. Ann Street. Despite this, the story of him being buried under Debenhams persists today.

We do not know how many actually took part in the rebellion. As well as those in Kent, there were 500 recorded indictments in Exeter, suggesting it was on a very large scale. They came from all walks of life and based on the 878 pardons issued afterwards by Richard, there were at least 12 nobles and over 200 clergy.

Brittany

The Bretons thought that death of Louis had put an end to the threat of immediate French military intervention and began to openly support Henry Tudor. Henry, prompted by letters from his mother and others, began to make plans to return to England at the same time as Buckingham's rebellion. After an oath-swearing ceremony in Vannes Cathedral officiated by Arthur Jacques, chaplain to the Duchess of Brittany, Duke François offered his support to Henry for the expedition. According to Vergil, Duke François gave Henry 15 ships and an army of 5,000 Bretons. However, the receiver-generals accounts only record seven ships and just over 500 men. One ship was supplied by Jean Dufou Admiral of Brittany, who was to command the small fleet, another came from Alain de la Motte, Lord of Les Fontaines, the vice-admiral with 60 soldiers. *Le Margarite* from Brest had 98 men, *La Michelle* and *La Marie* from Aurary had 75 and 69 men respectively. *La Tresoriere* and another from St. Malo had 50 and 40 men. Yves Millon, the Breton commissary-general, gave Henry 13,000 livres for wages and supplies as well as a loan of 10,000 *écus d'or*.

The fleet and men assembled at the fishing port of Paimpol on the northern coast. It was around this time that *The Ballad of Ladye Bessyie* suggests that Thomas Stanley sent Humphrey Brereton from Liverpool to 'Beggrames Abbey' in Brittany which was probably the Cistercian abbey of Begard near Paimpol, with letters and more funds. As we have already seen, Brereton may have been the author of the ballad, so this has a ring of truth about it. However, Henry did not leave Brittany until around 31 October, no doubt delayed by the same storms that were hampering Buckingham. Soon after leaving the harbour, fresh storms battered the fleet, forcing them back to Brittany or Normandy for shelter. Some, it appears, had been driven on the coast of Devonshire and Cornwall, and had been seized by the mayors of Dartmouth, Fowey, Plymouth and Penzance. Only two ships reached England as planned, including Henry's. The ships made landfall at Poole then sailed onto Plymouth at the beginning of November where they anchored and planned to meet with the rebel army. Unsure of what success Buckingham might have enjoyed, Henry sent a boat to reconnoitre the coast. A large group of men were waiting for him on the shore, saying they were Buckingham's followers and urged him to land. Henry erred on the side of caution, choosing to wait for more news. He then received word of Buckingham's execution. It had been a trap and the men on the shore were Richard's, so he raised anchor and put to sea again.

On the return journey the two ships were once again buffeted by storms and blown off course towards Normandy. One ship put in at Dieppe, the other at St. Vaast-la-Hogue on the Cotentin Peninsula. Vergil writes that once ashore, Henry:

> sent ambassadors to demand of Charles theight, king of Fraunce, who had succeeded Louis his father lately dead, leave to passe throwghe Normandy. The king pytying ther les fortune, dyd not onely grant him passage with good will, but also money to beare his charges. Howbeyt himself, trusting uppon the kinges courtesy, had sent his ships home before and was enteryd on his journey; yeat he had not gone fur whan thambassadors returnyd, so that greatly comfortyd by that benyfyt and replenished with good hope he returnyd into Brytayne, supposing that from thencefurth he must take another course.'

The Bibliothèque Nationale de France, MS Clairambault 473, suggests that after being met by François Lord of Lau, Henry was escorted to Saint-Sauveur de Redon monastery in Brittany by Henri Charbonnel. According to Alain Bouchard's *Grande Chroniques*, when Madame was told of Henry's accidental landing in France, he was invited to the French court where he was welcomed with honours, before returning overland to Brittany. However, Bouchard may be confusing this event with when Henry later fled into France from Brittany.

England

Without Henry or Buckingham, the rebellion faded away without a pitched battle and little bloodshed. Bodiam castle was still holding out under Sir Thomas Lewkenor on 8 November, for on that date the King issued a commission from Exeter to Richard Leukenore of Bramebilty, William Scote, Esq., and others, 'to summon the men of the counties of Kent and Sussex to besiege the castle of Bodyam, which the rebels have seized.' It fell soon after. In spite of the quick collapse of the rebellion. Many of the rebels quietly slipped out of England to Brittany and to Henry. Morton also escaped retribution, fleeing first to Ely and then taking a ship to Flanders where he continued to plot.

Brittany

According to both Hall and Vergil, when Henry reached Rennes, the capital of the Duchy, he was told of the death of Buckingham. Dorset and a number of other friends that had fled to Brittany in the aftermath of the rebellion had gathered at Vannes and awaited news of Henry's whereabouts. Henry sent a number of his retinue to fetch them. According to Vergil:

> They having knowledge that erle Henry was, after long wandering, returnyd safe into Brytayne, rejoysed woonderusly (for, being ignorant in what part of the world he was become, they fearyd least he had faullen into the handes of king Richard) and so reparyed to him in all hast thick and threefold.

After celebrating Henry's safe return, a council was held to discuss their plans for the future, and it was decided to make another expedition to England.

Fugitives from the failed rebellion continued to flee to Brittany, congregating around Henry at Vannes. How many joined out of fear of retribution if they remained in England, and how many went in genuine support for Henry, will never be known. However, out of the 300 or so defectors, there does seem to be a hardcore of Henry's supporters. There was of course, his Uncle Jasper. Then there was Sir John Risley, Seth Worsely and John Edward all from Thomas Stanley's household and another group connected to Margaret Beaufort including John, Lord Welles, her half-brother who was one of the first to join Henry along with Richard Pigot and John Browne from her household. John Cheyne, Edward IV's standard bearer and master of horse, who led the first rebellion against Richard and Sir Robert Willoughby were closely connected with both Margaret Beaufort and Lord Stanley along with Norfolk knight William Brandon, Edward's master of the bodyguard. All were colleagues and possibly annuitants of John Morton, Bishop of Ely and both Cheyne and Brandon attended Morton at his enthronement as Bishop of Ely in August 1479. The connection between the Brandons and Morton probably stretched back years as a William Brandon had been Master of Balliol College when John Morton was an undergraduate at Oxford. Brandon was also a Mowbray retainer from at least the mid 1450s serving the Duke of Norfolk as his chief councillor for many years, and as such was probably one of the few who knew of his French pension. More directly connected to Morton was his own nephew, Robert Morton, a 'kings servant' who also seems to have been in Brittany. Sir Giles Daubeney had been one of Edward's esquires of the body, but was connected to Reginald Bray, who had been Margaret Beaufort's estate officer for the last 20 years. Daubeney had also brought five yeomen with him. The Woodvilles were represented by the Dowager Queen's son from her first marriage, Dorset, and her brothers Lionel, the Bishop of Salisbury, Edward and Richard. Hastings' retinue was represented by John Harcourt, who had fought for Edward IV at Towton, Barnet and Tewkesbury.

Henry and his closest advisors probably acknowledged that his claim to the throne was weak, particularly as it was through an illegitimate female line. The decision was taken that uniting his claim with that of Edward IV's eldest daughter, Elizabeth of York, would bolster his acceptance as monarch and ensure the continuing loyalty of the Yorkist dissidents. The unification of the houses of York and Lancaster was not a new idea and it appears that John Morton had discussed it with Buckingham during his incarceration, although Henry's mother, Margaret Beaufort, might have proposed it much earlier.

On Christmas Day 1483, according to Vergil:

> first of all erle Henry uppon his othe promysyd, that so soone as he showld be king he wold mary Elyzabeth, king Edwards doughter; than aftir they swore unto him homage as thowghe he had bene already created king, protesting that they wold losse not onely ther landes and possessions, but ther lyves, before ever they wold suffer, beare, or permyt, that Richerds howld rewle over them and theirs.

Vannes Cathedral, Brittany. It was here that Henry Tudor pledged to marry Elizabeth of York. (Author)

Although the Breton chronicle says that this occurred at Vannes cathedral in the presence of the Duchess of Brittany, Vergil says it occurred at St. Pierre Cathedral in Rennes. Henry left the ceremony as a man with a small army that was willing to fight for him, or at least to fight against Richard III. For Henry, it meant that there was no going back.

Most of the men were around Henry's age and they set up their own little court in Vannes. On 22 November, Duke François authorised another loan of 10,000 gold crowns to his 'well-beloved cousin the lord of Richmond'. Deprived of any other income, they were given 2,500 livre tournois for their upkeep by the city burgesses. The canons of the Cathedral loaned them another 200 livres tournois which had still not been repaid 14 years later.

France

Hoping to be named regent, Orléans demanded that the Estates General be called. Two hundred and forty-seven delegates met at Tours on 15 January 1484. It was the first time that representatives of the *Tiers État*, the third estate, or commoners were invited. Madame was not allowed to attend, and she was not allowed to speak to the delegates. It was opened by William de Rochefort, chancellor of France. In his introduction to the assembly, he told them

> …without going farther for proofs of what I advance, examine what has lately passed in England. Edward, at his death, left two fair sons, the hopes of the nation; but instead of being suffered to ascend the throne of their ancestors, they have been basely massacred, and their assassin has been rewarded with the crown. You, Frenchmen, have no such act of atrociousness to blush for: open your annals, you

will there find that infant sovereigns have been more honoured and better served than the most absolute monarchs.

This information almost certainly came from Dominic Mancini's report although he had left England soon after Richard's coronation and whilst both the Princes were believed to be alive.

The parallels with what had happened in England and what was happening in France were uncanny. Like England, they had a boy King. Like the Woodvilles in England, they had a powerful family controlling the King. And, in Orléans, the French had a popular potential leader of the royal council, a position not unlike the Protector in England. However Anne of Beaujeu, who had been informed of what had happened in England by Mancini, was determined not to let Charles slip from her grasp and suffer the same fate as Edward's sons. Given the power struggle between her and Orléans, by claiming that Richard had murdered the boys and using it as cautionary tale for the French, it can also be seen as an attempt to gain popular support and a first strike against Orléans to stop him gaining control of the council. In any event, it is probably this moment that the suggestion that Richard murdered the Princes moved from gossip to 'fact' across Europe. It may also be what Richard was referring to in his December 1484 proclamation, when he said '…ancient enemies of France, by many and sundry ways, conspire and study the means to the subversion of this our realm, and of unity amongst our subjects, as in sending writings by seditious persons with counterfeit tokens, and contrive false inventions, tidings, and rumours.'

However, most of the representatives were more concerned with their own positions and how to curb royal power than the governing of the realm of France. King Louis had brought most of France under his control reducing the power of the nobles. After his death, they expected an immediate return to feudal policies where they had control over their own lands. Through their speaker, John de Masselin, the assembly urged a reduction of the armed forces. The standing army at the time consisted of 2,500 lances, 7,000 or 8,000 infantry, artillery, fortifications, and the royal-camp (presumably Pont de l'Arche). All had proved expensive to maintain. Masselin suggested that they no longer needed mercenaries, that lances should be reduced to 1,200 and that the royal-camp should be closed. In addition, he suggested several garrisons, particularly those in the centre of France, be reduced in numbers. There was no mention of the infantry or artillery.

In his conclusions, William de Rochefort responded to the proposed reduction of the armed forces by saying:

> Who will be able to check the turbulence of ambitious minds, if you take the troops from the king? Who will ensure the execution of the laws? Who will defend the widow and the orphan from violence and oppression? You have paid a just tribute of applause to Charles the Seventh, who first established regular companies; with what propriety then can you censure the king for wishing to keep them? If it were ever your intention to do good to your country, this is certainly the time to show it.

This exchange is critical in the story of Bosworth and the involvement of the French, for although many have suggested that the camp of Pont de l'Arche had been disbanded, it suggests the contrary.

Instead of reducing tax as the assembly hoped, the chancellor then introduced a new levy of 1500,000 livres in equal proportions on all the provinces. He then concluded by saying 'You may now retire, not to deliberate, for you have heard the king's will, but to prepare yourselves for expressing your gratitude in a becoming manner.' The assembly was stunned and soon were up in arms. Only the intervention of the Princes of the Blood prevented any bloodshed. Madame promised that the young king would come to the assembly the next day, however when the next day came, he did not arrive. The bad weather was blamed in preventing him from attending, though the Chancellor and the Princes had all arrived. In his closing speech Masselin remarked:

> Continue, august prince, to regulate your conduct by wholesome advice, but beware of the arts of those perfidious councillors by whom the princes of your blood are surrounded; they will tell you that a king is omnipotent; that he is never mistaken; that his will is law; these are monsters, objects of public execration; exterminate them without delay, or they will not only corrupt your heart, but will infect your court, and the whole body of the nation.

After settling the distribution of the taxes on the different provinces, the estates were dissolved on 14 March. Madame was already proving to be her father's daughter, and unlike Elizabeth Woodville she had successfully faced down those who would take the throne from the child she believed was the rightful heir.

England

In the aftermath of the rebellion, Richard sent orders to all the ports preventing anyone leaving England without his permission. Even Genoese and other Italian merchants, as well as a messenger of the Duke of Milan, were detained at Dover until they received a special letter of passage. In the New Year strict injunctions were sent out forbidding the wearing of any liveries except that of the King. The Cinque Ports were ordered to send out ships to watch the movements of Breton vessels and a strong fleet under Sir Thomas Wentworth was stationed in the Channel to guard the approaches to the English coast. John, Lord Scrope of Bolton, was nominated a captain and governor of the fleet and commissioners were appointed 'to take mariners in the king's name, for the furnishing of the ships, and to do service upon the sea.' These ships were called the *Andrew*, *Michael*, *Bastion*, and *Tyre*, and destined for service in the north. It was one of the earliest instances of seamen being pressed into the King's service.

Not long after we find merchants and others engaged 'to do the king service upon the sea against his enemies of France and Brittany.' A Spanish ship was purchased by the King for the purpose of 'making war upon the

Bretons'. In December, a number of Breton ships were captured including three which were laden with Spanish goods. One Breton ship appears to have been captured about or before the beginning of the new year and was brought into Calais. It was given by the King to Sir Humphrey Talbot, Marshal of Calais. Others were detained at Lowestoft. Four of the Breton prisoners were freed just before Christmas to arrange ransoms for themselves and those who were still incarcerated in England. Two French ships belonging to the Marshal of France were also captured and held at Sandwich with others taken kept in the West Country. In March 1484, a ship called the *Anne* of Topsham was captured by Bretons. Its crew of 52 was taken to Brittany and held for ransom.

Richard clearly suspected there were more rebels hiding in Kent as he issued a proclamation praising the loyalty of the people, many of whom had deserted the rebel leaders. It continued:

> And over this the king woll it be known that if any person harbour, lodge, comfort, succour, or keep within his house, or otherwise aid or resette wittingly any of the said traitors, and disclose them not, nor bring them to the king in all goodly haste possible after this proclamation, that then, he or they so harbouring, aiding, comforting, succouring, resetting, or lodging them or any of them, hereafter to be taken and reputed as the king's rebels and traitors ; and also that no man presume after this proclamation to keep any goods or chattels of the said traitors.

Statue of Richard III, Leicester, with the cathedral behind. (Author)

Soon after, Richard went into Kent himself and was at Canterbury on the 10 January and at Sandwich six days later.

Richard then returned to London for his one and only parliament which opened on 22 January at Westminster. King Richard opened it in person. The Bishop of Lincoln, as Lord Chancellor, made the customary speeches, On the following day, the Commons elected Sir William Catesby, Richard's Chancellor of the Exchequer, since 30 June 1483, as their speaker. Eighteen 'private' statutes which included the attainders against those involved in Buckingham's Rebellion, and 15 'public' statutes, were passed over the following month. The first of the private statutes was the *Titulus Regius* (the Title of the King) which reiterated why Richard and his heirs should be King. It was clear that people had concerns about the legitimacy of the June petition and Richard's election to the crown at a non-parliamentary meeting, and it was thought necessary to restate Richard's claim. It began:

> Where late heretofore, that is to say, before the Consecration, Coronation and Enthronization of our Sovereign Lord the King Richard the Third, a Roll of Parchment, containing in writing certain Articles of the tenor underwritten, on the behalf and in the name of the three Estates of this Realm of England, that is to wit, of the Lords Spiritual and Temporal, and of the Commons, by many and diverse Lords Spiritual and Temporal, and other Nobles and notable persons of the Commons in great multitude, was presented and actually delivered unto our said Sovereign Lord the King, to the intent and effect expressed at large in the same Roll; to the which Roll, and to the Considerations and instant Petition comprised in the same, our said Sovereign Lord, for the public weal and tranquility of this Land, benignly assented … And here also we consider, how the said pretensed marriage, between the above named King Edward and Elizabeth Grey, was made of great presumption, without the knowing or assent of the Lords of this Land, and also by sorcery and witchcraft, committed by the said Elizabeth and her mother, Jacquetta, Duchess of Bedford, as the common opinion of the people and the public voice, and fame is through all this Land; and hereafter.

The statute also suggests there was more evidence to be disclosed at a later date, when it said, 'if and as the case shall require, it shall be proved sufficiently in time and place convenient.'

It then continues:

> And here also we consider how that the said pretensed marriage was made privately and secretly, with edition of banns, in a private chamber, a profane place, and not openly in the face of the church, after the laws of God's church, but contrary thereunto, and the laudable custom of the Church of England. And how also, that at the time of the contract of the same pretensed marriage, and before and long time after, the said King Edward was and stood married and troth plight to one Dame Eleanor Butler, daughter of the old Earl of Shrewsbury, with whom the said King Edward had made a pre-contract of matrimony, long time before he made the said pretensed marriage with the said Elizabeth Grey in manner and form aforesaid. Which premises being true, as in very truth they been true, it appears and follows evidently, that the said King Edward during his life, and the said Elizabeth, lived together sinfully and damnably in adultery, against the law of God and his Church; and therefore no marvel that the sovereign Lord and head of this Land, being of such ungodly disposition, and provoking the ire and indignation of our Lord God, such heinous mischiefs and inconveniences, as is above remembered, were used and committed in the Realm amongst the subjects. Also it appears evidently and follows that all the issue and children of the said King, been (being) bastards, and unable to inherit or to claim anything by inheritance, by the law and custom of England.

One of the first acts of Henry VII's Parliament in November 1485 was to repeal Richard's *Titulus Regius* and orders were passed down to have it deleted from the Statute Book. As stated in the rolls of Henry's first Parliament, 'So that all things said and remembered in the said Bill and Act thereof may be for ever out of remembrance and also forgot.'

All copies were to be destroyed unread under pain of punishment. The intent was to wipe out the stain of illegitimacy on Henry's prospective wife, Elizabeth of York. Her legitimacy as an heir of Edward IV served to strengthen Henry's claim to the throne.

Although *The Croyland Chronicle* summarised the contents of the *Titulus Regius*, it was William Camden in the seventeenth century who discovered a lone copy of the long-buried Act of Settlement which had escaped Henry's purge, amongst private Acts filed away in the Tower. Cartographer John Speed printed more details from the *Titulus* in his book, *History of Great Britain* in 1611, and Sir George Buck used it as a source document for his better-known work, *The History of the life and reigne of Richard the Third*, written circa 1619.

After this, Parliament considered a series of attainders against those who took part in Buckingham's Rebellion, including Henry and his uncle Jasper Tudor. The first attainder was against a total of 92 men across the south of England. The second act was just for the clergy involved, John Morton, Lionel Woodville, Bishop of Salisbury and Peter Courtenay, Bishop of Exeter. '… for their greate and haynous Offences … have deserved to lose Lyfe, Land, and Goodes.' However, they were to be spared 'rigorouse punysshement.' The third was reserved for Margaret Beaufort. She was described as 'Countesse of Richmond, Mother to the Kyngs greate Rebell and Traytour. Henry Erle of Richemond' and was accused of having 'of late conspired, confederated, and committed treason' against the King, by 'sendyng messages, writyngs, and tokens to the said Henry, desiryng procurying and stirryng hym by the same, to come into this roialme and make Were ayenst oure said Soveraigne Lorde', and had also raised 'great sums of money' to be employed for the same purpose. Despite her obvious guilt, Richard was extremely lenient. He spared her the normal penalty of execution by burning and instead seized all her lands and gave them to her husband, Stanley, who could hold them for his lifetime after which they would revert to the Crown. Stanley was also ordered to keep his wife under strict control; to remove all her servants who had taken messages between Brecon, London and Brittany and prevent her from having further contact with her son and his supporters. Why Richard took this surprising decision that effectively let Margaret continue with her plotting and scheming whilst giving Stanley more power, has never been satisfactorily explained. It may have been due to the power vacuum it would have created. Stanley was one of the wealthiest men in England, controlled a huge number of estates and commanded a vast army of men. To execute Margaret at this stage would have only invited another rebellion, and whilst he was focused on Brittany and France, it was a risk he could not afford to take.

The second statute put an end to benevolences, the practice created by Edward IV that allowed for extra-Parliamentary taxation by 'requesting' gifts of money from wealthy subjects. The statute simply and plainly states: 'The subjects of this realm shall not be charged with any benevolences.' Parliament also enacted laws to curb corruption in the cloth trade and included anti-alien legislation that was popular throughout this period and was considered positive for English merchants.

Other statutes sought to drive out corruption and fraud from land transfers and are considered vital developments in English land law. Jurors were required to be men of substance, holding freehold land worth 20s or more or copyhold land valued at 26s 8d or more. This sought to ensure that jurors were men less prone to bribery or bullying, thus offering fairer trials. Richard also extended the rules of bail to apply to those not yet indicted. Before this, a suspect could be deprived of their goods and property including the tools of their trade, even before a judge had tried them. What is more, even if they were found to be innocent, there was no requirement to return the confiscated goods.

The remainder of the acts were related to the economy, including a series of statutes that sought to address the problem being faced by English merchants against what was seen as unfair foreign economic competition, and one that required Italian merchants to import 10 good bow staves with every butt of malmsey. A notable exemption from the anti-alien trade restrictions was the now well-established printing trade. Books arriving in England from Europe were not placed under the same restrictions as other goods. Richard's final act was the 'resumption of all grants, and estates of land etc made to Elizabeth Grey late Queen of England.' Parliament was then dissolved on 20 February.

According to *The Croyland Chronicle*, before the end of February Richard gathered almost all the lords spiritual and temporal as well as the knights and gentlemen of the King's household including the new Duke of Norfolk. Each 'subscribed his name to a kind of new oath, drawn up by some persons to me unknown, of adherence to Edward, the king's only son, as their supreme lord, in case anything should happen to his father.' It is also probably around this time that Richard arranged the marriage of his illegitimate daughter, Katherine, to William Herbert, Earl of Huntingdon and son of William, the 1st Earl of Pembroke who had been executed at Northampton by Warwick after the Battle of Edgcote.

On 1 March, in the presence of the Lords, the mayor and aldermen of London, Richard promised that he would protect Elizabeth Woodville and her five daughters if they would come out of sanctuary and place themselves in his care. He also promised that they would be treated honourably as his own kin and they would not be arrested. Richard agreed that Elizabeth could retire to the country and receive a 700 marks annuity, whilst her daughters would be married to men gentlemen born and each be given a dowry of 200 marks in land. It seems that the Woodvilles emerged from sanctuary soon after. Local legend suggests that Elizabeth and her daughters went to stay with Richard's Master of Horse, Sir James Tyrell, at Gipping Hall near Stowmarket. This was a significant moment and begs a number of questions, including, if Elizabeth was guilty of conspiring against Richard why did he let her off, and why if she was guilty, did she agree to come out? Furthermore, if Richard had murdered her sons, how could she trust his words and entrust her daughters to him, even after they had been declared bastards? Again, perhaps Richard showed her proof that at least one of the brothers were still alive or that someone else murdered them. Perhaps it was another of

Margaret Beaufort's plots that had implicated her, and Richard had proof to the contrary? Vergil writes:

> …that forgetting hir faith and promyse geaven to Margaret, Henry's mother, she first delyvered hir dowghters into the hands of king Richerd; than aftir by secret messengers advysyd the marquyse her soon, who was at Parys, to forsake erle Henry, and with all speede convenyent to returne into England, wher he showld be sure to be caulyd of the king unto highe promotion.

On the other hand it could be said that their coming out of sanctuary was proof that they were terrified of the consequences if they did not come out.

The next day, Richard created the College of Arms at Coldharbour on Upper Thames Street and in letters patent granted them £20 per year and 'perpetual succession and a common seal'. Here the heralds could for the first time store their heraldic record. Then, on 10 March he wrote to all his bishops telling of his plan to 'see virtue and cleanness of living to be advanced, increased and multiplied' and that he 'wished vices and all other things repugnant to virtue, provoking the high indignation and fearful displeasure of God to be repressed and annulled.'

Despite the *Titulus Regius*, the people of London were still unsure about Richard's claim to the throne as evidenced in the recent rebellions, as at the beginning of April 1484, he summoned the leading members of the London Livery Companies to Westminster to hear the 'King's title and right', starting with his descent from Henry II.

In another ceremony soon after, Richard gathered the nobles to swear allegiance to his son. *The Crowland Chronicle* notes that:

> By special command of the king there were gathered together in a certain downstairs room near the corridor which leads to the queen's quarters, almost all the lords spiritual and temporal and the leading knights and gentlemen of the king's household, the chief amongst whom seemed to be John Howard, whom the king had recently created Duke of Norfolk. Each person subscribed his name to a certain new oath, drawn up by persons unknown to me, undertaking to adhere to the king's only son, Edward, as their supreme lord, should anything happen to his father.

Scotland

In July 1483 the Scottish parliament attainted Richard's long-time friend the Duke of Albany. Before he left Scotland, he delivered Dunbar castle into the hands of the English. It was immediately besieged by the Scots. The following month, James III wrote to Richard proposing a cessation of hostilities. He offered to conclude an eight-month truce, or if Richard preferred, to send ambassadors with a view to a more permanent settlement. Richard at once agreed to the latter and offered to send a safe conduct for any ambassadors that the King of Scots should name. James accordingly named 11 persons for whom a safe-conduct was granted in November. However, no such embassy was actually sent, and the King of Scotland continued to besiege Dunbar.

The siege was still ongoing the following February when Richard began planning another invasion of Scotland. In a letter to Pope Sixtus IV, Richard wrote of 'this most serious war which we are waging with the very cruel and fierce people of the Scots.' On 18 February 1484, he sent orders to Sir John Mordaunt of Turvey, Bedfordshire and William Salisbury to be ready to serve in an expedition against Scotland by 1 May:

> Trusty and well-beloved, we greet you well. And, forasmuch as by the advice of the lords spiritual and temporal of this our land, late assembled at our palace of Westminster, we be fully determined, by God's grace, to address us in person with host royal toward the parties of our enemies and rebels of Scotland, at the beginning of this next summer, to subdue and do them all annoyance possible, both by sea and land, in saving as well this our land from such inconveniences (as else were like to ensue), as the honour of us and our blood, and true liege men, inhabited and inherited within this our land. We, having certain and perfect trust of your good will, aid, and assistance to this our great voyage, and knowing how useful and necessary your presence shall be to us in the same, will and desire you right effectually, and nathless charge you in the straitest wise that, incontinent upon the sight of this our writing, ye dispose you to serve us personally in the said voyage, accompanied and apparelled for the war, according to your degree.

In March another safe-conduct was granted for two ambassadors from Scotland, but it does not appear that they or any others came. On 13 March, the French renewed the *auld alliance* with Scotland and attacks on English shipping began again. The London merchants believed that a full-on war with France was likely that summer.

8

Preparations

There is no avoiding war; it can only be postponed to the advantage of others.
Niccolo Machiavelli

Brittany

By this time Duke François was seriously ill, and after an accident was described as being 'feeble in body and still more feeble in mind, so much so that his speech was scarcely intelligible'. According to contemporary accounts, Treasurer Pierre Landais was now running Brittany, and kept François shut up in his room, allowing none to have access to him but those about his person.

Smarting from his defeat, Orléans, aided by his sister the Abbess of Fontevrault, smuggled a messenger into Brittany. His instructions were to say that the Duke had more faith in the aid, support and favour of Duke François than in those of any other prince, and more importantly, that Orléans would immediately divorce his wife if he might secure the hand of the Breton heiress.

Early in the new year, a fresh invasion of England was being planned by Henry. After Henry promised he would repay any costs incurred, he was given a small fleet of six ships from Morlaix, St. Pol de Jean and Brest, including those of the Admiral of Brittany and the Lord of Auray with 890 men. According to the Breton receiver-general, the ships were fitted out in March and early April and payments were made for men and provisions showing that the plans were at an advanced stage. However, Henry's plans were to be overtaken by a dramatic turn of events in Brittany.

England

Richard seems to have received intelligence of Henry's new invasion plan, whilst the ships were being fitted out in Brittany. This does suggest that he had a spy in either the Breton or Henry's camp as the plans would have been carried out in relative secrecy. To prepare, Richard ordered that 20 new guns and two serpentines were to be purchased from Southampton merchants.

Richard's armourer, Vincent Tetulior, ordered 164 sets of harness from Breton and Genoese merchants at five marks each, with more purchased from Antwerp for the Tower.

As Richard did not know where Henry and his army would land he ordered a watch along the coastline and signal lamps to be built, especially in Wales. Vergil noted that Richard:

> … least he might be found altogether unready, he commandyd noble men and gentlemen dwellynge about the sea coste, and chiefly the Walshe men, to kepe watche by course after ther country maner, to thintent that his adversaryes showld not have ready recovery of the shore and coome a land; for thinhabytantes about the sea costes place, in the time of warre espcyally on the hylls adjoyning lampes fastenyd upon frames of timber, and whan any great or notable matter happeneth, by reason of all places, thapproche of enemyes, they suddanely lyght the lampes, and with showtes through towne and fielde geave notice therof; from thence others aftirward receave and utter unto ther neighbors notice after the same sort. Thus ys the fame therof caryed spedyly to all villages and townes, and both country and towne arme themselves agaynst thenemy.

The Croyland chronicler commented that 'The king was better prepared to oppose them in the present year than at any time afterwards, both by reason of the treasure which he had in hand … as well as particular grants which had been made and distributed throughout the kingdom.'

Richard and Anne then set out for Nottingham probably via Cambridge, Huntingdon, Stamford and Grantham. As before and after, this was possibly to be ready to counter any threat from any direction. Whilst at Cambridge University Richard wrote to the French king asking him to give free passage to Thomas Langton, Bishop of St. David's, to conclude a truce, then after finishing his negotiations in France, he was commissioned to go on to Rome to present the Pope Richard's compliments.

Brittany

On 5 April, a delegation from France arrived in Brittany led by the Bishop of Périgueux and the lords of Torcy and Argentan. Rather than a serious attempt at diplomacy, it seems their plan was to subvert Landais. They assured him that the French would give all the necessary aid to preserve the integrity of Brittany. However, following a previous request, they refused to pay a grant for 200 lances or surrender the three castles on the frontier which they said would lay Normandy open to invasion. They did, however, offer intelligence on current Spanish negotiations. They also offered intelligence on England as Richard's envoy Dr Thomas Langton was to stop in Paris as discussed above. Intriguingly they said, 'he would bring English news', and that it would be passed on to the Bretons. So, does this mean that Langton was a French spy or part of the Tudor conspiracy?

On 5 April Landais rival, Guillaume Chauvin, the deposed Chancellor of Brittany, died in prison. Two days later, a group of Breton nobles led by

Jean de Chalon, Prince of Orange, Jean de Rieux, the Marshal of Brittany, and the Vicomte de Rohan attempted to arrest or assassinate Landais in the ducal palace at Nantes, almost certainly encouraged and financed by the French ambassadors. De Rohan already had close connections with the French as he had previously been arrested by Landais for the murder of an equerry but had escaped from prison and sought sanctuary in France. It may be little more than coincidence but the fact that de Rieux had earlier held Henry Tudor and Rohan held Jasper raises some interesting possibilities. The conspirators, accompanied by a group of *seigneurs*, as well as friends and relatives of Chauvin and Rohan, entered the palace with weapons hidden under their cloaks. They quickly seized the gates and began searching for Landais. However, he was not there, and was in fact, at his house La Pabotière, a few miles away on the banks of the Loire. One guard managed to escape and sound the alarm. Soon the whole town was charging the castle. The attackers panicked and fired on the crowd, killing some of them before fleeing themselves to Rieux's stronghold of Ancenis on the Angevin border. The ringleaders then escaped into France.

On Easter Day, 18 April, Louis of Orléans, the Duke of Alençon and the Count of Dunois arrived in Nantes seeking support from Landais against the Beaujeu. Orléans also sent a request to the Pope to annul his marriage, so that he would be free to marry Anne of Brittany, Duke François' heir. Orléans had not been in Brittany long when Madame summonsed him back to Paris for the coronation of the new king. Sources suggest that around this time Orléans and Dunois also sought support from both Archduke Maximilian and Richard III in England. However, later, during Landais' interrogation after his arrest, he claimed that Orléans and Dunois were opposed to the idea of bringing English soldiers to Brittany. He continued that once Orléans had returned to France, he had decided that it would be useful to bring them to discourage any Breton lords from joining the dissidents. One immediate consequence of this sudden *volte-face* was that Landais could no longer openly support Henry and his allies. Therefore the plans for a new invasion of England were brought to an abrupt halt.

England

Richard had not been in Nottingham long when tragedy struck. He received the news that his only son, Prince Edward, had died at Middleham Castle. All the contemporary accounts tell of Richard's grief. The author of *The Croyland Chronicle* recounted that:

> In the following month of April, on a day not very far distant from the anniversary of king Edward, this only son of his, in whom all the hopes of the royal succession, fortified with so many oaths, were centred, was seized with an illness of but short duration, and died at Middleham Castle, in the year of our Lord, 1484, being the first of the reign of the said king Richard. On hearing the news of this, at Nottingham, where they were then residing, you might have seen his father and mother in a state almost bordering on madness, by reason of their sudden grief.

RICHARD III AND THE BATTLE OF BOSWORTH

The Church of St. Mary and St. Alkelda, Middleham. It was made a collegiate church in 1477 by Richard whilst he was Duke of Gloucester and may be the final resting place for his son, Edward. (Author)

There has been a lot of speculation concerning the whereabouts of Prince Edward's remains, as no surviving record exists of his burial place. York Minster, Jervaulx Abbey in East Witton, Coverham Abbey in Coverdale, and the Church of St. Helen and Holy Cross in Sheriff Hutton, have all been suggested as Edward's final resting place. However, the most likely candidate is Richard's Collegiate Church of St. Mary and St. Alkelda in Middleham itself.

Richard was now without a legitimate heir. Contemporary historian John Rous recorded that Richard declared his 10-year-old nephew Edward, Earl of Warwick, son of his brother George as his heir, although there is no other evidence to support this. George had been attainted and declared 'corrupted of blood', meaning that his son was disinherited and disbarred from claiming the throne. Rous also says that John de la Pole, 1st Earl of Lincoln, was given preference. He was clearly a potential threat as immediately after Bosworth Henry sent men to Sheriff Hutton and had the young earl brought back to London where he was held in the Tower.

On 27 April Richard left Nottingham for York, where he possibly held the funeral for his son. It was around this time that Richard reintroduced the mounted courier system last used during his brother's invasion of Scotland. With a station at 20 mile (32 km) intervals, news could travel 100 miles (160 km) per day. In May, Richard received intelligence that Sir Edward Woodville was preparing to attack either Dover or Sandwich and sent Lord Cobham to the coast to counter the threat. Receiving more invasion threats, he then spent the summer in his northern power base, first at Middleham, then at Pontefract, York and Durham. Early in May Richard was at Middleham when he received Nicholas von Poppelau, a Silesian ambassador of the Holy Roman Emperor, Frederick III. Von Poppelau was impressed by the court's splendour (in particular its music) and by Richard's generous and courteous behaviour. In his diary, he described Richard as 'a high-born prince, three fingers taller than I, but a bit slimmer and not as thickset as I am, and much more lightly built; he has quite slender arms and thighs, and also a great heart.' There was no mention of any deformity. The King dined with von Poppelau on eight occasions and conversation ranged widely but included the Hungarian victory over the Ottoman Turks at the Battle of Una the previous autumn. Ironically, Richard responded by saying, 'I would like my kingdom and land to lie where the land and kingdom of the King of Hungary lies, on the Turkish frontier itself. Then I would certainly, with my own people alone, without the help of other kings, princes or lords, properly drive not only the Turks, but all my enemies and opponents.' Within 18 months he would not be expelling a Great Muslim empire from Europe, but falling to a Welsh chancer with a weak claim to the throne in his own backyard.

As to the English people in general, von Poppelau noted that the cooking was poor and the women impudent, that they surpassed the Hungarians in brutality, the Poles in ostentation and pilfering, and the Italians in deceit!

On 8 June Richard, whilst at Pontefract, agreed to a truce between Brittany and England to last until 24 April 1485. One week later, a proclamation was sent to the sheriffs of the southern counties, telling them to publicly announce the dates of the truce, no doubt to try to stop the sea war that had been going on between the two sides.

Several English ships and their captains including Sir Thomas Everingham and John Nesfield were captured off the English coast near Scarborough Castle by the French. In June and July 1484 Richard personally directed naval operations from Scarborough against both the Scots and French. There was also trouble on the Scottish border and Richard was forced to despatch an expeditionary force to deal with it. On 24 July, Richard left Yorkshire but not before he re-established the Council of the North, first created by Edward in 1472. He made his nephew, the Earl of Lincoln, President, and Sandal Castle its base of operations. His other nephew, the Earl of Warwick, also seems to have had some involvement. It was laid down that it was to sit at least once a quarter in York to hear bills of complaint. Almost immediately it was called upon to deal with an enclosure riot in York and to deal with a forger of coin.

France

Support for Louis d'Orléans was growing. As well as Alençon and Dunois, the Duke of Lorraine had offered his support to Brittany against their rebellious subjects and to overthrow Madame, whilst the Count of Angouléme had withdrawn his forces from Normandy.

Charles VIII's coronation took place at Reims on 30 May 1484 and was followed by entertainments and fêtes. A few weeks later, the new King made his formal entry into Paris where more festivities took place. The dashing Orléans and the new king became close friends and according to some, Charles made no secret of his preference and implored Orléans to free him from his sister. Therefore, a plan was hatched for three of Charles' chamberlains to carry him off. However, word of the plot reached the ears of Madame. She burst into the Royal apartments, and in front of the King charged the chamberlains with treason. After warning him of the consequences of his actions, she placed the Duke of Orléans under house arrest at Gien. Then, as Paris was a centre of Orléanist influence, she moved the court to Montargis in the Loire Valley which is around 68 miles (110 km) south of Paris. It was the beginning of War of the Public Weal, or the 'Mad War' (the term was coined by Paul Emile in his *L'histoire des faits, gestes et conquestes des roys… de France…*, published in 1581).

After fleeing Brittany, the Prince of Orange, Peter de Villeblanche, and John le Bouteiller, lord of Maupertuis, travelled to Montargis, where they met Madame. There they promised and swore, that after the death of François they would acknowledge Charles as their lawful sovereign, and would devote their lives and fortunes to the advancement of his authority, on the following conditions.

1. That after the annexation of Brittany to the crown of France, justice should be administered in that province in the same manner as before, and by the magistrates of the country.
2. That the nobles, ecclesiastics and others, should have their privileges and franchises confirmed.
3. That the Duke's daughter should be married, with the advice of the estates, according to their rank. Madame then took the Breton nobles under French protection and immediately sent an order to Duke François, as a French vassal, to abstain from all further violence against them, and to repair the damages which they had already sustained.

The medieval St. Pauls in London. (Author's collection)

England

On 11 August Richard issued a stern proclamation prohibiting piracy against all nations, except, significantly, the French. Two days later, ships and troops set out to defend Calais against what was considered an imminent attack. Richard's problems were continuing at home. William Colyngbourne, a sergeant of the pantry under Edward IV and a tenant of Margaret Beaufort, posted a verse on the door of St. Paul's, it read:

The Ratte, the Cat, and Lovell our dogge,
Rule all England under the Hogge.

The satirical verse poked fun at Richard and his chief advisors, Richard Ratcliffe, William Catesby and Lord Lovell. Colyngbourne was caught and arraigned on 18 July 1484. Richard may have suspected that he was involved in a plot as in a letter of 3 June 1484 he asked his mother Cecily Neville, Duchess of York, that 'my lord Chamberlain … be your officer in Wiltshire in such as Colyngbourne had.' It emerged during the commission of enquiry held on 29 November that he had met with John Turberville, a relation of John Morton, around 3 July in the Portsoken ward of London although which year, either 1483 or 1484, remains a considerable contention, but may be connected to Henry's abortive invasion attempt in March 1484, or Buckingham's rebellion the previous year. According to his indictment he:

> among others offered a certain Thomas Yate eight shillings to go over into Brittany to the Earl of Richmond and his adherents, Dorset, Cheyney, and others, and To declare unto them that they should do very well to return into England with all such power as they might get before the feast of St. Luke the Evangelist next ensuing [18 October]; for so they might receive all the revenues of the realm due at the feast of St. Michael [29 September] next before the said feast of St. Luke. And that if the said Earl of Richmond with his part-takers, following the counsel of the said Colyngbourne, would arrive at the haven of Poole in Dorsetshire, he the said Colyngbourne and other his associates would cause the people to rise in arms and to levy war against King Richard, taking part with the said earl and his friends, so that all things should be at their commandments. Moreover, to move the said earl to send the said John Cheyney unto the French king to advertise him that his ambassadors sent into England should be dallied with, only to drive off the time till the winter season were past, and that then in the beginning of summer King Richard meant to make war into France, invading that realm with all puissance; and so by this means to persuade the French king to aid the Earl of Richmond and his part-takers in their quarrel against King Richard.

He was given a show trial at the Guildhall in London by two dukes, seven noblemen including Thomas Stanley, and five justices. He was executed soon after. The method was one reserved specifically for traitors; hanging, disembowelling and quartering. According to Robert Fabyan's chronicle he was first hung, then:

> cut down, being alive, and his bowels ripped out of his belly and cast into the fire there by him, and lived till the butcher put his hand into the bulk of his body, insomuch that he said in the same instant 'O Lord Jesus, yet more trouble,' and so he died to the great compassion of much people.

Turberville, on the other hand was just put in prison and later appears to have escaped to Brittany.

Brittany

Probably before May 1484, Maximilian sent Maître Antoine de Longueil, described as François' counsellor, with a representative of his own to Brittany.

Maximilian informed François that he was repudiating the Treaty of Arras which had been extracted from him unfairly in 1482 by Louis XI. Maximilian claimed had only given way because of the pressures brought on him by the rebellious Flemish cities. Longueil went on to become Bishop of St-Pol de-Leon and may have also led diplomatic missions to England.

Whilst Landais began to edge towards a new alliance with England, the Bretons continued to financially support Richard's opponents. In June Duke François made one payment to Henry of 3,100 livres. The Duke also gave the more senior members of the group individual pensions including 400 livres per month to Dorset and his men; 200 livres per month to John Halewell and 100 livres per month each to Edward Woodville and Robert Willoughby. It is no wonder that Commines noted how they were becoming a financial burden to the Duke.

As a result of the new treaty between England and Brittany which was concluded on 8 June and to commence from 1 July, Richard once again offered the Bretons English archers. According to Landais during his later interrogation, the offer was brought by the 'little Salazar' after Richard put a ship at his disposal for his passage to Brittany. 'Little Salazar' was the Basque Juan de Salazar, who was described by the chronicler Molinet as 'very experienced in war, bold, [an] enterprising and shrewd leader of men-at-arms'. Salazar had joined the Burgundian army in the early 1470s and became a leader of Burgundian resistance against the French, fighting with distinction at Guinegate. By 1480 he had been made captain of 100 lances and *conseiller et chambellan* to Maximilian. Maximilian had sent Salazar to Richard, although it is not clear whether it was as a diplomat, military 'advisor', or both. However, we do know he returned to England after the mission and was at Bosworth with Richard.

Instead of the 4,000 archers demanded by Duke François the previous year, Richard only agreed to send 1,000. As a sweetener, Richard possibly offered Duke François the revenue of the earldom of Richmond, which Henry Tudor had claimed for himself, and the lands of other rebels. In return, Richard asked that Henry be either placed under close arrest or extradited.

In September, *'le grand éscuier d'Engleterre'* ('The Great Esquire of England') who was possibly William Catesby, but more likely James Tyrell, Richard's master of the horse, was in Vannes and had made an offering in the cathedral. He, whoever he was, had probably been sent by Richard to oversee Henry's arrest. Landais also sent Jean Feuillet to recruit 2,000 Swiss mercenaries who he hoped to use against rebel Breton lords and to besiege the fortresses of Ancenis and Châteaubriant, which were in the hands of the Breton rebels.

By September, Richard's archers had still not arrived in Brittany. Salazar probably went to Brittany a second time, as an order by Richard authorises a ship to 'convey Saluzard' there in September 1484. By this time, news of the offer had reached the court of France and in September, the French sent Dunois to investigate rumours that 6,000 archers had arrived.

Probably in late September John Morton, who had escaped to Flanders in the aftermath of the rebellion, became aware of the plan to extradite Henry from 'friends out of England' possibly through Margaret Beaufort, who would have heard it from her husband. He despatched Christopher Urswick, Margaret's Priest and Confessor, to warn Henry, who by this time had been placed under house arrest at Vannes. Henry immediately sent Urswick to the French court, which was at Angers at the time, to request permission for the fugitives to enter France. Madame gladly agreed.

As soon as Urswick returned to Henry with the news, Henry began to plan his escape in utmost secrecy. Firstly, Jasper left Vannes under the pretence of visiting the Duke, but as soon as he got close to the French border, he turned aside and made straight for Anjou. Two days later Henry and five servants left Vannes under the pretext of visiting a friend in the country. Five miles outside the city, he turned off the road into a forest and changed into a serving man's clothes. With one of his servants acting as a guide, they too fled into Anjou.

When Landais heard of the escape, he immediately sent men after Henry. However, they were too late as Henry had crossed the border 'scarcely an hour earlier'. After 13 years, for some of which he was held in captivity, Henry had finally left Brittany for good.

Duke François, who appears to have recovered his strength around the same time, sent for Edward Poynings and Edward Woodville. He gave both of them and Sir John Cheyney, 100 livres tournois each and 20s for each of the 408 exiles still in Vannes from his own purse. He then allowed them to follow Henry.

Scotland

Border skirmishes continued between the English and Scots. Langton, Bishop of St. David's, who was with Richard at York, wrote:

> The Kyng of Scots hath sent a curteys and a wise letter to the kyng for his cace, but I trow ye shal undirstond tha I shal have a sit up or ever the kyng departe fro York. Thai ly styl at the siege of Dunbar, but I trust to God it shalbe kept fro thame.

Albany and the Earl of Douglas, along with an English army, probably led by Sir John Mordaunt and William Salisbury, and 500 horsemen advanced into Scotland in July. On 22 July they reached Lochmaben, just as the St. Mary Magdalen's Day fair was taking place. When they entered the townspeople took up their arms, believing this to be just another English raid. Soon a bloody battle was raging through the streets and the adjacent countryside, which continued from the middle of the day to dusk. News of the fight spread and the townspeople were reinforced by the local gentry, headed by Robert Crichton, Cuthbert Murray and John Johnstone. Unable to withstand the mounting pressure the English force broke and scattered. Albany fled once more to England, but the elderly Earl of Douglas was taken prisoner by Alexander Kirkpatrick. He was brought before King James who sent him to spend the remainder of his days in the seclusion of a monastery. Both the English commanders survived. Mordaunt later became an MP and fought for Henry VII at Stoke in 1487.

France

Madame sent Gilbert de Chabannes, Lord of Curton and Governor of Limousin to meet Henry and arrange for him to be 'housed in towns wherein he shall pass.' At the same time, Guy de Laval, a 'Monsieur de Sees' and a clerk were despatched with 2,000 francs for Henry's men. On 3 November, Madame sent a letter to towns across France telling how Henry and Jasper had arrived in France and that they intended to support Henry to 'recover the Kingdom of England from the enemies of the French crown.' Bizarrely, it also described Henry as the younger son of the late Lancastrian king Henry VI. Perhaps, knowing Henry's tenuous claim to the throne, it was done to give him more credibility. By the following day, the fugitives had reached Sens, 60 miles east of Montargis where the Monseigneur de La Heuze was instructed to 'house Richmond's people in the town' and give them what supplies they needed at a reasonable price.

According to Molinet, when Henry finally reached Montargis calling himself King of England, he was received with great joy and was well loved and looked after. However, he added that it was all show and was more to irritate Richard than in deference to Henry. The French knew full well how weak Henry's claim to the throne of England was. Commines remarked that Henry 'was a member of the house of Lancaster, but he was not the closest claimant to the crown', and Molinet noted that he was 'quite far removed from the crown of England regarding his bloodline'.

England

In August, messengers arrived in London from the French monarch. They brought a letter to Richard said that Charles regretted that it had been found impossible to arrive at any conclusion during Langton's stay, and was sending his Roussillon herald in reply, who was to ask for safe conduct for a French embassy that included 60 persons. Richard issued the passes on 1 September, but it seems that they never arrived. Shortly after, in a writ to the sheriffs of Wiltshire and a number of other counties, Richard proclaimed to his subjects that his 'friends and Confederates' were 'the kings of Spain and Portugal, the Dukes of Austria and Burgundy and the nations of Italy and Almain'. During his interrogation, Landais suggested that Richard's offer of archers for Brittany should be placed in the context of a triple alliance between the Duke of Brittany, Archduke Maximilian and Richard. It seems that the idea was first proposed during the summer of 1484. However, Landais thought it was not taken seriously until the extension was agreed in 1485.

Around this time, according to Harleian MSS 433, the docket book of Richard's Privy Seal, Sir James Tyrell, Richard's 'right trusty knight for our body and counsaillour' was sent 'over the See into the parties of Flaundres for diverse maters concernying gretely oure wele'. No further explanation is offered about this mission. Soon after his return, Sir James replaced Lord Mountjoy as Constable of Guisnes Castle, one of the two fortresses guarding

Calais. Despite being made Constable of Tintagel Castle and holding the post of Commissioner of Array for Wales, Sir James remained at Guisnes.

Maximilian seems to have given his ambassadors to Richard a lengthy set of instructions probably relating to the alliance negotiation. Although the date they were written is not known, the content suggests that it was shortly before a Breton embassy to England, but after the French had asked for letters of protection, and after Henry had fled to France. Others, however, have suggested it could have been as late as January 1485. A considerable part was concerned with the problems in Flanders and they asked Richard for 6,000 archers from the first day of April, as this was when Maximilian intended to march into Flanders. In recompense, they offered him 14,000 soldiers with which to attack France 'for the claim which he has to the crown or any other cause' and after two years 4,000 horse and 2,000 foot, until he had conquered France or finished his war against King Charles. If Richard chose not to attack France but to engage in war in Scotland or elsewhere instead, they were to offer him the half of the above number of men. The ambassadors were to urge Richard not to agree to a treaty with France because if he accepted one it would prevent him from any pursuit of the claim which he had to the crown of France. They were to tell him how the French feared him and if he accepted a treaty it would diminish any estimation the French held him in. They were to also say that Richard would never have so good an opportunity to invade as he has at present, as the King of France was young, and the kingdom governed by a number of princes who could not agree. As assurance that the Bretons would no longer support Henry Tudor, they offered Maximilian's surety and promise.

Relations with the French were continuing to deteriorate, and several naval battles followed. An assault on the last bastion of England in France, Calais, was also expected although it never materialised.

Meanwhile, in England, sporadic uprisings were continuing. On 2 November, Sir William Brandon and his sons led an armed revolt in Colchester which spread into Hertfordshire and involved Sir William Stonor, along with Thomas Nandyke, both of whom had rebelled in 1483, and Robert Clifford, Sir John Risley, an esquire of the body to Richard and his servant William Coke of Lavenham, Suffolk. Although details are scant, the plot was somehow connected to both Henry Tudor and the Earl of Oxford. When it failed, Sir William fled to sanctuary at Colchester whilst his sons Robert and William, along with Risley and Stonor, seized a ship from East Mersea to join Henry Tudor. Although many rebels fled to France to join Henry, others continued to plot Richard's downfall in England. Vergil makes it clear that one of the leaders was Thomas Stanley, saying:

> man of name passyd over dayly unto Henry, others favoryd secretly the parteners of the conspyracy. Emongest these principally was Thomas Stanley, William his brother, Gylbert Talbot, and others innumerable, whose inward mynde thowgh Richerd was ignorant of, yeat he trustyd never one of them all.

Stanley was already planning for Henry's return and 'that he might be ready to receave erle Henry as a frind at his coming'. Around the same time, Richard became aware of a plot to rescue John de Vere, Earl of Oxford, who had been held in Hammes castle near Calais since 1475.

King Edward had allowed John de Vere to succeed his father as the 13th earl, and on 18 January 1464 granted him licence to enter on his father's lands. On 26 May 1465 he was created a Knight of the Bath at the coronation of Elizabeth Woodville and officiated at the ceremony as both Lord Great Chamberlain, in the absence of the Earl of Warwick, and as Chamberlain to the Queen.

In November 1468 he confessed to plotting with the Lancastrians against the King but received a general pardon on 5 April the following year. However, within a year he had joined his brother-in-law, the Earl of Warwick, and King Edward's brother, the Duke of Clarence, in their first rebellion against Edward. De Vere fled overseas to the court of Margaret of Anjou and in September 1470 he joined Warwick and Clarence in the invasion of England which restored Henry VI to the throne. He was appointed Lord High Constable of England, and as such on 15 October tried and condemned for high treason the same Earl of Worcester who had in 1462 condemned Oxford's own father and brother. In March 1471, he prevented Edward IV's army from landing in Norfolk, and was in command of the right wing at the Battle of Barnet on 14 April of that year.

After Barnet, Oxford fled to Scotland with 40 men, accompanied by his two brothers, George and Thomas Vere, and Viscount Beaumont. From there he went to France, where he collected ships and engaged in privateering. His lands were confiscated, and his wife, Margaret, is said to have been subjected to great financial hardship.

On 28 May 1473 Oxford attempted an unsuccessful landing at St. Osyth in Essex. On 30 September 1473 he seized St. Michael's Mount in Cornwall, where he was besieged for some months by John Fortescue. After most of his men had deserted and he had been wounded in the face with an arrow, Oxford was eventually compelled to surrender on 15 February 1474, along with his two brothers and Beaumont. Oxford was imprisoned at Hammes Castle near Calais and was attainted early in 1475. His mother, the 12th Earl's widow, was forced to surrender her property to Richard who was still Duke of Gloucester. In 1478, whilst being held at Hammes, Oxford attempted to scale the walls. Whether he fell, was pushed, or deliberately jumped into the moat in a suicide attempt is unclear.

On 28 October Richard sent William Bolton, an usher of the crown, to bring Oxford back to England, however, he was too late. Oxford had persuaded the captain of Hammes, James Blount, to defect. Molinet suggests that Blount had been corresponding with Thomas Stanley about his defection for some time. Blount fled to Henry with John Fortescue, porter of Calais, leaving the garrison – which remained loyal to Blount – in charge of the castle. When Henry met Oxford in Angers 'he was ravished with joy incredible'. Not long after the escape, Lord Dinham, governor of Calais, laid siege to Hammes. Oxford was soon to return with a relief force and whilst he attacked the besiegers from the rear, Thomas Brandon led 30 men along a secret path through the marsh and into the castle. It would be the following January before Richard would recover the castle, and then only after he had issued a pardon to those inside.

PREPARATIONS

Meanwhile, the sea war with France was continuing. There was nothing unusual in hearing about clashes at sea. However, one clash stands out as it may have been a French attempt to disrupt the Anglo-Breton peace process. Sometime in early autumn, Jean de Coetanlem, a notorious Breton privateer nicknamed the *roi de la mer* (king of the sea), seems to have attacked an English fleet out of Bristol and may have gone on to burn and pillage Bristol itself. Coetanlem was a merchant and seaman operating from Morlaix and St. Pol-de-Leon in Brittany and a member of a Breton family heavily involved in shipping, customs and finance throughout the fifteenth century. There is no mention of this momentous clash in either English official records or English chronicles, although there are hints in English papers, as in February 1485 Richard gave a substantial remission of the fee farm in consideration of recent losses of ships and merchandise at sea. The only detail we have is from an inquiry by French officials over tax exemptions 55 years later. One of the witnesses, Guillaume le Borgne, recounted how Jean de Coetanlem had sold all he possessed to fit out ships against the English to do service to his prince and country. 'With money provided by his prince and the admiral, he did great damage to the English, taking ships and burning towns and other places on the coast.' He stated that in retaliation the English decided to fit out an 'army royal' from Bristol, to capture him. He told the officials that Coetanlem approached Bristol with his fleet and was spotted by the English who sailed to meet them. Although his crews were outnumbered five to one, he resolved to fight. He won. Coetanlem captured the English ships, then landed at Bristol, burnt and pillaged the city, and took off many rich prisoners to Brittany. Another witness, Giles Morice, adds further detail saying that at his own cost, Coetanlem fitted out several ships including *La Cullier* and *Le Singe*, whilst the English prepared three ships, *Trinity*, *Mary de Gracze*, and one other. All three were double crewed and heavily armed. He described how when the two sides met off the coast of Brittany, the battle raged for five or six hours. The English asked for a truce for two hours, which was granted. When battle recommenced, Coetanlem took the ships by assault. Yvon le Moal added that 'three well-armed warships had taken three great English ships; those English ships had been fitted out especially to deal with Coetanlem', but makes no mention of an attack on the city. Richart Henry also said he had been told by the crews that a great many ships were taken and agreed with Morice that the *Mary de Gracze* was one of the ships taken.

We know that there was a 300 ton *Mary of Grace* berthed at Bristol in 1480, as was the *Trinity,* which was of 360 tons with a crew of 34 including 12 soldiers and two gunners, which supports the possibility that the sea battle at least took place. What we don't know is whose flag Coetanlem was flying at the time and that gives rise to some interesting possibilities. Coetanlem seems to have sailed from Brittany, so it is probable that he was under their flag, although they had signed a peace treaty with England by this time.

At the beginning of November 1484, the King of France announced that his *gens de guerre* had inflicted great damage on the English who, like all Englishmen, had been accustomed to raid the coast of Normandy. That December there was a request to the King's Council from the Admiral of France, Louis de Bourbon, for his tenth of the booty captured from ships at La Rochelle. He claimed that he had equipped and supplied powder and weapons for certain ships belonging to 'Jehan Codelain' to make war on the English and other enemies of France. 'Codelain' had gained a good deal of booty, however, because many of his men were injured and his ships were badly battered, they had to put in at the port of 'le Plomb', close to La Rochelle on the Bay of Biscay. There is no mention of any prisoners taken. So, does this suggest that the French were behind the attack and not the Bretons? It seems likely that it was an attempt by the French to sow discord between England and Brittany. Further evidence for this is that in the aftermath of the battle, Coetanlem sailed on to Portugal and never returned to Brittany again. Sometime after, Duke François also wrote to Coetanlem demanding he returned the booty they had taken. No record survives of it being returned.

On 7 August whilst in London, Richard sent safe conducts for Scottish ambassadors to come to Nottingham to discuss a truce. The Chancellor of Scotland, Colin Campbell, 1st Earl of Argyll, William Elphinstone, Bishop of Aberdeen; Lords Robert Lyle and Laurence Oliphant; John Drummond, of Stobhall; and the King's own Secretary, Archibald Whitelaw, Archdeacon of Lothian presented their credentials to Richard in the Great Hall of Nottingham castle. Archibald Whitelaw gave a speech praising Richard's abilities, appearance and intentions, comparing Richard to a Prince of the Thebans and that nature never enclosed within a small frame so great a mind, or of such remarkable powers. Richard's delegation included Thomas Barowe, Master of the Rolls and Sir William Hussey, Chief Justice of the King's Bench. Five days later they agreed on a truce to last for three years. It included a marriage contract between the King's son and his own niece, Lady Anne de la Pole, daughter of the Duke of Suffolk, and sister of the Earl of Lincoln. After completion of the treaty, Richard remained in Nottingham. In October he wrote a letter to his Irish subjects, telling them of the actual date of the commencement of his reign. Richard's northern border was now secure, and he could concentrate his forces in the event of an invasion by Henry. By 10 November, Richard was back in the south, touring Kent before returning to London on 28 November.

The King had only been in London a few days when intelligence reached him that the French, despite their requests for a peace treaty, was still trying to undermine him. In Windsor and other towns 'seditious manifestoes' appeared, instigated by 'false inventions, tidings, and rumours' emanating from sources in France. Accordingly, on 6 December Richard addressed a letter to the Mayor of Windsor ordering him to check such attempts to foment discord and division between himself and his nobles:

> Forasmuch as we be credibly informed that our ancient enemies of France, by many and sundry ways, conspire and study the means to the subversion of this our realm, and of unity amongst our subjects, as in sending writings by seditious persons with counterfeit tokens, and contrive false inventions, tidings, and rumours, to the intent to provoke and stir discord and disunion betwixt us and our lords, which be as faithfully disposed as any subjects can suffice. We thereforewill and command you strictly, that in eschewing the inconveniences

> aforesaid you put you in your uttermost devoir of any such rumours, or writings come amongst you, to search and inquire of the first showers or utterers thereof; and them that ye shall so find ye do commit unto sure ward, and after proceed to their sharp punishment, in example and fear of all other, not failing hereof in any wise, as ye intend to please us, and will answer to us at your perils.

This letter was also published as a royal proclamation in other towns, and one of its first consequences was the arrest at Southampton of Sir Robert Clifford. Clifford was given a quick trial, taken to Tower Hill and executed, but not before his supporters had attempted a rescue en route. Richard's mention of 'our ancient enemies of France' in his proclamation raises some interesting questions, as they were publicly suing for peace with Richard at this time. With the political turmoil in France, were they in a position to do anything? It appears that Richard thought that there was a credible threat of an invasion, probably landing at Harwich as Sir Gilbert Debenham and Sir Philip Bothe were despatched with a strong force to defend it. But who was it that was going to invade, Henry or the French? And would anyone attempt a seaborne invasion in December? On 8 December, Richard issued a general Commission of Array, asking commissioners, to perform a head count and that all men were well horsed and harnessed. He must have thought an invasion was imminent, as 10 days later, instructions were issued to the Commissioner of Array for the counties of Surrey, Middlesex, and Hertford:

> to call before them all the knights, squires, and gentlemen within the said counties, and know from them what number of people, defensibly arrayed, every of them severally will bring at half a days' warning, if any sudden arrival forture of the king's rebels and traitors.

France

At about the same time, Henry began to write to his supporters and potential supporters in England. According to Molinet, urged on by both Oxford and Stanley he began to style himself as king, signing his letters 'H':

> Right trusty, worshipfull, and honourable good friends, and our allies, I greet you well. Being given to understand your good devoir and intent to advance me to the furtherance of my rightful claim due and lineal inheritance of the crown, and for the just depriving of that homicide and unnaturall tyrant which now unjustly bears dominion over you, I give you to understand that no Christian heart can be more full of joy and gladness than the heart of me your poor exiled friend, who will, upon the instance of your sure advertise what powers ye will make ready and what captains and leaders you get to conduct, be prepared to pass over the sea with such forces as my friends here are preparing for me. And if I have such good speed and success as I wish, according to your desire, I shall ever be most forward to remember and wholly to requite this your great and most loving kindness in my just quarrel.

On 17 November, the French royal council authorised 3,000 livres tournois 'to help him dress his people'. However, they pointed out this was 'for this time only'. More rebels seeking Henry arrived every week including Richard Fox, a noted cleric who was studying at the University of Paris. Not all the desertions were in Henry's favour, however, as in January 1485, Thomas Grey, the Marquis of Dorset, who had been with Henry since Buckingham's rebellion, tried to escape back to England. According to Vergil, Dorset was returning to the 'home of his mother's, partly despairing for that cause of Earl Henry's success, partially suborned by King Richard's fair promises.'

Shortly before his escape attempt, Dorset had sent Portuguese Ronald Machado to Flanders although the reasons why are unknown. Machado first appears in English sources in July 1471, as Leicester Herald, a royal herald in the household of Edward IV. He disappeared from the record in June 1483, so may have been involved in Buckingham's rebellion after which he fled to Henry, possibly with Dorset. Once in Flanders, Machado's *Memorandum Book* shows he rode for seven days from Bruges to Ghent to speak with a Monsieur Roumond and sold a total of £11 8s of the Marquis' silver. On 2 February 1485, he met and travelled with a Monsieur Jacques de Luxembourg, who was probably Jacques de Savoie, Comte de Romont, and a Madame de Mans from Bruges. It is unclear who Savoie was supporting at the time, but he had been a close adherent of Mary of Burgundy and was wounded fighting for Maximilian against the French at the Battle of Guinegate in 1479. After meeting Savoie, Machado rode for 10 days from Bruges to Laon in northern France with messages from the Marquis. Afterwards, he returned to Henry, and after Bosworth was made 'Richmond King of Arms of Norroy' which showed the high esteem in which Henry held him.

Once Henry heard of Dorset's escape, he sent Humphrey Cheney and Matthew Baker after him. They caught up with him at Lihons-sur-Santerre near Compiègne en route for France's northern border. Dorset was then 'persuaded' to return and had to remain in Paris during the invasion. Dorset never recovered his status after Henry was enthroned. In fact, he was confined in the Tower and not released until after the Battle of Stoke in 1487. Significantly when Richard issued his second proclamation against the rebels, Dorset was omitted. Was Dorset also one of Richard's spies, and was he trying to warn of the impending invasion?

The French still seemed to have no interest in supporting Henry at this time. *The Ballad of Ladye Bessiye* says that Henry, Oxford, Lord Lisle and Humphrey Brereton went to Paris but the French King, or in all probability, Madame, refused to help him return to England.

England

According to the *Diarium Burchard*, on 18 February French ambassadors had an altercation with those of Richard III in the presence of the Pope (*quia rex Anglie insuis literis nomina vitse regem Francie et Angli*). Soon after Christmas a Breton delegation, led by Bishop Longueil, arrived in England to negotiate an extension of the Anglo-Breton truce and no doubt to ask Richard where their archers were. With Henry's flight to France the immediate reason for military or financial aid to Brittany disappeared. Richard could afford to ignore his promises, albeit temporarily. Richard gave power to the Bishop of Lincoln, John Russell, the Lord Chancellor, and the Dean of Wells, John Gunthorpe, the Keeper of the Privy Seal to negotiate on his behalf. One of the conditions of the truce was that Richard sent the archers that he had been promising for so long. The truce was concluded on 7 March and ratified by Duke François on 9 April. The last cog in the triple alliance was now in place. A flurry of diplomatic exchanges with Maximilian seems to have followed, as in March Salazar's servants were given safe-conduct to Flanders and Brabant. A further safe-conduct was issued to another of Salazar's servants, Henry Delphant, along with two servants and as many horses, to go to the 'Duc of Ostriche' (Maximilian).

Richard needed extra funding if he was going to support the alliance and repel any invasion. His brother had raised money through 'benevolences' which were enforced loans that were rarely paid back. They had proved to be very unpopular and had been banned during Richard's only Parliament. To avoid making the same mistake, Richard sent out letters under the Privy Seal with the crown promising to repay the loan on fixed dates. They began:

> …And for such great and excessive costs and charges as we hastily must bear and sustain as well as for keeping the sea as otherwise for the defence of this Realm we desire and in our heartiest wise pray you to send to us by way of a loan by our trusty servant this bearer…

Another version said that the King and all his lords were thinking that every true Englishman will help him in this behalf. The letters were sent out between 21 February and 5 April, although it is not known how much money they raised, if any.

Richard remained in London but suffered another personal blow on 16 March when his wife Anne died. Polydore Vergil openly suggested that Richard had rid himself of Anne. He has Richard causing 'a rumour … to be spread abroad of the Queen his wife's death…' A short while later, Anne, 'whether she was dispatched with sorrowfulness, or poison, died…' In reality, Anne apparently suffered from some debilitating disease – possibly tuberculosis. John Rous later accused Richard of poisoning Anne Neville, and for good measure had Richard locking up Anne's mother, the Dowager Countess of Warwick, for the duration of her life. However, *The Croyland Chronicle* remarked that doctors had advised Richard to stay away from Anne's chambers, to avoid the contagion.

There is no contemporary evidence that Richard poisoned Anne. Richard's enemies spread such rumours after Anne died, and alleged that Richard intended to marry his niece, Elizabeth of York. Rumours that Richard was going to marry his niece had been circulating since Christmas and this only served to fuel them. Apparently, on the advice of Sir Richard Ratcliffe and Sir William Catesby, Richard issued a public declaration that he had no intention of marrying his niece. He spoke before the mayor and aldermen of London. A letter written by Richard was read out at the Guildhall in York (and probably other towns) on 19 April it said:

> Trusty and wellbeloved, we greet you well. And where it is so that divers seditious and evil disposed persons both in our city of London and elsewhere within this our realm, enforce themselves daily to sow seed of noise and slander against our person and against many of the lords and estates of our land to abuse the multitude of our subjects and avert their minds from us if they could by any means attain to that their mischievous intent and purpose; some by setting up of the bills, some by messages, and sending forth of false and abominable language and lies, some by bold and presumptuous open speech and communication one with another, where through the innocent people which would live and rest in peace and truly under our obeisance, as they ought to do,[they have] been greatly abused and oft times put in danger of their lives, lands and goods as often as they follow the steps and devises of the said seditious and mischievous persons to our great heaviness and pity … all other our officers, servants and faithful subjects wheresoever they be, that from henceforth as often as they find person speaking of us or any other lord or estate of this our land … or telling of tales and tidings whereby the people might be stirred to commotions and unlawful assemblies … the furnisher, author and maker of the said seditious speech and language be taken and punished according to his deserts, and whosoever first find any seditious bill set up in any place he take it down and without reading or showing the same to any other person bring it forthwith unto us or some of the lords or other of our council.

Richard had in fact already opened negotiations to marry Joanna of Portugal, sister of John II of Portugal. In Portugal she was known as 'The Holy Princess' for her strong religious beliefs. Joanne had previously had a number of marriage proposals, including Maximilian, heir to the Holy Roman Empire and the new King of France, Charles VIII, all of which she had all rejected. She was also a descendant of Philippa, a daughter of John of Gaunt, Duke of Lancaster, the sister of Henry IV, the first Lancastrian king, who had married into the Portuguese royal family. So the blood of Lancaster flowed strongly in Portugal. Edward Brampton, Richard's envoy, had left England soon after Anne's death and negotiations had continued through the summer of 1485. The Portuguese Council of State urged Joanna's brother, King John, to accept Richard's offer. King John tried bullying; his aunt, Philippa, tried persuasion. The fact that these negotiations continued until Richard's death shows that they were serious and possibly reaching their conclusion. According to Domingos Mauricio Gomes dos Santos, in his *O Mosteiro de Jesus de Aveiro* (Lisbon, 1962):

> Joanna retired for a night of prayer and meditation. She either had a vision or a dream of a 'beautiful young man' who told her that Richard had gone from among the living. The next morning she gave her brother a firm answer. If Richard were still alive, she would go to England to marry him. If he were dead, her brother John was not to press her again to marry. It is not necessary to believe in the supernatural to accept that Joanna may have had a premonitory dream of Richard's death. Within a few day of her decision, the news of Bosworth had reached Portugal.

Joanna never married and continued to support her brother. She died five years after Richard on 12 May 1490 at Aveiro. In 1693 she was beatified by Pope Innocent XII, to be known as Princess Saint Joan.

More importantly for Henry, the arrangement was to include Elizabeth's marriage into the Portuguese royal family to the King's cousin Manuel, Duke of Beja at the same time. Had the proposal been accepted, it would have thwarted Tudor's plans to combine the two houses in an instant. Time was running out.

In the spring of 1485, men-at-arms and archers put to sea under George Neville, Lord Bergavenny. Richard must have thought the invasion may come at Harwich as on 29 March he ordered 50 bows, 100 sheaves of arrows, a barrel of gunpowder, 50 spears and three carts of ordinance to be delivered there from the Tower. On 8 April an order was issued to under-treasurer Alfred Corneborough and six others to take musters 'in any convenient places of the realm', and to remain in readiness until 31 August.

Flanders

Maximilian's relationship with Flanders was rapidly deteriorating. The Knights of the Golden Fleece at Dendermonde deposed him as head of their Order and Bruges refused to admit him into their city with no more than a dozen people. The commander of the Flemish armies also proclaimed himself lieutenant-general in the name of Philip the Fair. Then, in November 1484, when Maximilian convened the States General, Flanders did not attend. So, in January 1485, Maximilian marched his army into Flanders and took Oudenaarde. He then defeated the forces of Ghent under their own walls. But when a mutiny broke out in his army, he was forced to retreat. The French responded by sending Philippe de Crèvecoeur, Lord of Esquerdes, into Flanders with 8,000 infantrymen, 650 lances, and 36 cannon from Pont de l'Arche. On 27 May 1485, the French army entered Ghent. However, instead of behaving like liberators, they behaved like conquerors and raped and pillaged the inhabitants. Crèvecoeur tried to calm the citizens by parading the young Duke Phillipe through the city. However, the people thought he was kidnapping the young prince and taking him to France. They rose against the French forcing them to withdraw somewhat ignominiously and, according to reports, were forced to abandon 1,200 halberds, salades (helmets), bows and aketons (a type of padded jacket) as well as a quantity of artillery. Twelve days later, on June 23, Charles VIII wrote to the aldermen of Ghent to ask them to send back his artillery.

Brittany

As a consequence of the extended treaty with England, Guillaume Guillemet was sent to Southampton with seven ships to transport the archers back.

The Franc-archers had been organised to take the field at the end of February and a body of cavalry had been gathered under Phillipe de

Montauban in readiness, as Landais knew that a full-scale invasion by rebels backed by the French was only a matter of time.

On 21 April, troops loyal to Landais laid siege to the castle of Ancenis, an operation which Landais had originally hoped to use the English archers for. The majority of the Breton rebels, however, were continuing to be a major threat from across the border in Angers. Landais placed additional troops in Dinan, Clisson and other fortresses to try to protect Brittany against them.

France

Orléans was still looking to Richard III and Maximilian, who had undertaken to invade Picardy, for support. During January, he came to Paris to enlist the support of *Parlement* in delivering the King from his evil influences. His pleas were turned down. Madame responded by issuing an edict that included an attack on Orléans saying: 'let the good towns distrust the Duke's representations, refuse him all support, arrest his emissaries and behave themselves with the vigilance and circumspection which the situation demanded.' With terrifying speed, she then marched on Paris. This was the type of warfare that her army had been trained for: mobile and fast. Orléans fled to Alençon's town of Verneuil where he summoned his supporters. Anne reached Paris on 5 Feb. Then, after securing the capital, her forces marched on Normandy and severed communications with Brittany. Denied the possibility of support, Orléans was forced to capitulate and submit to Madame at Evreux on 23 March. For the time being, he was contained.

On 14 April 1485, Charles made his formal entry into Rouen for the opening of the Norman Estates accompanied by Henry. However time was running out for the French. The coalition of Burgundy, England and Brittany had finally been agreed. It was only a matter of time before they overwhelmed France, so action was needed to be taken to disrupt their plans. Orléans was temporarily neutralised, Maximilian was preoccupied in Flanders, and Breton rebels were set to invade. So Madame turned her attention to destabilising England. In Henry Tudor and his supporters, they had the ideal way to neutralise the threat posed by Richard.

The attitude of the French towards Henry changed dramatically. Madame ordered that he should now be treated as a Prince of the Blood and described him as 'The Count of Richemont, they say the King of England'. On 28 April, Henry walked alongside the Royal Family at Rouen Cathedral where he was described as 'Princeps Anglie'.

Time was of the essence for Henry, 'such was the urgency of his need'. Richard's marriage plans for Elizabeth, Henry's intended bride, were reaching their conclusion and no doubt plans had already been put in place back in England. It was also around this time, that after receiving intelligence of Richard's marriage negotiations, Henry began to look for an alternative bride. He may have even given up on Elizabeth altogether. He set his sights on Katherine, sister of William Herbert, Earl of Huntingdon. Henry knew her from when he was at Raglan and in the earliest version of his manuscript,

Vergil had actually used the phrase that he knew her 'well and loved' but later deleted it. The proposed union would not be without its difficulties of course, as Herbert was married to Richard's illegitimate daughter, also named Katherine. It was suggested that as he was married to Maud, another of Herbert's sisters, the Earl of Northumberland could act as the intermediary. The fact that they were serious about the union can be seen in that Urswick was immediately despatched to make contact with Northumberland. However, he returned to France 'without accomplishing anything'.

At the beginning of May, Anne of Beaujeu finally offered Henry the support he needed to mount an invasion. It was announced in the French parliament that 'come to us our very dear and beloved cousin Henry of Richmond, requiring help to recover the Kingdom of England which belongs to him, and in whom in considering the proximity of lineage between us, also considering that he is of all the people in the world with the most apparent right to the throne of England, we will cater for him and his people for the time he spends here, and take the decision to help him in his business and deeds which may amount to a large sum of money.'

Molinet says that Charles gave Henry 60,000 francs, Commines on the other hand only says that Charles 'gave him and his companions a considerable sum of money'. A letter dated 1 March 1486, from Diego de Valera to Ferdinand and Isabella in Spain says that Charles lent Henry 'fifty thousand crowns'. However, the accounts of the receiver of finances in Normandy, Jean Lallement includes authorisation for a grant of 40,000 livres to cover the cost of Henry's expenses. Although, according to the French receiver-general's accounts for 1484–85, it appears that only one instalment of 10,000 livres was actually handed over.

Henry was still woefully short of funds to launch his invasion. He turned to Phillipe Luiller, Seigneur de Saint-Jean-le-Blanc, and Captain of the Bastille, for a loan for the balance of 30,000 livres. As surety he surrendered all his personal goods and possessions and left both the Marquis of Dorset and Lord FitzWarin as hostages.

Vergil's account of the financing of the invasion played down the involvement of the French only saying: 'obtaynyng of king Charles sclender supply, Pledges left and borowyng as well of him as of other pryvate frinds certane king of money, for the which he left sureties, or rather pledges, the marquyse and John Burschere.'

Thirteen years later on the death of Charles VIII, court poet Octavien de Saint-Gelais called on Henry to pay his respects to the King who had granted to him the rich land of England and his title to the kingdom. The French would have undoubtably wanted something in return for their support, although what this was, other than disrupting the English/Breton/Burgundian alliance has not survived. However, if Richard's proclamation of 7 December, is to be believed, it probably included the giving up the claim to the French throne, Normandy, Calais, Guînes and Hammes as well. In the years after Bosworth, a number of French writers complained of Henry's ingratitude, including Robert Gaguin who wrote in 1489 'Though you are ungrateful and careless of the nature of gratitude, You, an exile, by our help return to your native fields a victor.'

RICHARD III AND THE BATTLE OF BOSWORTH

A fleet of between 20 and 30 ships with the *Poulain de Dieppe* as the flagship was assembled at Harfleur on the mouth of the River Seine to take the army to England. According to the contemporary Diego de Valera, the fleet was commanded by a man called 'Colon'. Alfred Spont in his *La Marine Française* suggests that this was Guillaume de Casenove, also known as 'Coulon', a notorious pirate. Guillaume Coulon had been Louis XI's admiral, so the nickname was probably either in deference to the admiral, or his son or nephew. It was reported that three quarters of Coulon's men were foreigners, many of whom were probably Bretons. Closely associated with Coulon was George Palaeologus Disipatos, known as '*George le Grec*'. Jean Frotet of Honfleur and Jean de Porcon so these three may have captained some of the ships. Coulon and at least seven of his ships probably left soon after Henry came ashore, as on 20 August they captured four Venetian galleys en route for Flanders in the Bay of Biscay.

Whilst his army and fleet were made ready, Henry waited at Rouen. There, he was 'overjoyed' to receive news from England, sent by his mother through a messenger named John Morgan, that Rhys ap Thomas and John Savage had offered their support. Rhys had declined to support Buckingham's uprising. In the aftermath, when Richard appointed officers to replace those who had joined the revolt, he made Rhys ap Thomas his principal lieutenant in south-west Wales and granted him an annuity for life of 40 marks. Rhys was, however, required to send his son, Gruffydd ap Rhys ap Thomas, to the King's court at Nottingham as a hostage, but he excused himself from this obligation by claiming that nothing could bind him to his duty more strongly than his conscience. Savage was from Cheshire and one of Stanley's cousins. He fought with the Yorkists at the Battle of Tewkesbury and became a royal carver and knight of the body to Edward IV. In May Savage had been arrested at Pembroke, however he escaped or had been released just before Henry set sail. In addition, Morgan told Henry that Reginald Bray had secured 'not an inconsiderable sum' of money to pay soldiers' wages and urged him to make straight for Wales as soon as possible. According to Grafton Henry had a spy at the very top of Richard's administration: Morgan Kydwelly, the Attorney-General, who sent word that Lord Lovell was lying in wait at Southampton.

Late fifteenth century 'English' style armour based on the effigy of Sir Thomas Martyn (d.1485) in St. Mary's Church Puddletown. Illustration drawn by and © Gambargain.

Henry audaciously ordered six complete sets of armour, 12 pairs of brigandines and 24 sallets from a London draper called William Bret. This is significant as in France he would have had the opportunity to buy the best armour from anywhere in Europe. English-style armour was significantly different from that from Europe, so it is a clear statement that he wanted to be seen as English.

Madame also gave Henry a unit of between 1,000 and 4,000 French troops (depending on the source). Commines says that Charles 'paid for the passage of 3000 or 4000 men', and 'some pieces of artillery, and sent him out of Normandy to land in some part of Wales.' Scottish chronicler John Major writing in 1521, suggests that there were 5,000 men of which 1,000 were Scottish. Another Scot, Robert Lindsay of Pitscottie, in his *Scottish Chronicle* written sometime before 1585, says that there were 3,000 English, 6,000 French and 1,000 men-at-arms 'called the Scots company', sailing from Harfleur in 30 ships. Vergil on the other hand says that there were 2,000 armed men and noted in the original version that they were partly English and partly French. The letter from Diego de Valera also says that Charles granted Henry 'two thousand combatants'. The normally reliable Molinet says that at first, 1,800 men were assembled for the expedition and another 1,800 mustered at Honfleur just before they sailed.

Exactly where these French troops came from and their makeup is more difficult to ascertain. We do, however, have several pieces of documentary and circumstantial evidence that seem to explain. Firstly, we have a poetic funeral epitaph of Philippe de Crèvecoeur, Lord of Esquerdes which says:

par moyeust Richemont recouel en France terre,
Se fus le moienne urqu'il fut roy d'Engleterre

In other words it was Esquerdes that put Henry on the throne of England. It continues that he was 'ordained judge settler of the tournament'. He was also the commander of Pont de l'Arche and at the time of Henry's invasion of England, only just somewhat ignominiously returned from Flanders with his 8,000 infantrymen. We have also seen how Madame used her rapid reaction force to suppress Orléans. We know from a single surviving *lettres de remission* that Colinet Leboeuf, was an *archer du camp* (archer) serving under Gascon Perrot that fought at Bosworth and returned to France in September 1485. However, an *archer du camp* was only one of the four types of troops trained at Pont de l'Arche. On the other hand, we have the *Ballad of Bosworth Fielde* which says:

10,000 more spikes with all
& harquebusyers, throw lye can théth ringe
to make many a noble man to ffall

Clearly, there were a considerable number of 'pikemen' at Bosworth. Despite this, several modern historians have suggested that the French at Bosworth neither came from Pont de l'Arche as it had been disbanded nor were there 'pikemen' amongst them. Surviving evidence suggests the contrary. We have already seen how the request to close the camp was refused during the earlier meeting of the estates, although it may have been scaled down. We do know Pierre-Louis de Valtan had been appointed *capitaine general de la closure*, however, he was still there in 1485, with Esquerdes still in charge. When Commines referred to the French troops at Bosworth as 'as bad as could have been found anywhere' he was most likely referring to the men Esquerdes recently returned from Flanders where they gained such an unsavoury reputation (see below).

What better troops to send on the *voyage d'Angleterre*, than part of the self-contained, French rapid reaction force, trained and experienced in highly mobile warfare? They most probably took their tents and wagons with them too. And, as will be seen, it was their tactical skill that proved decisive.

It is highly unlikely that Esquerdes sailed to England with his men. Instead, command was given to Philbert de Chandée, a nobleman from Savoy, and described by Henry as 'our dear kinsman, both of spirit and blood'. Bernard André, Henry's biographer, described him as a man renowned for his military skill. Henry was to knight him once they arrived in England and on 6 January 1486 created him Earl of Bath. So could he have been in overall command of the army? Something that the Tudor chroniclers would be loathed to admit to. Perhaps he was Henry's trusted military advisor, his Rupert to his King Charles.

As already seen, there were around 1,000 Scottish soldiers with Henry's army as well. The Scottish chronicler Major names their commander as John, son Robert of Haddington (it has been suggested that this was an error and it was John Cunningham, captain of the Scottish archers in 1478), whilst Pitscottie suggests that Sir Alexander Bruce of Erlshall commanded the mounted troops and Henderson of Haddington the foot. Soon after the battle Bruce was rewarded by both James III and Henry, suggesting it was he who was in overall command of the Scottish. Another Scotsman who may have been present was Bernard Stuart, Lord of Aubigny, who had joined the French royal household.

If Sir George Buck's *History of the Life and Reign of Richard III*, published in 1646, is to be believed, it is also possible that the Bretons sent a number of men. We only know of one Breton taking part and that was Jean Perret. Hall, in his later account of the battle, has Richard saying just before the battle 'You see also what a number of beggarly Bretons and fainthearted Frenchmen be with him, arrived to destroy us, our wives and children.' Whilst Hall is famed for inventing speeches, he must have got the idea from somewhere. So it is possible, although it cannot be substantiated. And this was on top of his own followers, who by this time numbered in excess of 400 men.

On 25 June 1485, the Breton barons hostile to Landais denounced the Duke and the Treasurer at the Parliament of Paris. The same day, a letter in the name of Charles VIII announced that Richard had assembled a great army to invade France, which the Duke of Brittany had also mobilised, and that other lords and neighbouring princes had designs on the kingdom. The 'great army,' probably referred to the men that Richard was assembling at Southampton to support the Bretons. However, whether Madame knew that, and the intelligence was used to scare the French is not known.

England

By this time, Richard had received credible intelligence that the invasion was going to happen at a place called Milford. However, there were two

Milfords, one on the south coast, the other in Wales, and his intelligence did not specify which. According to *The Croyland Chronicle* on 22 May, Francis, Lord Lovell, was sent to Southampton 'there to deploy his fleet carefully so as to keep faithful watch on all the ports of those parts and not to miss the chance of engaging the enemy with the united forces of the whole neighbourhood if they tried to land there.' Richard had spent the last five months in London. On 2 June 1485 he was at Coventry where he attended the Corpus Christi celebrations. Then on 6 June he was at Kenilworth. On the same day, commissioners led by Lovell were finally appointed to muster the archers at Southampton that had been promised to Brittany. On 26 June John Grey, Lord Powis, was given the command. They were destined not to leave, however, as events in Brittany would overtake them.

With fresh threats of an invasion, Richard returned to Nottingham, arriving on 12 June. From there he could respond to threats in any part of the country. He then readied himself, and the country for war. On 16 June, three of Salazar's servants were sent to Maximilian on an undisclosed mission. On 22 June, letters were sent to Richard's sheriffs and Commissioners of Array instructing them to be ready to defend the realm against rebels and traitors, a copy of which has been preserved in *The Paston Letters*:

> Forasmuch as certain information is made unto us that our Rebels and traitors associated with our ancient enemies of France and other strangers intend hastily to invade this our Realm purposing the destruction of us, the subversion of this our Realm and disinheriting of all our true subjects ...
>
> Item, that the said Commissioners in all haste possible review the soldiers late mustered before them by force of the Kings commission to them late directed, and see that they be able persons, well horsed and harnessed to do the Kings service of war ...
>
> Item, that the Commissioners make proclamation that all men be ready to do the King service within an hour warning whensoever they be commanded by proclamation or otherwise ...
>
> Item, said Commissioners on the King's behalf give straightly in commandment to all knights, squires and gentlemen to prepare and ready themselves in their proper persons to do the Kings service upon an hour warning when they shall be commanded by Proclamation or otherwise.

It ended that:

> ... everyone of them to be loving and assisting the other in the King's quarrel and cause, showing them plainly that whosoever attempt the contrary, the King's grace will so punish him that all other shall take example by him.

Another letter was sent to every sheriff ordering that upon receiving their instructions from the Commissioners of Array, they were to remain within their shire town or at least ensure that their deputy was present.

The same day, in a long proclamation, Richard launched a blistering attack on Henry, it started:

> Forasmuch as the king our sovereign lord hath certain knowledge that Piers, Bishop of Exeter, Jasper Tydder [Tudor], son of Owen Tydder, calling himself Earl of Pembroke, John late Earl of Oxon, and Sir Edward Wodeville, with other divers his rebels and traitors disabled and attainted by the authority of the high court of parliament, of whom many be known for open murders, advoutres [adulterers], and extortioners contrary to the pleasure of God, and against all truth, honor, and nature, have forsaken their natural country, taking them first to be under th' obeisance of the Duke of Bretagne, and to him promised certain things which by him and his counsel were thought things greatly unnatural and abominable for them to grant, observe, keep, and perform, and therefore the same utterly refused. The said traitors, seeing the said duke and his council would not aid nor succour them nor follow their ways, privily departed out of his country into France, and there taking them to be under the obeissance of the king's ancient enemy Charles calling himself King of France … The said rebels and traitors have chosen to be their captain one Henry Tydder, son of Edmund Tydder, son of Owen Tydder, which of his ambitiousness and insatiable covetous encroacheth and usurpeth upon him the name and title of royal estate of this realm of England, where unto he hath no manner, interest, right, or colour, as every man well knoweth, for he is descended of bastard blood.

And it concluded:

> And over this our said sovereign lord willeth and commandeth all his said subjects to be ready in their most defensible array to do his highness service of war, when they by open proclamation, or otherwise shall be commanded so to do, for resistence of the king's said rebels, traitors, and enemies. Witness myself at Westminster, the 22d day of June, in the second year of our reign.

As part of his preparations on 24 July, Richard wrote to his Chancellor John Russell ordering that he should give the Great Seal to Thomas Barowe, Keeper of the Rolls, who should then bring it immediately to Nottingham. Without it, any proclamations or orders might be ignored. Russell handed it over in the Lower Oratory of the Old Temple in a white leather bag sealed with the Chancellor's eagle signet. It took another three days for Barowe to reach Nottingham. Barowe gave the Seal to Richard in the oratory of the chapel of the castle in the presence of the Archbishop of York, John, Earl of Lincoln, Thomas, Lord Scrope and George, Lord Strange. Richard then gave it back to him and immediately made him Keeper of the Great Seal.

On 28 July, the City of London, responding to Richard's letters, prepared to defend itself from Henry's army, mustering 3,178 of its citizens from 73 companies at Leadenhall under four overseers. First came two 'sad and discrete Communers with certeyn Officers assigned to them', then the archers on foot followed by two aldermen on horse. Next came the 'Bregandynes' in front of the mayor and the two sheriffs on horseback followed by the armed men, then finally behind the rest of the mounted aldermen came the *Jakkes*.

Richard could do no more except wait.

Brittany

At the end of June, as expected, Breton dissidents invaded the Duchy from France. The army that had been raised to oppose them refused to fight and demanded that Landais be surrendered to them. Despite many protestations, the Duke was forced to deliver Landais to be tried for various alleged crimes including extortion and causing the death of Chauvin. Under interrogation, he confessed to numerous other crimes. Pierre Landais was hanged on 19 July 1485 in the meadow of Biesse in Nantes. At his last interrogation, Landais denied having worked against the King of France, only that he had worked against the Beaujeu faction. On 9 August, a peace treaty was concluded between France and Brittany. The coalition was being picked off one by one, and England was next.

9

Invasion

I ask you, most gentle Lord Jesus Christ to keep me, thy servant King Richard. And defend me from all evil, from the devil and from all perils, past and to come, and deliver me from all tribulations, sorrows and troubles in which I am placed.

Richard III's Book of Hours

On 1 August 1485, Henry Tudor, self-styled King of England, sailed out of Harfleur to face Richard and take his Crown. Vergil says there was a soft southern wind. 'The weather being very fayre he came unto Wales… a lyttle before soone set,' on 7 August. There Henry took his first steps on Welsh soil for 14 years.

Henry and his army probably landed in Milford Haven at Mill Bay in Milford Sound, close to Dale. 'Nangle' (now called Angle), the place where Richard announced they landed, is on the opposite side of Mill Bay to Dale. It was not the first time that a French fleet and army had landed in Wales. In October 1402, during the Glyndŵr rebellion against King Henry IV, a force of French and Bretons said to be 1,200 strong by the French chronicler Monstrelet, landed at Carmarthen Bay. Once ashore they burnt the town and inflicted many casualties on its inhabitants. The fleet then sailed on to Tenby, where they joined Glyndŵr. It is not clear what happened to the French next, as some sources say they returned to France, others that they wintered in Wales. In early January 1404, a combined French and Welsh army led by Henry Tudor's ancestors Rhys and Gwilym ap Tudor ap Goronwy assaulted Caernarvon Castle which fell after six months' siege. Then, between 1 and 7 August 1405, 800 mounted men-at-arms, 600 crossbowmen and 1,800 infantry under the Marshal of France disembarked from 120 ships at Milford Haven and joined with Glyndŵr and his men. The combined Franco-Welsh army first marched on Haverfordwest then Carmarthen, where they laid siege to the castle. The army then marched into England, devastating the countryside as they went, and by 15 August was eight miles (123 km) northwest of Worcester at Woodbury Hill. An English army positioned itself on the other side of the valley, and for eight days the two sides faced each other. Whilst they stared at each other, a number of small skirmishes took place in the area with around 200 killed in the fighting. Eventually, appalling weather and a shortage of supplies forced the invaders to return to Wales. The French

Dale, near Milford Haven, Pembrokeshire, where Henry Tudor landed. (Author)

started to return home in November, although some infantry under '*le Begue de Belay*' did not leave until March the following year.

Robert Fabyan writing years later described how Henry kneeled down upon the earth and with 'meek countenance and pure devotion' began the Psalm 'Judge me O God and distinguish my cause,' before kissing the ground and making the sign of the cross. The scene was also remembered by Lewys Glyn Cothi in a eulogy to a Carmarthenshire knight who witnessed the landing. 'There were seen our gallant ones and a throng like York fair and a large and heavy host by the seashore, and many a trumpet by the strand, and guns around a red banner.'

Morale was shaky, and the French troops were reluctant to disembark. It is possible that a beacon at the nearby St. Anne's Head was lit to announce their presence. Perhaps, they saw the beacons on top of the hills being lit one by one across the landscape and realised they had not landed in secret. If we are to believe one Scottish chronicler, Henry even had to burn one of the ships to deter the others from sailing away prematurely.

When the French finally disembarked, they were 'marvellously well and kindly received' and given fresh provisions to cheer them up. Bernard André has Henry telling his men 'not to court any wrong on the common folk either to gain sustenance or to turn a profit, nor to take any property from any inhabitant without paying recompense.' Henry then knighted the French commander, Philbert de Chandée, his mother's half-brother Lord Welles, Edward Courtenay, John Cheyney, David Owen of Cowdray in Sussex, Edward Poynings, John Fortescue and James Blount.

Henry sent messages out to the Welsh gentry and nobility. One such letter, sent to John ap Maredudd ab Ieuan ap Maredudd from Eifionydd in South Caernarfonshire, survives today through his descendants the Wynns:

> Right trusty and well beloved, we greet you well. And where it is so that through the help of Almighty God, the assistance of our loving friends and true subjects, and the great confidence that we have to the nobles and commons of this our

principality of Wales, we be entered into the same, purposing by the help of the above rehearsed in all haste possible to descend into the realm of England not only for the adeption of the crown unto us of right appertaining, but also for the oppression of that odious tyrant Richard, late Duke of Gloucester, usurper of our said right, and moreover to reduce as well our said realm of England into his ancient estate, honour and prosperity, as this our said principality of Wales, and the people of the same to their original liberties, delivering them of such miserable servitudes as they have piteously long stand in. We desire and pray you and upon your allegiance straight charge and command you that immediately upon sight hereof, with all such power as ye may make defensibly arrayed for the war, ye address you towards us without any tarrying upon the way, unto such time as ye be with us wheresoever we shall be to our aid for the effect above rehearsed, wherein ye fail not hereof as ye will avoid our grievous displeasure and answer unto at your peril.

The south of Wales was firmly under Richard's control as was Brecon, so just like they did in 1405, the next morning Henry's army marched on Haverfordwest. This was probably because, just as Margaret of Anjou had marched towards Wales to join with Jasper Tudor after landing at Weymouth in March 1471, Henry and his army were probably looking to meet with the two Stanley brothers and their forces who were heading south. William Stanley was the Justicier of Anglesey, Caernarfonshire and Merioneth, whilst Thomas held extensive lands and offices in Cheshire and Lancashire,

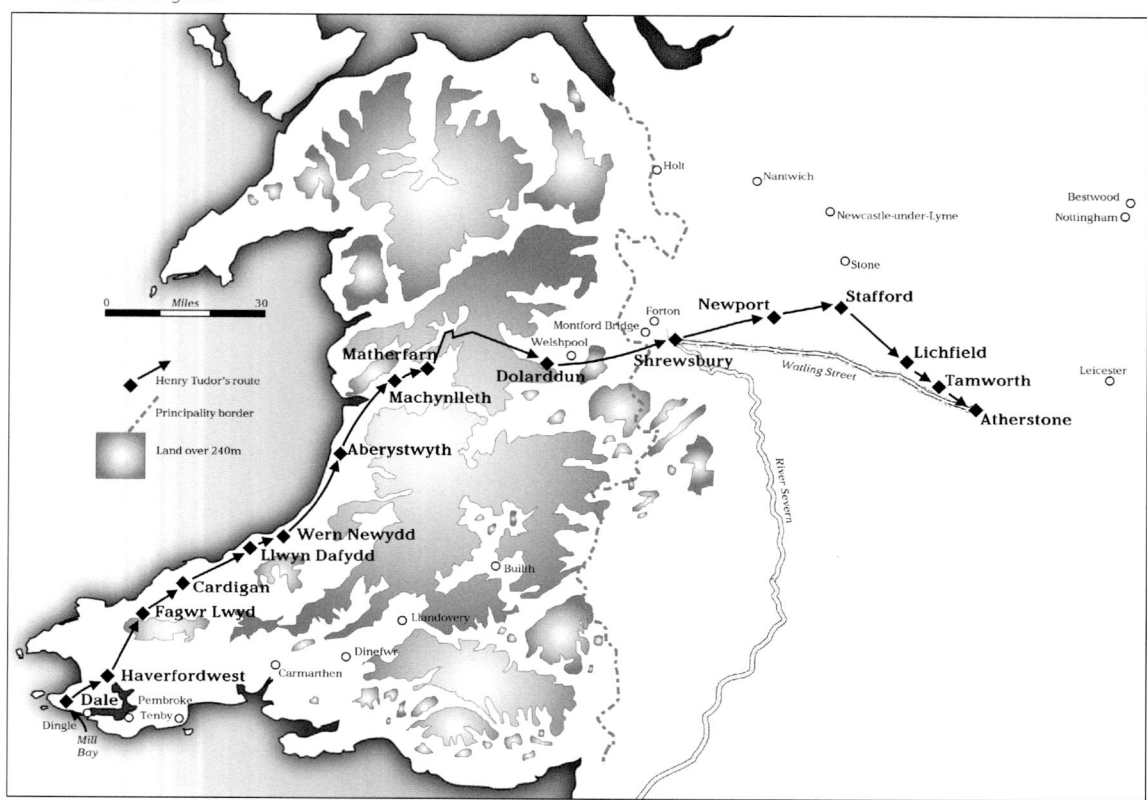

Henry Tudor's route across Wales and England.

so by going north they could expect a much friendlier welcome. Over the next 14 days, they would march around 225 miles, averaging 16 miles (26 km) each day.

According to Vergil when they reached Haverfordwest Henry was told that, despite assurances, both Rhys ap Thomas and John Savage had withdrawn their support. This is contrary to what Rhys ap Thomas' biographer wrote, claiming that the Bishop of St. David's offered to absolve him from his previous oath to Richard. The legend continues that Rhys stood under the Mullock Bridge about two miles (3.2 km) north of Dale whilst Henry marched over it. The biography was written in the 1620s after the family had fallen from grace and was a clear attempt to rehabilitate them, at best exaggerating Rhys's involvement in the campaign, at the worst reinventing it. Any content should, therefore, be treated with extreme caution. It was not all bad news, however. Arnold Butler arrived at their camp saying that the men of Pembroke were ready to support Jasper Tudor, their Earl.

We know little of the route they took until they reached Machynlleth on 14 August, over 80 miles (129 km) and five days later. Local legend suggests that they spent the next night near Cilgwyn. Vergil continues that when the army reached Carmarthen, rumours reached them that Rhys ap Thomas and Sir Walter Herbert were barring their way. Scouts were sent to investigate, only to find Richard Griffith, Sir John Morgan of Gwent, and a body of men waiting to join them.

Local tradition suggests they next stopped at the house of Dafydd ab Ieuan at Llwyn Dafydd. In return for their hospitality Henry supposedly sent the family the *Hirlas Horn* now in the possession of the Earl Cawdor (although this may be a later copy). A house four miles away at Wern Newydd, once the home Einion ap Dafydd Llwyd also claims that Henry stopped there too.

It was around this time that, according to Vergil:

> that he might advertise his frinds of his proceedinges, he sent unto Margaret his mother, to the Stanleys, to the lord Talbot, and others, certane of his most faythfull servants with secrete messages, theffect wherof was that he, trusting to the ayde of his frynds, had determynyd to passe over Severn, and throwgh Shropshire to go to London, and thcrfordesyryd them to mete him, with whom in place and time convenient he wold impart more of his intent.

The army presumably passed through Cardigan stopping at St. Hilary's church at Llanilar near Aberystwyth. According to Vergil's earliest version of the story, the small garrison at Aberystwyth castle opposed Henry's army who were 'forced to attack it and took it without much trouble'.

Henry reached Machynlleth on 14 August, where he wrote to Sir Roger Kynaston, the uncle of John Grey, Lord Powis. Kynaston was also constable of Harlech Castle and Merioneth and his family estates of Knockin and Middle had been acquired by Thomas Stanley's son.

> Trusty and well beloved we greet you well. And forsomuch as we be credibly informed and ascertained that our trusty and well beloved cousin the Lord Powis hath in time passed be of the mind and disposition that at our coming in to these

parts he had fully concluded and determined to have do us service, and now we understand that he is absent and ye have rule of his lands and folks, we will and pray you and upon your allegiance straightly charge and command you that in all haste possible ye assemble his said folks and servants and with them so assembled and defensibly arrayed for the war ye come to us for our aid and assistance in this our enterprise for the recovery of the of our realm of England to us of right appertaining.

It ended with the usual threat:

And that this be not failed as ye will that we be your good lord in time to come and avoid our grieves displeasure and answer to us at your peril.

We don't know if Kynaston answered the summons. Presumably Lord Powis was still at Southampton with the archers assembled for Brittany. They may have even left England *en route* for Brittany, only to find Landais had been executed.

From Machynlleth Henry and his army headed for England.

Richard III

The news of Henry's landing soon reached Richard Williams, Constable and Steward of Pembroke Castle. He immediately set off on the 210 mile journey to Nottingham, arriving on 11 August. He found Richard at the royal hunting lodge in Bestwood Park. According to *The Croyland Chronicle*, 'On hearing of their arrival, the king rejoiced, or at least seemed to rejoice, writing to his adherants in every quarter that now the longed-for day had arrived.' Vergil says that Richard believed that Henry:

… was utterly unfurnyshyd and feble in all thinges, contrary wyse that his men whom he had disposyd for defence of that province wer ready in all respectes. That rumor so puffyd him upp in mynde that first he estemyd the matter not muche to be regardyd, supposing that Henry having procedyd rashly consydering his smaule company, should surely have an evell ende when he showld coome to that place, wher ether he should be forcyd to fyght against his will, or taken alyve by Walter Herbert and Richard Thomas.

Richard immediately began to assemble his army. Vergil noted that 'he commandyd Henry erle of Northumberland, and other noble men that wer his frinds, who he hoped wold prefer his safety before all that ever they had, to make furth wyth muster of soldiers, and with ther forces furnysshyd to repare spedely to him.'

In 1480, John Howard was indented to provide 3,000 men for the Scottish campaign, then on 26 February 1484, as Duke of Norfolk, he promised Richard 1,000 men to 'be ready at all tymes at my lords wages.' In a list of 'men granted the king' for the forthcoming campaign that survives in his household book, Norfolk gives the names of 634 household men and servants, some bringing additional men, making a total of 760. Although the letter to Norfolk did not survive the ravages of time, one from Norfolk to Sir John Paston fortunately does, as it gives detail of not only Norfolk's movements but also Richard's. In it, he instructs Paston to join him at Bury St. Edmunds on Tuesday 16 August, with a company of tall men wearing the Duke's red livery as he had promised the King. He also informed Paston that Richard intended to leave Nottingham on the Tuesday after Lady Day, in other words, 16 August.

We do not know how many men were with Richard at Nottingham. By way of comparison Henry VI's excessive household had over 2,000 men in his when they left London for Leicester in 1455, whilst Edward IV had around 300, not including servants at the beginning of his reign. Horrox suggests that at the beginning of 1485, there were 600 men in Richard's household and that he had appointed 50 knights of the body, 48 esquires of the body, 60 esquires of the household and 138 yeomen of the crown. Some would have held other appointments at the same time, for example, Thomas Dalande, an esquire of the body, was also master of the tents and pavilions.

The Ballad of Bosworth Fielde only says that 'New messengers were made without delay, Soe farr into the West Countrye', *The Croyland Chronicle*, on the other hand, says that 'in manifold letters he despatched orders of the greatest severity, commanding that no men, of the number of those at least who had been born to the inheritance of any property in the kingdom, should shun taking part in the approaching warfare.' The chronicle continued that Richard warned them that if they failed to appear in his presence on the field, they could 'expect no other fate than the loss of all his goods and possessions, as well as his life.' Only one of these letters survives today, although in all probability he sent many more. The letter dated 11 August, was addressed to Henry Vernon, an esquire of the body, and said:

> Trusty and wellbeloved, we greet you well. And forasmuch as our rebels and traitors accompanied with our ancient enemies of France and other strange nations departed out of the water of Seine the first day of this present month making their course westwards, been landed at Nangle besides Milford Haven in Wales on Sunday last passed, as we be credibly informed, intending our utter destruction, the extreme subversion of this our realm and disinheriting of our true subjects of the same, towards whose re-countering, God being our guide, we be utterly determined in our own person to remove in all haste goodly that we can or may. Wherefore we will and straightly charge you that ye in your person with such number as ye have promised unto us sufficiently horsed and harnessed be with us in all haste to you possible, to us your attendance without failing, all manner [of] excuses set apart, upon pain of forfeiture.

The letter is also of interest as the level of knowledge of Henry's crossing indicates that Richard had been receiving up to date intelligence of Henry's movements. He was also receiving regular updates of Henry's movements, for example, on 18 August, Richard Alastre, the mayor of Nottingham paid Thomas Hall for 'ridyng forth to aspye for the town afore the feld'.

After the battle, both Roger Wake, Sheriff of Northampton and Catesby's brother-in-law, and Geoffrey Saint Germain claimed they had no choice but to come to the King's aid to avoid the threatened consequences. What they actually thought will never be known, as to say anything else would have meant incriminating themselves and would have invited some form of retribution from Henry.

About the same time, Richard wrote to York. The council agreed to send John Spooner, sergeant of the mace and John Nicolson to Nottingham to ask Richard how many men he wanted. It was proclaimed throughout the city that all freemen should be ready in 'their most defensible array' at an hour's notice. Nicolson was back in York on 19 August, and although Richard asked for 400 men, it was agreed to send 80 'with all haste for subduing the king's enemies.' However, it was probably too late, as the men of York appear to have not reached the battlefield in time. Why so few compared to what they had supplied in the recent past? The answer may lie in the will of Robert Morton of Bawtry made on 20 August. In it, he said he 'was going to maintain our most excellent King Richard III against the rebellion raised against him in this land.' If they and others in the country thought it was just a rebellion, it might explain why a number stayed away? Another possibility is that this was harvest time and those in the countryside would have wanted to bring their crops in first.

Letters were also sent to London. Richard summoned the Lieutenant of the Tower, Sir Robert Brackenbury, probably to bring some of the artillery that was stored there. According to Vergil, he was told to bring with him Thomas Bourchier, Walter Hungerford and others whom Richard did not trust.

Thomas Stanley was conspicuously absent from Richard's court at Nottingham. *The Ballad of Bosworth Fielde* says he was on the way to Nottingham when 'hee ffell sicke att Manchester'. Given that Stanley was central to the whole plot against Richard, it is Vergil's version of events that has a ring of truth about it when he said earlier that summer he had 'gone into his country, for his pleasure as he said, but indeed that he might be ready to receive earl Henry as a friend at his coming.' *The Croyland Chronicle* says that he 'made the excuse that he was suffering from an attack of the sweating sickness, and could not possibly come.' It continues that his son had prepared to desert from the King. Stanley and his son were certainly together in Lancashire on 18 July, when they both signed a document. Sometime after the arrival of the Great Seal, Lord Strange tried to leave Nottingham but was 'discovered by a snare and was seized'. The Croyland chronicler tells us that Strange then revealed to Richard that he, William Stanley and Sir John Savage had gone over to the side of Henry. Lord Strange, probably under duress, then wrote to his father, describing the 'danger to which he was exposed' and urged him to come to the King's aid with all his power. *The Ballad of Bosworth Fielde* recounts how Richard sent Stanley a message saying:

> Yonder cometh Richmond over the flood,
> With many allyants out of far countrye,
> Bold men of bone and blood;
> The crowne of England chalengeth hee.

You must raise those that under you bee
And all the power that yee may bringe,
Or else the Lord Strange you must never see,

Richard, in the meantime, declared Sir William Stanley and Sir John Savage traitors.

On 11 August, the mayor of London ordered a special watch of 101 men from 6:00 a.m. to noon and another 104 from noon to 7:00 p.m. Six days later it was announced that there would be a standing watch of 100 men from the livery companies 'wele and clenely harnest and wepened' in Cheapside, to continue daily until told otherwise. London was expecting Henry to appear at any time. They also supplied a further 1,200 men 'to continue daily unto that we have otherwise in commaundment'. The common council assigned four aldermen and 23 commoners to supervise the ordinance for the defence of the city. They could have easily just left the gates open for him if they disliked Richard's rule. However, the fact that the city took such a defensive posture shows that the aldermen and livery companies did not believe any of the rumours about him. Even whilst the battle was taking place at Bosworth, London was placed under what was in effect martial law. A curfew at 9:00 p.m. was put in place, if fighting occurred in the streets then all were to remain in their houses and 'every parsone householder & hopholder and of power to wayreharnes shall go daily in his harnes … for the save garde & suretie of this Citie.' Even two days after the battle, the city placed a watch of 196 men around the Guildhall, a watch of 204 men during the daytime and 183 at night. It was only when they had confirmation of Richard's death and that Henry was the new king, did they stand down.

Henry Tudor

Henry was heading for Welshpool, 30 miles away. Another local legend suggests he stopped at Dolarddun near Castell Caereinion where he was presented with a white horse which took him the rest of the way to Bosworth. Around this time Rhys Fawr ap Merududd from Golgynwal and the men of Gwynedd joined the ever-growing army. When they arrived at Welshpool, the army camped on Mynydd Digoll, which was also known as Long Hill, just 16 miles from England. It was here that according to Henry Rice his biographer, writing in the 1620s, that Rhys ap Thomas, under his black raven banner, met up with Henry. Rice says that Rhys brought with him 'a goodly number of soldiers,' estimated to be between 1,800 and 2,000 strong. Apparently they had been shadowing Henry since Dale. Vergil says that they only joined Henry's army after two days of negotiation that ended when Henry promised him the Lieutenancy of Wales in perpetuity (the promise was not kept). The Tudor chronicler Elis Gruffydd claimed that a great many men from Gwynedd joined before they reached Shrewsbury. Before the night was over, they were also joined by William Griffith of Penrhyn, Richard ap Howell of Mostyn in Flint and Rhys Fawr ap Maredudd from the Conwy valley. The town chronicle says that:

… the gates were shut against him and the portcullis let down. So the said Earl's messenger came to the gate, to say the Welsh gate commanding them to open the gates to their right king, and Master [Thomas] Mitton made and swore, being head bailiff and a stout wise gentleman, saying that he knew him for no king but only King Richard to whom he was sworn, whose life tenants he and his fellows were. And before he should enter there he should go over his belly, meaning thereby that he would be slain to the ground and so to run him over before he entered, and that he protested vehemently upon the oath he had taken.

The army withdrew to the village of Forton and camped on Forton Heath. Vergil notes that soon after, Christopher Urswick arrived laden with money and the news that all was safe with his friends and they were prepared to do their duty at the right time. Quite possibly this was the news Henry was waiting for – that the Stanley brothers and their armies were on the move.

The next morning another messenger was sent to the town but once again they reached an impasse. It was only broken by the timely arrival of Rowland Warburton who had been sent by William Stanley, 30 miles away at Holt, to persuade the burgesses to open the gates. A probably apocryphal story says that to get the bailiff's attention, he had to throw a message wrapped around a stone into the town. Whatever the message from Stanley said, the gates were duly opened. The local chronicle says what happened next: '…upon this they entered and in passing through the said Mitton lay along the ground and his belly upward and so the said Earl stepped over him and saved his oath and so passing forth and marching forwards…' It appears the army did not stop in the town, although local tradition suggests that Henry stopped at a house in Barracks Passage in Wyle Cop as he passed through. The ballad *The Rose of England* records that once the gate was open Oxford threatened to cut off Mitton's head, only to be stopped by Henry saying 'if we begin to head so soon, in England we shall bear on degree.'

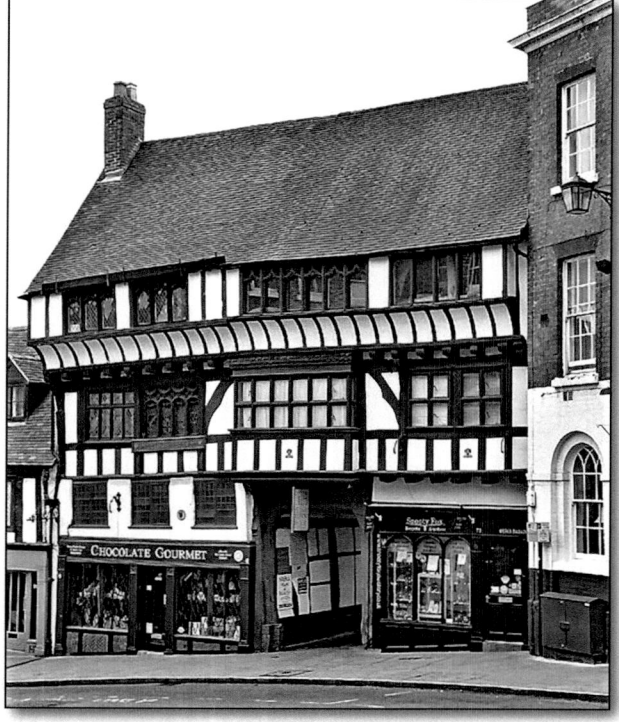

Henry Tudor House, Wyle Cop, Shrewsbury. So called because he is reputed to have stopped here en route to Bosworth. (Author)

Henry's next stop was on a hill outside Newport where he was joined by Gilbert Talbot with another 400 or 500 men. Soon after, Sir Richard Corbet, who had rescued Henry at Edgcote and was also Sir William Stanley's stepson came with another 800 men. They were also joined by John Hanley from Worcestershire and Robert Pointz from Gloucestershire. Sir William Stanley had by this time left Holt and according to *The Ballad of Bosworth Fielde*, 'Removed from Nantwiche to the towne of Stone', just eight miles (12 km) from Stafford with between 3,000 and 5,000 men.

On 19 August Henry had reached Stafford, where he finally met Sir William

Stanley. Sir William was going to act as Henry's vanguard, staying ahead of the main army for the rest of the journey. At this point, the army could have advanced directly on Nottingham to confront Richard, but instead turned south-east towards Lichfield. Was this part of the plan all along, bearing in mind that Thomas Stanley was ahead of them and that Bourchier and Hungerford seemed to know where to meet them?

Richard III

There was a growing sense of urgency in Richard's camp as, according to *The Croyland Chronicle*: 'The enemy making haste and moving day and night towards a direct confrontation with the king, therefore it was necessary to move the army, though it was not yet fully assembled, away from Nottingham and to proceed to Leicester.'

Richard left Nottingham on 19 August, just as Henry's army was entering Stafford. According to Vergil, they left in a square battle formation, with 'all impedimentes being gatheryd into the middest of tharmy, himself, with his gard, dydfolow the wings of horsemen ranging on both sydes; so keeping theraray, they came unto Leycester a little before the soonesett.' Richard had only stayed in Leicester four times his whole life, and those were all in 1483. A story by the writer and cartographer, John Speed, that first appeared at the end of the sixteenth century, has it that Richard stayed at the White Boar Inn (but renamed the Blue Boar after his death) in Northgate Street, reputedly in his own bed which he had brought with him. However the earliest reference to the inn is from the 1570s so it may not have even existed at the time. Although some have suggested that Richard stayed at the Blue Boar because the castle was in a poor state of repair, he had stayed at the castle in 1483, so it is unlikely it had deteriorated that much in two years. In addition, there were far more prestigious buildings in Leicester such as those in the Newarke where he could have stayed. The first castle was built around 1070. The Great Hall was built around 1150 by Robert de Bossu, 2nd Earl of Leicester and there is no evidence of any work until 1523 when it was extensively rebuilt, and the roof structure replaced. In 1695, it was given its brick frontage when it was used as a law court until 1992. It is now the Business School for De Montfort University.

During the fourteenth century, the earls of Leicester and Lancaster enhanced the prestige of Leicester itself when Henry, 3rd Earl of Lancaster founded a hospital for the poor and infirm in the area to the south of the castle now known as The Newarke (the 'new work'). His son Henry of Grossmont, the 1st Duke of Lancaster, enlarged and enhanced his father's foundation, and built the Collegiate Church of the Annunciation of Our Lady. It soon became a Lancastrian mausoleum, as Duke Henry had his father reburied there, and then was himself buried in the church, so too was Constance of Castile, Duchess of Lancaster (second wife of John of Gaunt) and Mary de Bohun (first wife of Henry IV, and mother of King Henry V). It also became an important pilgrimage site because it housed a thorn said to be from the Crown of Thorns, given to the Duke by the King of France. The church itself

RICHARD III AND THE BATTLE OF BOSWORTH

Victorian illustration of the Blue Boar in Leicester where legend says Richard stayed before the battle. (Author's collection)

was destroyed during the reign of King Edward VI, although a small part survives in the basement of the Hawthorn Building of De Montfort University.

Since Richard III's death, many other legends have arisen. One is that he could not sleep in strange beds and so, as noted above, brought his own with him from Nottingham to Leicester, where it was then set up for him in the White (Blue) Boar Inn. When Richard left Leicester, his bed remained behind ready for his return. So, the story goes, after his death the bed stayed at the Blue Boar, passing from tenant to tenant. Infamously in 1604 one owner, a Mrs Clark, was murdered because of a hoard of gold coins that she allegedly found hidden in the bed. The criminals, Thomas Harrison and Edward Bradshaw, aided by Mrs Clark's servant, Alice Grimbold, robbed and murdered the lady. They were quickly apprehended. Bradshaw was hanged, and Alice was burnt at the stake for their part in the crime in 1605. After the murder the bed became famous, and in 1611 'King Richard's bedstead' was included on a list of sights and exhibitions in England which could be seen for a penny. The bed was eventually acquired by Leicestershire Museums Service, and today it is on display at Donington Le Heath Manor House. However, for the most part, it seems to have been made in the seventeenth century.

Henry Tudor

Henry reached Lichfield on the evening of 19 August, his army camping outside the walls. The next morning, it marched through the city. According to *The Ballad of Bosworth Fielde*, it was greeted by old and young with guns 'cracken on high'. As Henry crossed Woosley Bridge, he was honourably received by the clergy as King, with entreaties. He also received news that Thomas Stanley had passed through the city three days earlier with a considerable army. He had apparently left Lathom on 15 August, passing through Newcastle-under-Lyme on the way, and was now further along Watling Street, at Atherstone, waiting for Henry to catch up. Vergil says that Stanley, 'understandinge of Henryes approche, went before, without delay, to a village caulyd Aderstone, meaning ther to tary till Henry showld draw nere.' This suggests it was part of the pre-arranged plan, and marching ahead he provided security for Henry's army following along behind, as the *Ballad of Bosworth Fielde* states:

> The vanward the Lord Stanley tooke hee;
> Sir William Stanley the rereward wold bee,
> And his sonne, Sir Edward, with a winge.
> The did remaine in their array.

Henry's army arrived at Tamworth on the evening of 20 August. Here he was joined by Walter Hungerford and Thomas Bourchier who had either escaped Brackenbury or were set free near Stony Stratford. According to Vergil:

> he herd that king Richerd, with an host innumerable, was at hand. While he thus, soomwhat sadd, folowyd alofe, all tharmy cam to Tamworth, and whan as by reason of the night which came uppon him he could not discerne the trace of them that wer gone before, and so after long wandering could not finde his company, he cam unto a certane towne more than thre myles from his camp, full of feare … Henry the next day after, in the gray of the morning, returnyd to the hoste, excusing himselfe that he was not deceavyd in the way, but had withdrawen from the camp of set purpose to receave soome goode newys of certane his secret frindes.

Who the secret friends were, has never been explained. Were they spies in Richard's army or potential defectors?

Richard III

On 21 August, having been informed of Henry's location by his scouriers, battle standards unfurled and ready to fight, Richard and his army marched out of Leicester, according to tradition through the West Gate and over Bow Bridge. Bow Bridge was 69 feet (21 metres) long but only 6 foot (1.8 metres) wide, built of stone with five semi-circular arches, and niches at intervals along both sides in which pedestrians could stand whilst allowing wagons to pass. Another one of those legends, once again first recounted by John Speed, is that as Richard left Leicester over the bridge, his heel struck the stone parapet. As always at times like this, an old wise woman appeared asking for alms. When Richard refused, she prophesied that 'where his spurre struck, his head should be broken.'

In another variation of the myth, perhaps drawing on local folk memory after the battle, it is said that he would next enter Leicester, with his head beneath his horse's back. The bridge was repaired in 1666, and again in 1784 when it was widened with brickwork but it was eventually demolished in 1861 and replaced with a wider iron bridge. The new bridge was designed as a memorial to Richard III with decorative ironwork showing the town's coat of arms (a white cinquefoil on a red shield) interspersed with roses and the coats of arms

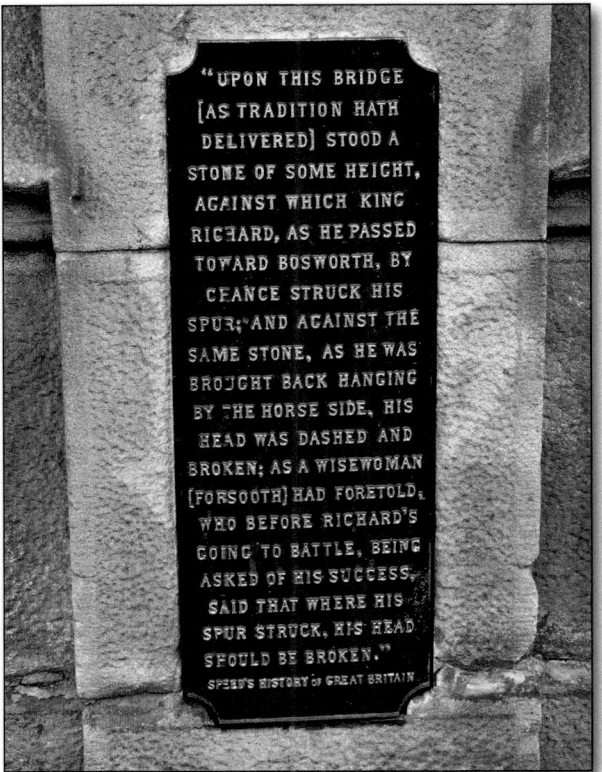

Plaque retelling the legend of the old wise woman on Bow Bridge, Leicester. (Author)

of Richard III and Henry VIII. However, whilst this had now been accepted as the gate from which he left Leicester, one 1644 account says he left from the south gate.

The Croyland Chronicle remarks on the procession that left Leicester as:

> On the Lord's day before the feast of Bartholomew the Apostle, the king proceeded on his way, amid the greatest pomp, and wearing the crown on his head; being attended by John Howard, duke of Norfolk, and Henry Percy, earl of Northumberland and other mighty lords, knights and esquires, together with a countless multitude of the common people.

The route Richard's army may have marched along to the battlefield is now lost. One possibility is they followed a now lost Roman road that passes close to Kirby Muxloe, the site of William Hastings' unfinished castle, to Peckleton and then Kirby Mallory where it continues as Fenn Lane near Dadlington before joining Watling Street. Another possibility is that they followed an ancient Salt Way, some of which continued as a green road in the eighteenth century. Local tradition has Richard's camp south of Stapleton, whilst Norfolk camped on Sutton Heath near Cadeby. When a wood there was cut down in 1748, it was reported that spears, swords, arrows, battle-axes, scull-caps, breastplates, and over a dozen knives were found. During

The modern Bow Bridge, Leicester. It was the medieval version of this bridge that Richard crossed on his way to Bosworth. (Author)

INVASION

the more recent survey of the area, a horse pendant with the arms of the Wake family, whom we know were at the battle, was discovered near to Cadeby. Was this from the camp or the rout? There was almost certainly a camp on top of Ambion Hill, although we do not know whether it was a small unit or a whole battle that camped there. At 400 feet (122 metres) above sea level, it was the ideal place to observe Henry's movements. It is likely that once night fell, they could even see the fires of at least one of Henry's camps, probably at Atterton, which was only three miles (five kilometres) away.

A battle the next day was now inevitable.

Henry Tudor

Exactly where Henry stayed the night before the battle is unknown. Many have suggested that it was at Merevale Abbey a mile away from Atherstone, although there is no evidence other than he visited the Abbey in 1503. In the south aisle of Merevale Church there is the stained-glass window of St. Armel dating from 1500–1525. When Henry returned to Merevale in September 1503, presumably to give thanks for his victory, he sanctioned a new stained-glass window to the saint. St. Armel was an obscure sixth century Breton saint whom Henry Tudor adopted as his own patron saint. Unlike other representations of St. Armel this is the only one with him wearing armour. He

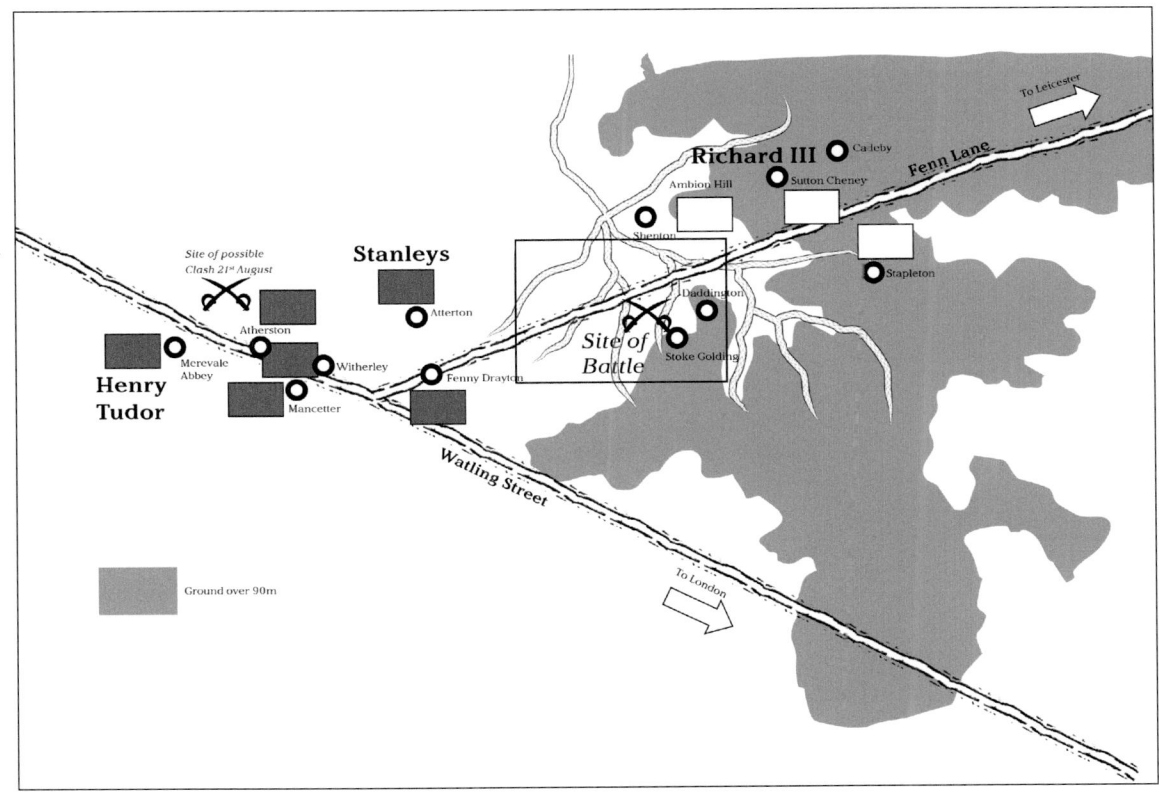

Bosworth, showing Richard III's and Henry Tudor's positions before the battle.

wears a large cope fastened by a morse, open at the front and underneath can be seen a breastplate and tassets with a skirt of mail. The head of a dragon can also be seen, peering out from a slit in his stole. Henry thought that St. Armel saved him from being drowned in a shipwreck and also saved his life on the Bosworth battlefield. However, there is also a field just east of Atherstone traditionally called 'Royal Meadow' with a 'Royal Clump' of trees on its edge, so equally he may have been there. A third tradition has Henry staying at the Three Tuns in Atherstone. This is also associated with Henry's meeting with the Stanleys. The Three Tuns name could alternatively be a simple allusion to three villages such as Atherstone, Atterton and Fenny Drayton or possibly Dadlington, Shenton and Sutton – the area of the battlefield. The Stanley brothers and their army were also probably at, or just outside, Atherstone. The 'Harley 542' version of *The Ballad of Bosworth Fielde* puts them in a dale, which could be in the valley at the confluence of the rivers Sence and Anker to the north of the town.

It appears from payments made 'by us and our company at our late victorious fields' after Henry had been crowned, that the army was dispersed around the area. By late August the majority of the grain would have been harvested and would have provided a plentiful supply of food for the army. Atherstone, Witherley, Mancetter, Fenny Drayton, Atterton and the Abbot of Merevale Abbey, all received compensation for loss of corn and grain with Witherley and Fenny Drayton being paid the most. This suggests that the army was dispersed over a wide area. However, as they were, in effect, in hostile territory, it is unlikely they were too far apart in case they were attacked. Therefore, the two most forward places, Fenny Drayton and Atterton, are more likely on the route the army took to the battlefield. The French, assuming that they brought their wagons, would have set up their own *laager* with tents in the centre. Another of the many local legends says that some of the men camped in the Outwoods, a mile to the east of Merevale Abbey. A mile to the south of the woods is Ridge Lane, in which an inn called the *White Hart* still stands, and before the battle, some of Henry's men drank the cellars dry.

There is tantalising evidence that an advance guard from Richard's army clashed with Stanley's men whilst at Atherstone. There are records of five men being killed on 20 or 21 August. These included Richard Boughton, Sheriff of Warwickshire and Leicestershire, and John Cock of Chadwell St. Mary in Essex, both dying on 20 August. John Kebell, Commissioner of Array for Rearsby in Leicestershire, William Curson of Brightwell in Suffolk and Thomas Hampden of Great Hampden in Buckinghamshire are all recorded as dying the following day. Some form of clash before the main battle is suggested by *The Song of Ladye Bessiye* which says:

> Now, is word come to Sir William Stanley there,
> Earley in the Monday in the morning,
> That the Earle of Darby, his brother dear,
> Had given battle to Richard the King.

This is collaborated by the *Ballad of Bosworth Fielde* which says:

> A messenger came to him straight
> And kneeled downe upon his knee,
> And saith, The Lord Stanley is his enemy nye,
> That are but a litleway from him.
> They will fight within these houres three
> With Richard, that is Englands Kinge.

In addition, on mid-eighteenth century maps of the area, there is a landmark called 'Bloody Bank' just north of the town. The name derives from an apparent discovery in 1766 of a number of bodies, a gilt spur engraved with a white rose pattern, and a wrought key with the cypher of RR. Is this where the clash took place?

It was now Sunday 21 August. Henry went to confer with Sir William and Lord Thomas Stanley, who was camped at Atherstone, where according to Vergil, they greeted each other cheerfully. Once again, local legend says it was at the Three Tuns or the nearby Hall Close. It was here that they probably planned the forthcoming battle saying 'they enteryd in cownsaylle in what sort to darraigne battayll with king Rycherd, yf the matter showldc oome to strokes, whom they herd to be not farre of.' No doubt, they were aware that Richard's army was much larger and that they needed some kind of advantage if they were to win. On 16 January 1486, Thomas Stanley testified that he had not known Henry well until 24 August. This is not surprising as he had not met his stepson before this point, and it was probably not until they reached Leicester after the battle that they got to know each other.

Molinet says that the place of battle was decided in advance, but not by whom. *The Song of Ladye Bessiye* has William Stanley say to one of Richard's heralds 'Say upon Bosseworth Field I mind to fight, Upon Monday early in the morning,' suggesting the place had already been chosen by Henry's forces. Having been in the area three days earlier, it was probably Thomas Stanley who had chosen the site, heeding Vegetius' advice that 'the wise commander will desire to be the first to take advantage of the terrain.' He knew that Richard had to come down the old Roman road now called Fenn Lane and it just so happened that there was a marshy flat plain, with a ridge of high ground running parallel with the road. The marsh would limit the use of cavalry and severely reduce the effectiveness of Richard's artillery. If they positioned troops on the high ground, they would control the road and force Richard to fight at a disadvantage.

According to *The Ballad of Bosworth Fielde* Richard sent a messenger to William Stanley ordering him to join him but instead replied:

> bidd him array him with royaltye
> & all the power that hee may bringe;
> ffor hee shall either flight, or fflee,
> or loose his liffe, if hee bee Kinge.

It was an open invitation to face him in battle, something Richard could not resist. Goaded by William Stanley, Richard was walking into a carefully planned trap.

10

The Battle of Bosworth Field 22 August 1485

A horse! A horse! My kingdom for a horse!
Richard III, Act V, scene vii

Henry Tudor

Dawn came at 5:00 a.m. on 22 August. According to Vergil, Thomas Stanley told Henry that 'the Earl should set his own forces in order while he would come with his array well appointed.' Vergil continues saying that it was not what Henry wanted to hear and 'to that which the oportunytie of time and weight of cause requyryd, thowghe Henry wer no lyttle vexyd, and began to be soomwhat appallyd, yeat withowt lingering he of necessytie orderyd his men in this sort.' This is one of those lines that has been used to suggest that the Stanleys had not made up their mind and were 'sitting on the fence.' We have already seen that this was not the case. What it possibly means is that not being a warrior and having no experience of war, he simply did not understand the plan and thought it might fail.

According to the *Ballad of Bosworth Fielde*, Stanley then lent Henry four of his best knights, Sir Robert Tunstall, Sir John Savage, Sir Hugh Persall and Sir Humphrey Stanley along with their retinues, something that he would have simply not done if he had not made up his mind. However, we have a variation in accounts here, as Vergil says that Savage had joined the Tudor army the previous day. Beaumont says in his poem that the Stanley camp was also visited by Brackenbury. We are told that Brackenbury commanded the Stanleys to join Richard's army or else Lord Strange would be executed. Thomas Stanley then replies that after the death of Hastings, they did not trust Richard and if Strange is executed, he had more sons. It is likely that the Stanleys had positioned themselves on the battlefield first thing in the morning, as Vergil says 'In the morning, he [Henry] ordered his soldiers to arm. At the same time he sent to Thomas Stanley, who had already arrived in the middle of the battlefield.' Translated literally, this last phrase says midway in the place of the fight. The battlefield was actually midway between Henry's and Richard's armies, so this implies that having chosen the battlefield, the Stanleys took up position first and waited for Henry to join them. Meanwhile, Henry then probably gathered his army at Witherley, as it was here that Henry knighted his standard bearer William Brandon, John Risley, John Hastoy, John Trenzy, William Tyler, Thomas Milborn and Richard Guildford whom he also made a master of ordnance, backdated to 8 August. Given that the army was probably dispersed, it would have taken some time to assemble, so they were probably not ready to leave before 7:00 a.m. We are told that Henry had local guides and although both John Cheyne and Robert Harcourt were from the area, a tradition in William Burton's family (as recalled in Nichols, *The history and antiquities of the county of Leicester*) suggests that John de Hardwicke, Lord of Lindley Manor, which overlooked the battlefield, and a commissioner of array for Leicestershire, was employed as a guide, bringing men and horses with him to get 'the advantage of the ground, sun and wind.' The route they took is unknown but could have either gone down to, then along, Watling Street, turning off onto Fenn Lane, or across the countryside to Atterton then down to Fenn Lane. As Henry paid reparations to both Fenny Drayton and Atterton afterwards, did they advance in two separate columns, the artillery and French needing better roads for their waggons taking Watling Street? Either route is around four miles (seven kilometres) and would have taken around an hour to get to the battlefield on foot.

Richard III

If Vergil and *The Croyland Chronicler* are to be believed, Richard, on the other hand, did not have a good start to the day. When he rose, he looked paler and more drawn than usual. Both say he told his followers that he had a bad night, his dreams plagued by visions of evil spirits or demons which Vergil ascribes to a guilty conscience. The Croyland chronicler also adds that his chaplains were not ready to celebrate mass nor was his breakfast ready, quite possibly because he was up earlier than expected. Richard may have had his faults, but he was unquestionably pious and would not have missed mass. A manuscript written around 1553 for Queen Mary called *Lord Morley on Transubstantiation* includes an account by Sir Ralph Bigot. Bigot was present at the battle and as knight of the body to Richard and master of his ordinance, ranked highly in his household. He would also go on to serve in the Countess of Richmond's, Henry's mother's household. He claimed that Richard 'callyd in the morning for to have had masse sayd before hym but when his chapelyne had one thing ready, evermore and they wanted another.' Richard's whole army would have said mass before the battle, so whether this refers to his personal mass when he awoke, or to his army before they marched to the battlefield or when they were taken by surprise by the Stanleys, is not known.

Tradition has it that he actually took his last mass at nearby Sutton Cheney church. This is another modern myth, started by the *Fellowship of the White Boar* (the forerunner of the Richard III Society) in the 1920s. However, the church has since become iconic in its own right with memorial services held

Memorial to Richard III in St. James' Church, Sutton Cheney. (Author)

Reconstruction of the Trevanion or Bosworth Sallet traditionally worn by one of the Trevanions who fought for Henry Tudor at Bosworth. From St. Mary's Church, Caerhays, Cornwall. Sadly the helmet was stolen in the 1950s and has never been recovered. (Armour Services Historical)

for Richard on the anniversary of the battle, and today drips with Ricardian symbolism. A gilded processional crucifix, which could be used as a portable mass cross, supposedly found in 1778 at an undisclosed location on the battlefield has been linked to Richard. The remains of a wooden pole with traces of paint and gilding had also been found at the same time. The crucifix is 23 inches tall and 11 inches wide (585 mm × 280 mm). It has an outer frame forming a foliated border, surrounding an inner cross made of strips of decorated metal with a Corpus (figure of Christ crucified) of bronze alloy. The arms of the crucifix end in roundels each of which is decorated with one of the symbols of the four evangelists, an eagle, a winged man, a winged lion, and a winged bull. On the back of each of the roundels is what appears to be a sun, reminiscent of the sun in splendour badge of Edward IV. The crucifix is now in the possession of the Society of Antiquaries in London.

An account by Pitscottie recounts that during the night, a servant of the Bishop of Dunkeld named Macgregor stole Richard's crown. There were two Bishops of Dunkeld at the time, Alexander Inglis and George Brown. Inglis had only been elected but not confirmed by the Pope, and Brown was probably either in or on his way back from Rome, so it was probably the former. Macgregor was quickly caught and brought before Richard. When he was asked why he stole it, he replied that his mother prophesied that one day he would be hanged and therefore decided it would be for something memorable. Impressed with the answer, Richard immediately pardoned him.

If Edward Hall's *Chronicle* is to be believed, Norfolk was given a warning of what would happen that day, for when he woke, he found a note pinned to his tent that said:

THE BATTLE OF BOSWORTH FIELD 22 AUGUST 1485

Jack of Norfolke be not to bolde,
For Dykon thy maister is bought and solde.

As we have already seen, Richard was marching into a trap that would have Richard fighting at a distinct disadvantage If this was true, then was this what the anonymous author of the note received by Norfolk was hinting at?

As Richard gathered his men, it was reported in *The Croyland Chronicle* that he told his followers that:

> to whichever side the victory was granted, would be the utter destruction of the kingdom of England. He declared that it was his intention, if he proved the victor, to crush all the traitors on the opposing side; and at the same time he predicted that his adversary would do the same to the supporters of his party if victory should fall to him.

We do not know the route Richard's army took from their campsites to the battlefield. One possibility is that they either came south from Ambion Hill or along Fenn Lane. As has been discovered at other battle sites because the vast majority of an army tends not to know where they actually are in the confusion of a rout, they tend to flee away from the enemy the way they came to the battlefield (e.g. as at Naseby in 1645). The trail of a debris field along Fenn Lane discovered by archaeologists and a cluster of finds at the nearby Dadlington windmill suggests this may be the direction of the rout and therefore the possible route to the battlefield. Given the number of finds in the vicinity, it may have also been where Richard pitched his camp before the battle.

Bosworth Battlefield. The view towards the battlefield from Ambion Hill. (Author)

The Two Armies

We do not know how many men faced each other that day. The Tudor based sources all wildly exaggerate the size of Richard's army, no doubt to emphasise how in the face of adversity, Henry overcame a much larger force. Apart from Norfolk, his son, Northumberland and Brackenbury, it is difficult to say who actually took part in the battle on Richard's side. It is relatively certain that Salazar was there, but whether he was alone or with a company of men, is more difficult to ascertain. He seems to have had a captain that took messages to Maximilian, which suggests he may have had a number of men with him, and there were Burgundian coins found in the debris field on the battlefield, however, this is only circumstantial. It is possible that he commanded a company of handgunners, as Burgundy had traditionally supplied in the past (e.g. Second Battle of St. Albans). There was also a considerable number of handgun balls (shot?), found on the site, but of course, these could be from anyone in either army.

The earliest version of *The Ballad of Bosworth Fielde* lists the names of 71 men who took part on Richard's side, including, one duke (Norfolk), six earls (Kent, Surrey, Lincoln, Northumberland, Shrewsbury, and Westmorland) and one viscount (Lovell), 15 barons and 48 knights. Where this list came from is not known and not everyone on it has been identified. There are also a number of omissions, and other versions have additional names. On 7 November 1485, 28 of Richard's supporters were attainted, i.e. declared guilty of treason by a bill of attainder. Several of those attainted are not included in the *Bosworth Fielde* list, despite them being known to be present at the battle such as William Catesby and Roger Wake. If we use numbers listed for Edward IV's invasion of France in 1475 as a guide to how many men could be mustered, then earls typically took 300–500 men, barons 100–200, and knights 20–50, based on a lance being a single man (see earlier discussion on the lance). Assuming that the ballad list is correct, then including Norfolk with 800 to 1,000 men and Richard's household of between 300–600 men, this then gives a range of 5,500–7,350 men. Catesby controlled vast swathes of land throughout the country, so probably brought a larger than an average number of men with him. None of the sources mentions troops raised by Commission of Array although undoubtedly some must have been there. We have already seen the letters sent out beforehand and there is a further clue in that Roger Wake who was known to have been at the battle, was Sheriff of Northampton, so in all probability brought the men of Northampton with him.

The length of the line of battlefield debris found during the recent investigations is around 1,000 yards (914 metres), so the battle-line must have been at least this long. If there were no gaps in the battle-line and that, according to Vegetius, men require three feet (one metre) of space each when fighting side by side, then we can estimate that there were around 1,000 men in the front line of the two vanguards. Given that Norfolk would have at least two or three ranks of archers and two or three ranks of infantry and knights, there must have been between 3,000–5,000 men in the vanguard. However, the vanguard could easily have been 10 ranks deep, given that the

Royal yeoman archers alone had raised 3,000 men in the past, which means that 7,000 men are not outside the realms of possibility. We can, therefore, estimate that Richard's army had between 10 and 15,000 men in total, which is not that different to most European sources (as the table below).

Table 1: Comparison of the size of Richard's Army by source

Source	Commander	Size of Force
De Valera	Richard III	7,000
	Norfolk	7,000
	Vanguard	10,000
Molinet	Richard III	60,000
	Norfolk	11–12,000
	Northumberland	10,000
Commines		Not recorded
Vergil	Richard III	Twice the size of Henry's Army
Bosworth Fielde	Richard III	43,000
Ladye Bessyie	Northumberland	30,000
	Norfolk	20,000
Spont Fragment	Richard III	15,000
Norfolk House Book	Norfolk	760

Henry's army is easier to estimate. We know that he returned to Wales with between 400–500 fugitives and between 2,000 and 3,600 French including around 1,000 Scottish. In addition, they probably gathered 2,000 to 3,000 en route. Then we have the Stanleys. William is generally suggested as having 3,000 men and his brother 5,000, although it can be read that William had 3,000 and Thomas 2,000. Vergil says Thomas Stanley only had 'one troup of horsemen, and a fewe footemen' because 'for the number of all his soldiers, all maner of ways, was scarce.' That gives a total army of between 8,000 and 12,000.

Unfortunately, we don't have a list of names of those who took part on Henry's side, as we do for Richard's army, and few are mentioned by name. However, we can get the names of some from those who were knighted or given rewards before and after the battle. A short time before his coronation on 30 October 1485, Henry created the Yeomen of his Guard, a formation of 50 archers under a captain to attend him, just like Louis XI, King of France. Records show that 15 of these had been 'present in our victorious journey' (culminating in the Battle of Bosworth) or had previous overseas service.

One of the biggest difficulties we have in reconciling Henry's army is that most Tudor sources go to great lengths to avoid mentioning the French altogether (see below) and to show the Stanleys as a separate entity, whereas in reality they were all one army. We are told that Henry's vanguard was slender but matched Norfolk's in length. It is unlikely that it was less than three men deep, or 3,000 to 4,000 men, as a line two men deep when faced with so many men would be quickly overrun. To these we must add approximately 2,000 to 3,000 French (and probably Scots) in their separate formation and around 5,000 men under Stanley. Therefore, if we take all the formations under Henry into account, we can see that the two armies were much more evenly matched than Tudor sources have led us to believe.

Table 2: Comparison of the size of Henry Tudor's Army by source

Source	Commander	Size of Force
De Valera	Henry Tudor	3,000
	French	2,000
	Lord Tamorlant (William Stanley?)	10,000
Molinet	Henry Tudor	60,000
	French	1,800 + 1,800
	Scottish	1,000
	Stanley	20,000
Commines	Henry Tudor (on leaving France)	3–4,000
	Thomas Stanley	1) 26,000 2) 25,000
Vergil	Henry Tudor	5,000
	Stanley (combined ?)	5,000
	Thomas Stanley	'one troup of horsemen, and a fewe footemen'
	William Stanley	3,000
	Gilbert Talbot	500
Ladye Bessyie	Thomas Stanley	20,000
	William Stanley	20,000
	John Savage	1) 15 2) 1,500
	Rhys ap Thomas	1) 8,000 2) 10,000
	Gilbert Talbot	10,000
	Edward Stanley	300
Bosworth Fielde	French? marespikes	10,000
The Stanley poem	Henry Tudor	500
John Major	Henry Tudor (on leaving France)	4,000
	Scots (on leaving France)	1,000
Pitscottie	Henry Tudor (on leaving France)	3,000
	French (on leaving France)	6,000
	Scottish (on leaving France)	1,000
Others	Rhys ap Thomas	1,800–2,000
	Richard Corbett	800

The Battlefield

Between August 2005 and August 2009 the Battlefields Trust undertook a major new study of Bosworth battlefield, on behalf of Leicestershire County Council. The Trust's project officer, Glenn Foard, a leading battlefield archaeologist in UK, led a team of national experts from the fields of military history, landscape history and battlefield archaeology aided by a team of volunteers. They eventually found the battlefield at the junction of the boundaries of the medieval villages of Dadlington, Stoke Golding, Upton and

Shenton. It was 2.5 miles (3.6 km) south-west of Ambion Hill, the traditional site of the battlefield and the location of the visitor centre. Here they found more than 33 lead and lead composite shot from artillery pieces of a variety of calibres as well as smaller roundshot from handguns. It was the largest group of cannonballs ever found on a medieval battlefield, and since then more have been found (see Appendix I for more details). The location was confirmed when a silver gilt boar badge that could have only come from one of Richard's retainers was discovered. The area where all the probable battle-related finds, and therefore the actual site of the battle is approximately 0.81 miles (1.3 km) long by 0.42 miles (0.68 km) wide and covers around 295 ha (729 acres) on the far western side of the registered battlefield.

From the finds we can determine that the area where the two sides met was centred on a flat plain, mainly comprising of fenland which was crossed by streams, with an area of peat marsh, known as Fen Hole, on the eastern side, south of the road. South of this marsh the ground gently rises 20 metres (65 ft) to a ridge, that overlooks the road. On the top of the ridge to the east is the village of Stoke Golding and approximately 650 yards (600 metres) further north east is the village of Dadlington. The ridge continues north-east towards Sutton Cheney with a westerly facing spur now known as Ambion Hill creating a shallow valley enclosed on three sides, before falling 98 feet (30 metres) back into the plain and the battlefield. The field to the south-east of the plain, which rises to Stoke Golding was known as 'Crown Hill' from before 1605 when it was included in a bill of sale. Records before 1484, gives its name as 'garbrodys' and 'below garbrodys'. As the name suggests, this is where Henry was probably crowned. It is therefore likely that it is to here that Vergil suggested Henry withdrew 'to the nearest [or adjacent] hill,' where he gave thanks to God, ordered that wounded and dead should be attended to, and received the royal crown after the battle. Another field that has battlefield connections is the field that rises to the top of the ridge behind the plain. This has been known as the 'Dining Table' (incorrectly spelt as Dinning Table on one of the maps) for many years as, according to local legend, it is where Henry ate after the battle.

Crucial to the understanding of the battle and how it unfolded was the discovery of a line of battle debris, running almost parallel with, and south of the old Roman road. The line was around 1,240 yards (1,132 metres) long, starting in the east with the now famous gilt boar badge close to the site of the now drained marsh known as Fen Hole. The line included coins, buckles, strap fittings, buttons and studs, a fragment of a gilded copper alloy cross-guard and a copper alloy chape from a sword scabbard, with the largest amount being found at the western end of the line. This must, therefore, be the line where the two battle-lines clashed in hand-to-hand combat and suggests that the heaviest fighting occurred at the western edge.

Another important consideration is the medieval ridge and furrow field system. Surviving ridges are parallel, ranging from three to 22 yards (three to 20 m) apart and up to 24 inches (61 cm) tall – but could be up to six feet high (1.8 m) in places. Research on the three battlefields of Northamptonshire (Edgcote, Northampton and Naseby) by the Northamptonshire Battlefields Society and the Naseby Battlefields Project suggests that battles all took place

RICHARD III AND THE BATTLE OF BOSWORTH

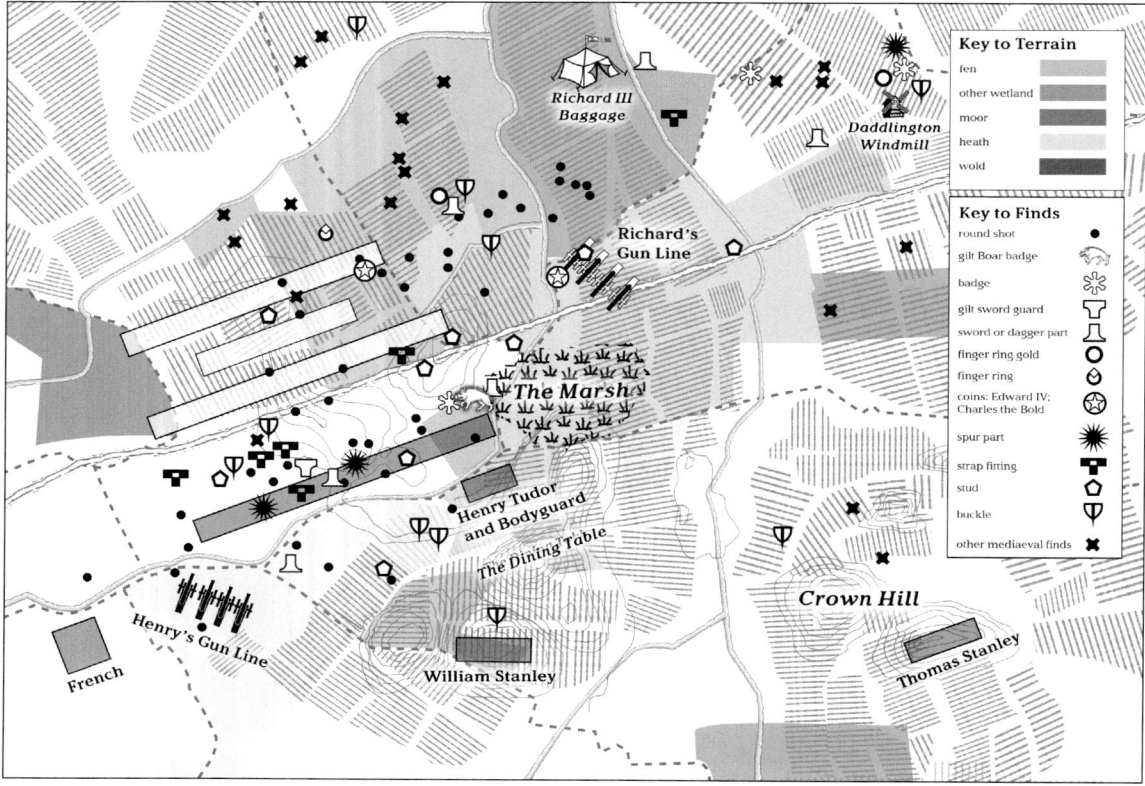

Bosworth battlefield showing the probable starting positions, finds, terrain, and the ridge and furrow field systems.

along the line of the ridge and furrow and not across it. Trying to cross them would have constituted a considerable obstacle and horses would have likely refused. At Bosworth, the ridge and furrow is, for the most part, 90 degrees to Fenn Lane, including down from the ridge. A separate strip also leads from the battlefield on to Crown Hill. Their identification, therefore, points to the direction of troop movements.

Deployment

Before discussing likely deployments, it is necessary to note that all the Tudor sources make no mention of the French or Scots in the battle. As already discussed, their importance was downplayed when they financed the invasion, and the same seems to have happened with regards to the battle. The only English source to even mention them is *The Croyland Chronicle*, and that only says that there was as many French as English, although we get a hint with the remark about the 10,000 marespikes in *The Ballad of Bosworth Fielde*. We therefore, have to rely on European sources for the part they played. As to the English sources, we then have to untangle the French from what seems to be included under the broad banner of the Earl of Oxford.

As already noted, it is likely that the Stanleys arrived on the battlefield first and assumed a blocking position on the rising ground overlooking the road. Whoever controlled the high ground controlled the road. The 'Harley

542' version of *Ladye Bessiye* implies that both of the Stanley divisions 'removed to a hyghe mountayne', although Thomas Stanley left the fighting to his brother, saying that he:

> *hove on this hill*
> *That fairebattell for to see*

The Ballad of Bosworth Fielde tells us that the Stanleys were in two separate formations:

> The Lord Stanley, both sterne and stout,
> 2 battells that day had hee…
> Sir William, wise and worthye,
> Was hindmust att the outsettinge…

It continues that William was positioned on the high ground:

> Then he removed unto a mountaine full hye
> And looked into a dale full dread:
> 5 miles compasse no ground they see
> For armed men and trapped steeds.
> Theyr armor glittered as any gleed;

As we have already seen, the only high ground is to the immediate south of the plain in which the battle was fought. Later in the ballad, it continues that:

> King Richard looked on the mountaines hye,
> &sayd, "I see the banner of the Lord Stanley."
> he said, "ffeitch hither the Lord Strange to me,
> ffordoubtlesse hee shall dye this day;

Richard would only have wanted to execute Strange if he saw the Stanleys as an immediate threat, and what bigger threat could they have posed than being positioned on the high ground. Whilst *The Croyland Chronicle* does not say where the Stanleys were, it does say Richard ordered Strange's execution as the two sides approached each other. There is another of those local traditions that says marks in the windowsill of Stoke Golding church, which is on the ridge, were made by men sharpening their weapons. However, it is far more likely that as at so many other churches around England, it was where men sharpened their scythes for harvest.

As there is no mention of Henry at this point, it is possible that Richard was next to arrive at the battlefield. With William Stanley on the ridge to the west of Crown Hill and Thomas further east near Stoke Golding, they would have blocked Richard's army from moving towards Watling Street or threatened his flank if moving either west or east along Fenn Lane. Richard would have had no alternative but to fight. The trap had been sprung. Richard, therefore, probably formed his army up in front of the Stanleys, parallel to, but on the other side of the Roman road.

Molinet tells us that Richard prepared his battles, 'where there was a vanguard and a rearguard; he had around 60,000 combatants and a great number of cannons. The leader of the vanguard was Lord John Howard … Another lord, Brackenbury, captain of the Tower of London, was also in command of the van, which had 11,000 or 12,000 men altogether.' We, therefore, have Norfolk in command of the first line, probably with his son Thomas, Earl of Surrey and Lord Brackenbury. *The Rose of England* suggests that Norfolk positioned himself on the left wing of his battle-line. As will be seen, opposite him was John Savage and could explain how Savage caught him at the windmill. Richard's battle-line must have been an impressive sight as Vergil describes it as:

> stretching yt furth of a woonderfull lenght, so full replenyshyd both with foote men and horsemen that to the beholders afar of yt gave a terror for the multitude, and in the front, werplacyd his archers, lyke a most strong trenche and bulwark.

Like the Battle of Towton, 24 years earlier, it appears that all the archers were brought to the front. Behind the vanguard was Richard and 'a choice force of soldiers'. This was no doubt his bodyguard, household troops, and personal retainers. Behind them was the Earl of Northumberland with what the Croyland Chronicler describes as a large company of reasonably good men. Vergil suggests that many would have changed sides or fled before the battle had even started, had it not been for Richard's *scurriers* (light cavalry) preventing them. Richard's array was, therefore, textbook Vegetius, with three battles one behind the other, used many times before both in England and Europe.

A number of historians have suggested that Richard's three battles were in a line, side by side, with Northumberland on the right. It has also been suggested that the reason that Northumberland does not get involved is that he is pinned in place by the Stanleys. Neither is likely because firstly, to get to Henry, we are told that Richard has to move past both vanguards. We have already seen that the vanguard contained archers, foot and horse. There is no mention of him passing Northumberland. Secondly, as we will see, we are told that Northumberland should have charged the French. This would have been impossible if he was on the opposite flank.

Although there is no record of what banners and standards Richard took to the battle, there are accounts of those he had obtained beforehand. These were 'one banner of Sarcenet of our lady' [soft silk in plain or twill weaves], 'one banner of the Trinity' and banners depicting St. George, St. Edward and St. Cuthbert. In addition, there were four standards 'of sarcanet with boars' and 'one of our own arms all sarcanet.' This was probably Richard's personal standard with the white boar and his personal motto which was in old French that said, 'Loyaulté me Lie' (Loyalty Binds Me). Another had 'three coats of arms beaten fine gold.'

Molinet says Richard had a great quantity of cannons at the battle. These would have been brought from London, possibly by Robert Brackenbury. It is *The Ballad of Bosworth Fielde* that suggest show Richard deployed them when it says:

> They had 7 score Serpentines without dout,
> that locked & Chained vppon a row,
> as many bombards that were stout;
> like blasts of thunder they did blow.

Why chain the guns together if they were in front of Richard's vanguard? The chains would certainly hamper if not stop the advance of the foot. Not only that but as the two sides moved to contact, once they had passed the gun line, they would have been useless. However, if they were on the flank in enfilade, they could rake Henry's lines with cannon fire and cause maximum destruction to his ranks right up to the point of contact. A line of cannons on the flank would also create an effective barrier, protecting it against attack. One potential danger of having guns on the flank, however, is that they could have been dragged off by Oxford's men during the battle, so it would make sense to chain them together to prevent this happening. In her updated version of Vegetius, Christine de Pizan wrote that 'in wing formation at their sides the firepower, cannoneers along with crossbowmen and archers similarly arranged.' Charles the Bold's plan for the Battle of Morat in 1476 placed his artillery on the left flank almost at a right angle to his battle-line in an attempt to destroy the Swiss with their longspears before they reached his army. It seems that both sides followed Pizan's advice for the firepower at least.

Having established the approximate positions of the battle lines, by examining the pattern of finds of cannonballs we can estimate the positions of artillery. The majority of the balls have been found towards the left of Henry's battle-line and to Richard's right (looking from the south). The natural target for the guns would be the centre of the line, so with this in mind, cones of fire emanating from Richard's and Henry's left flanks can be traced, passing through the opposing battle-line at an angle. In both cases, this would place the gun lines close to the roads. And, as guns were heavy and difficult to move across the country (especially across ridge and furrow), it would only be natural to place them as close to the road as possible. There is also some evidence to support this, as small groups of cannonballs were found close to the road, on Richard's left flank, just where you would expect the guns to be positioned. This is further supported by Molinet's comment about the French attack on Richard's right flank (see below); as from here, they would have been out the sight of the guns and their direct line of fire.

Once Richard had formed up in battle array, Henry's army was free to form up in front of them. Possibly arriving from the western side of the ridge. *The Ballad of Bosworth Fielde* tells that instead of the traditional English three division formation, Henry's army had four:

> theyr armor glittered as any gleed;
> in 4 strong battells they cold fforth bring;
> they seemed noble men att need
> as euer came to maintaine [a] King

It was a common Swiss and French tactic to form up in four battles, in 'echelon' (obliquely) and was successfully employed by the Swiss at the Battle of Morat nine years earlier to defeat Charles the Bold's massive advantage in artillery. Vegetius also said that this is a better option for when an army is impeded by numbers and a stronger foe. Henry's army was essentially a European one and Molinet goes as far as saying that Richard's army was English and Henry's French. The most likely explanation for the four battles that the author is referring to is those of Oxford, the French, and either the two Stanleys or Henry and William Stanley.

Vergil then tells us that: 'There was a marsh betwixt both hosts, which Henry of purpose left on the right hand, that it might serve his men instead of a fortress…'. The find of the gilt boar on the edge of the marsh during the archaeological investigation combined with Vergil's statement fixes the location of the right flank of Henry's battle-line on Fen Hole. Because of the description of Richard's charge and the location of the boar badge, the only possible location for Henry was positioned somewhere, to the right and behind his battle-line, probably behind the marsh. To support this, Beaumont says Henry was 'in the shadow of the hill'. With him was his personal retinue, which probably included his Uncle Jasper, John Byron, Walter Hungerford, John Cheyney and William Brandon, Henry's standard bearer. According to *The Great Chronicle of London*, when Henry eventually arrived in London, he offered up his standards in St. Paul's. We are told by its author 'oon was of the Armys of Seynt George,' the Patron Saint of England, on a red ground. The second 'a Red ffyry dragon peyntid upon whyte & Grene Sarcenet', powdered irregularly with red and white roses. Henry adopted the dragon as it had been used by Cadwallader, from whom he claimed descent. The third was 'a Baner of Tarteron bett with a Dun Cowe'. The first two speak for themselves and are images that Henry cultivated. The third is more obscure. 'Tarteron' was a silk, tabby-woven (usually striped) textile. The dun cow (or pied bull) was probably the mythical 'Dun Cow of Warwick', slain by Guy of Warwick on Dunsmore Heath near Coventry. Legend has it that its blade-bone hung on Coventry's north gate and that its ghost roamed the nearby village of Mickleton, bellowing (hence its nickname of the 'Mickleton Hooter'). However, how it was connected to Henry is not known.

We are then told by Vergil that Henry: 'made a sclender vanward for the smaule number of his people; before the same he placyd archers, of whom he made captane John erle of Oxfoord; in the right wing of the vanward he placyd Gilbert Talbot to defend the same; in the left verily he sat John Savage.' Vergil also suggests that Henry's battle-line was originally deployed south of the marsh, but advanced to contact 'whan the king saw thenemyes passyd the marishe, he commandyd his soldiers to geave charge uppon them.'

With such a long battle-line facing him, Henry would have no alternative but to match Richard's, or face the risk of being enveloped as the longer line wrapped itself around the sides. Vergil also says that it was done *'de industria'* (i.e. tactically). Richard may have had the larger army, but Henry already had two tactical advantages; his right flank was protected by the marsh, and he was on the higher ground. Both limited the effects of Richard's superior artillery, for as we have seen, a cannons maximum range was attained through bouncing, and cannonballs do not bounce well in marsh or uphill.

THE BATTLE OF BOSWORTH FIELD 22 AUGUST 1485

What has caused the greatest confusion in the working out of the deployment of Henry's army is the claim repeated in Vergil and the ballads that it was Oxford's battle that was the vanguard. In his earlier version, Vergil only ascribes a battle-line (*acies*) and not the vanguard (*prima acies*) to Oxford. Also, we have already seen how the French were written out of the narrative. Molinet says that the French were not part of the main army and that:

> The French also made their preparations marching against the English, being in the field a quarter league away … knowing by the king's shot the lie of the land and the order of his battle, resolved, in order to avoid the fire, to mass their troops against the flank rather than the front of the king's battle.

And, then there is a stanza in *The Ballad of Bosworth Fielde* and *The Rose of England* that says:

> Then the blew bore [Oxford] the vanguard had;
> He was both warry and wise of witt;
> The right hand of them [the enemy] he took
> The sunn and wind of them to gett

There is a further hint in Vergil when he says, 'both the vanwardes being arrayed, as soone as the soldiers might one sean other afur of, they put on ther head peces and preparyd to the fyght, expecting thalarme with intentyve eare.' In other words, Henry's vanguard was not in sight of the banners (the normal method of communication), which would have been visible to all in the plain, especially Oxford's men. As we have seen, it was only the French that were not with the army, and as they probably could not see the standards, were listening for a trumpet call before attacking.

It is therefore far more likely that it was the French who were the real vanguard, not Oxford. It is possible that because Oxford was placed in overall command of Henry's army, all the divisions come under his name. However, Chandée may also have been in command of the army, as Oxford's military reputation was chequered to say the least. At the opening of the battle, it seems they were hidden from Richard's view and waiting to the west, around three-quarters of a mile (1.2 km) away. We are not told in any source where the Scottish contingent was during the battle, although they were most probably with the French considering the commonality of weapons and fighting methods.

There is no mention of Henry's artillery at the battle other than he was given some by the French and collected several more en route. We do not even know how many cannons Henry had. If they were positioned on his left flank (as above), it would have helped to protect them, without hampering movement.

Another enduring puzzle is what time of day was the battle fought. Most historians have suggested the battle was fought in the early morning. However, the majority of the chroniclers agree that Henry's vanguard had the sun behind them during the battle. Having established that it was the French who were the vanguard, then the sun must have been in the west and behind

RICHARD III AND THE BATTLE OF BOSWORTH

the French. That the sun was to the west might also be what *The Ballad of Bosworth Fielde* suggests when it says:

> The Duke of Norfolke avanted his banner bright;
> Soe did the younge Erle of Shrewsburye
> To the sun and wind right speedylye dight

This then means that although the two sides possibly arrayed late in the morning, the actual battle was not fought until the afternoon.

The Battle

Despite being one of the most important battles in English history, it is one of the most poorly documented. All the contemporary or near contemporary sources only paint a broad picture of the actual battle, with Vergil supplying the most detail. So, for us to even begin to understand what happened, we have to pick out the relevant phrases and lines from all the others. A number of historians have described the battle as a clash between the old style (Richard) and the new, Continental style of warfare, and also that Richard did not know how to respond to Henry's tactics. Given that many of Richard's men had been fighting on the continent, this was almost certainly not the case. What Richard was not prepared for was the surprise attack on his right flank.

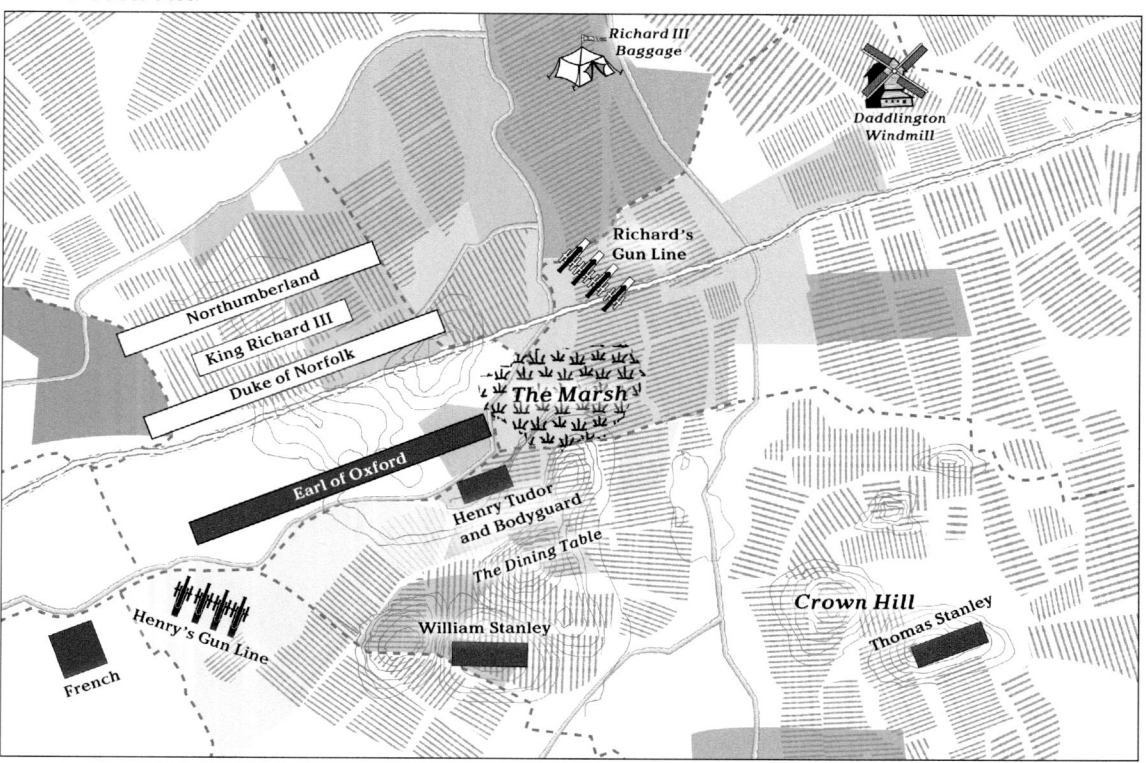

The Battle of Bosworth. The two sides close.

THE BATTLE OF BOSWORTH FIELD 22 AUGUST 1485

It seems that Henry must have advanced on Richard first, as the Croyland chronicler says that 'the earl of Richmond with his men proceeded directly against King Richard.' No doubt Richard's artillery opened fire as soon as they were in range, and Norfolk's archers would have followed suit. With the likely amount of firepower arrayed against them, Henry's men had no alternative but to advance or else be destroyed where they stood. Then, according to Vergil, when Richard saw Henry's army passing the marsh:

> … he commandyd his soldiers to geave charge uppon them. They making suddanely great showtes assaultyd the enemy first with arrowes, who wer nothing faynt unto the fyght but began also to shoote fearcely; but whan they cam to hand strokes the matter than was delt with blades.

Medieval warfare was face to face, bloody and brutal. With a resounding crash, the two sides would have come together: swords slashed, bills and halberds chopped and stabbed, the archers still with their bows, taking pot-shots where they could. The fully armoured knights with their retinues following behind carved their way through the lightly armoured men with sword or poll-axe, looking for equals. Small groups of lightly armoured men would pin down heavily armoured opponents looking for chinks in their armour, so they could deal the *coup de grâce*. The noise must have been deafening as metal clashing with metal mingled with shouts and cries, and the roar of cannon and handgun, the whole scene shrouded in a fog of gunpowder smoke.

Bosworth Battlefield. Looking west across the battlefield today, along the main battle-line where Oxford's and Norfolk's divisions fought. (Author)

RICHARD III AND THE BATTLE OF BOSWORTH

Bosworth Fielde describes the fighting between the two battle lines:

Then they countred together sad and sore:
Archers they lett sharpe arrowes flee;
They shott guns both fell and farr;
Bowes of ewe bended did bee;
Spring all spedd them speedy lye;
Harquebusiers pelletts throughly did thringe;
Soe many a banner began to swee
Then our archers lett their shooting bee;
With joyned weapons were growden full right.
Brands rang on basenetts hye;
Battell axes fast on helmes did light.
There dyed many a doughtye knight:
There under foot can the thringe. –
Thus they fought with maine and might.

The two sides then disengaged. After how long and why, is not clear from the texts. Oxford may have been attempting a feigned retreat to induce Richard's men to break their line and follow. If this was Oxford's plan, then it failed. Vergil tells us that:

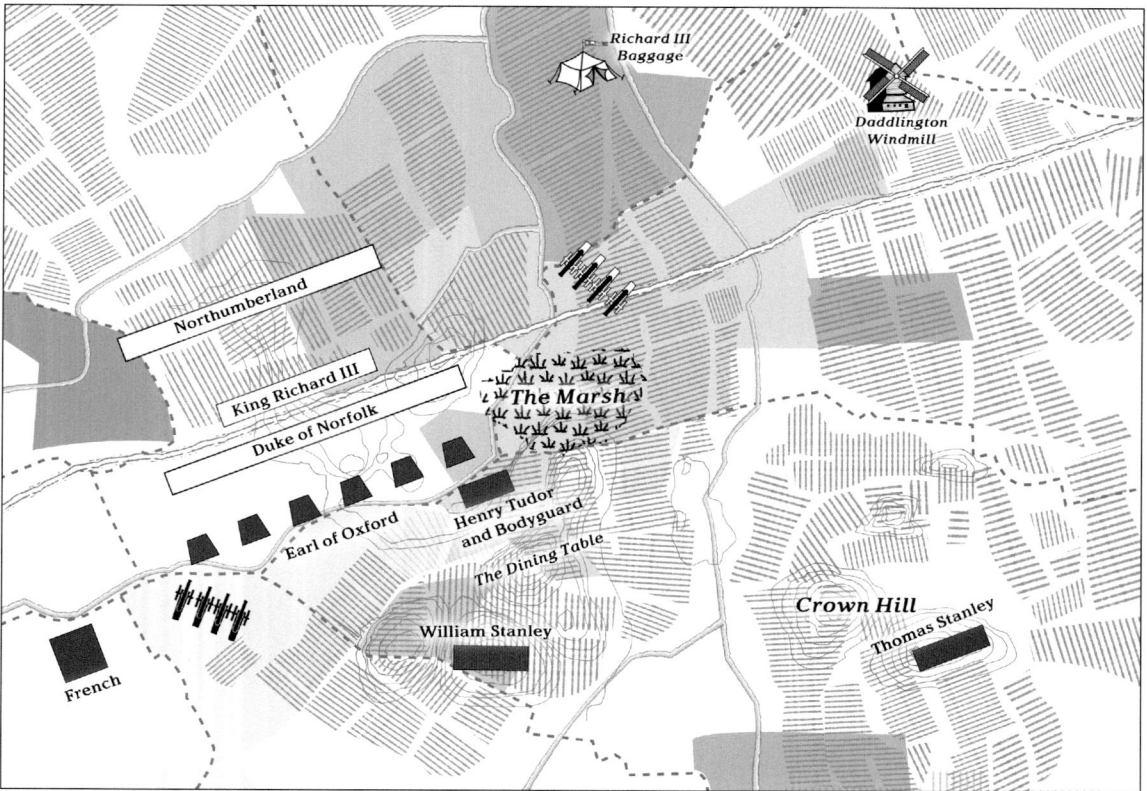

The Battle of Bosworth. Oxford's battle-line falls back and reforms in wedges.

fearing lest hys men in fyghting might be envyronyd of the multitude, commandyd in every rang that no soldiers should go above tenfoote from the standerds; … whan all men had throng thik togethers, and stayd a whyle from fighting, thadversaryes werther with a ferd, supposing soom fraude, and so they all forbore the fight a certane space … Than therle of Oxforth in one part, and others in an other part with the bandes of men closse one to an other, gave freshe charge uppon thenemy, and in array tryangle vehemently renewyd the conflict.

Here, Vergil's original expression is *Facto cuneo*, which although often read as a wedge, could also be read as a column. What is also important here is the line 'the others on the otherside made a wedge and simultaneously pressed on and renewed the battle.' What he is more probably saying is that although Oxford's men renewed their attack, it was a separate formation that attacked in a wedge or column. This must surely mean the French, who had been waiting some distance away for this moment.

It was probably during this lull in the fighting that Richard decided to carry out his threat to execute Strange. Both *The Ballad of Bosworth Fielde* and *Ladye Bessiye* give detailed accounts of what happened. They state that as he was about to be beheaded, a Lancashire gentleman called 'Lathum' was called for, who was perhaps one of his servants or even his executioner. He gave Lathum a ring from his finger, and asked him to give it to his wife, and saying that if Henry was to lose the field, she was to flee into exile with his son. As Strange put his head on the block *Ladye Bessiye* tells us that:

> A knight to King Richard then did appeare,
> The good Sir William of Harrington:
> "Let that Lord have his life, my dear
> Sir King, I pray you grant me this boone".

Beaumont's *Bosworth*, on the other hand, says that it was Catesby who was given the task of executing Strange, but was stopped by Lord Ferrers. Although the Croyland chronicler does not name Strange's saviour, he does say that it was because:

> The persons to whom this duty was entrusted, however, seeing that the issue was doubtful in the extreme, and that a matter of more weight than the destruction of one man was in hand, deferred performance of the king's cruel order, left the man to his own disposal and returned to the thickest of the fight.

It was at that moment according to *Ladye Bessiye* that:

> Then they blew up the bewgles of brass
> That made many a wife to cry, "Alas!"
> And many a wives child father-lesse.
> They shott of guns then very fast.

It was the signal for the French, who had been waiting out of sight, with the sun behind them to launch their attack on Richard's flank. In the area to the west of the battlefield, the ridge and furrow was parallel to the road, so they most likely advanced along it. Bristling with 22-foot *longspears* and screened by hand gunners and crossbow men, they crashed into his line. We have already seen that Molinet says that: 'knowing by the king's shot the lie of the land and the order of his battle, resolved, in order to avoid the fire, to mass their troops against the flank rather than the front of the king's battle.'

The French and Scots began to break Norfolk's line apart like a can-opener, the longspears forcing the line apart whilst the halberdiers and swordsmen behind hacked at dazed men. This was medieval shock and awe at its best and what the French were trained for. Further evidence of this can be found in a fragment of a letter written by a Frenchman soon after the battle. This long-lost letter, which was quoted in a paper written by Alfred Spont in 1897 for the journal *Révue des Questions Historiques* now known as the *Spont fragment*, says that Richard had shouted 'These French traitors are today the cause of our realm's ruin.' The only way they could have been stopped was with the artillery, however, this was on the opposite flank. The archers and handgunners may have stopped them, but these were already engaged in hand-to-hand fighting to their front. A third option would have been to charge them with Richard's cavalry, however, against the longspears, the chances of success were slim. This explains a second phrase mentioned in the *Spont fragment* which said 'he [Henry] wanted to be on foot in the midst of us, and in part we were the reason why the battle was won.' Clearly Henry

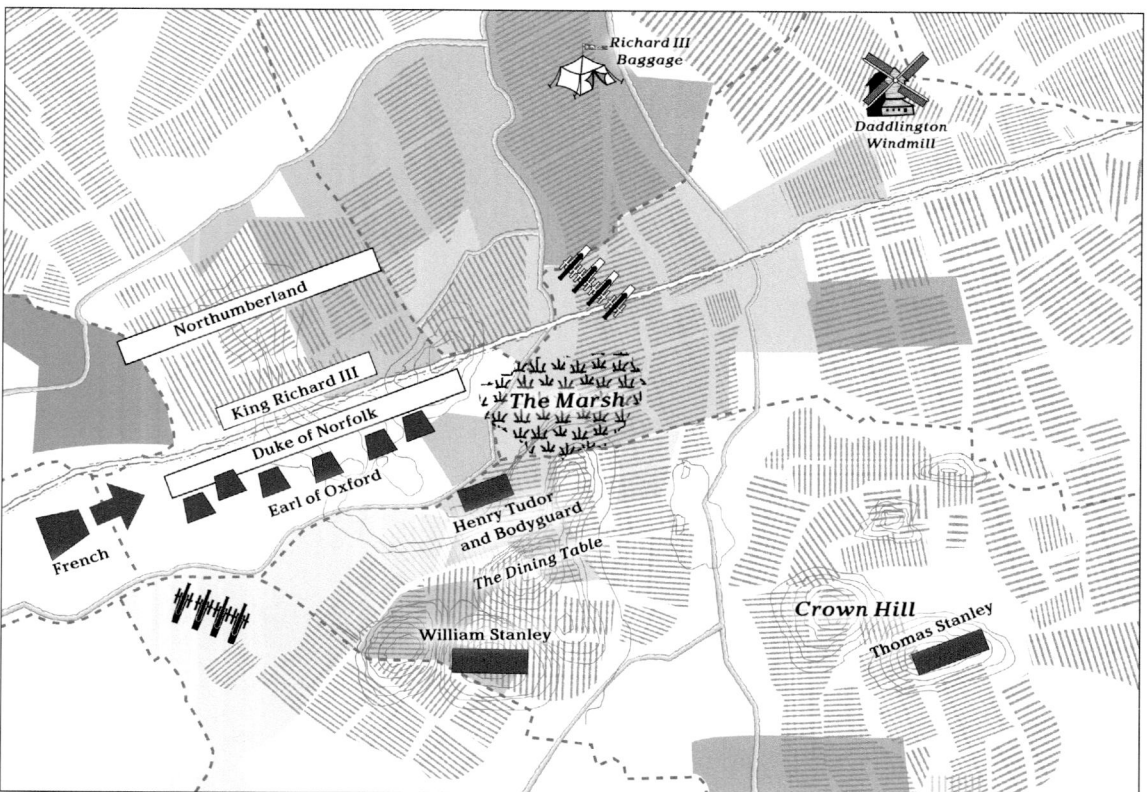

The Battle of Bosworth. Oxford's men renew their attack whilst the French launch their assault on Norfolk's flank.

thought the best place to be was in the middle of the French column. The French were, in effect unstoppable and Richard had been outmanoeuvred.

It is possible that one or two shots were fired at them from Richard's guns as they advanced. In April 2018, a metal detector survey was undertaken across five fields in the north of the new MIRA Horiba development on the battlefield. During the survey, they found a single 1.6 inch (41mm) lead shot related to the battle which stands out because it is outside the pattern of the other shot found. In other words, to the immediate west of the battle-line and on the likely route of the French advance. This was perhaps fired from one of the smaller, seven more portable serpentines on carts or one of the 28 'hacbushes' with frames that Richard ordered the previous year. A 0.7 inch (18mm) diameter lead musket shot was also found in the area, as well as a sword or dagger hanger. During a more detailed excavation during the summer of 2018 another single lead ball of approximately 0.47 inches (12mm) diameter was found. It is possible that both the smaller roundshot could have also come from the battle, but it is by no means certain.

Molinet suggests that: 'The Earl of Northumberland … ought to have charged the French, but did nothing except to flee,' Northumberland was in Richard's third line. The Croyland chronicler wrote that: 'In the place where the earl of Northumberland was posted, with a large company of reasonably good men, no engagement could be discerned, and no battle blows given or received.' Lacking any of the weapons or skills needed to stop them, to charge the French would have probably ended in disaster for Northumberland and his men. So probably seeing Norfolk's line disintegrating he chose to flee the battle. The word treason meant much more during this period, including warring on the King, not supporting the King, and providing aid and comfort to the King's enemies. So when Northumberland is accused of this, it most probably meant that he aided Richard's enemies by fleeing the battlefield. Molinet claims that Northumberland 'had an undertaking with the earl of Richmond, as had some others who deserted him in his need.' No other source mentions such undertaking with Henry. In fact, Northumberland was arrested and spent a short period in captivity after the battle, so it is unlikely that he had struck a deal with him beforehand. *Ladye Bessiye* makes no mention of the French, instead it substitutes Rhys ap Thomas for the French saying:

> Then Rees ap Thomas with the black raven
> Shortly he brake their array.

It does, however, agree that it was at this point that Northumberland fled the field.

> Then with thirty thousand fighting men
> The Lord Pearcy went his way.

This would not be the last time Henry used a flank attack. He may have used a similar tactic at Stoke in 1487. Then, at the beginning of 1497, a rebellion started in Cornwall over taxes. The Cornish army of around 9–10,000 marched

RICHARD III AND THE BATTLE OF BOSWORTH

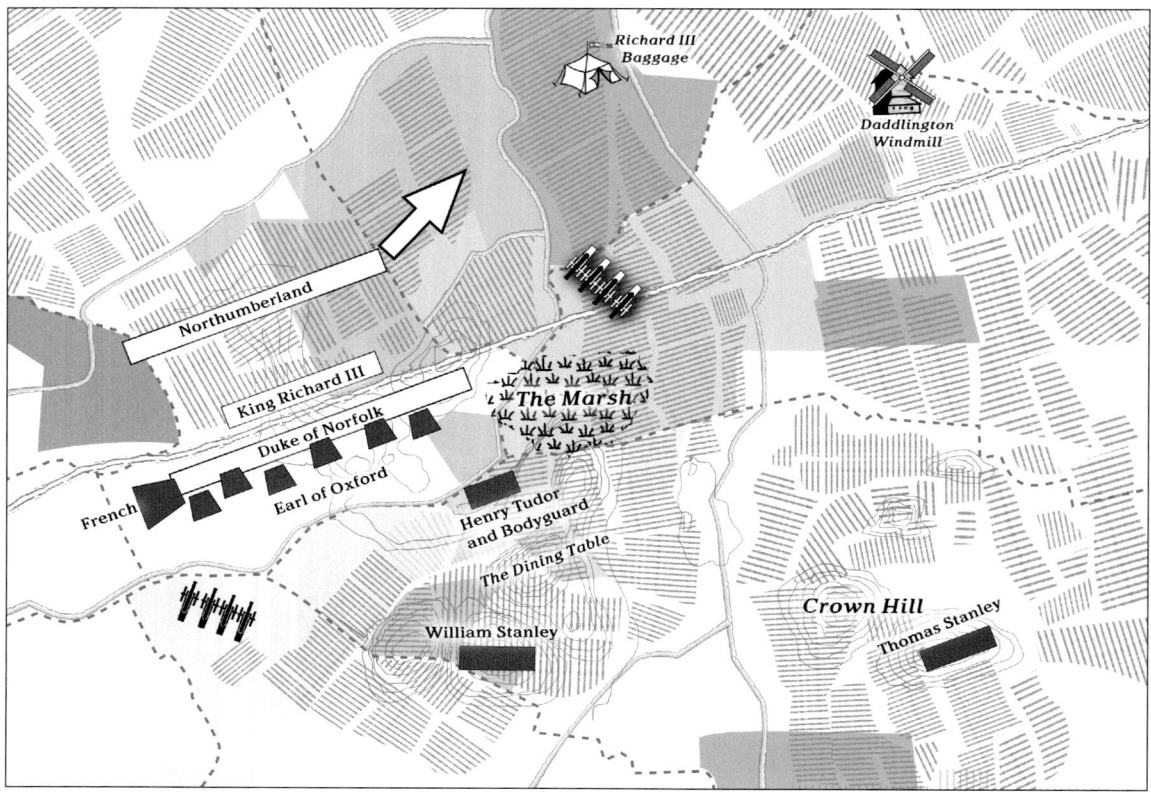

The Battle of Bosworth. Unable to stop the French, Northumberland flees the field.

to Blackheath outside London, where they made camp, Traditionally, it was said that their leader Michael Joseph (AnGof – the blacksmith), placed his tent on the mound once called the Smith's Forge but now known as Whitefield's Mount. Meanwhile, Henry had been assembling an army of over 25,000 men at Henley to counter the threat. After carefully spreading rumours that he would attack on the following Monday, Henry moved against the Cornish at dawn on Saturday 17 June 1497. Lacking cavalry and artillery, the Cornish placed a body of archers at the bridge at Deptford Strand with the rest of the army near to the top of the hill on Blackheath. Contemporary accounts describe how two of the three royal 'battles' under Lords Oxford, Essex and Suffolk, wheeled around the right flank and rear of the Cornishmen. Once they were surrounded, Lord Daubeney and the third 'battle' were ordered into a frontal attack. Lord Daubeney and his men poured across the bridge and engaged the Cornish head on. The two other battles then attacked, and the Cornish army was cut in pieces. Estimates of the Cornish dead range from 200 to 2,000 and a general slaughter of the broken army was well under way when AnGof gave the order to surrender. Angof, Audley and Flamank were all captured and suffered a traitor's death.

The situation for Richard on Bosworth Field must now have been dire. Norfolk's vanguard was collapsing, and Northumberland's men were fleeing. Fabyan states that whilst the battle raged, Richard looked for additional men. However, 'many toward the field refused him and went unto the other party, some stood hoving afar off until they saw which party the victory fell.' *The*

THE BATTLE OF BOSWORTH FIELD 22 AUGUST 1485

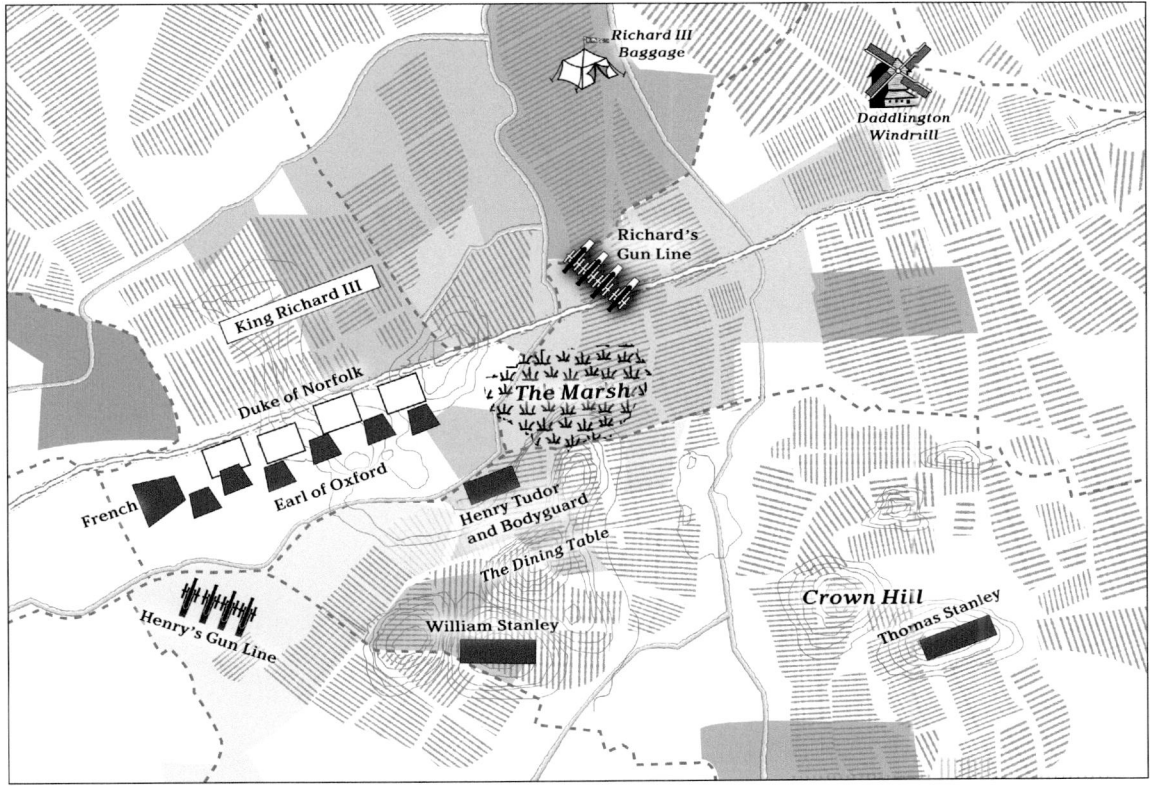

The Battle of Bosworth. Norfolk's line begins to collapse. As the two opposing battle-lines begin to open up, Richard spots Henry Tudor

Croyland Chronicle says something similar in that: 'deserters came from the ranks composed of many northerners, in whom especially, King Richard placed so much trust.' They both almost certainly refer to Northumberland's men.

It was at this critical moment of the battle that Vergil says that: 'king Richerd might have sowght to save himself by flight; for they who wer abowt him, seing the soldiers even from the first stroke to lyft up ther weapons febly and fayntlye, and soome of them to depart the field pryvyly'. Molinet also says that when Richard saw Northumberland leaving the field, he 'found himself alone on the field and thought to run after the others.' Vergil on the other hand says that around this time 'whan the matter began manyfestly to qwaile, they browght him [Richard] swyft horses.' *The Ballad of Bosworth Fielde* says it was at this point:

> then to King Richard there came a Knight,
> and said, 'I hold itt time ffor to fflee;
> ffor yonder stanleys dints they be soe wight,
> against them no man may dree'

The *Ballad of Bessiye* which repeats much of the *Ballad of Bosworth Fielde*, claims the knight to be Sir William Harrington. De Valera's Spanish report claims it was Salazar who tried to lead Richard from the battlefield saying, 'Now when Salaçar, your little vassal, who was there in King Richard's service, saw the treason of the king's people, he went up to him and said: "Sire, take steps to put your person in safety, without expecting to have the victory in today's battle, owing to the manifest treason in your following.'" It continues that Richard replied 'Salaçar, God forbid I yield one step. This day I will die as king or win.' And with that, Richard put on his coat of arms and his royal crown. The report also notes that the crown was worth 120,000 crowns and therefore very special. This may have been the original crown of Edward the Confessor, reputedly destroyed on the orders of Oliver Cromwell after the English Civil War. If it was this crown, then it was too valuable to be worn in battle, so it is more likely that he would have worn a simple gold circlet.

It is at this point that it came to Richard's attention that Henry was isolated from the rest of his army on the edge of the marsh. John Beaumont's poem suggests that it was Richard's original intention to support Norfolk's beleaguered right flank, but when he was told of Henry's isolation, he changed course:

> The King intended, at his setting out
> To helpe his vantguard: but a nimble scout
> Runnes crying. Sir, I saw not far from hence,
> Where Richmond houers with a small defence,
> And like one guilty of some heinous ill,
> Is cover'd with the shade of yonder hill

Vergil only says that Richard first received intelligence through his spies, 'than after drawing nerer he knew yt perfytely by evydent signes and tokens that yt was Henry.'

Bosworth Fielde says:

> Whyle the battayll contynewyd thus hote on both sydes
> betwixt the vanwardes, king Richard understood, first by espyalls
> wher erle Henry was a farre of with smaule force of soldiers
> abowt him; than after drawing nerer he knew yt perfytely by
> evydent signes and tokens that yt was Henry; wherfor, all inflamyd
> with ire, he strick his horse with the spurres, and runneth
> owt of thone syde withowt the vanwardes agaynst him.

If he could just reach Henry and kill him, then the battle would be over. So Richard gathered his household cavalry and infantry around him and launched the last charge of the Plantagenets.

Hall describes Richard's charge as:

> being inflamed with ire and vexed w outragious malice, he put his spurres to his horse & rode out of the syde of y range of his battaile, leuyng the auant gardes fightyng, & like a hungery lion ran with spere in rest toward him. Therle of Richmonde perceyued wel the king furiusly commyng toward him, and by cause the hole hope of his welth and purpose was to be determined by battaill, he gladly preferred to encountre with him body to body and man to man.

We do not know which route the charge took, however, the ground to the east of the marsh was boggy. As above, *The Ballad of Bosworth Fielde* says that they advanced 'owt of thone syde withowt the vanwardes.' Vergil agrees with this when he says: 'he strick his horse with the spurres, and runneth owt of thone syde withowt the vanwardes agaynst him.' Speed was of the essence, so he must have taken the shortest route with the marsh on his left and the two battle-lines to his right and the high ground with William Stanley to his front. Beaumont's poem says they charged uphill, which makes sense, as behind Henry was the high ground. The charge required split-second timing as Richard knew that once Stanley identified the threat, he and his men would charge down and attack him. Richard knew he only had moments to kill Henry and so save the battle.

Gathering momentum, Richard and his supporters crashed into Henry's bodyguard. Richard immediately killed William Brandon, Henry's standard bearer. The standard fell to the ground only to be picked up, according to Welsh tradition, by Rhys ap Maredudd (Rhys Fawr). Once his lance had broken, Richard would have taken up his side weapon which may have been a warhammer or battle-axe. *Bosworth Fielde* suggests the latter when it has Richard say 'Give me my battell axe in my hand.'

Richard III in the midst of his enemies. (Author)

Henry must have been close, because we are told by Vergil that next in Richard's path was the 6 foot 8 inch John Cheyney: '...a man of muche fortytude, far exceeding the common sort, who encountered with him as hecam, but the king with great force drove him to the ground, making way with weapon on every side'. Another of those spurious local legends says that Cheyne was riding to retrieve the standard when Richard struck him around the head with his broken lance. Cheyne lost his helmet, was unhorsed and stunned. When he recovered, he then took the skull from a nearby bull's carcass as a replacement helmet and re-joined the battle.

It has been suggested by some that based on the quotes in the *Spont fragment*, Henry was protected by a wall of French longspears. However, this is extremely unlikely as Brandon, as the standard bearer, would have been virtually thigh to thigh with Henry. So, if Henry and therefore Brandon, were behind the longspears, then Richard would not have got close enough to kill him.

According to *The Ballad of Bosworth Fielde*, during the attack, Sir Percival Thirwall, Richard's personal standard bearer, was unhorsed and his legs were cut from under him. Vergil tells us that at this moment 'Henry abode the brunt longer than ever his owne soldiers wold have wenyd, who wer now almost owt of hope of victory.' Holinshed says that Richard was no more than a sword point away from Henry, and Michael Drayton in his poem says they were 'scarce a lance length' apart. Victory was now within Richard's grasp.

RICHARD III AND THE BATTLE OF BOSWORTH

Bosworth Battlefield, looking south. The marsh and Fenn hole is on the hedge-line. It was in this area, probably near the centre, that Henry Tudor stood. Richard charged left to right across here. The possible site of Sandeford where Richard was killed is in the centre. (Author)

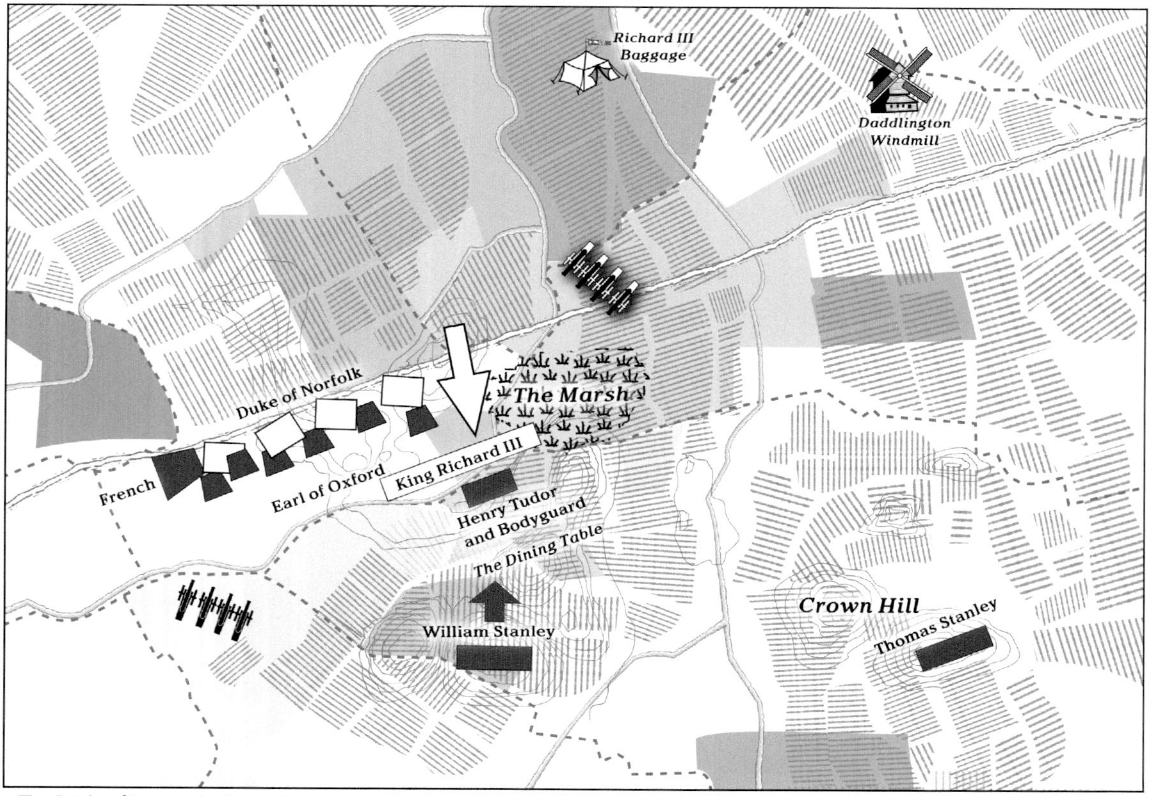

The Battle of Bosworth. Richard III charges into Henry Tudor and his bodyguard. William Stanley and his men charge down from the high ground to rescue Henry Tudor.

THE BATTLE OF BOSWORTH FIELD 22 AUGUST 1485

But at that moment, Richard's Wheel of Fortune turned again, as up to 3,000 fresh troops under William Stanley made a sudden charge down from the ridge into Richard's men. *The Rose of England* says that:

'And then came in the harts head;
A worthy sight it was to see,
The jacketts that were of white and redd,
How they laid about them lustilye.'

The Ballad of Bosworth Fielde only says that:

Downe att a backe then cometh hee,
And shortlye sett upon the Kinge.

There is a slight variation in the 'Harley 542' version of the ballad as it says at a 'banke' not 'backe'. Both suggest that they came off the high ground. Both also suggest that the final stages of the battle took place close to the marsh. One by one, Richard's followers were cut down in the *mêlée* that followed. And it was on the edge of the marsh that the famous gilt boar badge was found, probably no doubt coming from one of Richard's supporters during the fighting that ensued.

Another of the Bosworth puzzles is the description of the battle in a report written for the Spanish King and Queen, Ferdinand and Isabella, in March 1486 by Diego de Valera, a Castilian courtier, not least who was the mysterious 'Lord Tamorlant'. The account reads 'When King Richard was certified of the near approach of Earl Henry in battle array, he ordered his lines and entrusted the van to his grand chamberlain with 7,000 fighting men. My Lord Tamorlant with King Richard's left wing left his position and passed in front of the king's vanguard with 10,000 men, then, turning his back on Earl Henry, he began to fight fiercely against the king's van, and so did all the others who had plighted their faith to Earl Henry.' Many have suggested that he was Northumberland. However, if we remove just one small phrase – 'and passed' – then it makes more sense as it is describing William Stanley's charge against Richard. Stanley was in front and on the left of Richard's battle-line and when his men reached Richard's men, he probably had his back to Henry. Therefore, Lord Tamorlant was most likely William Stanley and the passage even has the correct title for him.

It was at this point that disaster struck. Molinet says that Richard's 'horse leapt into a marsh from which it could not retrieve itself.' No other contemporary account described exactly what happened next except to say it was at this point in time that Richard was killed. Exactly where Richard died is not known, although a proclamation by Henry soon after the battle says it was at a place known as 'Sandeford'. Where this was has been lost in time, although it was most likely south of the marsh at a crossing point on one of the streams that fed the marsh. His courage during his last moments is unquestionable. According to Vergil, he was 'killyd fyghting manfully in the thickkest presse of his enemyes', The Croyland chronicler writes that 'King Richard fell in the field, struck by many mortal wounds, as a bold and most

The possible site of Sandeford where Richard III was killed. (Author)

valiant prince.' Even his detractors were in agreement on Richard's valour, as the normally venomous John Rous says in his *Historia Regum Angliae*, he 'bore himself like a gallant knight and despite his little body and feeble strength, honourably defended himself to his last breath, shouting again and again that he was betrayed, and crying Treason! Treason!' *The Ballad of Ladye Bessyie* describes Richard's death in horrific detail saying:

> They beat his bassnet to his head,
> Untill the braine came out with blood;
> They never left him till he was dead.

So too does Guto'r Glyn's poem of around 1493 which says, 'killed the boar, shaved his head.'

The discovery of Richard's remains in Leicester allowed scientists and weapons specialists to discover the probable cause of Richard's death with modern forensic techniques, such as conventional CT and micro-CT scanning.

A total of eight separate wounds were found on Richard's skull, suggesting a frenzied attack possibly by more than one person. Although all were perimortem (before death) it is impossible to say in which order they took place because they were all distinct, without any overlap. However, the majority could have only occurred after his helmet had been removed. Bob Woosnam-Savage, Curator of Armour and Edged Weapons at Royal Armouries, suggests that Richard was on his knees with his head down when the fatal wounds were delivered from behind. What brought Richard to his knees will never be known. Perhaps he was already on his knees as he extricated himself from the marsh? He could have slipped in the mud? Or,

THE BATTLE OF BOSWORTH FIELD 22 AUGUST 1485

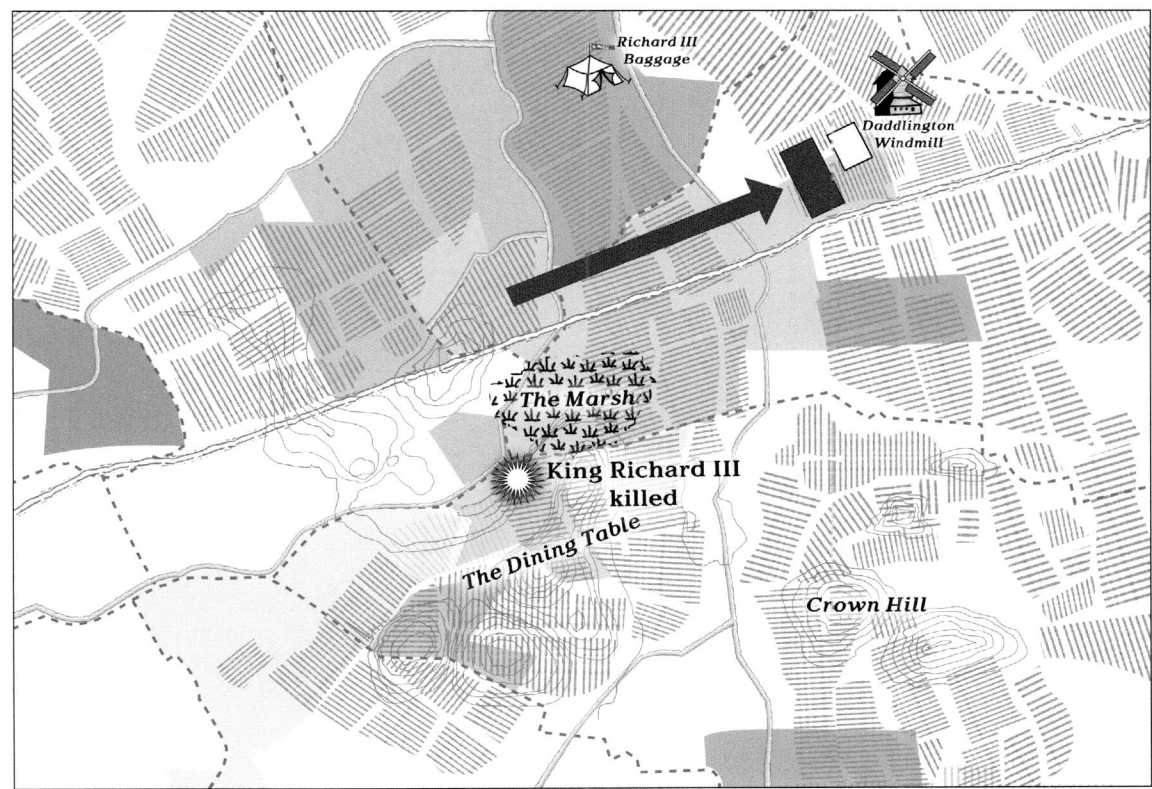

The Battle of Bosworth. Richard III is killed. Norfolk and his men make a last stand near or at Dadlington Windmill. Henry Tudor is crowned on what is now known as Crown Hill and according to legend stops to eat on a field now called 'The Dining Table'.

as suggested by the ballad, he was brought to his knees by a rain of blows to his helmeted head. A number of blows from a poll-axe, for example, would have certainly dazed him sufficiently to allow him to be overcome by his assailants. The absence of defensive wounds on his hands and arms suggest that he was still wearing armour at the time.

A narrow V-shaped cut 0.4 inches (10 mm) long was found on the bottom right side of the lower jaw, which is consistent with marks produced by knives and daggers. There was also a second small cut to the lower jaw, in line with the first but shallower. Both probably occurred when a blade was thrust up inside the helmet to slice the strap and forcibly remove his helmet. A 0.4 inches (10 mm) square hole in the right upper jaw that lined up with another hole through the back of the jaw was probably caused by a rondel-type dagger. Three shallow glancing blows caused by a sharp blade such as a sword or poll-axe sliced his scalp and shaved the bone, two on the left-hand side above the ear (looking from behind), and one on the top of the skull. None would have been immediately fatal. The pattern of the striations on the cuts suggest that at least two of the three were probably inflicted by the same weapon. On the top of the skull was a keyhole-shaped hole caused by an oblique thrust from a weapon delivered from above and behind, that caused two small flaps of bone on the inside of the skull. This injury could have been caused by the spike of a poll-axe or possibly a Rondel dagger. Although the injury would have caused a degree of external

RICHARD III AND THE BATTLE OF BOSWORTH

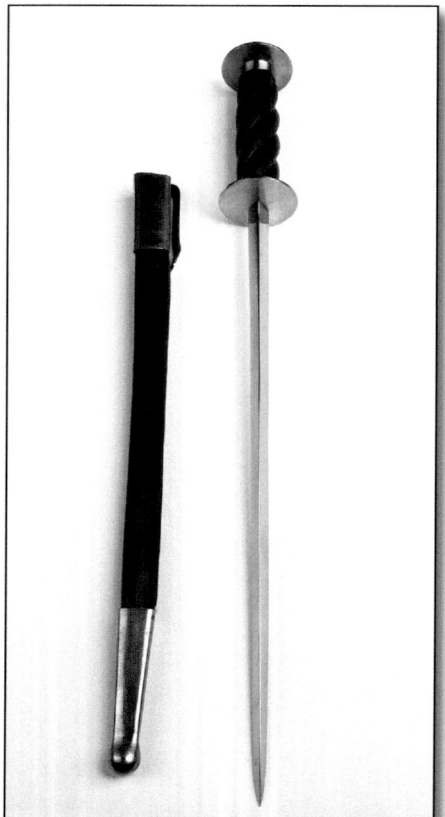

Reconstruction of a rondel dagger of the type that may have caused the hole on the top of Richard's head. (Matt Warden/MH Photographix)

and internal bleeding, even localised brain injury, in itself it would not have been immediately fatal.

In addition, there were two massive wounds to the lower rear of the skull. One 2.5 inches × 2.1 inches (65mm × 55mm) with smooth straight edges, sliced off part of the skull and was probably caused by a sword, halberd or bill. The other, was 1.2 inches × 0.7 inches (32mm × 17mm) with a radiating fracture and further damage on the opposite side of the skull, suggesting the weapon passed right through the brain. This wound is characteristic of a stab from the spike of a halberd or bill. Both wounds would have been fatal.

Who actually killed Richard is confused as a number of those present claimed credit. And in the confused heat of battle, it could have been any one of Henry's bodyguards or Stanley's men. Molinet only says 'One of the Welshmen then came after him, and struck him dead with a halberd'. A large proportion of William's men would have come from North Wales, so it could have been any one of them. The Denbighshire poet Tudur Aled claimed that it was Rhys ap Maredudd after he recovered Henry's standard. In another version of events the poet Guto'r Glyn implies that Rhys ap Thomas was responsible for killing Richard, although it is unlikely as he carried a halberd, but possibly could have had a poll-axe. This may only mean that one of Rhys ap Thomas' Welsh halberdiers killed the king, possibly, according to some traditions, Wyllyam Gardynyr. Rhys even had a bed lintel carved later in Henry's reign showing Rhys and Richard clashing on horseback with Richard's horse rearing up and losing a shoe. In between the two was a halberd. Another version is that it was Ralph of Rudyard, which is near the Stanley heartlands of Leek in Staffordshire, that dealt the fatal blow. Another claimant is Thomas Woodshawe, a tenant from Middleton Hall, near Tamworth. He was made bailiff and keeper of the park of Berkeswell in Warwickshire soon after in recognition for something. It is also worth noting at this point that the halberd was neither an English or Welsh weapon, so Molinet might have been using a generic term for a pole arm. However, if it was the weapon that killed Richard, then it was more likely supplied by the French and therefore carried by one of Henry's followers.

The Aftermath

With Richard's death any remaining resistance quickly ended. The battle had lasted no more than two hours. Many of Richard's men threw down their weapons and surrendered or were taken prisoner. Some we are told simply walked away and were allowed to leave as long as they did not return on Richard's side. Those who had not surrendered or had been captured were hunted down like animals as the rout began. Many would have been hacked down from behind as they ran. There is archaeological evidence of a rout in the form of a trail of battlefield debris heading east away from the battle site. Some of the fugitives may have reached Dadlington Mill, well over 1,000 yards away, as a livery badge of an eagle with wings, probably once owned either by a member of John Lord Zouche's household or the Duke of Norfolk was found close by. This is possibly where Norfolk, his son and the remains of the Royal army made its last stand. *The Ballad of Bosworth Fielde* says that:

> The Duke of Northfolke would have fledd with a good will
> With twenty thousand of his company.
> They went up to an windmillne upon a hill,
> That stood soe fayre and wonderoussehye.
> There he met Sir John Savage, a royall knight,
> And with him a worthy company.
> To the death was he then dight,
> And his son prisoner taken was he.

Molinet on the other hand suggests that Norfolk was captured, not killed in the fighting, then was sent by Henry Tudor to the Earl of Oxford who had him executed. In yet another version of events, Beaumont gives an entirely different perspective in his poem. He says that Norfolk recognised Oxford by his standard – a star with rays – and charged him. The lances of the two crossed, and each one shivered as they smashed against the armour of the other, which implies that they were fighting on horseback. Renewing their combat with their swords, Norfolk wounded Oxford in the left arm, Oxford then knocked Norfolk's bevor off. With the Duke's face exposed, Oxford chivalrously declined to continue the combat. At that moment Norfolk was struck in the face by an arrow and fell dead at Oxford's feet. *The Croyland Chronicle* simply says that Norfolk confronted Oxford and was killed in battle, but gives no details.

In 1841, the Rev. J.W. Darby wrote that he witnessed the opening of a vault under the tomb of Henry Fitzroy, Duke of Richmond (illegitimate son of Henry VIII) in Framlingham Church. As well as Richmond, five bodies were discovered. They were identified as the second and third Dukes of Norfolk, Anne of York (daughter of Edward IV, and wife of the third Duke) and Lady Mary Howard (daughter of the third Duke). The sixth was not embalmed but wrapped in lead sheet and had a large hole in the front of the skull. This, Darby speculated, was the remains of John Howard, the first duke, slain by an arrow at Bosworth. Beaumont may have taken artistic licence when describing this and other personal combats, however, the extraordinary detail into which he goes does have a ring of truth about it. And, if Darby was correct in his assumption, this gives further credence to Beaumont's version of Norfolk's death.

Beaumont continues by saying that Lord Surrey, having seen his father's death, set out to avenge him, but was stopped and surrounded by superior numbers. Sir Richard Clarendon and Sir William Conyers tried to rescue him but in turn were surrounded by Sir John Savage and his retainers and cut to pieces. In the meantime, Surrey came face to face with the veteran Sir Gilbert Talbot, who would willingly have spared the life of one so chivalrous and so young. Surrey was wounded but refused to accept quarter, and, when an attempt was made to take him prisoner, killed those who approach him. One last endeavour to capture him was made by a private soldier; Surrey, however, turned on him, collected his remaining strength, and severed the man's arm from his body. The brave Earl, worn out with loss of blood, then sank to earth, and seeing Talbot by his side, presented to him the hilt of his sword, imploring Sir Gilbert to slay him, lest he might die by some ignoble hand. Talbot, on the contrary, spared his life, and had him carried from the field.

Some, such as Lord Lovell and the Stafford brothers, managed to escape completely and fled into sanctuary at St. John's in Colchester. The cream of the Yorkist nobility was lying dead on the field including Norfolk, Lord Ferrers, Sir Richard Ratcliffe, Sir Robert Percy, Sir Robert Brackenbury, Sir John Sacheverell, and John Kendall. Catesby was not so lucky, he was captured either at the battle or soon after. Significantly, Catesby, along with two yeomen, both named Bracher from the West Country, were the only significant individuals to be executed after the battle, unlike the bloodbaths that followed the battles during the reigns of Henry VI and Edward IV. Perhaps it was because Catesby was Richard's closest advisor, and Henry felt he needed to make an example of him. On the other hand, he may have simply made too many enemies. In his will, made just after the battle on 25 August, Catesby asked to be buried in Ashby St. Ledgers church in Northamptonshire, and that the land he had 'wrongfully purchased' to be restored to their rightful owners. He then cryptically asked for the Stanleys to pray for his soul as they had not for his body, as he trusted in them. It reads as if Catesby had surrendered to the Stanleys, who had promised him protection, but then reneged and handed him over for execution. He may have been referring to an earlier deal as well, although exactly what he really meant will probably never be known.

Vergil says that 'Henry lost in that battayll scarce an hundreth soldiers.' The only notable casualty was William Brandon. Despite Richard's orders, Lord Strange was not executed. We do not know who else died that day. Vergil puts the numbers of dead from Richard's army as 1,000. Molinet says only 300 on either side whilst the Castilian Report says 10,000 in total. The truth probably lies somewhere in between. With the battle over, the victors looted Richard's baggage train. Richard's royal regalia was collected by Henry's officers and loaded onto his baggage train. William Stanley was offered the pick of the rest and took a set of Richard's tapestries which he proudly displayed at one of his residences, and Henry's mother was sent his personal prayer book.

Henry issued a proclamation either on the same day or the next that said:

> … the king ascertaineth you that Richard duke of Gloucester, late called King Richard, was slain at a place called Sandeford, within the shire of Leicester, and brought dead off the field unto the town of Leicester, and there was laid openly, that every man might see and look upon him. And also there was slain upon the same field, John late duke of Norfolk, John late earl of Lincoln, Thomas, late earl of Surrey, Francis Viscount Lovell, Sir Walter Devereux, Lord Ferrers,

THE BATTLE OF BOSWORTH FIELD 22 AUGUST 1485

Richard Radcliffe, knight, Robert Brackenbury, knight, with many other knights, squires and gentlemen, of whose souls God have mercy.

The *Historical notes of a London citizen*, written soon after the battle, recorded:

> This year the earl of Richmond and Jasper, earl of Pembroke ... came forth into England and met King Richard III at Redesmore, and there was King Richard slain and the duke of Norfolk and Lord Ferrers and Brackenbury, with many other. This battle was the 22 August 1485. Likewise, in this year the earl of Northumberland and the earl of Surrey were taken and brought into the Fleet of London, and there they were nine days, and then they were led into the Tower of London, and there they were two days, and after had to the castle of Queenborough in Kent.

Bernard André only says:

> I have learned somewhat of this battle from oral sources, but in this matter the eye is a more reliable witness than the ear. Rather than affirm anything rashly, therefore, I pass over the date, place and order of battle, for as I have said I lack the illumination of eye-witnesses. Until I am more fully instructed, for this field of battle I shall leave blank a space as broad...

The Battle of Bosworth memorial sundial on the top of Ambion Hill, the Bosworth Battlefield Heritage Centre.

According to Vergil, with the battle over, Henry gave thanks to God for his victory and withdrew to the nearest hill. Once again, at the time the ridge and furrow led away from the battlefield and up the hill. From here he thanked his commanders and nobles, knighted Gilbert Talbot, Rhys ap Thomas and Humphrey Stanley and gave orders that all the dead should be given an honourable burial. Vergil says that 'Thomas Stanley immediately placed Richard's crown, found among the spoil, on his head, as though he had become king by command of the people, acclaimed in the ancestral manner; and that was the first omen of his felicity.' *The Great Chronicle of London*, on the other hand, says, 'Sir William Stanley which won the possession of King Richard's helmet with the crown being upon it came straight to King Henry and set it upon his head saying, 'Sir, here I make you King of England.'

In August 1511, 26 years after the battle, Henry VIII visited the site, staying at Merevale Abbey. On 24 August whilst at Nottingham, he authorised a chantry chapel for those killed during the battle at St. James the Greater Church in Dadlington. This included the collection of alms for a period of seven years, in the dioceses of Lincoln, Chester, Worcester and Norwich to fund the stipend of a priest, to pray for the souls of those killed in the battle and 'for and towardis the bielding of a chapell of sainte James standing upon

RICHARD III AND THE BATTLE OF BOSWORTH

Looking across the battlefield towards Stoke Golding and Crown Hill. (Author)

The Church of St. James the Greater, Dadlington, where Henry VIII authorised a chantry chapel for the dead from Bosworth in August 1511.

a parcell of the grounde where Bosworth feld, otherwise called Dadlyngton feld,' A later Letter of Confraternity, stated that Henry VII had issued 'his letters patent', and granted indulgences and pardons for those that supported the 'buyldynge & meyntenaunce of Seynte James chapell where prayers were said for ye soules of them that weyr sleyne at bosworth feelde', and supported 'ye preestes and mynysters that beyth found ther to synge & rede & praye for ye seyde soules,' Whether it was completed remains a matter of debate. However, in 1868, it was reported that there were discoveries of multiple skulls and bones in a pit close to the churchyard entrance. Others were reported in 1900 and 1949.

Richard's body was recovered from the battlefield and taken to Leicester. According to Vergil, it was '… nakyd of all clothing, and layd upon an horse bake with the armes and legges hanginge downe on both sides.' Hall, although writing a while after, goes into more detail saying:

> Rycharde was as shamefully caryed to the towne of Leycester as he gorgiously the daye before with pompe and pryde departed owte of the same towne. For his bodye was naked and despoyled to the skyne, and nothynge left aboue hym not so muche as a clowte to couer hys pryue members, and was trussed behynde a persiuaunt of armes called blaunches englier or whyte bore, lyke a hogge or a calfe, the hed and armes hangynge on the one syde of the horse, and the legges on the other syde, and all by spryncled with myre and bloude, was brought to the grayfryers church within the toune, and there laielyke a miserable spectacle.

The Croyland chronicler simply said it was a 'miserable spectacle in good sooth.'

The probable gravesite for some of the fallen from Bosworth. The Church of St. James the Greater, Dadlington.

This was probably the first time that people saw Richard's scoliosis but grossly exaggerated by the angle that he hung over the horse. It would have looked like a hump and gave fuel to the later Tudor legends. It is also probable at the same time that his body received a humiliation wound when a narrow-bladed weapon was thrust into the right buttock and through the pelvic cavity.

As already seen above, Hall says that he was on the horse of his Blanc Sanglier Pursuivant, an officer of arms, ranking below a herald but having similar duties, but the *Great Chronicle of London* says it was a pursuivant called Norroy. John Moore was the Norroy King of Arms, a senior herald with jurisdiction north of the River Trent (Nottingham) and his son was at some point Blanc Sanglier, so it could have been either.

Henry wanted people to see that Richard was really dead. For years after his death, rumours that Richard II was still alive abounded and several rebellions in his name followed. In the absence of any images except for crude ones on coins, the only way to do this was to put his body on display at the last place he had been seen in public. And that was Leicester. For two days his body was put on public display at the Church of the Annunciation of Our Lady of the Newarke 'for all men to wonder upon'. As the church was a mausoleum for the House of Lancaster, it would have been an additional insult.

Vergil tells us that Richard's body was then 'two days after without any pomp or solmne funeral … in th abbey of the monks Franciscanes at Leycester.' In his *Historia Regum Angliae*, John Rous agrees stating that Richard was buried 'among the Friars Minor [Greyfriars] of Leicester, in the choir.'

The Newarke Gateway, Leicester. Richard's body was brought through here before being put on display at the Church of the Annunciation of Our Lady of the Newarke. (Author)

Richard's body was hurriedly interred in a crudely excavated hole without coffin or shroud against the southern choir stall at the far western end of the Choir in the Church of the Greyfriars. Probably as a result of the speed in which it was dug, the hole was made too small and the body was left hunched up in its grave. It is significant that he was not buried in the most prestigious part of the church, the presbytery close to the high altar at the eastern end. This kept the tomb away from public gaze and therefore could not become the focus of any new rebellion or cult.

Ten years after his death, Henry VII ordered that an alabaster tomb should be built over Richard's grave. The only description of it was given by George Buck in his *The History of King Richard the Third*, which he left in a damaged rough draft at his death. It described the tomb as 'mingled colour'd Marble, adorned with his Statue, to be erected thereupon'. What this statue looked like is also lost and could have been a full sculpture or simple brass plate. He also states that there should have been an epitaph that he had seen in a book in London's Guildhall, but for reasons unknown it was never added to the tomb. It was originally written in Latin and as well as Buck's transcription, two other written versions with translations are known to have existed. It is significant in that it states Richard fought bravely and that the death of the princes is not mentioned. In fact, Richard is described as 'an uncle ruling on behalf of his nephew'. A modern translation of Buck's original by the late John Ashdown-Hill reads:

> I, here, whom the earth encloses under various coloured marble,
> Was justly called Richard the Third.
> I was Protector of my country, an uncle ruling on behalf of his nephew.
> I held the British kingdoms by broken faith.
> Then for just sixty days less two,
> And two summers, I held my sceptres.
> Fighting bravely in war, deserted by the English,
> I succumbed to you, King Henry VII.
> But you yourself, piously, at your expense, thus honour my bones
> And you cause a former king to be revered with the honour of a king
> When [in] twice five years less four
> Three hundred five-year periods of our salvation have passed.
> And eleven days before the Kalends of September
> I surrendered to the red rose the power it desired.
> Whoever you are, pray for my offences,
> That my punishment may be lessened by your prayers.

11

King Henry VII

It is no doubt a good thing to conquer on the field of battle, but it needs greater wisdom and greater skill to make use of victory.

Polybius, *Histories*

Henry spent two days at Leicester before moving to Coventry where he stayed at the house of the mayor, Robert Onley. A note in the Coventry Annals records that 'K. Rich was shamefully Carryed to Leicester & Buryed their when he had Reigned 2 years 2 month & one day, the Earle being proclaimed King in the field Came to Coventry & the Citty gave A Hundred pounds…' From here he passed through Northampton then St. Albans towards London.

News of the battle reached York the following day and a Memorandum of a meeting in the council chamber on the Vigil of St. Bartholomew records, 'where it was shown by divers persons, and especially by John Sponer, sent unto the field of Redemore to bring tidings of the same to the city, that King Richard, late mercifully reigning upon us, was through great treason of the duke of Norfolk and many others that turned against him, with many other lords and nobles of this north parts, was piteously slain and murdered, to the great heaviness of this city.'

The York House Books show that a meeting of the council on 24 August decided that the mayor and others should meet with Sir Henry Percy to understand how they shall be 'disposed entent the king's grace Henry the event, so proclaimed and crowned at the feld of Redemore.' A messenger sent to the earl who they thought was at Wressle, returned with news that the Earl of Northumberland was with the king at Leicester. The entry also noted that Sir Roger Cotam, had come to the city but dare not enter it 'for fere of deth', the mayor and others, therefore, went to meet him and were reassured of Henry's graciousness. The following day, they agreed to send five men to Henry VII, 'beseeching his grace to be good and gracious lord unto this citie.'

Henry made a triumphal entry into London on 3 September, having been met by the Mayor and Aldermen at Hornsey, who, dressed in all their splendour, escorted him to St. Paul's cathedral. Henry then set about rewarding all those who had helped him. His uncle Jasper was made Duke of

Bedford, Philbert de Chandée was made Earl of Bath, Thomas Stanley became the Earl of Derby, Edward Courtenay, Earl of Devon and Sir William Stanley was also given key offices. With the old administration totally destroyed, Henry had to start again, and it was another month before the business of running the country began in earnest. Sir Robert Willoughby was sent to Sheriff Hutton to arrest Edward, Earl of Warwick, the son of the late Duke of Clarence and last of the male Plantagenets. Willoughby also brought with him Elizabeth the daughter of Edward IV and Henry's future bride. Elizabeth and her mother were escorted back to London. The 10-year-old Edward was made a prisoner in the Tower.

Henry's official coronation was held on 30 October. Eight days later he held his first Parliament. His first act was to repeal *Titulus Regius*, the statute that declared Edward IV's marriage invalid and his children illegitimate, thus legitimising his future wife. His second action was to declare himself king from the day before Bosworth Field. This meant that anyone who had fought for Richard would be guilty of treason. Surprisingly, only 28 of Richard's supporters were named in the Act of Attainder of 9 November 1485 and most were from the Midlands or the north of England. Richard's nephew, John de la Pole, Earl of Lincoln was spared, a decision that Henry would come to regret.

Henry honoured his pledge of December 1483 and married Elizabeth of York on 18 January 1486 at Westminster. This united the warring houses and gave his children a strong claim to the throne. His heraldic emblem, the Tudor rose, a combination of the white rose of York and the red rose of Lancaster, reflected the unification of the two houses.

After her son won the crown at the Battle of Bosworth Field, Margaret Beaufort was referred to in court as 'My Lady the King's Mother'. Throughout his reign, Margaret maintained close contact with her son, frequently accompanying him on royal visits or progresses. Royal household ordinances made provision for her accommodation at all the residences used by the crown. Margaret's rooms in the Tower were to be found next to her son's bedchamber and the council chamber. When they were apart, they were in frequent contact by letter, and the wording of these letters attests to their affection. One from Margaret begins: 'My own sweet and dear king and all my worldly joy', while another refers to him as 'My dearest and only desired joy in this world'. Later in her marriage, the Countess preferred living alone. In 1499, with her husband's permission, she took a vow of chastity in the presence of Richard FitzJames, Bishop of London. The Countess moved away from her husband Thomas Stanley, and lived alone at Collyweston, in Northamptonshire, ironically only a few miles from where Richard was born and grew up. She was regularly visited by her husband, who had rooms reserved for him. She died in the Deanery of Westminster Abbey on 29 June 1509, just over two months after the death of her son.

Henry demonstrated his gratitude to his 'right dearly beloved father' Thomas Stanley by creating him Earl of Derby on 27 October 1485, and the following year confirmed him in office as Lord High Constable of England and High Steward of the Duchy of Lancaster, besides granting him other estates and offices. In 1486 Stanley also stood as godfather to Henry's eldest son,

Arthur, Prince of Wales. He died at Lathom on 29 July 1504 and was buried in the family chapel in Burscough Priory, near Ormskirk in Lancashire. He had been predeceased by his eldest son and heir, George Stanley, Lord Strange, by only a few months and was succeeded by his grandson, Thomas Stanley, 2nd Earl of Derby. In his will of 28 July 1504, he ordained masses for 'the souls of himself, his wives, parents, ancestors, children, siblings, and, ever the good lord, them that have died in the service of my lord my father or of me.'

After Bosworth, Henry's main concern was to how to secure the throne. He did this by dividing and undermining the power of the nobility. His principal weapon was the Court of Star Chamber which revived an earlier practice of using a small group of the Privy Council as a personal or Prerogative Court, able to cut through the cumbersome legal system and act swiftly. Serious disputes involving the use of personal power, or threats to royal authority, were dealt with accordingly. Henry allowed the nobles to continue with their regional influence as long as they remained loyal to him.

These measures, however, were not enough. In September 1485, Robert Thockmorton, the newly appointed sheriff of Warwickshire and Leicestershire, petitioned the King for a pardon of fines and arrears touching his office on the grounds that there 'was within this your realme suche rebellioun and troble, and your lawes not stablysshed' that he had been unable to raise the customary revenues during his brief period in office. On 17 October, Henry wrote of his 'knowledge that certeyne our rebelles and traitours being of litell honour or substance conferred with our aunciennemyes the Scottes … made insurreccion and assemblies in the north portions of our realme'. Three days later, John de la Pole, Duke of Suffolk, notified John Paston, the sheriff of Norfolk and Suffolk, that rebels in the northern parts had been conferring with the King's Scottish enemies, and instructed him to have men of the counties of Suffolk and Norfolk at the ready for action at short notice.

Less than a year after he was crowned, whilst at Lincoln, Henry became aware of a rebellion by Francis Lovell, Richard's Lord Chamberlain, along with Humphrey and Thomas Stafford. Together they planned to raise troops and to kill Henry as he travelled to the north of England. Henry had them followed, finding the Staffords in Culham Church near Abingdon where they were arrested. Sir Richard Edgecombe and Sir William Tyler were sent to arrest Lovell. However, he managed to escape, first joining fellow rebels at Furness Falls and later fleeing to Richard's sister, Margaret in Flanders. Sir John Conyers, who was also suspected of being involved in the revolt, lost his stewardship of Middleham castle and had a £2,000 bond imposed.

Two years after Bosworth John de la Pole, Earl of Lincoln, fled to his aunt, Margaret, Duchess of Burgundy at Mechelen (Malines) on 19 March 1487. Here, Margaret provided him with financial and military support in the form of 2,000 German mercenaries, under Martin Schwartz. He was also joined by a number of Yorkist supporters including Lord Lovell, Sir Richard Harleston, the former governor of Jersey and Thomas David, a captain of the English garrison at Calais. In April, the army landed in Ireland claiming that a boy called Lambert Simnel, was the Earl of Warwick (who was, in reality, a prisoner in the Tower). On 4 June 1487 de la Pole, his army boosted by a body of Irish troops, crossed over to England. Here they were was joined by a

Stoke battlefield, 1487. Site of the last battle of the Wars of the Roses. (Author)

number of the local gentry led by Sir Thomas Broughton. In a series of forced marches, the Yorkist army, now numbering some 8,000 men, covered over 200 miles in five days. On the night of 10 June, at Bramham Moor, outside Tadcaster, Lovell led 2,000 men on a night attack against 400 men led by Lord Clifford. The result was an overwhelming Yorkist victory. On 12 June, de la Pole outmanoeuvred King Henry's northern army, under the command of the Earl of Northumberland by ordering a force under John, Lord Scrope to mount a diversionary attack on Bootham Bar, York. Lord Scrope then withdrew northwards, taking Northumberland's army with him.

De la Pole and the main army continued south. They met with a body of Tudor cavalry under Lord Scales outside Doncaster, and three days of skirmishing through Sherwood Forest followed. Eventually, Scales retreated to Nottingham. However, the fighting allowed Henry time to bring up substantial reinforcements under the command of Lord Strange, arriving at Nottingham on 14 June. The next day, they began moving north-east toward Newark after receiving news that Lincoln had crossed the River Trent. Around nine in the morning of 16 June, Henry's vanguard, commanded by the Earl of Oxford, encountered the Yorkist army on the brow of a hill by the River Trent at the village of East Stoke. The Yorkists surrounded on three sides, attacked immediately. However, the unarmoured Irish were cut to pieces and the German mercenaries, unable to retreat, fought to the last man. The battle lasted for three hours, de la Pole, Fitzgerald, Broughton, and Schwartz, were all killed in the fighting.

Only Lord Lovell escaped the fighting. One report suggests he drowned crossing the River Trent. Francis Bacon relates that according to one report he lived long after in a cave or vault, others say he fled to Scotland or Burgundy. In 1708, during building work at the Lovell mansion at Minster Lovell in

Memorial to the Battle of Stoke outside St. Oswald's Church, East Stoke.

Oxfordshire, workmen discovered a secret room. When they opened it, they supposedly found the skeleton of a man seated at a table with the skeleton of his dog at his feet surrounded by writing materials and a book. The remains of the skeleton and the papers then crumbled into dust when the air was let in. It was claimed that this was Lovell and he had hidden himself there and died of starvation. During his lifetime Lovell had hardly visited Minster Lovell and the manor had been granted to Jasper Tudor, Duke of Bedford, Henry Tudor's uncle, and was, therefore, an unlikely hiding place for Lovell. Whatever the case, whether he died or survived, Lovell leaves the picture completely and is no further threat to Henry.

Simnel was captured and made a servant in the royal kitchen by Henry, and eventually became the King's falconer. Twenty-eight Yorkists were attained in the aftermath but the Irish were pardoned. Following the death of his older brother, John, Edmund de la Pole became the leading Yorkist claimant to the throne. Henry allowed him to succeed as Duke of Suffolk in 1491, although sometime later, Edmund's title was demoted to the rank of Earl.

Soon after taking the throne, Henry began a deliberate policy of marrying the surviving female Yorkists to members of his own family. Margaret Pole, Countess of Salisbury, was the daughter of George, Duke of Clarence, the brother of Kings Edward IV and Richard III and uncle of Edward V. She was one of two women in sixteenth century England to be a peeress in her own right with no titled husband and by 1538, was the fifth richest peer in England. In 1487, she married Henry's cousin, Sir Richard Pole, whose mother was the half-sister of the King's mother, Margaret Beaufort.

In 1490 a man appeared in Burgundy, claiming to be Richard of Shrewsbury, Duke of York, the younger son of King Edward IV, although he was named as Perkin Warbeck by Henry. In 1491, he landed in Ireland but found little support. Returning to the European mainland, he was first received by Charles VIII of France but was expelled in 1492 under the terms of the Treaty of Étaples, in which Charles had agreed not to shelter rebels against the Tudors. However, The Duke of York, as Warbeck became known, was rapidly gaining popular support across Europe and was proving to be an embarrassment to Henry. Warbeck was even recognised as King Richard IV of England by Maximilian I. England began to fracture again. Many Yorkist supporters re-emerged believing 'Warbeck' to be the heir to the Yorkist dynasty. Others, discontented with Henry's rule joined them. Henry sent spies to Margaret of Burgundy in Flanders, claiming to be Yorkist supporters. Here they discovered the names of many of the conspirators, who were promptly arrested and charged with treason. The list included Lord Fitzwalter, Sir Simon Mountford, William Daubeney and Robert Ratcliffe as well as a number of priests. Significantly, the list also included Sir William Stanley who had helped Henry to the throne in the first place. Having been at court throughout Edward IV's reigns, if anyone knew who the man claiming to be the prince really was, it was he. William was beheaded on 10 July 1495.

A week earlier, before the execution on 3 July 1495, funded by Margaret of Burgundy, 'Warbeck' landed at Deal in Kent, but his small army was routed and 150 of his men were killed before he even disembarked. He was forced to return to Ireland and finding support from the Earl of Desmond, laid siege to Waterford. In the face of fierce resistance he fled to Scotland where he received support from the King, James IV. An army was raised, crossing the River Tweed at Coldstream on 19 September 1496. They were at Hetoune (Castle Heaton) on 24 September, where miners demolished four towers. However, in the face of an army under Lord Neville advancing from Newcastle and dwindling supplies, the army returned home. After signing a peace treaty with England, James sent 'Warbeck' back to Ireland where he once again laid siege to Waterford. This time four English ships chased him away after only 11 days.

A marker for the Burrand Bush where Henry Tudor supposedly planted his standard after the Battle of Stoke in 1487. (Author)

Under what is now known as 'Morton's Fork' (although it may have been invented by another of Henry's supporters, Lord Privy Seal, Bishop Richard Foxe), Morton raised additional funds for his King by holding that someone living modestly must be saving money and, therefore, could afford taxes, whereas someone living extravagantly obviously was rich and, therefore, could afford taxes.

In 1495, Henry introduced 'The Council Learned in the Law' to defend his position as the feudal landlord and to maintain his revenue and exploit his prerogative rights. The brainchild of Sir Reginald Bray (the close associate of Henry's mother), the council was run by a number of Henry's key legal advisors. Officially, it was a secondary department of the Star Chamber, although it was not legally constituted, outside normal law, and only answerable to the King himself. According to Edmund Dudley, Henry said he 'wanted many persons in danger at his pleasure bound to his grace for great sums of money.' Fed by a network of spies and informers, the council often used obscure or fabricated laws to force people into massive bonds to guarantee good behaviour. It struck fear into the hearts of noble and commoner alike. Following Bray`s death in 1503, Richard Empson from Easton Neston in Northamptonshire became president. With Edmund Dudley, the two formed a feared combination of able bureaucrats who raised the extraction of money into a fine art and created many enemies amongst the nobility and key advisors of the King. They sold offices, wardships, and licences to marry the widows of tenants-in-chief; pardons for treason, sedition, murder, riot, retaining, and other offences. In less than four years they collected some £219,316 in cash and bonds for future payment. For the first time since William the Conqueror, with the combination of 'The Council Learned in the Law' and 'Morton's Fork', the nobility and barons were brought to their knees and firmly under Henry's control.

Three days after Henry VII's death, the council was abolished and both Empson and Dudley were thrown into prison by order of the new king. They were charged with the crime of constructive treason. Empson was convicted at Northampton in October 1509. Their attainder by Parliament followed, and both were beheaded on Tower Hill on 17 August 1510. The downfall of the pair brought rejoicing in the streets.

At the beginning of 1497, another rebellion was fermenting in Cornwall, this time over heavy taxation to raise money for a campaign against Scotland. Tin miners were angered as the scale of the taxes overturned previous rights

Effigy of Edward Stafford, 2nd Earl of Wiltshire, Lowick Church, Northants (d. 1499). He was with the forces which fought against the Cornish rebels at Blackheath on 17 June 1497.

granted by Edward I of England to the Cornish Stannary Parliament, which exempted Cornwall from all taxes of 10ths or 15ths of income. Michael Joseph (AnGof – the smith), a blacksmith from St. Keverne and Thomas Flamank a lawyer of Bodmin, incited many of the people of Cornwall into armed revolt against the King. An army of 15,000 gathered at Bodmin and marched into Devon. From there they headed for Kent where they hoped to gain additional support. En route they were joined by James Touchet, Baron Audley who acted as a 'political' leader.

After being rebuffed by the men of Kent, the army marched on London arriving at Guildford on 13 June. The Royal family moved to the Tower of London for safety whilst in the rest of the City, there was a feeling of panic. It was said that there was a general cry of 'Every man to harness! To harness!' as citizens armed themselves and lined the walls and gates. Lord Daubeney sent out a force of 500 mounted spearmen and they clashed with the Cornish at 'Gill Down' outside Guildford on 14 June 1497. The Battle of Blackheath which followed has already been described above.

On 7 September 1497, hoping to capitalise on the Cornish people's resentment in the aftermath of their uprising, 'Warbeck' landed at Whitesand Bay, near Land's End, in Cornwall. He proclaimed that he would put a stop to extortionate taxes levied to help fight a war against Scotland and was warmly welcomed. He was declared 'Richard IV' on Bodmin Moor and his Cornish army some 3,000 strong marched on Exeter where they were twice beaten off. Lord Daubeney was sent to deal with the rebellion, but when Warbeck heard that scouts were at Glastonbury he panicked and fled to sanctuary in Beaulieu Abbey in Hampshire. 'Warbeck' eventually surrendered and was imprisoned first at Taunton and then the Tower. Henry reached Taunton on 4 October 1497, where he received the surrender of the remaining Cornish army. The ringleaders were executed, and others fined. Initially 'Warbeck' was only held under house arrest and lived in comparative luxury.

Henry had been trying to arrange a marriage between his son Arthur and the daughter of Ferdinand and Isabella of Spain, Katherine of Aragon. The Spanish monarchs had raised their fears about sending their daughter to England before the Tudor dynasty was secured by the removal of rival claimants to the throne. Due to his Yorkist descent, Edward, Earl of Warwick, the son of George Duke of Clarence, and 'Warbeck' posed the largest threat to the Tudor claim to the throne. 'Warbeck' was moved to the Tower alongside Warwick. In 1499, a plot was hatched whereby an escape attempt would be engineered involving Warwick and Warbeck, who would then be hastily recaptured. By escaping they were committing treason, and this was sufficient to have them both executed.

In his confession, possibly obtained under torture, 'Warbeck' said he was Flemish, born to a man called John Osbeck (also known as Jehan de Werbecque) in Tournai. In 1491, aged about 17, he was taken to Cork in Ireland where he learned to speak English. He then claimed that upon seeing him dressed in silk clothes, some of the citizens of Cork who were Yorkists demanded to '[do] him the honour as a member of the Royal House of York.' He said they did this because they were resolved in gaining revenge on the King of England and decided that he would claim to be the younger son of

King Edward IV. Despite the confession, his true identity is still a mystery and a number of historians have suggested that his story was to try to avoid execution. However, on 23 November 1499, he was drawn on a hurdle from the Tower to Tyburn, London, and was hanged as a commoner, after reading out the confession. Five days later Edward was beheaded. Edward may have been mentally retarded as his sister Margaret later said that 'he did not know a goose from a capon'. It is more likely because he had been held prisoner most of his short life, he had probably not seen the outside world or had an education.

Not all of Richard's supporters stayed loyal to the Yorkist cause. Thomas Howard, Earl of Surrey, spent three years in prison after Bosworth, but eventually was restored to the Earldom. In 1499, he was recalled to Court and accompanied the King on a state visit to France in the following year. Surrey was an executor of the will of King Henry VII and played a prominent role in the coronation of King Henry VIII, in which he served as Earl Marshal. He would also go on to command the English army at the Battle of Flodden in 1513, crushing a larger Scottish army. On 1 February 1514, he was created Duke of Norfolk. Meanwhile, Edmund de la Pole, who was now the Yorkist heir, had fled England in 1501 with the help of Sir James Tyrell, seeking the help of Maximilian. In 1506, Maximilian's son, Phillip of Burgundy, was blown off course while sailing to Castile, and unexpectedly became a guest of Henry VII. Whilst in England, Phillip was persuaded to hand Edmund over to Henry on the proviso that he would not be harmed.

On 21 April 1509, Henry died of tuberculosis at Richmond Palace and he was buried at Westminster Abbey. His second son, Henry VIII, succeeded him and ruled for the next 45 years. There remained a Yorkist party within the court led by Henry Courtenay, Marquess of Exeter and Lady Salisbury, Margaret Pole daughter of the Duke of Clarence. The Marquis was the son of Katherine, the youngest daughter of Edward IV, and therefore heir to the throne, after the Tudors.

Margaret Pole's own favour at Court varied. When Prince Arthur married Katherine of Aragon, Margaret became one of her ladies-in-waiting, but Katherine's entourage was dissolved when Arthur died. In 1520, Margaret was appointed Governess to Henry's daughter, Princess Mary but was removed the following year, then restored by 1525. When Mary was declared a bastard in 1533, Margaret refused to give Mary's gold plate and jewels back to Henry. Her first son, Henry Pole, was created Baron Montagu, another of the Neville titles, and spoke for the family in the House of Lords. Her second son, Arthur Pole, had a generally successful career as a courtier, becoming one of the six Gentlemen of the Privy Chamber. Margaret's third son, Reginald, studied abroad in Padua and became a dean in Exeter and Wimborne Minster in Dorset as well as a canon in York. In 1537 Reginald, despite not being ordained, was created a Cardinal. Her youngest son Geoffrey, married Constance, daughter of Edmund Pakenham, and inherited the estate of Lordington in Sussex.

Like his father, Henry VIII faced a number of rebellions, but he was not so forgiving as his father and would eventually eradicate the Yorkist line. Edmund de la Pole remained a prisoner in the Tower. His younger brother,

Richard, found safe refuge at Buda with King Ladislaus II of Bohemia and Hungary. When Louis XII of France went to war with England in 1512, he recognised Edmund's claim to the English throne and gave Richard a command in the French army. In 1513, after the execution of Edmund, Richard assumed the title of Earl of Suffolk. Now the leading Yorkist claimant to the throne of England, in 1514 he was given 12,000 German mercenaries, ostensibly for the defence of Brittany, but really for an invasion of England. His army prepared for the invasion at St. Malo, but at the conclusion of a peace treaty between France and England, they were prevented from leaving. As a consequence of the treaty Richard was required to leave France and he established himself at Metz, in Lorraine, where he built a palace at La Haute Pierre, near St. Simphorien. Richard de la Pole had numerous interviews with King Francis I of France, and in 1523 along with John Stewart, 2nd Duke of Albany, the Scottish regent, he began to arrange a new invasion of England, However, he was with Francis I at the Battle of Pavia on 24 February 1525, where he was killed in the fighting, putting an end to the invasion.

In May 1536, Reginald Pole broke with the king when Pope Paul III put him in charge of organising assistance for the Pilgrimage of Grace, an effort to organise a march on London to install a conservative Catholic government instead of Henry's increasingly 'Protestant' one. It was the greatest threat to Henry's rule and 9,000 men marched on London.

In 1538, Henry Courtenay, Marquess of Exeter, grandson of King Edward IV, nephew of the Queen Consort, Elizabeth of York and a first cousin of King Henry VIII was accused of a plot to depose Henry. During the investigation that followed, Margaret Pole's youngest son, Geoffrey, was implicated in the plot and he was arrested in August 1538. Under interrogation, Geoffrey admitted that his eldest brother, Lord Montagu, and the Marquess had been parties to his correspondence with Reginald. Henry Pole, 1st Baron Montagu, Exeter, and Margaret were arrested in November 1538.

Sir Geoffrey was pardoned, and Montagu and Exeter were tried for treason, while Reginald Pole was attainted in absentia. Courtenay was beheaded with a sword on Tower Hill on 9 January 1539 along with Montagu and their cousin Edward Neville. Margaret Pole was also arrested for her alleged involvement in the plot. On the morning of 27 May 1541 aged 68, she was executed at the Tower of London, on Henry's orders. Frail and ill, she refused to lay her head on the block. As she struggled, the inexperienced executioner's first blow made a gash in her shoulder rather than her neck. It took 10 more blows to complete the execution. The Plantagenets were no more.

Epilogue

The *Renaissance* had already started in England when Henry Tudor claimed the throne. William Caxton had begun to publish books under the patronage of Lord Rivers, Sir Anthony Woodville and then Richard III. An Act of 1484, under Richard III, had specifically exempted 'merchant strangers' from any restrictions on either printing in England or bringing in books from abroad, introducing new ideas and ideals. After Richard's death Margaret Beaufort became Caxton's main patron, and in 1490 he printed the statutes of the first three Parliaments of Henry VII, the first time statutes of England were produced in English rather than legal French.

Henry VII's descendants would be responsible for changing England. Besides being remembered for his six marriages, his son, Henry VIII (1491–1547) was instrumental in the separation of the Church of England from the Roman Catholic Church, and the Dissolution of the Monasteries. Henry VII's granddaughter, Queen Elizabeth I (1558–1603) ushered in a period now known as the 'Golden Age'. It was a time of national pride through classical ideals an age of exploration and international expansion. It was the height of the English Renaissance and saw the flowering of poetry, music and literature. The era is also famous for theatre and the playwright William Shakespeare.

On Elizabeth's death, James VI of Scotland (1566–1625) succeeded to the English throne as James I, joining the two countries for the first time. It was also the time of the 'Gunpowder Plot' which was led by Robert Catesby, a descendant of William Catesby, Richard III's right-hand man.

Throughout the Tudor age, plots, conspiracies and rebellions continued to haunt its rulers, although the Protestant/Catholic divide was often at their heart. After Bosworth, all the kings and queens still believed in the right of divine rule and although parliament grew in power during the period, it was not strong enough to challenge the ruler. It would be 157 years before it could do that, and it led to another bloody civil war.

Appendix I

Finding the Battlefield

Early records associated the Battle of Bosworth with 'Brownehethe', 'bellum Miravallenses' and 'Dadlyngton field'. The record in the York books dated 23 August 1485 said that it was fought 'on the field of Redemore.' A letter from a few years later also mentions 'Redesmore' as the site. Henry VII describes the battle as taking place at Bosworth and at some point before 1510, it became to be known as 'Bosworth Fielde.' Early in the seventeenth century, local antiquarian William Burton wrote in his *Description of Leicester Shire*, that the battle was, 'fought in a large, flat, plaine and spacious ground, three miles distant from this town, [Bosworth] between the Towne of Shenton, Sutton, Dadlington and Stoke.' He also recorded that 'divers peeces of armor, weapons and other warlike accoutrements' were found near Stoke Golding when it was enclosed at the turn of the century. A number of maps were subsequently published that included 'King Richard's field' or similar but as cartography was in its infancy, they were vague and only gave the general area. King Richard's Well first appeared on Prior's map of 1777, other new maps followed and started to include it. It was William Hutton who wrote the first detailed study of the battle, *The Battle of Bosworth-Field* in 1788. Often using local hearsay as sources, he placed the location of the battle west of Ambion Hill on the north side of the River Sence. His theory seems to be largely based on the site of the well and the comment in Holinshed's chronicle written in 1577 that: 'King Richard pitched his field on a hill called Anne Beame, refreshed his souldiers and took his rest.' Hutton's ideas were developed and continued in John Nichols' *The history and antiquities of the county of Leicester*, Vol. 4, published in 1811. In 1813, a cairn was built over the well and a plaque was added proclaiming:

> Near this spot on August 22 nd 1485, at the age of 32, King Richard III fell fighting gallantly in defence of his realm & his crown against the usurper Henry Tudor. This cairn wa erected by Dr. Samuel Parr in 1813 to mark the well which the king is said to have drunk during the battle. It is maintained by the Fellowship of the White Boar.

Later authors continued to follow Hutton. Gairdner added a marsh on the slopes of Ambion Hill in 1896 and Burne also continued the Ambion Hill

King Richard's Well, Ambion Hill, where legend has it Richard drank before the battle. (Author)

version of events in the 1950s. In the early 1970s Danny Williams persisted with the Ambion Hill theory, putting Richard on the top of the hill, Henry attacking from the west and the Stanleys to the north.

Based on the theories available in 1973, Leicestershire County Council chose Ambion Hill Farm to be the location for the country's first Battlefield Interpretation Centre and it opened its doors in 1974. A walking trail around the hill was developed, a stone marked the spot where it was thought Richard died and flags marking the initial positions of each of the three armies were positioned were added. Since then, there have been a number of revamps, including extensions, new galleries and exhibits, including the award-winning exhibition seen today.

In 1985, Colin Richmond pointed out that Ambion Hill did not fit the contemporary accounts of the battle. In 1990, Peter Foss also demonstrated that the battle could not have been fought on Ambion Hill and proposed a site between Stoke Golding and Dadlington to the south of Ambion Hill. When English Heritage first compiled its Register of Historic Battlefields in 1994, because of all the potential sites for Bosworth, they included all of them, including Ambion Hill, Foss's theory of where it was fought, and Crown Hill within its boundary. Despite finding the actual battlefield on the western extremity of the registered battlefield, the boundary of the registered battlefield has still not been updated 19 years later.

By 2004, there were at least four potential sites for the battle. Metal detector surveys of some of them including Ambion Hill had been carried out over at least a 15 year period but the actual battlefield remained elusive.

With so many possible sites, the Battlefields Trust was commissioned by Leicestershire County Council to resolve the issue. Partly funded with £154,000 from the Heritage Lottery Fund, for the first time, a team of specialists from various disciplines were brought together under archaeologist Glenn Foard to search for the battlefield. The work they carried out would ultimately set new standards for battlefield archaeology.

After reviewing the original documentary evidence for the battle and the armies. the historic landscape was reconstructed from documentary sources and archaeological evidence. Soils were analysed, as were peat deposits to discover the locations of any marsh and when it disappeared. After the battlefield had been found, further help came from the University of Leeds, Cranfield University and the Royal Armouries. A systematic archaeological survey by a team of volunteers was carried out across all the potential sites using metal detectors. From September 2005 to February 2009, 716 acres

APPENDIX I

(2.9 km2) was investigated, almost all on 10 metre (10.9 yard) transects (gridded lines). However, nothing was found.

Then on 1 March 2009, during the last week of a six month extension to the project, a single 1.18 inch (30 mm) diameter round shot was discovered two miles (3.2 km) from Ambion Hill. A week later, another was found. This was sufficient for a further extension to the project and by December 2010 they had found a total of 34 lead balls fired by cannons, some of which had iron or stone cores. Most were over, 0.78 inches (20 mm) diameter and the largest was 3.8 inches (97mm), of which at least one was fired by a breach loading cannon and another three by a muzzle-loader.

On top of these, 37 coins from 1460–1485, including three from Burgundy, were found. Part of a gilded copper alloy cross-guard from a sword and a copper alloy sword scabbard chape were discovered. There were also two gold finger rings, 36 buckles and 25 strap ends, but again these could not be securely dated. However, the most important find was a 1.06 inch (27 mm) silver gilt boar badge. This was found on the edge of the marsh and could have only come from one of Richard's supporters, most likely lost during his final charge. Bosworth Battlefield had finally been found.

A further survey in 2016 revealed seven new pieces of round shot, all within the existing scatter. Another survey undertaken in 2018, as part of MIRA's planning application for a test track, to the immediate west of the battlefield, revealed another 1.6 inch (41mm) round shot, a smaller 0.7 inch (18 mm) round shot and a fifteenth century sword or dagger belt hanger.

It is important to differentiate between the actual and Historic England's registered battlefield. This is because the later encompasses over 1,078 ha (2,664 acres), and not only covers the actual battlefield but also outlying areas such as Sutton Cheney and Ambion Hill and the site of the battle proposed by Danny Williams, despite it being proved wrong by the latest research. This has the cumulative effect of making the battlefield seem much larger than it actually is. They are all important places in the story of the battle, but not where it was actually fought!

The largest cannonball (97mm) found on Bosworth battlefield during the investigation. (Peter Burton)

Reproduction of Richard III's boar badge. It was a similar gilt badge found on the edge of Fenn Hole that led to the identification of the battlefield. (Author)

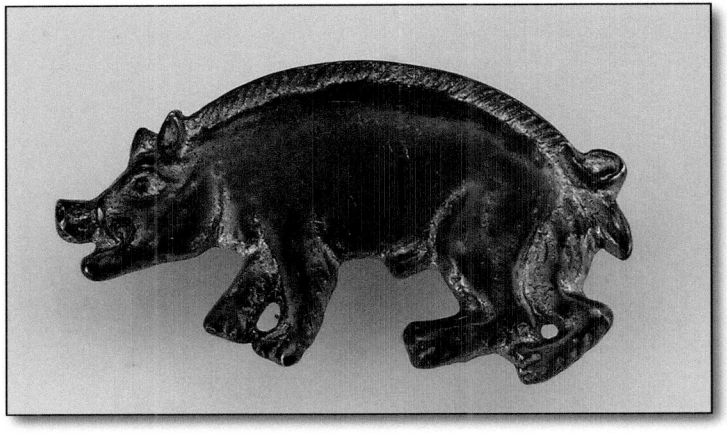

In 2018, it was announced that MIRA Horiba was going to build a driverless vehicle test track on the extreme western edge of the battlefield, only a short distance from the end of the battle-line. It was where the French probably waited to attack, and their route to the battlefield. A last-minute desperate attempt was staged by historians, the Battlefields Trust, the Richard III Society and many thousands of ordinary people from around the world tried to stop the development on the tranquil, largely unspoilt countryside. The local council did not listen and approved the application. Part of one of the most important battlefields in England, which had been lost for so many years, and only found eight years earlier, was to be lost again.

Appendix II

Finding Richard

In November 1538, the Greyfriars friary suffered the same fate as many others and was dissolved. Over the next eight years, the buildings were dismantled, and its stone sold. The site was sold to two Lincolnshire property speculators and was later acquired by Robert Herrick who would be the Mayor of Leicester three times. Herrick built himself a mansion with a number of buildings and a large ornamental garden. Herrick was well aware of the site of Richard's grave as in 1612, Christopher Wren (father of the famous architect Christopher Wren) recorded that in part of the garden there was 'a hansome Stone Pillar three feet [1 m] high with the inscription, "Here lies the Body of Richard III, Some Time King of England."'

Herrick's mansion remained in the possession of his family until it was sold in 1711. During the 19th century, the site was redeveloped, and the mansion was finally demolished in 1871. In 1863, the Alderman Newton's Boys' School was built on part of the site of the old Greyfriars. Then in 1915, a large proportion of the site was acquired by Leicestershire County Council where during the 1920s and 1930s they built their offices. In 1944, the site of Herrick's old garden was turned into a staff car park.

Leicester was already famous as the burial site of Richard III in the early 1600s. In 1611, antiquarian John Speed wrote in his *Historie of Great Britaine* of a stone coffin outside a 'common inn' which had been 'converted to a cistern at which (I think) cattle drink.' Celia Fiennes wrote in 1700 that she had seen 'a piece of his tombstone he lay in, which was cut out in exact form for his body to lie in; it remains to be seen at ye Greyhound in Leicester but is partly broken.' William Hutton also noted in 1758, that a coffin that had 'not withstood the ravages of time,' was kept at the White Horse Inn on Gallowtree Gate. During the 1980s, another purported 'coffin' was discovered in a garden in Earl Shilton and put on display at the Bosworth Visitor Centre in 2009, where it can still be seen today.

Speed's story was further embellished with the Blue Boar legend. However, more importantly, he added that local tradition said that Richard's body had been 'borne out of the City, and contemptuously bestowed under the end of Bow Bridge, which giveth passage over a branch of Soare upon the west side of the town.' The story was widely accepted and was still believed by many, even in the late twentieth century. In 1856 a large carved stone memorial

The carved stone memorial plaque erected in 1856 next to Bow Bridge, by Benjamin Broadbent. (Author)

plaque was erected next to Bow Bridge by Benjamin Broadbent, a local builder, stating, 'Near this spot lie the remains of Richard III the last of the Plantagenets 1485.'

In 1975 an article by Audrey Strange was published in the Richard III Society's journal, *The Ricardian*, suggesting that his remains were buried under one of the three car parks near Leicester County Council's offices. One of these was the City Council's car park. Five years later a memorial to Richard by David Kindersley was set in the floor of the choir of Leicester Cathedral. The Richard III Society also commissioned James Butler to make a life-size bronze statue of Richard, which was placed in Castle Garden next to the river. In 1986, historian David Baldwin speculated, 'It is possible (though now perhaps unlikely) that at some time in the twenty-first century an excavator may yet reveal the slight remains of this famous monarch.'

In 2005, John Ashdown-Hill announced that he had discovered the mitochondrial DNA sequence of Richard III after identifying a British-born woman who had emigrated to Canada after the Second World War. Joy Ibsen (née Brown), was a direct descendant of Richard's sister, Anne of York (and therefore Richard's 16th-generation great-niece). He also determined, like Audrey Strange, that the ruins of the priory church at Greyfriars were under the City Council's car park. Philippa Langley, secretary of the Scottish Branch of the Richard III Society, independently carrying out research in Leicester for a Richard III screenplay, came to the same conclusion. Philippa's research highlighted the northern end of the car park. A small, almost un-noticeable green plaque was placed next to Broadbent's original beside Bow Bridge stating 'This plaque, originally erected by Mr B. Broadbent ... records the 17th-century tradition, now generally discredited, that at the dissolution, of the monasteries the body of Richard III was disinterred...'

An archaeological dig in Grey Friars Street during 2007, which was key to Langley's research, found little which suggested that the remains of the friary church were more likely where Strange, Langley and Ashdown-Hill suggested. This was also the conclusion of Annette Carson, in her 2008 book *Richard III: The Maligned King*. Langley and Ashdown-Hill met in Edinburgh in February 2009 when Langley decided to launch the 'Looking for Richard Project'. Langley teamed up with Richard III Society members Dr David Johnson and his wife Wendy to launch a project with the objective 'to search for, recover and rebury his mortal remains with the honour, dignity and respect so conspicuously denied following his death at the Battle of Bosworth.' In 2011, Langley also brought in Ashdown-Hill and Carson in the search for more evidence. By February 2012, Ashdown-Hill agreed with the location for the church and grave being in the northern end of the car park.

Although it was outside the remit for 'Time Team', because of Philippa's persistence, the project eventually gained the backing of Leicester City Council. Langley was now the named client and received permission to undertake a radar survey and archaeological dig.

In August 2011, using ground-penetrating radar (GPR), the modern utilities crossing the site, such as pipes and cables were identified but little else. The proposed excavation was announced in the June 2012 issue of the *Ricardian Bulletin*, the Richard III Society's magazine, but a month later one of the main sponsors pulled out. Through the Richard III Society Langley launched an appeal for the shortfall in funding which resulted in donations of £13,000 in just two weeks (making £17,367). Leicester University gave £10,000, Leicester Shire Promotions agreed to pay £5,000 and Leicester Adult Schools a further £500. The University of Leicester Archaeological Services (ULAS) was also appointed as the project's archaeological contractor.

On 24 August 2012, a press conference held in Leicester announced the start of the work the next day. Because most of the Greyfriars site had been built on, only 17 percent of the friary was available to excavate. Even then, due to the limitations of the project's funding, the area to be investigated was only one per cent of the actual site. Co-Director of ULAS and lead archaeologist Richard Buckley (who later received an OBE for his services to archaeology) admitted that although he thought there was a reasonable possibility that they would find the friary buildings, there was only an outside prospect that they would find the choir, and they had no chance of finding Richard's

The site of Richard III's grave soon after it was discovered. (Author)

remains. He considered the latter possibility so remote that he offered to eat his hat if they did.

Under site director Mathew Morris, it was decided to open two trenches in the Social Services car park, with an option for a third in the playground. Almost immediately, in the very first trench, two human leg bones were discovered about 16 ft (5 metres) from the north end of the trench about 4.9 ft (1.5 metres) down, suggesting an undisturbed burial. Against all the odds, (although it was not known with any certainty until much later) Richard's remains had been found in six hours 34 minutes. The bones were covered temporarily to protect them while excavations continued further along the trench. Over the next few days, evidence of medieval walls and rooms was uncovered. Thought to be the bones of a friar in the nave of the church, exhumation of the remains began following a further payment by Langley from the proceeds of the appeal. It soon became clear that the bones found on the first day lay inside the east part of the church, possibly the choir, where Richard was thought to be buried.

The bones were uncovered by Jo Appleby, the project osteoarchaeologist, on 4 September. The grave was slightly too small meaning the skull was propped-up. More importantly, the spine was curved in an S-shape. The skeleton's arms were also crossed over the right hip, suggesting they were tied together at the time of burial. On 12 September, the University of Leicester team announced that they had possibly found the remains of Richard III.

The bones were taken to a laboratory for examination. Turi King, a geneticist at the university led the work on Richard's DNA. In addition to the work by Ashdown-Hill, Kevin Schürer traced a second individual in the same family line. Joy Ibsen had died in 2008, leaving three children. Her son Michael, now a cabinet maker based in London, gave a sample of his DNA. It was an almost exact mitochondrial match between the exhumed skeleton, Michael Ibsen, and a second direct maternal line descendant, Wendy Duldig,

Richard III's tomb in Leicester Cathedral. (Author)

an Australian resident in England. At a press conference on 4 February 2013, Richard Buckley, Jo Appleby, Turi King, Lin Foxhall and Kevin Schürer finally confirmed that the skeleton was that of Richard III.

A week later, the University of Leicester announced a project led by Turi King to sequence the entire genome of Richard III and Michael Ibsen. The Richard III Society then commissioned Caroline Wilkinson, Professor of Craniofacial Identification at the University of Dundee, to reconstruct the face.

On Sunday 15 March 2015, Richard's remains including all the samples taken by the university were placed first in a lead ossuary made by Jonathan Castleman, then in a simple golden English oak coffin made by Richard's descendant Michael Ibsen. Carved on the lid by Anna Louise Parker was simply, 'Richard III 1452–1485' and a rose. The funeral procession began at Fenn Lane pausing for ceremonies on Ambion Hill, and Market Bosworth. The coffin was transferred from a motor hearse to a four-horse-drawn hearse for entry into the city of Leicester. The cortege entered Leicester over Bow Bridge and wound its way through the streets lined by an estimated 35,000 people.

From 23 to 25 March 2015, the remains lay in the cathedral. Waiting times to view the coffin were reported to exceed four hours. Then on Thursday 26 March 2015, Richard was finally laid to rest in Leicester Cathedral, in a brick-lined vault beneath the cathedral crossing along with a small box engraved like the coffin in which were three glass Kilner jars containing soil from Fenn Lane, Fotheringhay and Middleham. The vault was sealed with a fossil-rich slab of Swaledale limestone from Yorkshire incised with a cross on a dark Kilkenny-marble plinth inscribed with Richard's name, dates, motto, emblems and royal arms.

Appendix III

Order of Battle

THE ROYAL ARMY

Overall Commander: Richard Plantagenet, King Richard III

The Vanward

Commander: John Howard, 1st Duke of Norfolk
Thomas Howard, Earl of Surrey
Robert Brackenbury

The Mainward

Commander: King Richard III
Standard bearer: Sir Percival Thirwall
Juan de Salazar

The Rearward

Commander: Henry Percy, Earl of Northumberland

Peers

Sir George Talbot, Earl of Shrewsbury
Edward Grey Earl of Kent
Ralph Neville Earl of Westmorland
Thomas de la Pole, Earl of Lincoln

APPENDIX III

Barons

John Lord Scrope of Boulton
Thomas Lord Lumley
Lord FitzHugh
Lord Dacre

From Henry VII's Attainder of 9 November 1485

Francis Viscount Lovell	Richard Ratcliffe	William Catesby
Walter Devereux, Lord Ferrers	John Lord Zouch of Harringworth	Richard Watkins, Herald
Robert Harrington	Richard Charlton	William Berkeley
Robert Middleton	Thomas Pilkington	Sir William Sapcote
James Harrington	Walter Hopton	Humphry Stafford
William Clerke	Geoffrey Saint Germaine	Roger Wake
William Brampton of Burford	Thomas Pulter	John Welsh a.k.a. Hastings
John Kendall secretary	John Bucke	Andrew Ratte
Richard Reuell		

Listed as taking part in the battle according to the ballads and other contemporary sources:

Lord Ogle	Lord Lumley	Lord Greystoke
Lord Maltravers	Lord Welles	Lord Grey of Codnor
Lord Grey of Powys	Lord Audley	Sir William Lord Berkeley of Uley
Lord Ferrers of Chartley	Lord Dudley	Lord Fitzhugh
Lord Scrope of Masham	Lord Scrope of Bolton	
Sir Ralph Harbottle of Beamish	Sir Henry Horsey	Sir John Grey
Sir Thomas Montgomery of Faulkborn	Sir Richard Charlton of Edmonton	Sir Thomas Markenfield
Sir Christopher Ward of Givendale	Sir Robert Plumpton	Sir William Gascoigne of Gawthorpe
Sir Marmaduke Constable of Somersby	Sir Martin De La Sea	Sir John Melton of Ashton
Sir Gervase Clifton	Sir Henry Pierrepoint	Sir John Babington of Dethick
Sir Humphrey Stafford of Grafton	Sir Robert Ryder	Sir Brian Stapleton of Carleton

Sir John Norton	Sir Thomas Mallyvere of Allerton	Sir Christopher Moresby of Windermere
Sir Thomas Broughton	Sir Richard Tempest of Bracewell	Sir Ralph Ashton
Sir Robert Middleton of Dalton	Sir John Middleton of Belsay	John Neville of Liversedge
Sir Roger Heron	Sir Henry Vernon	Sir Robert Manners of Etal
Sir Thomas Strickland of Sizergh	Sir William Parker	Sir Robert Percy of Scotton
Sir Thomas Windsor of Stanwell	Sir John Sacherverel	Sir Archibald Rydley
Sir William Staffertone of Windsor	Sir Gilbert Swinborne of Nattertone	Sir John Walsh
Sir Richard Watkins	Sir Richard Williams	Sir Thomas Kendall of Smisby
Sir John Ratte	Sir John Kendal	Sir John Joyce of Windsor
Sir Richard Revel of Ogston	Sir John Pudsey of Arnford	Sir John Huddleston
Sir Thomas Poulter of Downe	Sir Robert Mortimer of Thorpe le Soken	Sir Christopher Mallory of Studley
Sir William Musgrave of Penrith	Sir Thomas Metcalfe	Sir Walter Hopton
Sir Thomas Gower of Sittenham	Sir William Gilpin of Kentmire	Sir Edward Franke
Sir John Ferrers	Sir John Conyers of Hornby	Sir William Conyers
Sir William Clerk	Sir John Buck of Harthill	Sir Richard Boughton of Lawford
Sir William Brampton	Sir William Bracher	Sir William Allington
Sir RichardMallivere	Sir John Audley of Markeaton	Humphrey Beaufort of Barford St. John
Henry Bodrugan	Robert Rither	John Huddleston
Sir John Hortton	Sir Roger Bigod	William Gilpen
Robert Claxton	Alan Fulthorpe	Thomas Stafford
Sir William Ratcliffe	Sir Thomas Ratcliffe	Sir John Willmarley
Sir Robert Swayley	Sir Richard Rosse	Sir Robert Utridge
Sir Robert Sturley	Sir Thomas North	Sir Martin Wardley
Sir Robert Conway	Sir Oliver Horsley	Sir Robert Clotten
Sir John Spencer	Sir William Ward	

APPENDIX III

Henry Tudor's Army

Overall Commander: Henry Tudor, Earl of Richmond, future King Henry VII

The Mainward – English and Welsh

Commander: John De Vere, Earl of Oxford
Right Wing: Gilbert Talbot
Left Wing: Sir John Savage
Sir Robert Tunstall
Sir Hugh Persal
Humphrey Stanley

Henry Tudor's Bodyguard (also see below)

Jasper Tudor, Earl of Pembroke
Sir John Cheyne of Falstone Cheney
Standard Bearer – Sir William Brandon of Soham

The Vanward – French and Scottish

Commander: Philibert De Chandée
including Gascon Perrot and Colinet Leboeuf
Scottish under command of Alexander Bruce and John of Haddington

The Rearward

Sir William Stanley

The Reserve

Sir Thomas Stanley

The list of those who took part in the battle, or were present at the time on Henry's side, comes primarily from contemporary sources and awards after the battle.

John Lord Welles of Maxey	James Blount	Rhys Fawr ap Maredudd
John Hastoy	William Blount	John Morgan of Gwent
John Trenzy	John Fortescue	John Treffry of Fowey

William Tyler	Humphrey Cheyne	Richard Griffith
Thomas Milborn	Rhys ap Thomas	John Perret
Richard Guilford (master of ordnance)	Giles Daubeney	Sir Edward Woodville
William Griffith of Penrhyn	Reginald Bray	Mathew Baker
Richard ap Howell of Mostyn in Flint	Rhys Fawr ap Maredudd	Richard Fox
Rowland Warburton	Sir Robert Tunstall	Roger Tocotes
Richard Corbett	Sir John Risley of Laenham	Owen ap Griffith
John Rygby	Thomas Idem	Thomas Nandyke
Roger Acton	Brian Sandford	John Spicer
Thomas Croft	John Harpere	Jevan Lloyd Vaughan
John Hanley	Sir Thomas Bourchier	Richard Nanfan
Robert Pointz	Sir William Berkeley of Beverstone	Ronald Machado
John Farrington	William Frost	William Coke of Lavenham
William Sommaster	John Turbevill	Robert Clifford
John Biconnel	Robert Willoughby	Robert Cotton
Owen Lloyd	John Denton	John Pylton
Morris Lloyd	Stephen Calmady	Christopher Urswick
Piers Curteys	Simon Digby	Walter Hungerford
John Fosse	John Heyton	Retherth ap Rhys
Maurice ap Owen	Rees ap Llewellen ap Hulkyn	Robert Crompe
Richard Owen	Christopher Savage	James Savage
Thomas Bevercotes	Hugh Brown	John Brown
Ralph Vernon	Thomas Morton	John Turberville of West Knighton
Richard Ashton	Richard Bagot of Blithfield	John Bicknell of South Perrott
Robert Willoughby of Beer Ferrers	Arnold Butler of Dunraven	John Byron of Clayton
Edmund Carew	William Case	William Chetwynd of Ingestre
Humphrey Cotes	Sir Edward Courtenay	Piers Courtenay; Bishop of Exeter
Matthew Cradock of Caerphilly	John Crokker	Richard Tunstall
Hugh Eardswick	Richard Edgecumbe	Sir John ap Ellis Eyton

APPENDIX III

John Fortescue	William ap Griffith ap Robin	Sir Robert Harcourt
John Hallwell of Bigbury	Edmund Hampden	John Hardwick of Lindley
Richard Guildford of Cranbrook	Reginald Hassall	Thomas Havard of Caerleon
Phillip ap Howel	Richard ap Howel	Sir Walter Hungerford
Roger Kynaston ?	Nicholas Latimer	Thomas Leighton of Stretton-en-le-Dale
Piers Legh of Lymm	Morris Lloyd of Wydegada	Thomas Lovell of Barton Bendish
Thomas Milbourn	John Wogan of Wiston	John Mortimer of Kyre Magna
John ap Meredith	John Mordaunt of Turvey	Edmund Mountfort of Coleshill
David Myddleton of Denbigh	John Mynde	William Norris
David Owen of Cowdray	Thomas Perrott of Haroldston	James Parker
David Phillip of Thornhaugh	Phillip ap Rhys	Ralph Ponthieu
Henry De Vere of Great Addington	John Waller the Younger	John Williams of Burghfield
John ap Thomas	Roland De Veleville	William Willoughby cf Broke
Brian Sandford of Thorpe Salvin	William Tyler of Snarestone	Edward Courtenay

A number of men described as being present in the victorious journey or on overseas service, are listed in the records of Yeoman of the Guard when they were formed shortly after the battle. They were probably Henry's bodyguard at the battle.

Sir Charles Somerset	John Edwardes	Piers Lloydt
Robert Bagger	Thomas Fulbroke	Richard Pigot
William Brown	Thomas Gaywood	John Rothercomme
Henry Carre	Robert Jay	John Rigby
John Carre	Thomas Kingman	Richard Selman
William Cheseman	Thomas Leche	

Colour Plate Commentaries

Unarmoured Burgundian handgunner. By the time of Bosworth handguns were commonplace and a number of small roundshot were discovered on the battlefield. It is probable that Maximillian I sent a contingent of men including handgunners under Juan de Salazar to support Richard.

French longspear. Anne of Beaujeu, the French regent, sent a force of around 2,000 troops from Pont de l'Arche to England with Henry Tudor. These included men armed with longspears, halberds and handgunners. They wore little armour in battle. The illustration shows one of these men with his longspear but without the breastplate he would have worn in combat.

John de Vere, 13th Earl of Oxford, Standard: The motto translates to 'Nothing more true than truth'. De Vere had been held prisoner at Hammes Castle outside Calais since 1474 but escaped to join Henry Tudor in France soon after Henry Tudor arrived there. He commanded Henry's battle-line (mainward) at Bosworth.

Francis Lovell, 9th Baron Lovell, 6th Baron Holand, later 1st Viscount Lovell, Conjectural Standard. The motto translates to 'Time shows all things'. Lovell was a childhood friend of Richard and one of his leading supporters. He fought at Bosworth possibly in Richard's personal retinue and escaped Bosworth to lead several rebellions against Henry VII. He disappears from the historical record after the Battle of Stoke in 1497.

Sir Gilbert Talbot, Banner. Talbot was a younger son of John Talbot, 2nd Earl of Shrewsbury and 2nd Earl of Waterford. Talbot supported Henry Tudor at Bosworth where he possibly commanded the left wing of Oxford›s battle-line.

Henry Tudor, King Henry VII, Standard. According to The Great Chronicle of London, when Henry arrived in London, he offered up his standards in St. Pauls. We are told by its author 'oon was of the Armys of Seynt George', the Patron Saint of England, on a red ground. The second 'a Red ffyry dragon peyntid upon whyte & Grene Sarcenet', powdered irregularly with red and white roses. Henry adopted the dragon as it had been used by Cadwallader, from whom he claimed descent. The third was 'a Baner of Tarteron bett with a Dun Cowe'.

Sir John Savage IV, Banner. Savage's mother was the sister of Thomas Lord Stanley. He declared for Henry Tudor as soon as he landed and raised a considerable body of men wearing the Savage family's distinctive livery of white hoods. It is probable that Savage commanded the right wing of Oxford's battle-line.

John Howard, 1st Duke of Norfolk Banner. Howard was a loyal supporter of Richard III, commanding his vanguard at Bosworth. He was possibly killed near Daddlington Windmill in the rout that followed.

Rhys ap Thomas, Banner. Thomas and a large force of men seem to have only joined Henry Tudor before his army crossed into England. His exact location in the battle is confused and could have either been in Oxford's battle-line or with Henry Tudor. The Welsh poet Guto'r Glyn implies that Rhys himself was responsible for killing Richard.

Richard III, Standard. Although there is no record of what banners and standards Richard took to Bosworth, there are accounts of those he had obtained beforehand. These were 'one banner of Sarcenet of our lady', 'one banner of the Trinity', and banners depicting St. George, St. Edward and St. Cuthbert. In addition, there were four standards 'of sarcanet with boars' and 'one of our own arms all sarcanet'. This was probably Richard's personal standard with the white boar and his personal motto in old French that said, 'Loyaulté me Lie' (Loyalty Binds Me). There was also 'three coats of arms beaten fine gold' (probably the Royal banner).

Richard III Royal Banner (see Richard III, Standard)

Thomas Lord Stanley, Standard. Lord Stanley was Henry Tudor's stepfather. He marched ahead of Henry's army towards Bosworth but appears to have played little part in the battle.

William Catesby, Banner. Catesby was one of Richard's close supporters immortalised as the 'cat' in the rhyme 'The cat, the rat and Lovell our dog'. His position on the battlefield is unknown but he was captured in the aftermath and was the only noble to be executed.

William Stanley, Banner. William acted as Henry's rearguard on the road to Bosworth. He then commanded Henry's division on the high ground behind Henry's main position. It was his division that rescued Henry when Richard III charged. Sometime after, William was executed for his involvement with 'Pekin Warbeck' who claimed to be Edward IV's son Richard (younger of the two 'Princes in the Tower').

Richard III's skeleton (top photo). Richard III's skeleton showing the sideways curvature of his spine (Idiopathic adolescent-onset scoliosis). The feet were destroyed sometime in the past, possibly by gardeners working on the site. There is no evidence of a withered arm or limp. Image: University of Leicester.

Richard III's skull (centre photo). There were two wounds to Richard's face. One is a cut to the jaw and possibly caused when the straps of Richard's helmet were cut before it was pulled off. The other is a small rectangular wound to the right cheek and may have been a symbolic 'punishment blow' to the King's body after his death. Image: University of Leicester.

Richard III's skull (bottom photo). Eight wounds have been identified on Richard's skull, suggesting a frenzied attack. There are three slicing wounds on the back of his skull probably caused by a bill, halberd or poll-axe and would not have been immediately fatal. Two of the wounds were probably caused by the same weapon. A fourth wound can be seen on the crown of the head. It was probably caused by a sharp blow from a pointed weapon such as a Rondel dagger or the point of a poll-axe. The fatal wound was probably a slicing blow to the base of the skull from a bladed weapon such as a halberd. Image: University of Leicester.

Bibliography

Sources

A Castilian report, translation in E.M. Nokes and G. Wheeler, 'A Spanish account of the battle of Bosworth', *The Ricardian,* 2, no. 36 (1972)
Chroniques de Jean Molinet (1474–1506), 3 vols., ed. G. Doutrepont and O. Jodogne (Brussels: Palais Académies, 1935–37)
John Rous of Warwick. *Historia Johannis Rossi Warwicensis de Regibus Anglie,* ed. T. Hearne, 1716
Memoirs of Philippe de Commines, 3 vols., ed. L.M.E. Dupont (1840)
Parliamentary record, Act of Attainder, November 1985
Rotuli Parliamentorum, Vol. VI, ed. J. Strachey, 1767–83
The Croyland Chronicle Continuations, 1459–1486, ed. N. Pronay and J. Cox (London: Richard III and Yorkist History Trust, 1986)
The Great Chronicle of London, ed. A.H. Thomas and I.D. Thornley (London: Guildhall Library, 1938)
The Anglica Historia of Polydore Vergil, ed. and tr. D. Hay, Camden Society, 3rd series, 74 (London, 1950)
Tudor Royal Proclamations, Vol. I, *The Early Tudors,* ed. P.L. Hughes and J. P. Larkin (New Haven: Yale University Press, 1964)
Green, R.F., 'Historical Notes of a London Citizen 1483–4', in *English Historical Review,* vol. 96, 1981
Hall, Edward, *The Union of the Two Noble Families of Lancaster and York* (London, 1550)
Mancini, Dominic, *The Usurpation of Richard III,* ed. and tr. C.A J. Armstrong (Gloucester: Sutton, 1984)

All the original texts can also be found on the American branch of the Richard III Society website, <http://www.r3.org>

The Battle

Bennett, M.J., *The Battle of Bosworth* (Stroud: Sutton, 2000)
English Heritage (1995) *Battlefield Report: Bosworth 1485*
Foard. G., 'Discovering Bosworth', *British Archaeology,* May/June 2010
Foard. G., and Curry, A., *Bosworth 1485: A Battlefield Rediscovered* (Oxford: Oxbow Books, 2013)
Foard, G., 'Reassessment of Bosworth Battlefield' (Bosworth Battlefield Project report, 2005)
Foss, P. *The Field of Redemore: The Battle of Bosworth, 1485* (Leeds: Rosalba Press, 1990)
Hammond. P., *Richard III and the Bosworth Campaign* (Barnsley: Pen & Sword Military, 2010)
Hammond, P.W., & Sutton, A., *Richard III: The Road to Bosworth Field* (London: Constable, 1985)
Ingram, M., *Bosworth: Battle Story 1485* (Stroud: The History Press, 2012)
Jones, M.K., *Bosworth 1485: Psychology of a Battle* (Stroud: Tempus Publishing, 2002)
Rodríguez, M.G., *An Intensive Metal Detector Survey for land at MIRA-TICIT development proposal Higham on the Hill Parish and Witherley Parish,* Leicestershire, ULAS Report Number 2018–113

Skidmore, C., *Bosworth: The Birth of the Tudors* (London: Weidenfeld & Nicholson, 2014)

Richard III and Henry VII

Bridge, J., *A History of France from the death of Louis XI: Vol. 1, Reign of Charles VIII, Regency of Anne of Beaujeu* (Oxford: Clarendon Press, 1921)
Carson, A., *Richard III: Maligned King* (Stroud: The History Press; reprint edition 2009)
Carson, A., *Richard Duke of Gloucester as Lord Protector and High Constable of England* (Horstead: Imprimis Imprimatur, 2018)
Chrimes, S.B., *Henry VII* (London: Methuen, 1972)
Davies C.S.L., 'Richard III, la Bretagne et Henry Tudor (1483–1485), in *Annales de Bretagne et des pays de l'Ouest*, Tome 102, numéro 4, 1995
Dockray, K., *Richard III: a source book*, (Stroud: Sutton, 1997)
Gairdner., J. (ed.), *Letters and Papers Illustrative Of The Reigns Richard III. and Henry VII*. Vol. 1 (London: Longman, 1861)
Gairdner., J. (ed.), *Letters and Papers Illustrative Of The Reigns Richard III. and Henry VII*. Vol. 2 (Longman, 1863)
Gifford. J., *History of France, from the earliest times, to the accession of Louis the Sixteenth* (London: Lowndes, 1793)
Gill, L., *Richard III and Buckingham's Rebellion* (Stroud: Sutton, 2000)
Gillingham, J. (ed.), *Richard III: A Medieval Kingship* (London: Collins and Brown, 1993)
Griffiths. A., and Sherborne, J., *Kings & Nobles in the Later Middle Ages* (Gloucester: Alan Sutton, 1986)
Griffiths, R., and Thomas, R., *The Making of the Tudor Dynasty* (Stroud: The History Press, 2013)
Halsted. C., *Richard III, as Duke of Gloucester and King of England*, Volume 2 (Carey and Hart, 1844).
Hanham, A., *Richard III and His Early Historians* (Oxford: Clarendon Press, 1975)
Jones, M., and Underwood, M., *The King's Mother: Lady Margaret Beaufort, Countess of Richmond and Derby* (Cambridge: Cambridge University Press, 1993)
Hicks, M., *Richard the Third* (Stroud: Tempus, 2001)
Horrox, R., *Richard III: A Study in Service* (Cambridge: Cambridge University Press, 1989)
Kendall, P.M. (ed.), *Richard III: The Great Debate* (New York: W.W. Norton, 1992)
Kendall, P.M., *Richard the Third* (New York: W.W. Norton, 1956)
Lewis, M., *Richard III: Loyalty Binds Me* (Stroud: Amberley Publishing, 2018)
Penn, T., *Winter King: The Dawn of Tudor England* (London: Allen Lane, 2011)
Pollard, A.J., *Richard III and the Princes in the Tower* (New York: St. Martin's Press, 1991)
Ross, C., *Good King Richard III* (London: Eyre Methuen, 1981)
Nichols, J., *The History and Antiquities of the Country of Leicester*, Vol. I. Part II (Nichols, Son & Bentley, 1815)
Various, *The Ricardian* (The Richard III Society)

The Wars of the Roses

Bicheno, H., *Blood Royal: The Wars of the Roses: 1462–1485* (New York: W.W. Norton & Company, 2019)
Carpenter, C., *The Wars of The Roses: Politics and the Constitution in England: c.1437–1509* (Cambridge: Cambridge University Press, 1997)
Evans, G., *The Battle of Edgcote – 1469: Re-evaluating the evidence* (Northamptonshire Battlefields Society, 2019)
Haigh. P., *Military Campaigns of the Wars of the Roses* (Stroud: Sutton, 1995).
Hicks, M., *The Wars of the Roses 1455–1485* (Oxford: Osprey Publishing, 2003).
Kendall, P.M., *Louis XI: The Universal Spider* (New York: W.W. Norton & Company, 1971)
Lander, J.R., *The Wars of the Roses* (Stroud: Sutton, 1990).
Lewis, M., *The Wars of the Roses: The Key Players in the Struggle for Supremacy* (Stroud: Amberley Publishing, 2016)
Pollard, A.J., *The Wars of the Roses* (Basingstoke: Macmillan Education Ltd., 1988)

Ross, Charles, *The Wars of the Roses: A Concise History* (London: Thames and Hudson, 1976)
Royle, T., *The Wars of the Roses. England's First Civil War* (London: Abacus, 2010)
Scofield, C., *The Life and Reign of Edward the Fourth: King of England and France and Lord of Ireland: Vol. 2* (Stroud: Fonthill Media; Reprint edition, 2016)
Vaughan, R., *Phillip the Bold* (Woodbridge: The Boydell Press, 2002)
Vaughan, R., *Charles the Bold: The Last Valois Duke of Burgundy* (Woodbridge: Boydell Press, 2014)

Military Aspects

Boardman, A.W., *The Medieval Soldier in the Wars of the Roses* (Stroud: Sutton, 1998)
Contamine, P., *War in the Middle Ages* (Malden, Mass.: Wiley Blackwell, 1986)
Goodman, A., *The Wars of the Roses: Military Activity and English Society*, 1452–97 (London: Routledge, 1990)
Goodman. A., *The Wars of the Roses: The Soldiers' Experience* (Stroud: The History Press 2006)
Pizan, C. (ed. C. Cannon Willard, trans. S. Willard), *The Book of Deeds of Arms and of Chivalry* (University Park, Pa: Penn State Press, 1999)
Smith, R.D., and Devries, K., *The Artillery of the Dukes of Burgundy 1363–1477* (Woodford: Boydell Press, 2005)
Strickland, M., and Hardy, R., *The Great Warbow* (Somerset: Haynes Publishing, 2011)

Finding Richard

Ashdown-Hill, J. *The Last Days of Richard III and the Fate of his DNA* (Stroud: The History Press; Reprint edition, 2013)
The Greyfriars Research Team, *The Bones of A King: Richard III Rediscovered* (Chichester: Wiley Blackwell, 2015)
Langley. P., and Jones, M., *The Search for Richard III: The King's Grave* (London: John Murray, 2012)
Langley., P., Carson, A., Ashdown-Hill, J., Johnson, J. and Johnson, W., *Finding Richard III: The Official Account* (Horstead: Imprimis Imprimatur, 2014)
Morris, M., and Buckley, R., *Richard III The King Under the Car Park. The Search for England's last Plantagenet King* (Leicester: University of Leicester Arhcaeological Services, 2013)
Speed, J., *The history of Great Britaine under the conquests of ye Romans, Saxons, Danes and Normans* (H. Hall and J. Beale, 1611)

Websites

The Battlefields Trust <http://www.battlefieldstrust.com>
The Richard III Society <http://www.richardiii.net/>
American branch of the Richard III Society. A useful resource for all things related to the Wars of the Roses, <http://www.r3.org/>
University of Leicester, <https://www.le.ac.uk/richardiii/>

Places to Visit

Anyone interested in the story of Richard III has to visit the quiet village of Fotheringhay in Northamptonshire, 3 1/2 miles (5.6 km) to the north of the market town of Oundle and close to Peterborough. It is also easily accessible from the A1. Here are the remains of the castle where Richard was born and grew up. The Church of St. Mary and All Saints is the burial place of his his father, mother and uncle, Edward, Duke of York. It also has an impressive pulpit donated by Richard's brother, Edward IV.

RICHARD III AND THE BATTLE OF BOSWORTH

A visit to the Bosworth Battlefield Visitor Centre is essential for anyone interested in the battle and the period. Sited on Ambion Hill, and with something for all ages, there is a large exhibition of the battle with interactive maps, displays of weapons and equipment etc. There are battlefield walks and regular tours of the area, a gift shop and restaurant. On the anniversary of the battle, the Centre holds the Bosworth Festival which includes re-enactments of the battle. For more details, see <http://www.bosworthbattlefield.com>

Another must is the award-winning King Richard III Visitor Centre, Leicester, a modern museum featuring interactive exhibits on King Richard III's life, death & grave discovery. For more details, see <https://kriii.com>. Richard's final resting place at the Cathedral is just across the road, see <http://leicestercathedral.org>.

Index

PEOPLE

Albany, Alexander Stewart, 1st Duke of Albany 44, 79, 101–103, 171, 181, 261
André, Bernard 111, 114, 196, 201, 247
Angus, 5th Earl of, see Archibald Douglas
Anne of Beaujeu, 'Madame la Grande' 155, 162, 164–166, 175, 177–178, 181–182, 188, 192–193, 195–196
Anne of York 29, 43, 245
ap Goronwy, Goronwy ('Goronwy Fychan') 105
ap Goronwy, Tudor ('Tudor Hen') 105–106
ap Maredudd, Rhys Fawr 207, 239, 244
ap Thomas, Rhys 77, 90, 194, 203, 207, 222, 235, 244, 247
ap Tudur, Maredudd 106–108
ap Tudur, Owain ap Maredudd 106–108, 198
Argyll, 1st Earl of, see Colin Campbell
Armagnac, Count of 34, 117
Armel (Saint) 213-214
Arthur, Prince of Wales 28, 35, 161, 254, 259–260
Audley, Lord 38, 55, 142

Bacon, Francis 146, 255
Barowe, Thomas 99, 186, 198
Bayeux, Bishop of 41, 115
Beauchamp, Anne de, Dowager Countess of Warwick 40, 189
Beaufort, 4th Duke of, see Edmund Beaufort
Beaufort, 5th Duke of, see Henry Somerset
Beaufort, Edmund, 2nd Duke of Somerset 36–38, 107, 131
Beaufort, Edmund, 4th Duke of Somerset 36–38, 48, 92–93, 107–109, 111, 114, 131
Beaufort, John, 1st Duke of Somerset 107, 109
Beaufort, Margaret, Countess of Richmond 83, 108–110, 113–115, 119, 131, 134–136, 142, 147, 149, 156–157, 163–164, 169, 171, 178, 180–181, 203, 217, 253, 256, 262
Beaumont, Lord 42, 54, 108
Bedford, 1st Duke of, see John of Lancaster, Jasper Tudor
Berkeley, William, 2nd Baron Berkeley 27, 133
Blount, James 184, 201
Bourchier, Henry, 1st Earl of Essex 42, 97, 236
Bourchier, Thomas, Archbishop of Canterbury 42, 138, 142, 206, 209, 211
Brackenbury, Sir Robert 94, 206, 211, 216, 220, 226, 246–247
Brampton, Edward 133, 190
Brandon, Sir William 163, 183, 217, 228, 239, 246
Bray, Reginald (Raynold) 113, 157, 163, 194, 257
Brereton, Humphrey 161, 188
Brittany, Duchess of 161, 164
Buchan, 2nd Earl of, see John Stewart
Buck, Sir George 129, 145, 169, 196, 251
Buckingham, 2nd Duke of, see Henry Stafford
Buckingham, Duchess of, see Katherine Woodville
Butler, Eleanor 138–139, 168

Cade, Jack 27, 37
Cambridge, 3rd Earl of, see Richard of Conisburgh
Camden, William 108, 161, 169, 281
Campbell, Colin, Earl of Argyll 103, 186
Canterbury, Archbishop of, see Thomas Bourchier
Catesby, Sir William Snr 135, 139
Catesby, Sir William 134–135, 139, 167, 178, 180, 189, 220, 262
Catherine of Valois 31, 106–108
Caxton, William 54, 83, 262

285

Chandée, Philbert de 196, 201, 253
Charles the Bold, Duke of Burgundy 41–43, 51, 55, 67, 71, 77, 89, 95, 115, 118, 120, 123, 128, 141, 227–228
Charles VI of France 31–32, 34, 37, 106
Charles VII of France 31, 34–35, 51, 76, 79, 109, 116–118
Charles VIII of France 122, 126, 155–156, 162, 177, 190–191, 193, 196, 256
Charlotte of Savoy 117, 155
Chauvin, Guillaume 123, 125–126, 174–175, 199
Cheyne, Sir John 96, 149, 163, 217
Clarence, Duke of, see George Duke of Clarence
Clifford, Sir Robert 159, 183, 187
Coetanlem, Jean de 185–186
Colyngbourne, William 178–179
Commines, Philippe de 44–45, 51, 55, 65, 78, 96, 119, 124, 136, 144, 180, 182, 193, 195, 221–222
Constance of Castile 29, 209
Constance of York 29–30, 209
Coppini, Francesco 47, 117
Corbet, Sir Richard 113–114, 208
Courtenay, Henry, Marquess of Exeter 89, 260–261
Courtenay, Peter, Bishop of Exeter 142, 158, 169, 198
Courtenay, Sir Edward 158, 160, 201, 253

Dacre, Thomas, Lord Dacre of Gilsland 73, 98
Daubeney, Sir Giles, Lord Daubeney 157, 163, 236, 259
de Crèvecoeur, Philippe, Seigneur d'Esquerdes (Lord Cordes) 124, 132, 150, 191, 195–196
de la Pole, Edmund, 3rd Duke of Suffolk 145, 236, 256, 260
de la Pole, John, Earl of Lincoln 52, 109, 142, 176–177, 186, 198, 220, 246, 253–255
de la Pole, William 1st Duke of 109, 140, 142, 145, 186, 254, 256
de Mowbray, John, 3rd Duke of Norfolk 48, 140, 163, 245
de Mowbray, John, 4th Duke of Norfolk 41, 47, 60, 91, 95–96, 99, 136, 141
de Pizan, Christine 54, 67, 227
de Valera, Diego 193–195, 221–222, 237, 241
de Vere, John, 12th Earl of Oxford 99, 111
de Vere, John, 13th Earl of Oxford 42, 48, 92, 183–184, 187–188, 208, 224, 227–229, 232–233, 236, 245–246, 255
d'Esquerdes, Seigneur, see Philippe de Crèvecoeur
Devereux, Sir Walter, Lord Ferrers 89, 109–110, 113, 159, 246–247

Dinham, Lord 42, 184
Donne, John 89, 123
Douglas, Archibald, 5th Earl of Angus 44, 101, 103, 129, 186
du Quélennec, Jean, Vicomte du Faou 121–122
Dudley, Edmund 257–258
Durham, Bishop of 97, 153
Dynham, John 150, 156

Edmund of Langley, 1st Duke of York 28–31
Edmund, Earl of Rutland 33, 38–39, 84–85, 97
Edward (prince, son of Henry VI) 38–39, 41, 92–93
Edward (prince, son of Richard III) 89, 153–154, 170–171, 175–176
Edward I 28, 47, 49–50, 105, 140, 259
Edward II 28, 105–106, 141
Edward III 28–30, 38, 106–107, 131, 157
Edward IV 27, 38–49, 51–53, 55, 60, 65, 70–72, 84–86, 89–96, 98–99, 101–103, 112, 117–118, 124, 128, 130, 132, 134–145, 149, 152–154, 157–158, 163–165, 168–169, 177–178, 184, 188, 194, 205, 218, 220, 245–246, 253, 256–257, 260–261
Edward of Norwich, 2nd Duke of York 29, 30–33
Edward V 27, 41, 45, 93, 125, 129–135, 139–140, 142, 145, 148, 256. See also, Princes in the Tower
Edward, Earl of Warwick (son of Duke of Clarence) 42, 176–177 253–254, 259
Elizabeth of York 28, 122, 126, 157, 164, 169, 189, 253, 261
Elne, Bishop of 123–125
Elrington, Sir John 102–103
Ely, Bishop of, see John Morton 134
Essex, 1st Earl of, see Henry Bourchier
Everingham, Sir Thomas 43, 124, 177
Exeter, Bishop of, see Peter Courtenay
Exeter, Duke of, see Sir Henry Holland
Exeter, Marquess of, see Henry Courtenay

Fabyan, Robert 144, 179, 201
Falstolf, John 58, 60, 85
Ferdinand and Isabella, Spanish monarchs 77, 145, 149, 193, 241, 259
Ferrers, see Walter Devereux, Lord Ferrers
Fisher, John, Bishop of Rochester 110, 113
Flamank, Thomas 236, 259
Foard, Glenn 222, 264
Fortescue, John 42, 74, 184, 201
François II of Brittany 108, 112, 118–123, 125–126, 134, 142, 151–152, 161, 164, 173, 175, 178–181, 186, 189

INDEX

Frederick III, Holy Roman Emperor 43, 76, 146, 176
Froissart, Jean 28, 30, 60, 106, 109, 115, 133
Fulford, Sir Thomas 133

George, Duke of Clarence 29–30, 40–43, 84–86, 91–94, 96, 99, 113–114, 131, 137–139, 176, 184, 253, 256, 259–260
Gloucester, Duke of, see Humphrey of Lancaster, Thomas of Woodstock, Richard III
Gloucester, Thomas of Woodstock, 1st Duke of Gloucester 28, 38, 131
Glyn Cothi, Lewis 90, 113
Glyn, Guto'r 112, 242, 244, 279
Glyndŵr, Owain 30, 106, 200
Goldwell, James, Bishop of Norwich 43, 142
Grafton, Richard 103, 135, 160, 194
Gregory, chronicler 74, 110
Grey, Andrew, Lord Grey 38, 103, 111, 130, 166
Grey, John, Lord Powis 197, 203–204
Grey, Sir Richard 39, 129–131, 140
Grey, Thomas, Marquess of Dorset 39, 96, 101, 130, 132–134, 138, 160, 163, 179, 180, 188, 193
Greystoke, Ralph, Lord Greystoke 32, 98, 102–103, 139, 160, 217, 244
Griffith, Richard 203, 276
Gruffydd, Elis 106–107, 110, 207
Guildford, Richard 157–158, 217

Habsburg, Maximilian 43, 77, 123–126, 148, 156, 175, 179–180, 182–183, 188–192, 197, 220, 256, 260
Halewell, John 133, 180
Hall, Edward 53, 102–103, 157–158, 163, 196, 218, 238, 249–250
Harcourt, John 136, 163
Hardyng, chronicler 29, 35
Harrington family 90, 95
Harrington, James 90, 95, 102
Harrington, Robert 90, 95, 103
Hastings, William, Lord Hastings 41, 52–53, 72, 78, 91–93, 95–96, 130, 132, 134–139, 156, 163, 212, 216
Henry IV (Henry of Bolingbroke) 28, 30–31, 91, 106–107, 190, 200, 209
Henry V 31–32, 40, 82, 106, 110, 209
Henry VI 27, 32, 35–39, 41–42, 54, 56, 91–92, 107–112, 114, 131, 135, 182, 184, 205, 246
Henry VII (Henry Tudor) 27–28, 41, 48, 51, 53–54, 60–61, 74–75, 77–78, 83, 89–90, 105, 107–108, 110–116, 119, 121–122, 125, 131–132, 134–136, 144–147, 149, 151–152, 157–164, 168–169, 171, 173–174, 175–176, 179–183, 186–189, 191–198, 200–210, 212–216, 218, 220–222, 225–231, 233–241, 244–262
Henry VIII 62, 107, 113, 212, 245, 247–248, 260–262
Herbert, William, 1st Earl of Pembroke 40, 89, 109–113
Herbert, William, 2nd Earl of Pembroke, later Earl of Huntingdon 89, 142, 160, 170, 192–193
Holinshed, Raphael 93, 144, 239
Holland, Sir Henry, Duke of Exeter 92, 111
Howard, John, Lord Howard (Duke of Norfolk from 1483) 44, 124, 140–142, 158, 170–171, 204, 212, 218–221, 226, 230–231, 234–236, 238, 245–247, 252
Humphrey of Lancaster, Duke of Gloucester 32, 107, 160–161, 167, 188, 216, 247, 254
Hungerford, Sir Walter, 1st Baron Hungerford 106, 206, 209, 211, 223
Huntingdon, Earl of, see William Herbert
Hutton, Dr Thomas 143, 151

Isabeau of Bavaria 34, 106
Isabella of Castile, Duchess of York 31, 149

Jacquetta, Duchess of Bedford 39, 137, 168
James I of Scotland 116
James III of Scotland 44, 101–103, 120, 125, 129, 171, 181, 196
James IV of Scotland 44, 257
John II of Portugal 79, 190
John of Gaunt, 1st Duke of Lancaster 28–30, 107, 109, 190, 209
John of Lancaster, 1st Duke of Bedford 32, 39–40
John the Fearless, Duke of Burgundy 34, 71
Joseph, Michael 236, 259

Katherine of Aragon 259–260
Katherine Swynford 30, 107
Katherine, daughter of Richard III 170, 193
Kent, Earl of 97, 142
Kynaston, Sir Roger 203–204

Landais, Pierre 122, 125–126, 152, 173–175, 180–182, 192, 196, 199, 204
Langton, Dr Thomas, Bishop of St. David's 174, 181, 203
Leicester, Maud, Countess of 29, 193
Lincoln, Bishop of, see Thomas Rotherham, John Russell
Lincoln, Earl of, see John de la Pole

Lionel of Antwerp, 1st Duke of Clarence 28–30
Lisle, Thomas Talbot, 2nd Viscount Lisle 27, 140, 188
London, Bishop of 133, 253
Longueil, Maître Antoine de 179–180
Louis I, Duke of Orléans 34, 155, 177
Louis XI 35, 40–41, 43–44, 70, 78–79, 95–96, 101, 108, 111, 115–121, 125, 136–137, 150, 152, 155, 180, 194, 221
Lovell, Francis, Viscount Lovell 86, 102, 137, 142, 145, 159, 178, 194, 197, 220, 246, 254–256, 273, 277–279

Major, John 195, 222
Mancini, Dominic 39, 43–45, 49, 59, 99, 104, 129–134, 137, 139, 144–145, 149, 165
March, 3rd Earl of, see Edmund Mortimer
March, 4th Earl of, see Roger Mortimer
March, 7th Earl of, see Edward IV
Margaret of Anjou 36–39, 41, 48, 70, 89, 92, 102, 110–112, 114–115, 117, 137, 184, 202
Margaret of Scotland 44, 116
Margaret of York, Duchess of Burgundy 43, 84, 89, 118, 141, 254, 256–257
Margaret Pole, Countess of Salisbury 42, 256, 259–261
Mary, Duchess of Burgundy 123, 125–126, 188
Middleton, Sir John 55, 102
Milan, Duke of 117, 166
Molinet, Jean 83, 146, 180, 182, 184, 187, 193, 195, 215, 221–222, 226–229, 234–235, 237, 241, 244–246
Mordaunt, Sir John 172, 181
More, Sir Thomas 134, 136
Morgan, John 194, 203
Mortimer, Edmund, 3rd Earl of March 29, 31–32
Mortimer, Edmund, 5th Earl of March 31–32
Mortimer, Roger, 4th Earl of March 30–31
Morton, John, Bishop of Ely 96, 123, 134, 137, 145, 154, 156–157, 162–164, 169, 179–180, 257–258
Morton, Robert, 154, 163, 206
Mytton, Thomas 160, 208

Neville family 27, 37, 40, 86–87, 91, 98, 153
Neville, Anne 40–41, 43, 86–87, 93–94, 97–98, 137, 141, 153–154, 171, 174, 189
Neville, Cecily 32–33, 44, 84, 98, 179
Neville, George, Archbishop of York 40, 42, 47, 86
Neville, George, Lord Bergavenny 47, 86, 154, 191
Neville, Isabel, Duchess of Clarence 40, 42–43, 86–87
Neville, John, 1st Marquess of Montagu (prev. Earl of Northumberland) 39, 41, 48
Neville, Ralph, 1st Earl of Westmorland 32, 272
Neville, Ralph, 2nd Earl of Westmorland 32, 98, 103, 139, 160, 217, 244
Neville, Richard, 16th Earl of Warwick 37–41, 48, 67, 86–91, 93, 112–115, 117–118, 137, 139, 157, 170, 184
Neville, Richard, 5th Earl of Salisbury 37–38, 93, 117
Neville, Thomas, 'the Bastard of Fauconberg' 41, 93
Norfolk, 1st Duke of (from 1483), see John, Lord Howard
Norfolk, 3rd and 4th Dukes of, see John de Mowbray
Norwich, Bishop of, see James Goldwell

Paston, John 59, 83, 119–120, 158, 205
Percy family 27, 37–38, 93
Percy, Henry, 2nd Earl of Northumberland 38, 111, 142, 212, 252
Percy, Henry, 4th Earl of Northumberland 44, 95, 97, 101–104, 111, 134, 140, 142, 160, 193, 204, 212, 220–221, 226, 235–237, 241, 247, 252, 255
Philip III of Burgundy, 'the Good' 34–35, 76, 117, 148
Philip IV of France, 'the Fair' 126, 150, 191
Philippa, 5th Countess of Ulster 29–30
Pitscottie, Robert Lindsay of 195–196, 218, 222
Pius II 35, 77, 117
Poppelau, Nicholas von 88, 129, 146, 176
Poynings, Edward 181, 201
Prince of Orange 155, 178
Princes in the Tower 143–147

Ratcliffe, Sir Richard 103, 134, 140, 189, 247
Ratcliffe, Sir Robert 44, 101, 130, 133, 257
Rice, Henry 90, 207
Richard II 30, 106–107, 250
Richard III (prev. Duke of Gloucester) 27, 29, 31, 40–41, 44–49, 51, 54, 59–61, 63, 66–67, 69–70, 72, 74, 76, 83–104, 107–108, 111–112, 115, 127–154, 156–194, 196–198, 200, 202–221, 223, 225–244, 246–254, 256, 260, 262

INDEX

Richard of Conisburgh, 3rd Earl of Cambridge 29, 31–32
Richard of Shrewsbury, Duke of York (son of Edward IV) 99, 125, 132, 140–141, 145–146, 256. See also, Princes in the Tower
Risley, Sir John 163, 183
Robin of Redesdale 40, 112, 141
Rochefort, William (Guillaume) de 144, 164–165
Rochester, Bishop of, see John Fisher
Rohan, Vicomte de 121, 175
Romont, Jacques de Savoie, Comte de 124, 188
Rotherham, Thomas, Bishop of Lincoln 97, 133
Rous, John 93, 129, 140, 146, 157, 176, 189, 242, 250
Russell, John, Bishop of Lincoln 133, 159, 167, 189, 198

Salazar, Juan de 180, 189, 197, 220, 237
Salisbury, 5th Earl of, see Richard Neville
Salisbury, Bishop of, see Lionel Woodville
Salisbury, William 172, 181
Savage, Sir John 194, 203, 206–207, 216, 222, 226, 228, 245
Saye, Lord 41, 91
Schwartz, Martin 254–255
Scrope, John, 5th Baron Scrope of Bolton 98, 102, 135, 166, 255
Scrope, Thomas, Lord Scrope of Masham 32, 98, 142, 198
Shaa, Dr Ralph 139–140
Shakespeare, William 88, 93, 129, 144, 262
Sixtus IV 103, 172
Somerset, Henry, 5th Duke of Beaufort 29–30
Spont, Alfred 194, 234
St. David's, Bishop of, see Thomas Langton 174, 181, 203
Stafford, Henry, 2nd Duke of Buckingham 27, 38, 40, 53, 83, 85, 90, 110, 113, 115, 119, 131–134, 136–147, 149, 154, 156–164, 167, 169, 179, 188, 194
Stafford, Humphrey 160, 246, 254
Stafford, John, 1st Earl of Wiltshire 36, 110
Stafford, Sir Henry 83, 110, 113–115, 119
Stafford, Thomas 246, 254
Stanley family 89–90, 95, 203, 214, 216–217, 221, 224–226, 246
Stanley, Edward 90, 103, 210, 222
Stanley, George, Lord Strange 137, 159, 198, 254
Stanley, Humphrey 216, 247
Stanley, Sir William 53, 60, 90, 98, 130, 147, 202, 206–208, 210, 214–215, 222, 225, 228, 239–241, 246–247, 253, 257

Stanley, Thomas, Lord Stanley 41, 60, 90–91, 95, 97, 101–102, 119, 134–135, 142, 159, 160–161, 163, 179, 183–184, 203, 206, 209–210, 215–216, 221–222, 225, 247, 253–254
Stewart, John, 2nd Earl of Buchan 79, 261
Stonor, Sir William 139, 159, 183
Stow, John 103, 148, 158
Strange, Lord, see George Stanley
Suffolk, 1st Duke of, see William de la Pole
Suffolk, 3rd Duke of, see Edmund de la Pole
Suffolk, Elizabeth, Duchess of 87, 142
Surrey, Thomas Howard, Earl of Surrey (Duke of Norfolk from 1514) 47, 141–142, 226, 245–247, 260

Talbot, John, 3rd Earl of Shrewsbury 41, 91, 95, 138
Talbot, Sir Gilbert 183, 208, 222, 228, 245–247
Thirwall, Sir Percival 239, 272
Tudor, Edmund 107–110, 198
Tudor, Jasper 41, 91, 108–112, 114–115, 119, 121–122, 163, 169, 175, 181–182, 198, 202–203, 228, 247, 252, 256
Tyler, Sir William 217, 254
Tyrell, Sir James 103, 144–145, 160, 170, 182–183, 260

Urswick, Dr Christopher 156–157, 181, 193, 208

Vaughan, Sir Thomas 129–130, 140, 160
Vegetius 54, 215, 220, 226–228
Vergil, Polydore 45, 93, 107–108, 111, 114, 116, 119, 127–128, 134, 138, 144–146, 154, 156–157, 161–164, 171, 174, 183, 188–189, 193, 195, 200, 203–204, 206–211, 215–217, 221–223, 226, 228–233, 237–239, 241, 246–247, 249–250

Wake, Roger 206, 220
Warbeck, Perkin 146–147, 256–257, 259
Warwick, 16th Earl of ('The Kingmaker'), see Richard Neville
Welles, John, Lord Welles 97, 110, 113, 133, 149, 163, 201
Welles, Lionel de, 6th Baron Welles 110, 113
Welles, Richard, 7th Baron Welles 113–114
Welles, Sir Robert 40, 113–114
Westmorland, 1st and 2nd Earls of, see Ralph Neville
Whitelaw, Archibald 129, 186
Willoughby, Sir Robert 163, 180, 253
Wiltshire, 1st Earl of, see John Stafford

289

Woodville family 40, 43, 99, 129-131, 135-136, 138, 154, 157, 163, 165, 170
Woodville, Anthony, Lord Rivers 39-41, 44, 74, 89, 91, 101, 120, 129-131, 136, 140, 158, 214, 262
Woodville, Edward 102, 120, 132-134, 136, 143, 176, 180-181
Woodville, Elizabeth 39-41, 96, 119, 129-132, 134-135, 137-138, 154, 157, 160, 163, 166, 170, 184
Woodville, Katherine, Duchess of Buckingham 85, 131, 157
Woodville, Lionel, Bishop of Salisbury 28-30, 110, 113, 132, 154, 160, 163, 169

Worcester, John Tiptoft, 1st Earl of Worcester 41, 91, 111, 184
Wrangwysh, Alderman Thomas 101, 134

York, 1st Duke of, see Edmund of Langley
York, 2nd Duke of, see Edmund of Norwich
York, 3rd Duke of, see Richard Plantagenet
York, Archbishop of, see George Neville
York, Richard Plantagenet, 3rd Duke of 29, 31-34, 36-39, 41, 55, 76, 84-85, 97-98, 109, 117, 119, 132

PLACES

Aberystwyth 109-110, 203
Agincourt 31-32, 46, 55, 110
Alençon 175, 177, 192
Ambion Hill 213, 219, 223, 247, 262
Ancenis 118, 120, 175, 180, 192
Angers 111, 181, 184, 192
Anglesey 105-107, 111-112, 202
Anjou 36, 181
Aquitaine 86, 140
Artois 124, 126
Atherstone 75, 210, 213-215
Atterton 75, 213-214, 217
Austria 64, 148, 182
Aveiro 190-191

Bamburgh Castle 44, 101, 112
Barnard Castle 94, 99, 101-102, 134
Barnet 41-42, 48, 67, 81, 83, 86, 92, 99, 119, 132, 141, 163, 184
Bay of Biscay 186, 194
Baynard's Castle 84-85, 108, 140
Beauvais 42, 96, 120
Bedfordshire 107, 109, 172
Berwick 72, 101-103, 134
Blackness Castle 44, 101
Blore Heath 38, 48, 55
Blue Boar inn, Leicester 209-210, 267
Bohemia 64, 261
Bootham Bar 97, 255
Bosworth 46-48, 51, 53-55, 59-60, 63-65, 67-70, 72, 74-78, 83, 89, 111, 135, 141, 144-145, 166, 176, 180, 188, 190, 193, 195, 205-208, 210, 212-216, 218-222, 224-227, 229-234, 236-241, 243, 245, 247-249, 253-254, 260, 262
Bourges 34, 116
Bow Bridge, Leicester 211-212
Brabant 126, 189
Brecknock Castle 137, 160
Brecon Castle 156, 159-160
Brecon 137, 156, 158-160, 169, 202
Brest 119, 161, 173

Bristol 37, 91, 97, 185
Brittany 42, 52, 83, 96, 108, 111-112, 116, 118-123, 125-126, 134, 136, 143, 149, 151-152, 157, 161-164, 166-167, 169, 173-175, 177-182, 185-186, 189, 191-192, 196-197, 199, 204, 261
Bruges 59, 85, 95, 188, 191
Burgundy 35, 41-43, 46-47, 51, 71, 76-78, 83, 85, 89, 95-96, 102, 112, 114, 117-119, 121, 123-126, 141, 182, 192, 220, 255-256

Cadeby 212-213
Caernarfonshire 105, 201-202
Calais 37-38, 40-42, 62-63, 66, 70, 77-78, 86, 95, 102, 111, 115, 126, 130, 132-133, 136, 145, 150, 156, 167, 178, 183-184, 193, 254
Cambridgeshire 98, 110
Canterbury place 42, 61, 167
Carmarthen 89-90, 109-110, 115, 200, 203
Castillon 37, 67, 140
Channel 86, 156, 160, 166
Château d'Amboise 41, 114
Château de l'Hermine 119, 122
Château de Largoët 121-122
Cheshire 194, 202
Chester 70, 93, 95, 97, 122, 247
Chinon 34, 111
Church of the Greyfriars, Leicester 250, 251
Cinque Ports 39, 142, 166
City of London x, 51, 66, 158, 190, 198
Colchester 141, 183, 246
College of Arms 145, 171
Collegiate Church of St. Mary and All Saints, Fotheringhay 31, 33
Compiègne 35, 188
Coventry 38, 41, 61, 65, 74, 85, 89, 91-92, 94, 160, 197, 228, 252
Coverham Abbey 98, 176

INDEX

Crécy 28, 46, 55
Cumberland 93, 97, 104

Dadlington 212, 214, 219, 222–223, 243, 245, 247–249
Dale 200–201, 203, 207, 214, 225
Dartmouth 114, 137, 162
De Montfort University 209–210
Denbigh 108, 112
Devon 41, 91–92, 119, 158, 162, 253, 259
Dieppe 124, 162, 194
Dorset 89, 179, 260
Dover 156, 166, 176
Duchy of Lancaster 89, 93–94, 154, 253
Dunbar 44, 171, 181
Durham 94, 97, 99, 153, 176

Edgcote 40, 54–55, 89, 112, 160, 170, 208, 223
Edinburgh 44, 103
Empingham 40, 113
Essex 42, 158, 184, 214
Exeter 92, 111, 142, 158, 161–162, 169, 198, 259–261

Fen Hole 223, 228
Fenn Lane 212, 215, 217, 219, 224–225
Fenny Drayton 75, 214, 217
Flanders 56, 83, 123–124, 126, 148, 150–151, 162, 180, 182–183, 188–189, 191–192, 194–196, 254, 256
Flodden 47, 260
Florence 77, 125
Forth 44, 101
Fotheringhay 30, 33, 44, 84–86, 89, 97–98, 100, 102–103, 119, 149, 153
Fowlmere 98–99
France 28, 31–32, 34–37, 39–44, 48, 51–53, 56, 61, 72–73, 76–79, 91, 95–96, 102–103, 106, 108–109, 112, 114–123, 125–126, 132–133, 136–137, 140, 143, 147, 149, 151–152, 155–156, 162, 164–167, 169, 172, 174–175, 177–200, 205, 209, 220–222, 256, 260–261

Germany 52, 56, 68, 71, 102
Ghent 156, 188, 191
Gloucester 89, 159
Gloucestershire 43, 90, 208
Grafton Regis 40, 62, 131
Grantham 160, 174
Gravesend 158–159
Guildford 115, 217, 259
Guildhall, London 140, 145, 179, 207, 251
Guinegate 78, 124, 180, 188
Guînes 77, 145, 193

Hague, the 91, 147
Hammes 42, 184, 193
Harlech 112, 203

Harwich 187, 191
Hereford 90, 97, 110, 113, 156
Herefordshire 109, 113
Hertfordshire 31, 107, 183
Holland 29, 91–92, 141
Holt 90, 208
Hornby Castle 90–91
Hornsey 132, 252
Hull 91, 96

Ireland 30, 36, 38, 54, 85–86, 106, 140, 149, 254, 256–257, 259
Italy 29, 52, 65, 77, 117, 125, 182

Jersey 119, 254

Kent 29, 37, 85, 149, 158, 161–162, 167, 186, 247, 257, 259
King's Lynn 41, 91
Kirby Muxloe 137–138, 212

La Rochelle 79, 186
Lancashire 90, 159, 202, 206, 233, 254
Lathom 159, 210, 254
Leadenhall, City of London 51, 198
Leicester 29, 32, 38, 53, 61, 63, 92, 127–128, 137, 149, 159–160, 167, 188, 205, 209–212, 215, 217, 242, 246, 249–250, 252
Lichfield 209–210
Lincoln 156, 159, 247, 254
Lincolnshire 40, 90, 110, 113
Lochmaben 102, 181
Loire Valley 34, 178
London 37, 39, 41–44, 51, 53–54, 56, 59, 66, 68, 70–72, 84–86, 89, 92–95, 97, 99, 104, 107, 113–114, 128, 130, 132–136, 139–141, 144–146, 148–149, 154, 157–158, 161, 167, 169–172, 176, 178–179, 182, 186, 189–190, 194, 197–198, 203, 205–207, 218, 226, 228, 236, 247, 250–253, 259–251
Ludlow 31–32, 37–38, 84, 129–131, 145, 147
Luxembourg 39, 75, 188

Machynlleth 203–204
Maine 36, 118, 232
Mancetter 75, 214
Maxey Castle 110, 113, 149
Merevale Abbey 75, 213–214, 247
Merioneth 202–203
Micklegate Bar, York 101, 153
Middleham 42, 86–87, 93, 97–100, 140, 153–154, 175–176, 254
Milan 29, 56, 59, 117, 166
Milford Haven 74, 200–201, 205
Montargis 178, 182
Morat 55, 67, 227–228
Morlaix 173, 185

Mortimer's Cross 39, 110

Nancy 43, 55, 117, 124
Nantes 119, 121, 175, 199
Naseby 219, 223
Netherlands 58, 126, 148
Neuss 55, 95–96
Newark 89, 255
Newarke, Leicester, the 209, 250
Newcastle upon Tyne 102–103, 257
Newcastle-under-Lyme 210
Newport, Shropshire 110, 208
Norfolk 163, 184, 254
Normandy 36, 42, 76, 78, 118, 120, 124, 161–162, 174, 177, 185, 192–193, 195
North Wales 89, 105–106, 133, 244
Northampton 38–39, 54, 67, 85, 92, 110, 113, 130–133, 157, 170, 206, 220, 223, 252, 258
Northamptonshire 30, 40, 84, 110, 112, 135, 149, 223, 246, 253, 258
Nottingham 61, 89, 92, 174–176, 186, 194, 197–198, 204–206, 209–210, 247, 250, 255

Orléans 34, 118

Paris 34–35, 44, 60, 95, 106, 109, 115–116, 118, 124–126, 133, 174–175, 177–178, 188, 192, 196
Picardy 78, 95, 126, 156, 192
Picquigny 42, 70, 96, 122, 138
Plymouth 114, 162
Poitiers 28, 46, 79
Pont de l'Arche 78, 152, 155, 165–166, 191, 195
Pontefract Castle 30, 94, 131, 140, 154
Poole 162, 179
Portchester 31, 133
Portugal 82, 182, 186, 190

Raglan 110–111, 192
Reims 34–35, 116, 118, 177
Rochester 42, 113, 158
Rouen 34–36, 61, 78, 120, 139, 192, 194
Royal Armouries 53, 63

St. Albans 27, 38, 39, 48, 92, 132, 157, 220, 252
St. George's Chapel, Windsor 45, 153
St. Jakob an der Birs 76, 117
St. Malo 119, 122, 161, 261
St. Michael's Mount 42, 184
St. Osyth 42, 184
St. Paul's Cathedral 72, 134, 139, 178, 228, 252
St. Paul's Cross 138–139
Salisbury 89, 149, 158, 160–161
Sandal 55, 94–95, 177
Sandwich 38, 41–42, 111, 167, 176

Scarborough 96, 102, 177
Scotland 44, 70, 79, 101–104, 106, 110–111, 116, 120, 125–126, 129, 135, 137, 171–172, 176, 181, 183–184, 186, 255, 257–259, 262
Severn (River) 159–160
Shenton 214, 223
Sheriff Hutton 86, 93, 104, 140, 176, 253
Shrewsbury 82, 113
Somerset 89, 119
South Wales 89, 110, 133
Southampton 31–32, 42, 93, 102, 132, 154, 173, 187, 191, 194, 196–197, 204
Southwark 42, 85
Spain 54, 65, 77, 145, 182, 193, 259
Stafford 208, 209
Stamford 27, 174
Stoke Golding 222–223, 225, 248, 263–264
Stoke 27, 181, 188, 235, 255–257
Stony Stratford 130–131, 133, 211
Suffolk 144, 183, 214, 254
Surrey 114, 149, 158, 187, 220
Sussex 37, 149, 158, 162, 201, 260
Sutton Cheney 214, 217–218, 223
Switzerland 76, 102

Tadcaster 153, 255
Tamworth 211, 244
Tenby 115, 119, 200
Tewkesbury 41, 43, 55, 72, 92–93, 99, 115, 121, 134, 137, 144, 163, 194
Three Tuns, Atherstone 214–215
Touraine 111, 116
Tours 79, 111, 116, 155, 164
Tower Hill 111, 113, 187, 258, 261
Tower of London 37, 39, 42–43, 56, 68, 70, 85, 94, 102, 130, 132, 134, 136–139, 141, 143–148, 157, 169, 174, 176, 188, 191, 206, 226, 247, 253–254, 259–261
Towton 39, 47, 55, 61, 73, 81, 82, 85, 113, 137, 154, 163, 226
Trent (River) 94, 250, 255
Tyburn 43, 260

University of Cambridge 36, 86, 98–100, 174
University of Leicester 128, 269–270
University of Oxford 43, 111, 163

Vannes 119, 122, 161, 163–164, 180–181
Verneuil 46, 79, 192

Wakefield 39, 55, 85, 90, 92, 101, 117
Wales 28, 30, 32, 41, 89–90, 92–94, 105–110, 112–114, 122, 129–130, 133, 153, 158, 160, 174, 183, 194–195, 197, 200, 202, 205, 207, 221, 244, 254
Warwick 42, 92, 149, 228
Warwickshire 40, 110, 214, 244, 254

INDEX

Watling Street 130, 210, 212, 217, 225
Weobley 113–114, 159–160
Westminster Abbey 41, 108, 113, 132, 141, 146, 253, 260
Westminster Hall 140, 142
Westminster 32, 41, 99, 108, 113, 132, 134, 138, 140–142, 146, 167, 171–172, 198, 253, 260
Westmorland 87, 104, 220
Weymouth 41, 92, 202
Wiltshire 89, 179, 182
Windsor 43, 45, 101, 107–108, 115, 143, 148, 186
Witherley 75, 214, 217
Woking 114–115
Worcester 61, 157, 200, 247

York Minster 86, 98–99, 130, 153, 176
York 41, 89, 91, 97–98, 101, 104, 130, 134, 142–143, 153–154, 159, 166–177, 181, 190, 201, 206, 252, 255, 260
Yorkshire 81, 89, 91, 93–94, 134, 160, 177

CONTEMPORARY SOURCES

Annales of England 148, 158
The Arrivall of Edward IV 92–93

Ballad of Bosworth Fielde 67, 78, 195, 205–206, 208, 210, 214–216, 220–222, 224–227, 229–230, 232–233, 237–239, 241, 245
Ballad of Ladye Bessyie 161, 242

Chroniques 162, 281
Croyland Chronicle 39, 44, 85, 109, 126, 130–131, 138, 140, 143, 157, 159, 169, 175, 189, 197, 204–206, 209, 212, 219, 224–225, 236, 245

The *Great Chronicle of London* 71, 139, 144–145, 228, 247, 250

Hall's *Chronicle* 102–103, 158, 218. See also, Edward Hall
Historia regum Angliae 242, 250
Holinshed's Chronicles 93, 144. See also, Raphael Holinshed

Knyghthode and Bataile 54, 74–75

The Song of Ladye Bessiye 214–215
Stanley Poem 90, 103, 222

Titulus Regius 167–169, 171, 253

Warkworth Chronicle 42, 93

GENERAL TERMS

Battlefields Trust 222, 264, 266
Bridport Muster Roll 57, 60, 62, 64, 67

DNA 29, 84, 128

Great Seal 99, 132, 159–160, 198, 206

House of Lancaster 28, 30, 38, 182, 250
House of York 28, 33–34, 38, 60
Hundred Years War 28, 30, 46, 53–54, 78, 83, 103, 116

Jack Cade's Rebellion 27, 37

scoliosis 87–88, 127, 250
Swiss troops 43, 46–47, 63–64, 67, 75–78, 117, 124, 155, 180, 227

Trinity (ship) 134, 185, 226
Treaty of Arras 35, 45, 76, 118, 126, 180
Treaty of Picquigny 42, 70, 122, 138
Treaty of Troyes 31–32

White boar device 60, 86, 94, 209, 217, 226

293